ANGLISTISCHE FORSCHUNGEN
Band 463

Begründet von
Johannes Hoops

Herausgegeben von
Rüdiger Ahrens
Heinz Antor
Klaus Stierstorfer

SARAH BRIEST

Married
to the City

The Early Modern
Lord Major's Show
Between Emblematics
and Ritual

Universitätsverlag
WINTER
Heidelberg

Bibliografische Information der Deutschen Nationalbibliothek

Die Deutsche Nationalbibliothek verzeichnet diese Publikation
in der Deutschen Nationalbibliografie;
detaillierte bibliografische Daten sind im Internet
über *http://dnb.d-nb.de* abrufbar.

Dissertation Ruhr-Universität Bochum, 2016

UMSCHLAGBILD

Fools milking the breasts of the world in book one,
emblem twelve, of Francis Quarles' Emblemes, Divine and Moral (48).
Image by courtesy of Penn State University Libraries.

ISBN 978-3-8253-6889-0

© 2019 Universitätsverlag Winter GmbH Heidelberg
Imprimé en Allemagne · Printed in Germany
Druck: Memminger MedienCentrum, 87700 Memmingen

Gedruckt auf umweltfreundlichem, chlorfrei gebleichtem
und alterungsbeständigem Papier.

Den Verlag erreichen Sie im Internet unter:
www.winter-verlag.de

To the right honorable and worshipful R. W.

Table of Contents

Introduction

In late 1613, on the occasion of Welsh-born Grocer Thomas Myddleton's inauguration as Lord Mayor of London, the sizeable model of a rhinoceros arrived in St Paul's church-yard; red-robed Envy, astride the creature, hugged a snake to her bared breast while simultaneously feeding on her own bloody heart.[1] In so far as anthropologist Clifford Geertz is right in purporting that it is moments of fascination and bewilderment in equal measure which trigger inquiries into the rituals of other cultures, the rhinoceros and its rider constitute the starting point of this present study of the methods, themes, and ritual functions of the early modern Lord Mayor's Show. The past, of course, quoting novelist L. P. Hartley, "is a foreign country: they do things differently there."[2] What they did, in this instance, was to celebrate the annual installation of a new mayor with episodes of entertaining and identity-affirming pageantry; in this particular case betraying an overt indebtedness to the morality play (by the end of the day Envy and Error would be defeated – burned to the ground – by the agents of Truth).

Various scholars have argued – and innumerably more merely stated casually – that these pageant episodes, enacted in the course of a typical early 17th-century Lord Mayor's Show, are "emblematic" in character. In his significant 2003 study of *English Civic Pageantry 1558-1642*, David M. Bergeron outlined the following plan:

> Because the representation of these persons [allegorical personifications appearing in Lord Mayor's Shows] and their thematic significance closely link with the technique of the popular emblem books, I intend to explore the relationship between emblems and civic pageants, which should help in defining pageantry's soul as well as offering us a different perspective on the interrelationship of civic pageants with other non-dramatic literary and visual traditions (Bergeron, Civic Pageantry 263).

Bergeron's analysis, although very insightful and the most thorough of its kind, is far from exhaustive, with only a total of 32 pages devoted to the relationship between emblems and civic pageantry – a limitation which is acknowledged by the author himself.

---

[1] On the scene, Tracey Hill muses that "[s]ome local butcher must surely have supplied the supposedly 'human' heart that Envy eats whilst seated on her rhinoceros" (Pageantry 179).

[2] Richard Homan has previously argued for taking up Geertz's so-called "thick description" in investigations of theater history (303). He proposes "that the information we have about medieval theatres, and perhaps theatres of other historical periods, can be treated in the way an anthropologist treats field notes: as the pretext for the interpretation of another culture" (315). Miri Rubin also advocates Geertz' concept of thick description in her examination of the festival of Corpus Christi in England (4), and Tracey Hill has looked at Lord Mayor's Shows through the lens of Geertz's *Local Knowledge*, in which the latter analyzes strategies of implementing and justifying authority by means of royal pageantry in Europe, Africa, and Asia (Anthony Munday 154).

Bergeron reproduces three woodcuts from Geffrey Whitney's immensely popular emblem book *A Choice of Emblemes* (1586) – depicting personified Envy, Ulysses, and Orpheus – as well as representations of personified Truth, Fame and Virtue from Henry Peacham's *Minerva Britanna* (1612) which he considers relevant to his purpose of demonstrating affinities between the techniques and themes of emblems and pageants. Notwithstanding Bergeron's indisputable interest in and knowledge of both formats under discussion, he offers neither a clear definition of the emblem nor of the exact nature of 'emblematic' strategies at work in pageantry. Yet, despite this vagueness scholars unceasingly refer to the emblematic character of pageantry in general and the Lord Mayor's Show in particular. Glynne Wickham influentially declared that "[p]ageantry is itself the quintessence of emblematic art" (Vol. 1.1, 209) – although by "emblematic" he meant primarily "non-realistic" –, while Peter M. Daly notes that coronations, royal entries, progresses, and other pageants "were so often emblematic in character" (2). Anne Lancashire describes the "presentation mode" of the Lord Mayor's Show as consisting of "emblems, personifications, and allegory" (Comedy 7), while Hardin Craig writes matter-of-factly of "emblematic displays staged along the processional route" tread by the lord mayor and his entourage (19).[3]

In her recent thorough and highly engaging account of the early modern Lord Mayor's Show, Tracey Hill accepts the received opinion by commenting that "[t]he use of emblems, in particular, shows how widespread was the cross-fertilisation between civic pageantry and other theatrical forms of culture in this period" (Pageantry 23), and by mentioning, offhandedly "emblematic tableaux, music, dance and speeches" (ibid. 1), "emblematic figures" (ibid. 3), "emblematic pageants, featuring speeches and songs" (ibid.), "the use of conventional 'morality' emblems" (ibid.), "[h]eraldic emblems" (ibid. 192) and more formulations of this type.[4] In her sub-chapter on "emblems and symbols in the Shows" (ibid. 161-68), Hill notes "how important emblems and imagery were to these productions" (ibid. 118), and reproduces two emblems, featuring personified Envy and the self-sacrificial pelican, from Geffrey Whitney's *Choice of Emblemes*. As interesting as these emblems are, the discussion here suffers somewhat from the absence of a definition of the emblem; at the same time it is not too surprising that two early modern commonplaces which appear in Whitney's emblem book also appear in Lord

---

[3]   Caitlin J. Finlayson, too, mentions "emblematic pageant devices" (840), and Sheila Williams refers to pageant tableaux as "three-dimensional emblems closely related to the two-dimensional ones of the popular emblem-books" (504). Finlayson elsewhere refers to some pageants as "wholly visual emblems that invite the reader's interpretation" (Finlayson, Jacobean Foreign Policy 595), which contradicts the explicitly visual *and* verbal nature of the emblem. These "visual emblems", she goes on, contrast with pageants that have "their significance explicated by a personification or, as in Heywood's pageant books, by lengthy authorial commentary" (ibid.).

[4]   Cf. Hill: "The emblems employed in the Shows were thus taken from a range of places" (Pageantry 162); "hence the emphasis one finds in all of his [Munday's] productions on conventional emblems which one would hope would be readily interpreted by onlookers" (ibid. 143); "Munday's 1616 Show for the Fishmongers incorporated emblems associated with the Goldsmiths" (ibid. 167); "symbolic and emblematic sophistication" (ibid. 219); "emblematic participants" (ibid. 242); "the careful use of selected figures and emblems" (ibid. 271).

Mayor's Shows by Middleton (Envy) and Munday (pelican). It adds to the confusion that the term "emblem" is used to refer to Whitney's emblems a well as to any commonplace notions or symbols – a terminological ambiguity that occurs in both early modern and modern discourses. Moreover, Hill refers to Munday's supposed adoption "of the inherent economy of the emblem: its ability to encapsulate meanings which when expressed verbally might be 'tedious' to the onlooker" (ibid. 172), which turns a blind eye to the interplay between the verbal and the visual at the heart of the emblem.

With regard to common cultural sources, drawn on by both emblematist and pageant poet, Bergeron maintains that

> we can direct our attention to studying parallels between specific emblems and specific pageants without worrying over the problem of possible indebtedness. The greater indebtedness of both forms goes obviously to iconographical traditions that aid in the problem of visual representation (Civic Pageantry 265).

However, Bergeron uses the above argument, reasonable as it is, to sideline any 'iconographical traditions' in his approach and to insist on the kinship of pageantry and emblem books. This effectively undercuts his own *caveat*.[5]

The early modern use of the term "emblem" also contributes to the problem of semantic imprecision today. Not only was the word used to refer specifically to those tripartite compositions, combining verbal and visual codes, compiled in emblem books, it also frequently served as a more general label for any "symbol" or "representation". For example, in the pamphlet commemorating his Lord Mayor's Show *Chrysanaleia* (1616), Anthony Munday refers to fishing as "the absolute Embleme of our present intendment" (B), meaning nothing more than that the activity is represented and is connected to the Fishmongers. In the same pamphlet personified Virtues and Vices who are riding in a pageant chariot, which principally carries impersonations of King Richard I (1189-99) and an angel, are described as "best observed by their severall Emblems and properties, borne by each one" (B4). These "Emblems and properties" are objects – some symbolically charged – by which their bearers can conceivably be identified. Munday clearly does not refer to emblems as they appear on the pages of Whitney's or Peacham's emblem books. John Dixon Hunt recognizes that definitions of "emblem" and "emblematic" remain fuzzy in scholarly discourse (156) and further concurs that "[c]ritics often blur their analysis by failing to distinguish the emblem as a vehicle of commonplaces from the emblem as a verbal-visual construct" (ibid.). Hunt considers it a lure of "emblematic elucidation" that "it allows criticism to think that it has pinned down the meaning of a difficult text" (161). However, he rejects "the assumptions that word and image somehow function identically on the stage and on the page of the emblem

---

[5] For the same reason, i.e. the existence of common cultural sources, Michael Bath has previously warned against "the dangers of snatching a random analogue from emblem books or mythologies to serve as a gloss on a literary text" (234). Mario Praz has referred to the "unoriginality of emblem-writers" (210), and likewise commented on difficulties in ascertaining the influence of emblems on other forms of literary and artistic expression due to the fact that many similarities may be explained by an indebtedness to common sources (206).

book" (156), and concludes "that emblems are too static for dramatic use" (167).[6] Hunt's assertion that medium matters is valid, as is his disapproval of the fact that this has generally been ignored in the context of emblem-stage comparisons.

Emblem Books

Even before a vogue for *imprese* or "devices" took hold in Italy around the turn of the 15th century, an interest in Egyptian hieroglyphics (with their pictogrammatic blending of language and the visual arts) anticipated the popularity of the emblem (Praz 25).[7] The *impresa* bore a close resemblance to the emblem but, whereas a 'normative' emblem consisted of three interdependent parts (motto, picture, and explanatory verse), the device only combined motto and picture. The device or *impresa's* more personal application in comparison with the universal aspiration of the emblem is echoed in the etymology of the former: The term derives from Italian *imprendere*, meaning to undertake or to intend to do something (Warncke 32), and, in fact, *imprese* conveyed aspirations or sentiments only applicable to their individual bearers (Praz 68, 80). They allowed for a playful freedom of expression, displaying everything from the proud lion rampant, to "ermines in copulation" (Praz 70). It should be noted that, while related forms, *imprese* were not identical with the familial coats of arms of the nobility. While these were generally stable identifiers, "*imprese* were really ad hoc armory" (Day 102). Like the *impresa,* the 'proper' emblem initially developed on the European mainland, specifically in Italy and, a little later, in France and the Low Countries. While it was in these countries that the fashion was strongest (cf. Diehl 49), the English also developed a taste for books of emblems and devices. Before the first English translations of the anthologies of Jan van der Noot, Paolo Giovio, or Lodovico Domenichi were available, the educated classes had already pored over the Latin, Italian, or Dutch originals. Indeed, Cambridge scholar Gabriel Harvey despaired of students more interested in emblem books than the works of Aristotle (ibid.).

The emblem tradition proper is commonly held to begin with the publication of the *Emblematum Liber* in 1531 by the Italian lawyer Andrea Alciato, of which 140 editions were produced in the 16th century alone (ibid.). Alciato's emblems set the standard of the genre which most emblematists opted to imitate in his wake. His emblems are composite entities consisting of a motto (also commonly referred to as *inscriptio* or *lemma*), a picture (alternatively known as *pictura, icon, imago* or *symbolon*), and a short textual explanation below the picture, also called *subscriptio* or epigram (Hill, What is an Emblem? 262; Schöne 18-19).[8] Alciato placed his woodcut prints in between motto and verse, reflecting

---

[6] Hunt, who believes the rivalry of the arts – *paragone* – to be at the heart of Shakespeare's *Timon of Athens* (156, 159, passim.), argues further that "the presence of tableaux" in a play "does not in itself authorize the relevance of emblems" (160).

[7] The late antique *Hieroglyphica* of Horapollo – offering a wealth of generally inaccurate descriptions of Egyptian ideographs – became a significant text among Florentine humanists and in the developing emblem tradition after a version of the manuscript reached Florence in 1422 (Praz 23; Warncke 20).

[8] John Manning suggests that this placement of elements does not originate with Renaissance emblems but may rather derive from a prior manuscript tradition of arranging content (6).

the emblem's etymological descent from "emblema", which originally referred to an inlay "such as a mosaic or low-relief decoration" in Greek and Roman art (Hill, What is an Emblem? 261). Emblem books enjoyed equal popularity among Protestants and Catholics, with the former not averse per se to the use of pictures as "commemorative aids" (Diehl 56), as long as the images themselves did not inspire worship and thereby externalize religion (ibid. 55).[9] This position echoed widespread Protestant equivocation on the nature and worth of allegory in general.

In the following chapters I will be referring to "the two major English emblem books of the time" (Madelaine 146), Geffrey Whitney's 1586 *A Choice of Emblemes* and Henry Peacham's *Minerva Britanna* (1612) with particular frequency because both emblem books were widely known in England and have been cited by scholars who attest to the emblematic propensities of the Lord Mayor's Show. Whitney's anthology is often identified as the first English emblem book. Although *A Choice of Emblemes* was published in Leiden, Whitney was an Englishman whose emblems – while adapted from a variety of sources – were no mere translations (Daly and Raspa 84). Like Alciato, Whitney sandwiched a picture in between a corresponding motto and verse. His verse generally refers to both picture and motto and thereby establishes a meaningful connection between these two, otherwise not explicitly linked, constituent parts of the emblem.[10] He selected his woodcuts from stock owned by his publisher, the Plantin Press, and used some cuts as they were while he had others reworked to better suit his creative needs (ibid.). While artisans on the European mainland had become adept at producing copper engravings by the end of the 16th century, their English counterparts lagged somewhat behind (Freeman 45). Therefore, while French, Italian, and Dutch composers of emblems habitually commissioned artists to produce woodcuts or engravings to suit their texts, it was more common for English writers to choose from existing blocks and either use these in their original conditions or commission alterations (Hill, What is an Emblem? 262). Against this trend, Henry Peacham produced his own woodcuts for his *Minerva Britanna*.[11]

---

[9] For this reason, Diehl notes, "writers of English emblem books frequently describe the function of their emblems as being aids to memory, and thus pointing to invisible truths beyond the pictures themselves" (57). The prefaces to Renaissance emblem books indeed often claim the superior goal of moral instruction as a justification of their image-heavy means (Praz 169), a strategy still employed by John Bunyan in his justification of the use of allegory in *The Pilgrim's Progress*. Thus, the emblem arguably achieved a wholesome fusion of "[t]he sensuous and the didactic" in a single unit (ibid. 16).

[10] While emblem mottoes were commonly phrased in Latin, English emblematists generally formulated verse elucidations in the vernacular (Hill, What is an Emblem? 262).

[11] In the preface to *Minerva Britanna* Peacham speaks up for the creativity of English emblematists, claiming, with a view toward the writers of southern Europe, that "we are not so dull as they would imagine us, not our Soile so barren as that we neede to borrow from their Sunne-burnt braines, our best Invention" (Minerva A4).

The Lord Mayor's Show

The field of scholarly engagement with early modern Lord Mayor's Shows – and, indeed, civic pageantry in general – is characterized, and divided, by two broad approaches. On the one hand, scholars consider conflicts and tensions as intrinsic to the production of pageantry and stress its normative and restrictive enforcement of established social norms and hierarchies. On the other hand, scholars who follow a 'consensus school of thought' emphasize pageantry's potential to facilitate solidarity and social cohesion. For example: Lawrence Manley and Anne Lancashire assess early modern Lord Mayor's Shows as essentially inclusive events (Lancashire, Comedy 6), whereas Kathleen McLuskie argues that the shows, even if they were "quintessentially city events", should not "be regarded sentimentally as events which overcame the deep divisions of status and wealth which existed in seventeenth-century London" (77).[12] Adherents of the conflict school variously detect friction between authors and sponsors of pageants, between mayor and administration, aldermen and livery companies, big companies and minor guilds, merchants and manufacturers, city dwellers and suburbanites, or shopkeepers and pedlars; whereas consensus school publications stress the capacity of civic pageantry to overcome antagonisms – or at least put them aside temporarily – in the service of a joint project. In the following chapters I will, on the whole, side with the consensus school and demonstrate the ways in which the Lord Mayor's Show is an attempt at communal integration.

At the beginning of the 17th century the City of London was governed by a Court of 26 Aldermen, each of whom represented one of the 26 wards of the city. At the same time as the Court of Aldermen was a powerful institution and the guilds remained significant organizations, the economic hegemony of the livery companies was increasingly coming under strain, with business thriving outside the city walls and, thus, outside the control of mayor and aldermen (Hill, Anthony Munday 162).[13] Consequently, scribes like Thomas Middleton, Anthony Munday, and Thomas Heywood were still "working for merchant princes, but for worried merchant princes" (Heinemann 127). Tracey Hill confirms that "[a]lthough the companies still dominated the urban scene in this period, their survival was never absolutely guaranteed" (Pageantry 28).

---

[12] McLuskie perceives "the separation of a ruling oligarchy from an increasingly proletarianised working population" in early 17th-century London (58), and consequently believes that attempts to create unity among disparate groupings were bound to fail. According to Michael Berlin, "[t]he early dominance of the mercantile élite in London mitigated the need felt in other towns to perform ceremonies which publicly integrated the various parts of the whole" (qtd. in McLuskie 78). McLuskie supports this view and further argues that in Dekker's and Heywood's mayoral pageants, "[t]he iconography of the main shows and the importance of the speeches rehearsed the values of a mercantile élite, making them, rather than the populace as a whole, responsible for the perpetuation of the virtues of justice and mercy and good government" (78). Her assessment, however, passes over the authors' and organizers' explicit catering to a highly diverse audience.

[13] Cf. Brenner on the Court of Aldermen: "Election to this body was not merely an entree to the most important municipal political decision-making body, it was also a sign of elite socio-economic position." (63)

As a rule, aldermen were chosen from the ranks of the twelve great livery companies –
Mercers, Grocers, Drapers, Fishmongers, Goldsmiths, Skinners, Merchant Taylors, Haberdashers, Salters, Ironmongers, Vintners, and Clothworkers[14] – and although they were
nominated in their respective wards, the Court of Aldermen held the power to reject
nominees and, thus, held an effective monopoly over city administration (Seaver 65-66).
In matters of taxation and legislation the Common Council, a body of 212 representatives
elected by the freemen[15] of the wards, had to consent to aldermanic propositions but since
the body met in the presence of the aldermen it was also privy to their influence (ibid.
66). Lord Mayors were elected from among the aldermen and so traditionally belonged
to one of the twelve major companies.[16] In the rare case that a likely candidate for the
mayoral office belonged to one of the lesser guilds his transferal to a major company prior
to taking up office was expected. In the early 1500s a system of election was established
whereby the most senior alderman who had already served as sheriff would inevitably be
elected (Berlin 18). A period of circa ten years would generally elapse between a
magistrate's term as sheriff and his election to the mayoralty. This fairly predictable
system allowed pageants tailored to company and individual candidate to be devised
before the actual election took place.[17] In the first half of the 16th century it also became
the custom to bestow a knighthood on every mayor. At the same time, the grander
appellation of "lord mayor" came to replace the simpler "mayor" (ibid.).

London government was organized in a ceremonial year consisting of a secular
semester from the end of June until the end of October and a religious semester, beginning
on 1 November and lasting until 29 June (Manley 299). By the second half of the 15th
century the last day of the religious semester had become the occasion of the Midsummer
Marching Watch, the biggest annual civic festivity of its day and originally a "grand
military muster" (Hill, Pageantry 29). This guild-sponsored parade was led by the Lord
Mayor and two sheriffs along a fixed route and by the mid-16th century displays of
pageantry had become incorporated into the procession (Manley 299). In the course of

[14]   This order of precedence among the twelve great livery companies of London was fixed in 1523
      (Berlin 18). Contemporaries did not refer to livery companies as "guilds" but as "companies"
      (Hill, Pageantry 12).
[15]   Achievement of the freedom of the city – by apprenticeship, purchase, or patrimony – was the
      condition for citizenship (Lobanov-Rostovsky 888). The freedom of London gave citizens the
      right to carry out any trade of their choosing in the city (Seaver 65).
[16]   From 1475 the right to participate in civic elections was restricted to members of the livery and
      "[e]ntry into the livery was restricted to those members of the yeomanry who were able and
      willing to fulfil various ceremonial obligations as so-called bachelors in foynes and budge or
      'rich bachelors' as they were sometimes known" (Berlin 17). Bachelors "in foins" were com-
      pany members allowed to don "pine-marten fur", while "budge" refers to lamb's wool (Hill,
      Pageantry 54).
[17]   Hill states that "[c]ommonly, the sub-committee for planning the Show was established only at
      the beginning of October; at the earliest, the detailed preparations did not generally commence
      until late September, for the Lord Mayor was elected on Michaelmas Day, 29 September"
      (Pageantry 24). Yet, since, as stated, "these elections were generally a formality", some
      planning could take place beforehand (ibid. 72). An alderman who had already served as mayor
      was said to have "passed the chair" (ibid.).

the 16th century livery companies also started investing in spectacle and pageantry on the occasion of the mayor's inauguration, which marked the end of the secular semester. By the middle of the century, committees entrusted with the planning of the Midsummer Watch and the Lord Mayor's Show had begun commissioning pageant scripts (ibid. 302-03): Candidates submitted their outlines to the responsible authorities for consideration, awaiting rejection or approval.[18] On the heels of this innovation the decline of the Midsummer Watch set in and early in the reign of Elizabeth I the Lord Mayor's Show had succeeded the Watch as London's premier annual civic event (Lancashire 328).[19] The Midsummer Watch lost favor and was eventually abandoned altogether (Manley 303).

Each Lord Mayor's Show was financed by the livery company of which the incoming mayor was a member (ibid. 307).[20] Bachelors (those company members who had not joined the elite ranks of the livery) formed committees to organize the particulars of the upcoming event and to raise funds; like many early modern misers or spendthrifts, those unwilling to contribute to the costs could quickly find themselves in debtors' prison (Bergeron, Civic Pageantry 256). At the same time as committee members were under the obligation to curb expenses where possible, they were faced with "a concomitant need to be *seen* to spend lavishly" (Hill, Pageantry 57). In recompense of the company's outlay – the average cost of an early Stuart Lord Mayor's Show amounted to just over £700[21] – the pageants paid homage not only to London's administrative institutions and the new mayor but also to the history and traditions of the sponsoring company specifically (Bergeron, Civic Pageantry 256). The fact that both dramatist and chief artificer (responsible for the construction of stage sets and props) conducted negotiations with the sponsoring company about the details of their contracts, their rights and responsibilities, demonstrates the considerable importance of the artificer vis-a-vis the writer in these endeavors (ibid. 240). Hill refers to the close collaboration between these two parties as

---

[18] This "new articulateness", argues Lawrence Manley, reflects a contest for ideological domination between Watch and Lord Mayor's Show (303). Tracey Hill notes that "[a]s well as having historical antecedents, the Shows had synchronic relations with other forms of ceremonial" (Pageantry 34), such as "the celebration of the election of a livery company's new master and wardens" (ibid. 35) or "the investiture of Princes of Wales, Henry and Charles, in 1610 and 1616" (ibid. 37).

[19] Theater historians generally apply the term "Lord Mayor's Show" to the pageantry and ceremonial surrounding the mayor's inauguration from the 1550s onward (Lancashire 328). Tracey Hill comments: "The livery company records for the period prior to the 1550s [...] indicate that music was part of the procession even if speeches were a later development" (Pageantry 33).

[20] Bachelors were themselves raised from the yeomanry to the livery in mayoral years (Manley 307). The Grocers provide an example of the numbers involved: 20 percent of members, i.e. circa 140 men, belonged to the livery of that company (Levin 1254). Bergeron posits that bachelors might have been elevated to the livery as a method of generating further funds toward an upcoming Lord Mayor's Show (Civic Pageantry 255).

[21] Hill notes that "£180, the sum often received by the writer and artificer in this period, is around £16,000 in modern terms" (Pageantry 60).

"the 'writer and artificer' arrangement" (Pageantry 37).[22] However, very often the exact contributions made by authors, artificers and others to the finished 'product' of a Lord Mayor's Show are impossible to disentangle. Creative partnerships of various types, sometimes uncredited, add complexity to questions of authorship, and, as Hill points out, the fact "that a single name appears on a printed work does not necessarily mean that uncomplicated authorship, or sole authorship, occurred" (Pageantry 68), – a phenomenon certainly not unknown in the wider field of early modern literary production.

The election of the mayor traditionally took place on Michaelmas, a month before the new incumbent's oath-taking and official inauguration on 29 October, the day after the religious feast of Saints Simon and Jude (Manley 299).[23] At eight a.m. on the day of the festivities the mayor was met by the aldermen at his personal residence and escorted by them to the Guildhall, then on to the river bank, from whence he departed upstream to Westminster for his oath-taking before representatives of the Exchequer. The newly elected mayor swore his oath in the presence of his predecessor, the Lord Chief Baron, and the Lord Treasurer (ibid. 134-35). Occasionally, during outbreaks of plague, the mayor was sworn in at the Tower instead (ibid. 33). The oath-taking procedure signaled the subordination of mayor to monarch (Manley 295), although it was in practice often the monarch who depended on the mayor in matters of finance.[24] This could cause complications such as those experienced by John Leman in the course of his mayoralty, when in early 1617 the crown demanded a loan of £100,000 from the city which it failed to repay fully (Ashton n. pag.). Already on the way to and from Westminster the mayor was met by more or less elaborate water entertainments on the Thames. The first pamphlet text which records entertainments taking place on the river is George Peele's 1591 *Descensus Astraeae* which was also the first such show to bear a distinct title (Bergeron, Introduction 1766). One significant aspect of the water entertainments was the galley foist, a barge equipped with guns, the main purpose of which "was simply to make a tremendous racket" (Hill, Pageantry 157). On land, portable pageant stages and performers accompanied the mayor and his entourage of guild representatives, whom eye witness Abram Booth referred to as "represent[ing] the corpus and community of the city" (qtd. in Lusardi/Gras 22). Generally, the liverymen proceeded in "traditional reverse order of seniority (the youngest and least important went first)" (Hill, Pageantry 134). On the nature of the pageant stages, Hill sums up "[t]he general consensus [...] that the pageants were peripatetic, joining the procession at its end once their function as venues for

---

22 Hill remarks that "[b]y the 1620s the artificers often received the total payment and it is not often possible to tell how the responsibility was spread, if at all" (Pageantry 87).

23 In his *Triumphs of Re-united Britannia*, Munday tells the Lord Mayor to "bethink thee how on that high Holiday, / Which beares Gods Champion, th' Arch-angels name, / When conquering Sathan in a glorious fray, / Michaell Hels-monster nobly overcame, / And now a sacred Saboath being the same, / A free and full election on all parts, / Made choice of thee, both with their hands and harts" (C4). Along with the mayoral election, the swearing in of the new sheriffs also took place on Michaelmas (Manley 299).

24 In Thomas Dekker's *The Dead Tearme*, a personification of Westminster tells her fellow city London approvingly that "thy Princes call thée Their Treasurer and thou art so" (B).

tableaux and speeches was concluded" (Pageantry 146). The exact movements of the pageants varied, however, from show to show.

Following the mayor's return from Westminster, his party proceeded to move along a fixed route through the city which generally took its beginning at Baynard's Castle or at Paul's Wharf (Manley 306), picking up pageants and performers as they went.[25] In 1611 the Goldsmiths hired as many as 100 porters to carry and watch over pageant sets before and during that year's Lord Mayor's Show (Robertson and Gordon 84). Frequently these constructions bore child actors, who constituted a lighter load than adults.[26] Adult thespians certainly also participated in the pageantry but they did so, often, from the back of a horse, the mode of transportation also used by the mayor himself. Whether women or girls participated in the pageantry is uncertain, yet, "contemporary evidence reveals that women played parts in London's annual Midsummer Shows" (Rice and Pappano 197-98). Female contribution to the Lord Mayor's Show, therefore, cannot be ruled out despite the fact that actresses were taboo on the stages of the public playhouses.

From the banks of the Thames, the mayor and his entourage proceeded northward to Paul's Chain, through Paul's Churchyard, and eastward onto Cheapside. Past the Little Conduit and the Standard, the procession made its way to the Guildhall, via St Lawrence Lane, for a banquet.[27] While the mayor and his guests feasted, actors and others involved in staging the entertainments and controlling the crowds took the chance to rest. Spectators, meanwhile, assembled outside the Guildhall doors, waiting for the pageantry to resume (Levin 1261). After the feast, the procession moved back to St Paul's Cathedral along the same route as previously taken, by which time, "given that it was late October, darkness would have fallen" (Hill, Pageantry 3), and myriads of candles lighted to

[25] The actual size of pageant wagons used in Lord Mayor's Shows is somewhat contested in scholarly debate. Morrissey argues that they would have been significantly smaller than 14 by 23 feet, since "from the beginning, pageant-wagons had to negotiate small lanes and alleys, as well as the doorways of various guildhalls" (361). Company records relating to the 1624 Lord Mayor's Show mention the sum of 16 shillings paid to "Nicholas Edmonds, the city carpenter, for taking down and setting up 23 signs, 14 signposts, and 6 tavern bushes, in divers streets where the pageants were to pass" (Robertson and Gordon 108). This reinforces Morrissey's argument but also indicates that artisans exhausted the space available to them.

[26] Cf. Hill: "[T]he performers were usually, but not always, children, and girls may have performed some female roles, for many of the symbolic figures were gendered female" (Pageantry 138). Withington argues that guild records from the 1550s and 1560s indicate that it was the rule rather than the exception for children to act in inaugural shows (11). Company records also announce the involvement of underage actors by way of repeatedly listing among the duties of pageant authors their responsibility for providing "breakfast for the children" (Bergeron, Civic Pageantry 159). The duties of writers hired by the companies were diverse: Not only did they devise pageant episodes, hire performers, provide costumes as well as meals for child actors, they were also in charge of having the pageant texts printed (Bergeron, Civic Pageantry 159; Robertson and Gordon xxxi).

[27] The Standard in Cheapside held symbolic importance as the place where Wat Tyler in 1381, and Jack Cade in 1450 had executed victims (Manley 301). The Standard itself was shaped as a pillar, with statues decorating its sides and a figural representation of Fame blowing a trumpet on top. It also served as a marker of ward boundaries (Hill, Anthony Munday 14).

18

illuminate the procession. Following the church service, the mayor was escorted back to his personal residence and so back to the very starting point of the day's events, where he was presented with a final, torch-lit, farewell speech by a mythological, moral, or historical character.[28]

The typical audience of an early modern Lord Mayor's Show was not only multitudinous but also highly diverse: All along the show route citizens and non-citizens of all persuasions hung from doorways and windows or gathered at street level to see the entertainments. Hill affirms the wide appeal of the pageants and related amusements, such as dances and fireworks, for "an audience of all comers" (Pageantry 38). In their attempts to close in on pageants and remain close to the parade, Londoners prompted flamboyant means of crowd control. In his account of the inaugural celebrations of 1613, Russian ambassador Aleksei Ziusin describes masked men carrying "palms with fireworks" which "threw from them sparkling fire on both sides because of the great press of people, that they might give way. And before them and behind them went soldiers, and on both sides, turning quickly and waving swords and sabres so that people would get out of the way" (ll. 129-35). Not only a broad spectrum of Londoners turned out each year for the event but "many strangers of all Countries [...] come to be spectators of these Annuall Triumphs", notes Thomas Heywood in the pamphlet recording his *Londini Artium & Scientiarum Scaturigo* (London's Fountain of Arts and Sciences) (C3).[29] To accommodate such a diverse audience, Heywood made a point of including in each of his Lord Mayor's Shows an entertainment entirely devoid of scholarly ambition. The third pageant episode in his *Londini Speculum*, he explains

> consisteth of Anticke gesticulations, dances, and other Mimicke postures, devised onely for the vulgar, who are better delighted with that which pleaseth the eye, than contenteth the eare [...]: neither are they altogether to be vilefied by the most supercilious, and censorious, especially in such a confluence, where all Degrees, Ages, and Sexes are assembled, every of them looking to bee presented with some fancy or other, according to their expectations and humours. (312)

Popular accessibility and the eclectic range of entertainments may have contributed to the scholarly reputation of the Lord Mayor's Show as generally irrelevant in comparison with the ostensibly more profound contemporary drama of the public playhouses. Hill has wittily voiced her justified exasperation at this attitude toward civic entertainments, pleading that "[t]he mayoral Show cannot fairly be likened to a 'municipal' entity like a

---

[28] As Henry Machyn's diary suggests, this processional route was already established by 1553 (Bergeron, The Elizabethan Lord Mayor's Show 270). Machyn, who made his living as an undertaker (Hill, Pageantry 132), left personal records covering the period from 1550 to 1563 (Bergeron, The Elizabethan Lord Mayor's Show 270).

[29] As many of these foreign visitors were "such as can iudge of Workmanship" (C3), it was some comfort to Lincolnshire-born Heywood that his creative partner, artisan Garrett Christmas, yearly delivered handiwork that not only achieved good likenesses but was constructed from materials more durable than wicker and paper. Tracey Hill points out that, in contrast to Heywood, the majority of pageant poets entrusted to plot mayoral entertainments were "Londoners born and bred" (Pageantry 94).

public toilet" (Pageantry 15). Applying the standard of the public stage to civic pageantry, critics have eagerly looked for dramatic action and unified plot and, with few exceptions, come away empty-handed. Even Bergeron has commented with some derision on the absence of dramatic interaction and coherent plot in most Lord Mayor's Shows and singles out for praise – as most scholars do – the entertainments of 1612 and 1613 for their indebtedness to the morality play. Dekker's *Troia-Nova Triumphans* (1612), commends Bergeron, "adds up to good theatre with dramatic unity being achieved despite the obstacles" (English Civic Pageantry 170). Yet, he bemoans that "this high point of achievement of 1612 was not duplicated in Dekker's other mayoral pageants" (ibid.). He finds Dekker's 1628 and 1629 shows "sorely lacking" (ibid. 177), even "a sad spectacle" compared with his masterpiece of 1612 (ibid. 178). Following the same pattern, Bergeron praises Middleton's dynamic *Triumphs of Truth* (1613) but is less enthused about the dramatist's other pageants; like the "rather undistinguished work" of 1617 (*The Triumphs of Honour and Industry*), which just "does not measure up" (ibid. 186), these shows are significantly less dramatic and plot-driven.[30] This, however, makes them much more typical Lord Mayor's Shows, which do not, in fact, continually fall short of the standards of the public stage but operate to a different set of standards. Lancashire, too, stresses that criteria applied to the Elizabethan and Jacobean public theater are unsuitable measures when gauging the quality or success of a Lord Mayor's Show (Comedy 6); a point of view that is shared by Hill, who argues persuasively that "the widespread critical preference for Middleton's first mayoral text quite possibly derives from the fact that more than some of its peers it resembles a stage play, the cultural form with which a number of commentators are most comfortable" (Pageantry 5). However, the expectations and value judgments brought to the Lord Mayor's Show should take into account the ritualistic function of the pageants and associated proceedings.

The ceremonies and celebrations observe a magistrate's status elevation from alderman to mayor, but in their regular annual recurrence they are also akin to calendrical, communal rites[31] – involving not only the mayor himself and his immediate affiliates but

---

[30] Bergeron also praises Munday's 1611 entertainment because its portrayal of the resurrection of former mayor Nicholas Faringdon "brings us further in the direction of a meaningful dramatic action" (English Civic Pageantry 150). Demonstrating a similar mindset, Sergei Lobanov-Rostovsky judges Middleton's and Dekker's contributions to the genre as superior to Munday's. While the former two supposedly employ dramatic strategies to favorable effect, the latter only perfects the "emblematic tableaux" (879). Tracey Hill counters Lobanov-Rostovsky's argument that Dekker's and Middleton's shows are dramatic, theater-influenced, and dialogue-driven while Munday's are more static and disconnected and therefore 'worse'. Hill believes Lobanov-Rostovsky to be deliberately creating differences between Munday and more critically acclaimed writers where there are none. In her apt assessment Lobanov-Rostovsky "typefies" an approach that treats "Heywood, Dekker, Taylor and Munday, in particular, [...] as a plebeian bunch of hacks" (Pageantry 5).

[31] In his *Literature and Culture in Early Modern London*, Lawrence Manley calls the inaugural celebrations "a calendrical rite, a periodic collective ceremony" (260).

principally all city dwellers.[32] Arnold van Gennep famously subdivides rites of passage into phases of separation (preliminal phase), transition (liminal phase), and incorporation (postliminal phase) (11). The Lord Mayor's Show understandably favors themes of incorporation as it attempts to knit an incumbent to his new office, to his livery company, to the Court of Aldermen and Common Council, and to suggest and celebrate the unity of the city. A shared meal and ceremonial greetings along the processional route, identified by Van Gennep as common elements of rites of incorporation (20, 32-33), are just some of the means by which the mayor's passage is consummated. Tracey Hill asserts that "[c]orporate feasting was an important 'bonding' activity for the Companies" (Pageantry 62), and points out that other companies also regularly hosted dinners in their own halls on inauguration day (ibid. 138), affirming and strengthening their own communal and professional bonds.

Bearing in mind that a theme of union between mayor and city runs prominently through a significant number of Lord Mayor's Shows, it is perhaps not surprising that the mayor's incorporation into his office in many ways mimics a wedding – a rite of passage which also traditionally favors motifs of incorporation. By conceptualizing London in terms of body (a strategy certainly not unique to the place, period, or genre), the mayor's position vis-a-vis the city can be rendered in concrete, material terms, and the idea of a collective body further offers an opportunity for Londoners to cohere into an organically defined community. A comparable effect was achieved by the earlier religious tradition of Corpus Christi which had also constituted (Christian) society "in terms of body" (James 4).

Although the Lord Mayor's Show was primarily intended not to be read (of) but to be experienced with all senses, for obvious reasons it is necessary to work with the surviving textual and sparse visual records. By far the most important of these are the extant commemorative pamphlets commissioned by the sponsoring companies and distributed to a select clientele.[33] The pamphlets – going by their entry dates into the Stationers' Register[34] – were generally ready for distribution within days of the event (Williams 510). However, despite this urgency, there seems not to have been an actual market in Lord Mayor's Show pamphlets.[35] Hill concludes that the pamphlets were sometimes distributed to company members and guests on the day of the event and sometimes handed out at a later date (Pageantry 233). She concedes that "we do not know whether the printed texts of Shows were actually sold or simply given away" (ibid. 230), but notes that "there does seem to be a degree of congruence between the number of copies of

---

[32]   Supporting a theme of status elevation, Palmer sees in the resurrection of Walworth in Munday's *Chruso-thriambos* a symbolic raising: "'raising' is the theme of this spectacle: the raising of the dead and the raising of a goldsmith to the office of lord mayor." (377)

[33]   Williams speculates that, for the most part, the pamphlets were handed out to company members as souvenirs of the event which they had already witnessed (510). Before the Restoration there is no evidence that poets had more copies produced than stipulated by the company in order to sell them for personal profit (ibid.).

[34]   Yet, "[o]nly rarely were the printed Shows entered in the Stationers' Register" (Hill, Pageantry 229).

[35]   For example: When Thomas Heywood published his *Collected Works*, none of his Lord Mayor's Shows were included.

Shows printed in this period and the number of livery members of the Companies that commissioned them" (ibid. 220). Considering this, however, the "extreme scarcity in Company Halls" of show pamphlets does seem odd (ibid. 258).

Some other points have to be acknowledged: While, certainly, "publication thwarts disappearance" (Bergeron, Civic Pageantry 9),[36] what author and sponsor chose to commit to posterity by means of a commemorative pamphlet may deviate to a greater or lesser extent from the actual performance of a Lord Mayor's Show. Explanations and digressions offered by the voice of the author/narrator in the pamphlets may offer valuable insights to scholars but at the same time it is important to recall the obvious fact that these would not have been available to spectators, even privileged ones, on the day of the festivity. At the same time, elements present on the day may have been omitted from the pamphlet for one reason or another (their seeming inconsequence, a desire to exclude more trivial occurrences or mishaps from the official record).[37]

There are further unavoidable limitations which arise from working with the pamphlets: tantalizingly, narrators hint at sounds and sights available to contemporary spectators but unavailable to modern readers. A sea chariot in Heywood's *Londini Emporia* is described as "visible to all" and, therefore, not in need of "any expression from me" (B), while the "peales of Ordinance" in Munday's *Himatia-poleos* professedly "make better report in the aire, then they can be expressed by pen" (B4). Additionally, the manner in which most spectators experienced the shows, excepting perhaps only the mayor himself, would have differed markedly from the manner in which pamphlets present their material. Although narrative cohesion was not at the heart of the Lord Mayor's Show – most shows consisted of a sequence of separate rather than overtly interconnected pageant tableaux –, it is worth keeping in mind that Londoners, in the main, would have experienced only fragments of the complete entertainment as recorded in the pamphlets. In addition to practical restrictions in visibility and acoustics, the ordinary spectators' view of the entertainments differed from the mayor's experience in as far as the mayor himself was perceived as an actor in the pageants whose movements along the processional route prompted character speeches and other developments. This was sometimes also true (to a lesser extent) of the new sheriffs. Effectively, in Hill's words, "a larger group of spectators were watching a smaller one" (Pageantry 128).

The only visual records of Lord Mayor's Shows prior to the Civil War are the sketches of Dutch eye witness Abram Booth and a set of drawings depicting pageant devices featured in Munday's 1616 *Chrysanaleia*, in the possession of the Company of Fishmongers and known as the "Fishmongers' Pageant Roll" (Hill, Pageantry 234). These latter illustrations were more likely conceptual than commemorative, according to

---

[36] The publication of the pamphlets, in Hill's words, offers "a kind of immortality (or at least a greater longevity than that of a fleeting day) through the medium of print" (Pageantry 193).

[37] Based on comparisons of pamphlets and company records, Hill speculates: "In sum, it seems to me most likely that in the majority of cases – particularly with Dekker's Shows – the main body of the printed works was based, sometimes with very little amendment, on the writer and artificer's scenario for the Show as commissioned by the livery company in question." (Pageantry 250) Scott Trudell certainly agrees that the pamphlet text was completed in advance of the actual performance in the case of Munday's 1605 show (241).

Robertson and Gordon, "not working drawings, but clearly a set executed for submission to the Company for their approval" (xliii-xliv). Hill speculates "that similar illustrations" may have been "produced for other Shows as part of a team's 'project' but not kept" (Pageantry 234). Booth's sketches offer impressions in pencil and ink of pageant episodes from Thomas Dekker's 1629 *Londons Tempe*. Remarkably, the differences between the Dutchman's account – both in word and image – and Dekker's own narration are slight, indicating either a privileged position as a spectator on the day or access to a pamphlet. The circumstance that there are so few visual records of the shows may be due to a relative lack of English expertise in the production of woodcuts and engravings (compared to the conditions in mainland Europe) as much as time constraints in the production of the pamphlets, since these had to be ready for distribution close to the date of the event (Hill, Pageantry 255).

Based on the evidence which the pamphlets afford, it is my aim in the following chapters to demonstrate the ways in which Lord Mayor's Show pageantry cannot adequately be described as "emblematic" when that designation is understood as relating specifically to emblem books and the tripartite text/image compositions found on their pages. This is a project which challenges assumptions repeated in the majority of scholarship on English civic pageantry. The corpus of Lord Mayor's Shows under examination includes all extant texts from the Jacbobean and Caroline periods prior to the Civil War, beginning with Munday's 1605 *Triumphes of Re-United Britannia* – which had to be restaged on All Saints Day due to inclement weather on the original date (Bergeron, Munday n. pag.; Hill, Pageantry 6)[38] – and concluding with Heywood's 1639 *Londini Status Pacatus*, a plea for peace inspired by the ravages of the Thirty Years' War and, arguably, growing political tensions at home.[39]

Following a brief investigation of formal differences between emblems and the mayor's inaugural entertainments in chapter one, chapter two is concerned with thematic discrepancies between these two formats. In chapter three, beginning with a brief survey of terms and concepts, I explore the ritualistic function of the Lord Mayor's Show and devote particular attention to the ubiquity of feminized personifications, notably the "speaking female city" or *urbs invictissima* (Paxson 152). These personifications directly relate to the strong presence of marriage imagery in mayoral pageants. This double phenomenon [personifications and allusions to marriage] has not heretofore received much scholarly attention, and it will form the backbone of my discussion of the Lord Mayor's Show as a unifying ritual. In the third chapter I also examine the processes of (a) enforcing control through naming and (b) expediting integration via "serious punning". Further, I substantiate my claim that Victor Turner's "communitas" concept,

---

[38] Bad weather on and around the day of the show was proverbial. In Middleton's and Dekker's *The Roaring Girl* a character called Trapdoor, on being asked whether he knows the eponymous roaring girl Moll, answers in the affirmative: "[a]s well as I know 'twill rain upon Simon and Jude's day next" (1.2.203-04).

[39] Cf. Bergeron: "The ravages of the plague prevented a pageant in 1603. But in October 1604 Ben Jonson and Munday collaborated in producing the mayor's pageant. [...] Although the guild spent £1 10s. for 'printing the bookes of the device', none has survived." (Munday n. pag.)

according to which disadvantaged groups are endowed with ritual powers, may be profitably drawn on in order to gauge the function(s) of mayoral pageantry.

1 Structural Differences between Emblem and Pageant: Representation and Interpretation

The present chapter challenges – on a formal level – the widely undisputed assumption that Lord Mayor's Show pageantry can unproblematically be dubbed 'emblematic'. A brief résumé of the emblem's key properties will serve as a point of departure. According to emblem-scholar Karl Josef Höltgen, representation and interpretation are two characteristic functions of the emblem which it shares with other allegorical forms of expression (24). German philologist Albrecht Schöne, too, detected in the three-part structure of the prototypical emblem "eine Doppelfunktion des Abbildens und Ausle-gens" [a double function of representation and interpretation] (21). In Höltgen's view each part of the emblem – picture, motto, and explanatory verse – can "share in the double function of representation and interpretation" (ibid.). In general, however, the represen-tational function is fulfilled by the picture while interpretation, i.e. the application of moral to image, is effected by the verbal components of the emblem. Admittedly, the verse very often does incorporate descriptive elements or recounts anecdotes referenced by the picture before moving on to interpretation. The picture, on the other hand, seldom has an overt share in its own interpretation. Significantly, the verse refers back to both picture and motto and so elucidates the connection between these otherwise unrelated components, spelling out the relationship between target (tenor) and source (vehicle) of the metaphor. This strategy sets the emblem apart from other forms of allegory.

In an appraisal of the emblematic qualities of the Lord Mayor's Show, Bergeron has likened pageant tableaux to emblem pictures and character speech to their accompanying verse interpretations. He contends that "the tableaux that constitute [Thomas Middleton's 1613] *The Triumphs of Truth* resemble movable emblems" (Introduction 966) and notes with reference to the character of Zeal that in emblem books, "the verses interpret the symbolism of the emblem, much as Zeal's speech does in the pageant" (ibid. 967). Zeal's elucidation of the hidden qualities signified by the outward appearance of Truth is indeed reminiscent of a type of emblem which presents allegorical personifications and offer verbal interpretations of their attributes (e.g. Truth, Fame, Opportunity etc.). Yet, this instance cannot be taken as a representative sample of the methodology of the Lord Mayor's Show. Bergeron's contention that "[i]n keeping with allegory", the "emblematic method [...] becomes the basic tool for all writers of pageant entertainment" (The Elizabethan Lord Mayor's Show 283), is overly general and somewhat unhelpful in that no explanation is offered as to what constitutes the emblematic method in this context.

Kate D. Levin's account of Anthony Munday's Lord Mayor's Shows corresponds to Bergeron's comment on the role of personified Zeal as a stand-in for an emblem's explanatory verse. Levin defines Munday's shows as "a succession of 'inventions,' from which one figure emerges as a kind of narrator or presenter. At some point toward the end of the pageant this figure explains to the Lord Mayor and his entourage the iconography of all the devices they have seen" (1251). In this case, too, the observation is not unfounded but it bears qualification since interpretation offered in the absence of the referenced pageants comes with its own problems – not to mention that interpretations offered by characters in Lord Mayor's Shows are often partial at best.[1] Frequently, too, sets are so crowded with characters, coats of arms, and other symbolic properties that any attempt at coherent interpretation must fail and is often simply not made. The apparent contrast between a represented personage, object or unfolding scene, on the one hand, and its covert, allegorical meaning, revealed via explicit interpretation, creates the tension at the heart of an emblem. The same is not true for the Lord Mayor's Show, in the context of which the opposition and resolution of two separate planes of expression – the visual and the verbal – is not very significant: Allegorical meanings are generally supposed to be self-explanatory (whether or not that approach always proved successful is another matter). At the same time, one type of pageant made frequent use of in the Lord Mayor's Show (to be discussed in more detail in chapter three) does not so much employ allegorical strategies as a method one might be tempted to call *parvae pro toto* – based on the Merchant Taylors' motto *concordia parvae res crescunt* – by which an idealized vision of small scale craftsmen, tradesmen and laborers was created, inviting spectators of middling and lower socioeconomic standing to feel incorporated into the livery companies' conception of London. At the same time, these episodes or tableaux suggested the existence of a set of values and beliefs shared by the city's merchant elite and less privileged sections of the population. In general, while some pageants were colorfully overcrowded, others deviated from the emblem format by means of their dramatic structure and interactivity.[2]

1.1   Overcrowded Pageant Stages

One chief reason for the non-fulfillment of the "double function of representation and interpretation" in the Lord Mayor's Show is the overcrowding of pageant stages with historical characters, personified Virtues, props, coats of arms or personalized *impresa* – all, of course, amassed for the glory of London – which seriously impedes interpretation. Granted, this is not true for every pageant but it is the case so frequently that most sets cannot comfortably be described as 'emblematic'. Emblems certainly make use of a variety of picture types, including renderings of personifications. However, those emblems which feature personifications generally focus on a single personage and the metaphorical meanings of its physical attributes. Larger groups of personifications in

---

[1]   When Caitlin Finlayson claims that "[e]ach of the 'mount' devices [in Squire's 1620 *Triumphs of Peace*] functions as an emblem, which invites and requires the reader to unfold it", she brushes off the structure of the emblem by using the term as vaguely synonymous with "symbol" or "metaphor" (Jacobean Foreign Policy 597).

[2]   Bergeron has noted "the potential ingredients for drama" in the Lord Mayor's Shows of the Elizabethan period, i.e. "live actors, speeches, a type of stage. What we can witness through the Elizabethan era is a refinement and sophistication of these native components of the incipient dramatic form" (The Elizabethan Lord Mayor's Show 271). Where the Lord Mayor's Show resembles a public stage play most closely, Bergeron is most convinced of its qualities.

contemporary English emblem books are rare. One exception to the rule is Time's vindication of Truth in Whitney's *Choice of Emblemes* – but even here motto and verse very clearly identify the two protagonists and their allegorical significance.

Pageant tableaux, on the other hand, frequently swarm with personifications. Hill, too, has remarked on "the large numbers of protagonists required by some of the individual pageants" (Pageantry 151), and notes that "many of the pageants piled significance upon significance in a way unlikely to be readily or fully accessible to onlookers" (ibid. 176). In Munday's *Chrysanaleia*, for instance, the pageant referred to as the Chariot of Triumphal Victory carries 15 personified vices and virtues, yet no interpretation or moral is formulated. The chariot is drawn by mermen and mermaids – the Fishmongers were the sponsors – while the "triumphing Angell" rides inside the chariot: "[w]ith one hand (King Richard sitting in a degree beneath her) she holds his Crowne on fast […], inferring thus much thereby: By mee Kings reigne, and their enemies are scattered" (B4). In the front of the chariot, lower than monarch and angel, are placed Truth, Virtue, Honour, Temperance, Fortitude, Zeal, Equity, and Conscience as well as Treason and Mutiny. "Behind and on the sides" sit Justice, Authority, Law, Vigilance, Peace, Plenty, and Discipline, who, notes Munday-as-narrator, are the "best props and pillers to any Kingly estate" (ibid.). All personifications "are best observed by their severall Emblems and properties" (B4); they are to be recognizable without further verbal elucidation and, indeed, none is forthcoming. The chariot pays homage to the Fishmongers, to a well-ordered, virtuously governed commonwealth and further implies the monarch's dependence on London and its merchant administrators for a secure reign. In confirmation of the latter, *Chrysanaleia* also commemorates the death of Wat Tyler, leading figure in the Peasants' Revolt of 1381, at the hand of Mayor William Walworth. The historical episode is referenced as an example of the loyalty of London's dignitaries to the crown. In this, no individual importance pertains to any one of the personifications nor to their props and a unified, coherent message or moral is not verbally ascribed to, or drawn from, the materially represented Chariot of Triumphal Victory.

In Munday's *Sidero-thriambos*, a pageant set termed Mount of Fame, wherein "is figured, a modell of London's happy Government" (B4), is also occupied by circa 15 personifications.[3] In the most prominent place sits Fame – "seeming as if she sounded her Golden Trumpet, the Banner whereof, is plentifully powdred with Tongues, Eyes and Eares" (ibid.). Somewhat lower than Fame and to her right sits Expectation who proceeds to tell the newly inaugurated Mayor Sebastian Harvey that he is to be "like a Beacon on an Hill" for his urban constituents. Hope, seated on Fame's left, observes that since Sebastian Harvey's father, Sir James Harvey, had been lord mayor of London before him

---

[3] Following the death of his parents sometime before 1571, Munday was placed under the guardianship of the City of London (Hill, Anthony Munday 29). He was apprenticed to printer John Allde in 1576 and made free of the Drapers' Company by patrimony in 1585. Although Munday was in the habit of signing his publications as "Citizen and Draper", he may have also been free of the Merchant Taylors' Company (Bergeron, Munday n. pag.). Munday's son Richard, a painter and stainer, was made free of the Drapers in 1613, at which time he became involved in the production of props and banners for the Lord Mayor's Show, a side business he persisted in for 25 years (ibid.).

(in 1581), hopes for the son's mayoralty are particularly high. Personified Hope goes on to point out the virtues which "gave his father comfort in his Magistracy", namely Justice and Fortitude. These are shown as conquerors of Ambition, Treason, and Hostility. Fame's "sober sisters Fear and Modesty" are placed on a lower rung behind their many-eyed, -eared, and -tongued sibling. In the show pamphlet, Munday asserts that Vigilance, Providence, Care, Courage, and Council also do their part to protect the Mount and that, "for beter understanding, the personages have all Emblemes and Properties in their hands, and so neere them, that the weakest capacity" should be able to recognize them without any explicit explanation (C2). The pageant tacitly posits that the presented qualities are necessary for the achievement of fame and that new mayor Harvey (of course) already possesses them. In the process, the relation of Harvey to the personified concepts is much more crucial than the interplay between verbal and visual/material components.

Fig. 1: The busy Chariot of Triumphal Victory featured in Munday's *Chrysanaleia* (1616). Plates based on the original drawings were published by J. G. Nichols in 1844. The set of drawings pertaining to *Chrysanaleia* and Abram Booth's diary sketches remain the only extant visual records of 17th-century, pre-Restoration Lord Mayor's Shows. © The British Library Board.

With its 14 personifications the population density of London's Triumphant Mount in Middleton's *Triumphs of Truth* is similar to that of Munday's Mount of Fame. The struggle between Truth and Error, enacted on and around the Mount, is dynamic and, unusually, continues almost throughout the entire show – ending only at the mayor's own residence at night with the final destruction of the antagonist. On the pageant mount, Fame is represented with her trumpet, Liberality holds a cornucopia, Meekness a lamb and Simplicity a dove. Three other personifications are to be identified by their differently colored garlands. The Virtues and Vices associated with the Mount pageant are neither distinguished from one another by a speaker, nor are the meanings of their costumes and properties elucidated, nor even the point of their presence. Once more, their support of merchant London and relation to the new mayor – in 1613 Thomas Myddleton of the Grocers – is imperative, whereas the relation between representation and interpretation is only ancillary.

Furthermore, Bergeron's claim, that "with slight variation Middleton's Truth could have walked off the pages of Peacham's *Minerva Britanna* and into the pageant" (Introduction 967) is exaggerated since nudity and sunbursts – features which both representations share – are conventional characteristics of personified Truth, present in countless other renditions. Peacham's version, moreover, is presented with a book (the Bible) and a globe. From what we can tell, Middleton's Truth is in possession of neither of these items. What is more, Zeal in *Minerva Britanna* is a winged woman with a flaming chest, (Aa3) and, thus, diverges clearly from Middleton's version of the same personage. Although these findings have no bearing on general questions of method, they do at least indicate that Middleton did not use Peacham's *Minerva Britanna* in particular as a sourcebook for his cast of moral personifications.

In Middleton's *The Triumphs of Honour and Industry* (1617) Reward, Justice, Truth (with a sun and a fan), Antiquity (with a scroll), Harmony (with a lute), Fame (with a trumpet), Desert (lacking a prop but supposedly "glorious through her own brightness"), Good Works ("expressed with a college or hospital"), Honor (with a star), Religion (with a temple), Piety (with an altar) and Commiseration (with a heart) linger on top of or in the vicinity of the "Castle of Fame or Honour" in Cheapside and await the approach of new mayor George Bowles (alternatively spelled Bolles) (ll. 225-34). Yet, no speech explains the import of the personified Virtues and their physical attributes to Bolles. Thus, the interface of interpretation and representation, the latter certainly sumptuous and colorful in its own right, again fails to be of much concern. The five personifications riding in the Chariot of Fame in Middleton's third Lord Mayor's Show, *The Triumphs of Honour and Virtue* (1622) are dealt with in a similar manner. Another pageant device in the same show (i.e. a stage construction, not to be confused with *impresi*) is referred to as the Globe of Honor. Inside this pageant globe, which is encountered by new mayor Peter Proby (a Barber-Surgeon turned Grocer) and his entourage after the customary service at St Paul's, are revealed personified Clear Conscience, Divine Speculation, Peace of Heart, Integrity, Watchfulness, Equality, Providence, and Impartiality (Beaven n. pag.). These are identified in the pamphlet as parts of the inward man, though the precise moral import of this for Proby, his colleagues and constituents remains implicit and vague. Outside the device are placed the cardinal virtues Wisdom/Prudence, Justice, Fortitude/Courage, and Temperance/Restraint. Over all of them, Honor keeps watch. All personifications are, according to Middleton, "expressed" by their "proper illustration", yet, what these are and in how far 'illustration' and meaning correlate, Middleton does not disclose.[4] At the Little Conduit, Proby and company are met by the Chariot of Fame, inside of which rides "Antiquity, a grave and reverend personage with a golden register-book in his hand" (ll. 13-15). Antiquity is not alone:

> Next beneath Antiquity sits Authority, placed between Wisdom and Innocence, holding a naked sword, a serpent wound about the blade thereof, two doves standing upon the cross-bar of the hilt, and two hands meeting at the pummel, intimating Mercy and Justice; accompanied with Magistracy, who holds in his hand a key of gold (l. 186ff.).

Antiquity, Authority, Wisdom, Innocence, and Magistracy all presumably contribute to fame and are present for the glorification of Mayor Proby and the City of London. The exact nature of their function and meaning is not elucidated, however, and their individual props remain relatively inconsequential. The same is true of the characters riding in the Chariot of Honor, both the first and final pageant device of Middleton's *Triumphs of Health and Prosperity* (1626) – and recycled from his *Triumphs of Integrity* (1623). In "the most eminent seat" perches a personification of Government, "it being the proper virtue by which we raise the noble memory of Sir Henry fitz Ailwin [the first mayor of London]" (ll. 119-21). Sir John Norman is represented "under the person of Munificence" and Sir Simon Eyre, "under the type of Piety" (ll. 124-27). Yet, exactly how this is achieved and on which grounds concepts and eminent historical mayors were matched is not communicated. The chariot itself is drawn by two golden pelleted lions, in allusion to the heraldic felines supporting the Drapers' arms. Power and Honor "have their seats upon the lions" and showcase "the one in a little streamer or banneret [...] the arms of the present lord mayor; the other of the late" (ll. 128-33).

Government/Fitz Ailwin gives a speech from the chariot which postulates that London is for the whole of England as the heart is for the human body, while the monarch compares to the head, the "counsellors of state" to the eyes, churchmen to the lips, and the "defensive part of men" to human arms (ll. 151-56). The message of incorporation is very much relevant to the festivities – and will be discussed in detail in chapter three – but the way in which it is presented here does not conform to emblem conventions since no body parts whatsoever are represented to form the material part of the equation (incidentally, the heart became a frequent subject in 17th century religious emblems). The analogy of body and state (containing both representation and interpretation), thus, remains restricted to the verbal sphere, while the material presences of Government/Fitz Ailwin, Munificence/Norman, and Piety/Eyre do not relate explicitly to what is stated. The second pageant in Dekker's *Brittannia's Honor* (1628), sponsored by the Worshipful

---

[4]   A globe featured as a major set piece in Ben Jonson's 1606 court masque *Hymenaei* from which emerged eight performers, impersonating the Four Humors and Four Affections (Bergeron, Middleton's No Wit 69). Another globe device had been a part of Dekker's triumphal arch for the Royal Entry into London of James I; that globe had been accompanied by personified Justice, Virtue, Fortune, Envy, the remaining Cardinal Virtues and the Four Elements, while inside the globe were represented the "states" of the land, in a hierarchy ranging from noblemen down to poor laborers (ibid. 67).

Company of Skinners, is New Troy's Tree of Honor. The arbor set is home to Minerva (Athena) and Bellona, signifying wisdom and martial force respectively, as well as to personified London, Peace, Religion, Civil Government, Justice, Learning, Industry, and Honor.[5] In addition to these ten personifications, an assortment of coats of arms is placed in and around the Tree of Honor. The device implicitly attributes the assembled qualities to New Troy, i.e. London, and stresses the metropolitan importance of the venerable organizations invoked by their arms. Once more individual personifications and their props are of secondary importance as is the interface of visual appearance and its verbal conditioning. The same is true of the show's fourth device – Britannia's Watchtower – which harbors not only Britannia herself but four angels, a shipwright, Edward the Confessor, kings Richard I, John, Henry III, as well as personified Magnanimity and Victory. Dekker's last device is a flowery arbor called the Sun's Bower for its primary occupant, Roman sun god Sol (Helios to the Greeks, and frequently conflated with Apollo). "[W]ith golden Beames about his Face", the deity sits amid personified Spring, Summer, Autumn, and Winter, all in their "proper Habiliments" (C2). Below Sol and the Seasons, furry animals commingle, "some grinning, with lively, naturall postures" (C2), among them "Beare, Wolfe, Leopard, Luzerne, Cat-A-Mountaine, Foxes, Sables, Connies, Ferrets, Squirrels" (ibid.). Above these beasts a scroll declares: "Deus ecce Furentibus obstat. See, for all some Beasts are fell, There's one, that can their curstnesse quell." (ibid.) Sol gives a speech from the pageant stage in praise of London but does not offer a coherent interpretation of himself, his companions or surroundings. The scroll comes close to functioning as an emblem motto – stressing the civilizing power of the mayor – but Sol's speech does not further clarify the relation between motto and pageant tableau, nor offer any interpretation of the physical setup, as the verse part of an emblem generally would. Rather, Sol's main function is to represent a strongly beneficial – and almost divine – influence on London, analogous in nature to that attributed to and expected of new mayor Richard Deane.

In Munday's *Himatia-poleos* a chariot, drawn by golden pelleted lions and golden "Woolves Ermimois after the manner of the triumphall Chariot of the Romaine Emperours", carries "the supposed shape of King Richard the first" and with him personifications of several cities including London, "chiefe Mother and matrone of them all" (B2). The chariot implicitly commemorates the creation of the office of mayor of London under Richard I and simultaneously validates the current-day office and its newly inaugurated incumbent. There is, however, no dissimilarity or tension between this implication and the physically manifest chariot and its crew which might then be verbally

---

[5] Peace holds a dove in one hand and a palm branch in the other, Religion wears a glossy white robe and a coronet of stars. In one hand she holds an open book (the Bible), in the other a golden ladder (Jacob's) (B2). Civil Government wears a robe covered with eyes and holds a dial, intimating vigilance (B3). Justice holds a sword, Learning a book and Jacob's staff (B3). Industry carries a golden hammer and "a Sea-mans Compasse, as taking paines to get wealth, both by Sea and Land", while Honor is purposefully dressed in scarlet as is the mayor himself (B3). Yet, these descriptions are given only in the pamphlet and the multitude of characters again distracts from the relationship between form and meaning in the individual personification.

31

resolved. Another matron and her retinue are lodged on the show's third pageant stage, which is a "goodly Monument figuring the whole estate of London's Draperie" (B2). With personified 'Drapery', known as Himatia (referencing the ancient Greek wrap-around garment), are her daughters: Personified "Carding, Spinning, Weaving, Rowing, Fulling, Shearing, Dressing, Dying, Tentering" (ibid.). Furthermore, "Peace, Plentie, Liberalitie, Councell and Discreet Zeale, doe supporte the florishing condition of Himatiaes Common-wealth" (B2). While the pamphlet allows no final conclusion as to whether these five personifications were also impersonated by actors on the pageant stage, based on the evidence other pageants provide (their tendency to carry plenty of characters), it appears likely that they would have been. No explicit interpretation accompanies Himatia's "goodly Monument" with its ten to fifteen personifications – all of whom, notes the character of John Norman later in the day, the mayor's "well iudging eye may easily conceive [...] by their apt distinguishment" (C2).

The second device in Munday's *Metropolis Coronata* (1615) is a "Sea Chariot" on the Thames which, so narrator-Munday informs, is provided by Neptune himself for the sole reason of rendering the day's festivities "more magicall" (A4). Inside the contraption, "shaped like to a Whale, or the huge Leviathan of the Sea" (ibid.), ride "the shadow of Sir Henry Fitz-Alwine"[6] and a band of eight personified 'Royal Virtues'. These carry the heraldic shields of eminent members of the Drapers' Company, by name "Poultney, Cromer, Aeyre, Wotton, Sidney, Bullen, Campbell, Champion"; but the ways in which virtues and Drapers correspond is not spelled out. The pageant also contains "Fame triumphing in the top, and Time guiding the way before" (B). From his chariot, Fitz Ailwin greets Mayor John Jolles and confesses himself pleasantly surprised that for a second, consecutive year a Draper has been elected to the city's highest office. He then turns his attention to the show opener, a pageant Argo carrying Jason, Medea, Hercules, Telamon, Orpheus, twins Castor and Pollux (appearing to sailors as St Elmos's Fire) and Calais and Zethes (sons of the north wind), plus attendant eunuchs. "You are our Jason, London's glorie," Fitz Ailwin tells Jolles on his way to Westminster, "Now going to fetch that fleece of Fame, / That ever must renowne your name" (B2). While Fitz Ailwin steps into the role of tableau commentator for the Argo pageant – tapping into the association of merchants and venturous Argonauts – his own busy sea chariot remains uninterpreted. Certainly, the device lauds the venerable history of London's civic administration in general and the Worshipful Company of Drapers in particular but it does so implicitly (yet firmly) without exploiting a solvable discrepancy between the 'seen' and its unseen allegorical meaning.

The first pageant elements encountered by the mayor on land, following his return from Westminster, are a ship named "Ioell" ('seriously punning' on the mayor's name), Neptune seated on a pelleted lion, personified Thames on a "Sea-Horse", as well as "a goodly Ramme or Golden Fleece [...] having (on each side) a housewifely Virgin sitting, seriously imployed in Carding and Spinning Wooll for Cloth" (B3). Having transitioned

---

[6]   Hill argues that Munday presents Fitz Ailwin's guild membership with deliberate ambiguity in *Metropolis Coronata* due to an earlier mistake regarding his company affiliation (172). It is also possible that Munday simply chose to put a convenient spin on the matter on both occasions.

from water to land, the Argo follows in the wake of the ram. Thus, St Paul's becomes the backdrop for an eclectic medley of elements: The "Ioell" and its crew, Neptune, Thames, and the 'spinning virgins' amount to four separate pageants, composed of multiple parts each. All of these components, it seems reasonable to conclude, contribute to a celebration of shipping and land-bound lines of work in the production of cloth. Beyond this tacit understanding no speech draws any concrete messages from the pageants, let alone connects them all. A similar potpourri of pageantry in the vicinity of St Paul's was provided by Dekker in 1612: At Paul's Chain, early in *Troia-Nova Triumphans*, Neptune, moon goddess Luna, mermaids, ships and – not least – horses costumed as dolphins commingled.

Another pageant episode in *Metropolis Coronata* centers on Robin Hood, here "Earle Robert de la Hude, sometime the noble Earle of Huntington", made by Munday "Sonne in Law (by Marriage) to olde Fitz-Alwine" in order to justify his presence at the civic event (B3).[7] Earl Robert initially exhibits churlishness at being 'resurrected', typical of Munday's Lord Mayor's Show characters, before perking up and fulfilling his dedicatory role. "[L]ittle John Scathlocke, Much the Millers sonne, Right-hitting Brand, Fryar Tuck", all armed with bows and arrows, are among the earl's band of yeomen outlaws (ibid.). All together they form a choir and offer some musical entertainment following the show's farewell speech, delivered at the mayor's gates. The episode constitutes a highly unusual coda which falls outside of the conventional structure of the Lord Mayor's Show. Yet, while the merry spectacle is broadly community-affirming in its accessibility, it does not point at 'truths' beyond its material self. In Dekker's *Londons Tempe* (1629), the fourth pageant stage bears the "Lemnian Forge" where Vulcan (Hephaestus to the Greeks) and his cyclopes – sporting shaggy black manes and leather aprons – swing their hammers while singing a work song (B). Dekker had previously conjured the image of Vulcan as a happy and eager workman, when writing of diligent "yong shopkeepers [...] plying their business harder all day then Vulcan does his Anvile" (The Seven Deadly Sinnes 20). In *Londons Tempe*, while the cyclopes are industriously hammering, Cupid is on the receiving end of a steady supply of golden and silver arrows from the smithy which he proceeds to shoot into the sky (B3). Somewhere above perches Jove (Jupiter), always in need of thunderbolts – fresh from the fire – with which to put down roarers Pride, Avarice, Ambition, and War. The episode honors the Company of Ironmongers and is paradigmatic in its use of characters and setting. Cyclopes, Vulcan, Cupid and even Jupiter are presented, in a playful manner, as well-wishers and supporters of the city. Despite its personnel – Jupiter and, in particular, Cupid are recurrent emblem book characters –, the pageant is far from being a three-dimensional emblem. No concrete moral or message is drawn from it, neither on the spot nor later on, and there is no crucial interplay between visual and verbal elements.

---

[7] Munday had previously written two successful stage plays about Robin Hood: *The Downfall of Robert, Earl of Huntington* and *The Death of Robert, Earl of Huntington* were not published until 1601 but one or both plays were performed at court in 1598 (Bergeron, Munday n. pag.).

Fig. 2: Self-love (Philautia) holds a mirror to her face but still remains "in her Imperfections blind" in Peacham's fifth emblem. The mirror and serpent held by her are elucidated below the image in the form of a dialogue. Philautia was evoked often and commended highly in Erasmus' The Praise of Folly. Image by courtesy of the David M. Rubenstein Rare Book & Manuscript Library, Duke University.

The same is the case on the 'Orferie' set in Munday's *Chruso-thriambos* (where Chthoon/Terra, Gold, Silver, Antiquity, Memory, Experience, and Goldsmith Dunstan implicitly attest to the virtue inherent in mining and metalworking) and numerous other sets across the Lord Mayor's Shows of Middleton, Munday, Dekker, Squire, Taylor and Heywood. Pageant episodes frequently do not rely on the tension between visual and verbal components as emblems do and, at the same time, stages are often so overcrowded with well-wishers and supporters that focus necessarily shifts away from individual characters. As mentioned previously, a subset of emblems centers on the depiction of personifications (see for example fig. 2 below) and the written elucidation of their significant attributes but this process is rarely realized in the corpus of Lord Mayor's Shows under examination. Furthermore, allegorical personifications were by no means a prerogative of the emblem book but were a staple of early modern visual and literary culture. Other types of emblem depict and interpret anecdotes, fables, plants, animals, architectural elements, or everyday objects (singly or grouped together) but this is not a mode of operation generally utilized in the Lord Mayor's Show.

1.2 Dramatic Structure and Reciprocity

Some pageant episodes deviate from the 'emblematic mode' by their interactivity and dynamic structure. In Munday's *Chruso-thriambos* (1611)[8] personified Time, who can "[r]ecall[...] to the present sight of Sunne / Actions, that (as forgot) have lien at rest" (B3), temporarily resurrects two former civic dignitaries. First, Leofstane – "a Gold-Smith, the first Provost that bare authoritie in London" (A4), and grandfather to London's first mayor Henry fitz Ailwin – is ordered to spend the day in the retinue of new mayor James Pemberton. Leofstane complies although he admits that, having spent the past five hundred years entombed, the extent of Time's control over worldly matters (including, apparently, dead matter) had receded from his mind and now comes as an inconvenient surprise. Time gives Mayor Pemberton a brief account of the history of London's mayoralty, with special reference to the sponsoring company of Goldsmiths. The procession then moves to a pageant stage which presents the tomb of Goldsmith and former mayor Nicholas Faringdon. Here, Time announces, "sleepes one, / Whom in this urging, and important case, / (He being Gold-Smith too, and long since gone / Out of this world, old Nicholas Faringdon, / Foure times Lord Maior) I may not well omit" (B4). He strikes the tomb with his silver wand and thereby causes Faringdon to revive. Time, Leofstane and Faringdon not only interact with each other but also incorporate Pemberton into their group, validating his venerable position within the Worshipful Company of Goldsmiths and the providential history of London itself. There is, however, nothing particularly emblem-like about the episode.

A "goodly Ramme or Golden Fleece, with a Sheepheard sitting by it", awaits new mayor Thomas Hayes on his return from Westminster in Munday's 1614 *Himatia-poleos.*

---

[8]   There is a good possibility that Munday's *A Briefe Chronicle of the Successe of Time*, also published in 1611, which depicted the Goldsmiths in a positive light, gained him the commission for that year's Lord Mayor's Show (Hill 81).

The shepherd addresses Hayes directly and tells him of the debt of gratitude shepherds from the Cotswolds – an area famous for its own "longwooled and large-boned" breed of sheep (Harmer) – supposedly feel they owe to London Drapers. As a gesture of thanksgiving, he goes on to explain, these shepherds traditionally send their best ram to London when a member of the Drapers' Company is inaugurated as Lord Mayor (B4). The pageant episode depends crucially on the presence of Hayes who has to acknowledge the gift of the sheep and thereby symbolically affirm the mutually beneficial economic relations between London merchants in the cloth and wool trade and shepherds and weavers in other parts of the kingdom. Another 'unemblematic' pageant episode in *Himatia-poleos* is presented to Hayes even earlier in the festivities. On the Thames a vessel called "Barke-Hayes" in his honor is "supposedly laden with woollen sloathes" (B2). On board are a "Captaine, Maister, Mate" (B2), representing professions involved in the shipping of goods to and from London. More generally the Barke-Hayes expresses the boon of commerce and hints at the innumerable, diverse livelihoods dependent on it. While the pageant pays tribute to Hayes and features multiple characters in action, it does not depend on his active participation. Still, with no contrast or tension between the material elements and their import (neither glossed by a character nor interpreted in the pamphlet) the emblematic mode is not invoked. Rather the crew aboard the ship represent London's working population and elevate them to a place of importance in the ideology of the city. The same applies to the fishing boat in Munday's *Chrysanaleia* with its laboring crew (fig. 3) and the above example of the Cotswolds shepherd and his ram (which honors shepherds and associated occupations). In Heywood's *Porta Pietatis* (1638) a shepherd – with his flock and his dog – is placed on a "plat-forme adorn'd with flowers, plants, and trees, bearing sundry fruits" (267). In his speech, the shepherd praises "the profits of your trades commerce" (267), these being the means "[b]y which all states, all common weales subsist" (268). Simultaneously, he articulates his appreciation of the humble sheep which renders valuable services to mankind by being an accommodating source of wool, milk, and meat. Except for the reduced role of the mayor, who is not asked to accept a ritual gift in Heywood's scenario, the pageant functions as Munday's shepherd pageant does.

Another point of departure from the emblem is the widely practiced custom to distribute small gifts from pageant stages, in a manner reminiscent of throws from carnival floats. These gifts were generally company related and intended to raise the sponsoring company's profile among Londoners. In Munday's *Chruso-thriambos* personified Gold and Silver, along with their mother Terra, alternately identified as Justice in the Goldsmiths' records, "dispers[ed] money abroad" from their pageant mountain (Robertson and Gordon 81). In 1613 the Grocers spent £3 on "nutmegges, Gynger, almonde in the shell, and sugar loves" to be "throwen abowt the streetes by those w[ch] sate on the Gryffyns and Camells" in that year's *Triumphs of Truth* (ibid. 88). The same amount was again spent on sugar loaves, dates, ginger roots, almonds, and nutmegs in 1622 (ibid. 104). Early in *The Triumphs of Re-united Britannia* Neptune and his wife Amphitrite make an appearance, seated astride a lion and camel respectively. They throw pepper, cloves, and mace to onlookers. In *Chrysanaleia* the "King of Moores" flings coins about him from the back of a golden leopard (B2), and fishermen distribute free fish from a "beautifull fishing Busse, called the Fishmongers Esperanza, or Hope of London" (B), demonstrating the goodwill and largesse of Goldsmiths (coins) and Fishmongers (fish).[9] Interactive episodes like these were a staple of the Lord Mayor's Show and were sure to engage spectators as much as canvas for their allegiance.

Fig. 3: Fishermen on Munday's "beautifull fishing Busse" distribute their catch with notable abandon. © The British Library Board.

In Munday's *Chrysanaleia* the "imaginary body of Sir William Walworth" is laid out on a tomb, like an effigy of the departed (a common funerary practice among the wealthy), in St Paul's churchyard (B3).[10] The stage on which the tomb is erected is dressed as "a goodly Bower" and near the pageant wait five knights as well as "Londons Genius" on

---

[9] The "King of Moores" pageant episode was intended as a tribute to the Goldsmiths since a traditional friendship bound them to the Fishmongers. In Munday's *Chruso-thriambos* Time refers to this traditional friendship but makes sure to point out that the expense for the day's show was covered entirely and solely by the Goldsmiths (C2-3).

[10] In Dekker's and Middleton's play *The Roaring Girl*, dashing gallant Jack Dapper recalls being compared to "a painted alderman's tomb" at an ordinary (5.1.29). The humorous anecdote testifies to the grandeur of city magistrates' funerary monuments – which would have inspired Munday and his artificer-partner in planning their tomb set.

horseback.[11] The latter carries the severed head of Peasants' Revolt leader Wat Tyler "on Walworth's Dagger" (ibid.). With the following incantation – as well as the help of a magic wand and the blast of trumpets – the Genius causes Walworth to wake from his death-like slumber: "Though yet thou sleep'st in shade of death; / By me take power of life and breath. [...] / Londons Genius gives thee leave, / An ayrie substance to receive." On regaining consciousness, Walworth offers "to doe what gracefull helpe I may / Unto that band of worthy men, [the Fishmongers] / That were, and are my Brethren". The episode brings civic hero William Walworth back to life so that he can praise the sponsoring company, London's civic administration as a whole, and highlight the good relations between crown and city. The means employed in the endeavor are neither those of the emblem nor even allegorical. The episode is a dramatic interlude, set in motion by the mayor, which interweaves past and present, real life and play, as the historical Walworth is 'brought to the present' by Time to interact with new mayor John Leman.

In *Triumphs of Truth*, Truth's Angel and Zeal, two of the show's main characters, welcome new mayor Thomas Myddleton back to the city after his oath-taking in Westminster and immediately pull him into the action. The entire show is uncommonly dramatic and consecutive pageant episodes relate to and build on each other to an unusual extent. At Paul's Chain, Truth's antagonist, Error,[12] appears – along with his "infernal ministers" – and attempts to corrupt Myddleton by suggesting to him the manifold ways in which he might abuse his office for personal profit, i.e. for "revenge or gain" (l. 273). Error's head is "rolled in a cloud, over which stands an owl", while "a mole [perches] on one shoulder, a bat on the other, [...] mists hanging at his eyes". These attributes are all identified by Middleton as "symbols of blind ignorance and darkness" in the commemorative pamphlet. Outside of the pamphlet, however, no comment is uttered on the relationship between Error's outward attributes and inward qualities or moral import. Error's ally is Envy, who is seated astride a rhinoceros and gnaws on a human heart – proverbially her own (ll. 251-52). Her left breast is bared and on it suckles a snake; in her right hand she carries a bloody dart (ll. 252-54). In the *psychomachia* for Myddleton's soul (with the outcome of the conflict between Truth and Error never in doubt), what is ultimately important is the affirmation of London's civic administration and Myddlton's status elevation.

Envy also plays a part in Dekker's *Troia-Nova Triumphans* (1612), the structure of which resembles *Triumphs of Truth*. At the Little Conduit, Envy holds the "Forlone Castle", "attired like a Fury, her haire full of Snakes, her countenance pallid, meagre and leane, her body naked, in her hand a knot of Snakes, crawling and writhen about her arme". She is accompanied by Ignorance, Sloth, Oppression, and Disdain, all of whom carry bows and arrows with which to shoot at Virtue. At the castle gate two club-carrying

---

[11] The genius of the city had also greeted newly-crowned James I at the first pageant arch encountered on his Royal Entry through London. The arch, conceived by Ben Jonson, had also displayed a miniature model of the City of London across its top (Bergeron, Turks 261). The genius of the city makes a further appearance in Heywood's *Londini Status Pacatus* (1639).

[12] In Spenser's *Fairie Queene* personified Error appears "[h]alfe like a serpent horribly displaide, / But th' other halfe did womans shape retaine" (book 1, canto 1, stanza 14). She is black-blooded like the dragon which is slain at a later point in the first book (ibid., stanza 24).

giants, by name Riot and Calumny, stand guard (B4). When Virtue's chariot passes by the castle it manages to do so unharmed. The arrows of Envy's minions miss their purported mark and explode in fireworks (C1). Triumphant Virtue then leads new mayor John Swinnerton to the House of Fame which is placed near the Cross in Cheapside;[13] here a selection of eminent historical personages, in bygone times free of the Merchant Taylors, have already taken their place. Fame herself urges Swinnerton to continue following Virtue since "in this Court of Fame / None else but Vertue can enrole thy Name". She goes on to list exemplary personages free of the Merchant Taylors, among them Henry VII, "who made both Roses in one Branch" by his marriage to Elizabeth of York (C2). Eventually pistol shots cause Envy and her companions to vanish. A very similar dynamic characterizes *The Triumphs of Truth* and Middleton almost certainly drew inspiration from Dekker's 1612 show. Both entertainments are relatively coherent moral allegories but neither of them demonstrates a heightened concern with visual-verbal relations, i.e. the separate levels of representation and interpretation which constitute the emblem according to Höltgen, Schöne and others.

---

[13] Geoffrey Chaucer had found the *House of Fame* in his eponymous 14th-century dream vision not in Cheapside but, more precariously, built on a foundation of ice (1135).

2   Merchant Heroes and Merchant Monkeys: Themes of Mayoral Pageantry and Popular Emblem Books

As previously mentioned, the supposition that the pageant tableaux of English Renaissance festivities "were three-dimensional emblems closely related to the two-dimensional ones of the popular emblem-books" (Williams 504), is almost universally accepted. David Bergeron renders the assumption in concrete and colorful terms: "At times it is as if some of these figures in civic pageants have merely stepped from the pages of the popular emblem books" (English Civic Pageantry 161). In this tradition, a close affinity between the pageant tableaux of early modern Lord Mayor's Shows and the popular emblem anthologies of the age has been propounded by scholars. This apparent consensus on the compatibility of emblem book and real-life festivity, however, is unsubstantiated in the case of the Lord Mayor's Show of the first half of the 17th century. A close examination of pageant pamphlets, eye-witness accounts, and emblem books reveals that the themes which run through the emblem collections of the likes of Geffrey Whitney and Henry Peacham, on the one hand, and those which permeate the Lord Mayor's Shows by Munday, Middleton, Dekker et al., on the other, are frequently incompatible, sometimes even antithetically opposed. I do not deny at all that some of the communicative strategies deployed by emblematists are also at work in festive pageant tableaux, nor that some topics are taken up and some personages appear in both contexts. However, these similarities – based on recourse to contemporary systems of knowledge and a common image stock – should not obscure the fact that there are also significant differences.

Here is a scenario: If the characters who appear in Lord Mayor's Shows had, in fact, stepped from the pages of such popular emblem books as Whitney's *A Choice of Emblemes* (1586) or Peacham's *Minerva Britanna* (1612) and exhibited their emblem book personalities in the streets of London, the nature of the show would have been significantly transformed. Jupiter would not have bowed to any mayor but caused murder and mayhem, punishing human pride and vanity or simply exercising his almighty – and destructive – powers for no humanly conceivable reason at all. Meanwhile, the splendid barges of civic dignitaries would not have arrived in triumph at Paul's Wharf but suffered shipwreck on the Thames. Crowds would not have been united in their celebration of London and in their eagerness to be a part of the spectacle but would rather have turned against each other. Some merchants and company dignitaries might even have found themselves metamorphosed into monkeys – a scenario suggested by Peacham's 168th emblem.

The frailty and ineffectiveness of humankind when confronted with the forces of a darkly chaotic world is a recurrent theme on the pages of Whitney's and Peacham's anthologies, whereas the Lord Mayor's Show projects a conception of the cosmos as harmonious and benevolent into the streets of the capital and beyond. Moreover, spectators are invited to feel a part of an integral community of Londoners which flourishes in these conditions and which even absorbs a variety of ethnic 'others' into its

41

fabric. Conversely, Whitney's and Peacham's emblem collections insist on the ever present potential for conflict in human interaction and tend to ascribe inherent depravity to non-Europeans. Furthermore, while popular emblems invite readers to ponder the sin of pride, vilify ambition, and scorn the accumulation of material possessions, pride in civic identity is obviously essential to the celebrations surrounding the mayor's inauguration. Here, industry and ambition, too, are lauded as qualities which deserve to be rewarded and wealth is understood as the deserved consequence of industry, serving not just those who have it but the have-nots and the entire metropolitan community, too. The fact that a contingent of poor men were traditionally clothed in blue garments and included in the mayoral parade – i.e. "[t]he temporary inclusion of representatives of 'the poor' into the corporate body of the livery" – contributes to the "putative inclusiveness" and charity broadcast by the Lord Mayor's Show (Hill, Pageantry 192).

Another major difference between emblem books and mayoral pageantry lies in the treatment of ships and seafaring: In the Lord Mayor's Show ships signify the entrepreneurship of merchants and the forms of social organization accruing around it in the city. In emblems, however, the topic functions as a metaphor for the precarious mortal journeys of men and women through their earthly lives: seafaring is frequently linked with the uncertainty of human undertakings in the face of ungovernable forces, of time, and mortality. In his emblem book *A Theatre for Worldlings*, Jan van der Noot articulates this daunting perspective on life in the sobering phrase that "nought in this worlde but griefe endures" (emblem 8, 15). Lord Mayor's Shows, on the other hand, embrace a view of life that is distinctly less foreboding. The mood of the show is buoyant: exotic displays, dances, fireworks, idealistic representations of working people and merchant culture all contribute to a cheerful communal event for Londoners and visitors alike. Eye-witness Abram Booth reports music, fanfares and fireworks (22). Chariots, temples, and idyllic arbors are commonplace sets while gods, personified virtues, and reverent forbears are recurring characters. While English emblem books may incorporate all of the above, they have a side, too, – conveniently ignored by a majority of scholars of Renaissance pageantry – which is dark, misanthropic, even reveling in gruesome minutiae.

Furthermore, compounded by the circumstances of reception, emblems invite detached introspection while Lord Mayor's Shows are communal events which hinge on immediate, collective engagement. In a foreword to Peacham's *Minerva Britanna*, William Segar affirms that in contemplating Peacham's offerings, insight "doth yeild to reason what is due" (B3). To Segar, it is Peacham's aim to nurture the "good insight" of his readers (ibid.). This bias toward reflection is countered by an impulse toward immediate involvement in the reception of Lord Mayor's Show pageants. All of this, it might be argued, is rather self-evident, yet, previous approaches to the matter would suggest otherwise.

As suggested above, the powerlessness of man in the face of fate, chance, or god's incomprehensible will is a motif frequently encountered in English emblem books. The books make no clear distinction between fate, fortune, or chance but construe them all as seemingly random developments which affect human beings, often to their detriment, which cannot be anticipated and which are not generally regonizable as part of a divine plan, though they may be. Lord Mayor's Shows, on the other hand, present the antithesis to apparent chaos: a well ordered world in which everything has its proper place, plans come to fruition, the good prosper, and the bad are chastised for misdemeanors. "Time, and Industry attaine the prise", states the character of Edward III in Webster's *Monuments of Honour*, expressing the sentiment succinctly (B3). The mayor's journey itself is represented as the epitome of personal accomplishment and reward. Correspondingly, Manley has found "annual self-renewal and the historical providence that culminated in the crowning achievements of an individual citizen" to be typical themes of mayoral pageantry (308). Each new mayor, so the consensus, has led a life of merit and his promotion is no more than a deserved consequence of his previous achievements and conduct.

Contrarily, the cruelty of unknowable, uncontrollable fate is invoked in Whitney's 22nd emblem, "Nullus dolus contra Casum/No cunning against chance", which combines the image of a fox adrift on an ice float with the moral that "no subtill crafte will serve, / When chance doth throwe the dice" (111). No preparation, neither shrewdness nor goodness can prevent calamity from striking. There is no order that cannot be overthrown by chance. "That evell happes, unlooked for doe comme", is the message of Whitney's emblem 185, under the motto "Semper praesto esse infortunia/Misfortunes are always at hand" (275). The emblem picture shows three women playing dice around a central table. They play, explains the verse, in order to find out which of them will be the first to die. Yet, the player for whom the outcome of the game promises a long life is killed by a falling tile while still seated at the table. Life, this implies, can be short and cruel and the only certainty it offers is uncertainty. In a similar vein, one of Thomas Combe's emblems shows Hercules fighting Hydra in illustration of the precept that dangers often come when they are least expected (380).[1] Peacham's emblem 76 (M2) invokes the concept of the wheel of fortune according to which men, even kings, are subject to the ups and downs of fortune regardless of their own provisions. The emblem picture shows a wheel with four crowns fastened to its outer rim, one on top, one at the bottom, and one on each side, to indicate the turmoils of fortune that even sovereigns are subject to. That fortune does not favor the virtuous over the wicked is the tenor of Whitney's emblem 76, "Fortuna virtutem superans/Fortune vanquishing virtue", which illustrates the suicide of Marcus Junius Brutus following the battle of Philippi and annotates the image with the words "[t]hat fortunes force, maie valiant hartes subdue" (164). How even the strongest and wisest are not immune to the cruelty of random chance is expressed in Peacham's emblem 197 which shows the Olympian Pallas Athena trapped in a net. Elucidating the image, the

---

[1]   Thomas Combe's 1593 emblem book, *The Theater of Fine Devices*, is a translation and adaptation of Guillaume de la Perrière's 1539 *Le Theatre des Bons Ensigns* (Silcox 328).

verse states that even the wise can be fooled and virtue itself must "stoope to Fortunes ficklenesse" (Ee1). That people are mere playthings to fortune is reaffirmed by Peacham's emblem 153, "Sors" (Y3), which relates the story of two men whose trajectories in life are ironically, cruelly inverted: One man, in a state of despair, is prevented from committing suicide only by the unexpected discovery of a treasure, hidden underneath a rope – the very rope which he would have used to hang himself with. When the rightful owner of the treasure returns and finds it gone, he despairs and proceeds to take his own life, using the rope that remains in the place of his treasure.

The futility of some endeavors, however diligently pursued or well-intended, is expressed by Whitney in his emblem 48, "Labor irritus/Labour in vain", which shows a donkey munching on one end of a rope which a rope maker is meanwhile in the act of producing. The verse states in matter of fact misogynist terms that "[t]he Asse declares a wicked wastfull wife: / Whoe if shee maie, she quicklie spendes and spoiles / That he with care, was getting all his life" (137). Defying this portrayal of a futile enterprise, industry always has positive connotations in Lord Mayor's Shows and is, in fact, celebrated as the cornerstone of London society.

In opposition to the caprioles of a cruel and unpredictable universe, the Lord Mayor's Show embraces a world view that is orderly and has as its perpetual telos the inauguration of the lord mayor into London's highest civic office.[2] The show's regular recurrence not only emphasizes the tradition and clockwork reliability of city administration, it also regenerates 'exhausted social energy', a function integral to Arnold van Gennep's understanding of ritual (182). Lawrence Manley's observation that the Lord Mayor's Show effects a kind of "annual self-renewal" reiterates Van Gennep's claim and suggests that the impact of the yearly event is not confined to the 29th of October, the day of the inaugural entertainments, but has longer lasting social implications. The show creates a cosmology inside of which the lord mayor, as himself and as an actor inside the narrative, is raised into his rightful place – within the city and within the realm (the ritual aspects of this preferment will be further scrutinized in chapter three). The invariability of the lord mayor's route through the city reflects the notion that his advancement is as much destined as deserved and should therefore proceed along clear and predictable lines. As an enactment of a journey that is territorially as well as socially defined, the Lord Mayor's Show conforms to van Gennep's assessment that a rite of passage from one social position to another is often translated into a territorial passage or crossing (192). At the same time, the mayor's passage clearly favors rites of reincorporation over those of separation and transition, i.e. the in-between state, a weighting which goes hand in hand with the show's encouragement of communal integration.

Historical and mythic personages as well as personifications of abstract concepts or places – frequently of London 'herself' – are appropriated by the pageant writers in an

---

[2] In the "Epistle Dedicatory" to Heywood's *Londini Speculum*, the author explains that it is "thus concluded by the Learned, that the Dominion of the *greatest Magistrates* which are *Kings* and *Princes*, ought to be perpetuall; but of the lesse which be *Praetors*, *Censors*, and the like, only *Ambulatory* and *Annuall*" (304). This expresses a fundamental belief in the rightfulness of the configuration of London politics as they are, based on the incontestable opinions of "the Learned" and historical precedent.

effort to validate the status and add to the renown of mayor, company, and city. Sometimes it is personified, anthropomorphous Time 'himself' who points the mayor invariably toward his destiny. In Munday's *Chruso-thriambos* Time confirms the justness of the mayor's status elevation and leads the characters, most explicitly Faringdon and Leofstane – the latter played by King's Man and Goldsmith John Lowen (Bergeron, Munday n. pag.) – through the streets and through the day. In *Himatia-poleos* the character of former (and first) mayor and civic hero Henry fitz Ailwin (d. 1212) corroborates the preordained state of city administration, to the advantage of the sponsoring Drapers, when he augurs that "Time reserveth in his store, / For the like honour [the mayoralty], many more [Drapers]" (C2). In his *Chrysanaleia* pamphlet, Munday gives as the "[r]eason of our present Shewe" the fact of "*Time* hauing turned his yearely Glasse, for election of a Magistrate, a Brother of the *Fishmongers* Societie" (B). The blessed inevitability of developments is also invoked by Heywood who defines his triumphal show for Ralph Freeman, *Londini Emporia*, as warranted by time and confirmed by custom ["as Time warranteth, so Custome confirmeth", (Q2)]. In the same show personified Prudence notes how Time brings about and approves of the specific nature and arrangement of London society: "all such things / As Custome (by Time strengthened) hath made good, / You should maintaine, with all your livelyhood" (C). Freeman is simultaneously lauded as a predestined mayor and instructed to play his part in the continuation of the civic arrangements, as providentially decreed.

The premise that merit is the foundation of the mayor's advancement is an important aspect of this simple but affirmative cosmology. In the "Epistle Dedicatory" to his *Londini Artium* Heywood informs the newly elected Nicholas Raynton that "Now Time and your owne Demerit Right Honourable, have raysed you to this Eminence and Dignity" (A3). Along the same lines, he addresses Ironmonger Christopher Clitherow in his *Londini Sinus Salutis* pamphlet with the words that "Time, and your Merit, have call'd you to this Office and Honor" (285). In reward and as a consequence of his merit, Time tells the new mayor in Taylor's *Triumphs of Fame and Honour* that, "*Time* shall transport your Marchandise and wares, / *Time* shall assist you in your great'st affaires: / *Time* shall be alwaies yours Auspitiously, / And *Time* will bring you to Eternity" (qtd. in Williams 516). The esteemed precedent of Rome is habitually invoked, too, as historical validation of London's administrative organization. In typical fashion, Heywood claims the precedent of classical antiquity for the Lord Mayor's Show (even if it had only existed for a handful of decades in its then-current spectacular form): "it is derived unto from Antiquity, and I wish it may continue to all Posterity." (Londini Emporia, A2) London, however, even surpasses the exemplar as "Rome it selfe when the Monarchy of the world was under her sole Iurisdiction, never received her Praetor, Consul, or Dictator with the like Pompe and Solemnity" (A2). Certainly, there is an element of 'invented tradition', as outlined by Eric Hobsbawm and Terence Ranger, inherent in the conceptualization of the Lord Mayor's Show as an ancient civic ritual, based on the precedent of Rome. Meanwhile a hereditary line of descent from Rome to London is rejected in Peacham's emblem 88 which suggests that it would be a fruitless endeavor to attempt to "ione by art in one, Our *Thames* with *Tyber*" (N4).

In almost all shows before the Civil War a feminine personage is the pinnacle of the inaugural celebrations, its main attraction and highlight. It is the mayor's confrontation with this personage, their metaphorical union, which forms the climax of the show. The moment of communion between new mayor and feminine personage, who combines aspects of goddess, mother and, above all, wife, is the moment the mayor ascends to his office in ritual terms, within the cosmology of the Lord Mayor's Show. It is not strange at all that the mayor's inauguration should be allegorized in terms of a marital union, considering that marriage and, resulting from it, well-ordered families were widely regarded "as essential not least as foundation and mirror of a well-ordered commonwealth" (Dwyer Amussen 86). The mayor was understood to serve as the head of the city, exercising duties of care and correction, in the manner of a husband and head of a family. This conception of the mayoralty presupposed a stout belief in the virtue, dependability and orderliness of family life, applicable both to the microcosm of the actual family and the macrocosm of city and state. Marriage and familial relations in emblems, on the other hand, were often envisaged as less than ideal. The state of matrimony itself is defined as being unhappily bound to a situation that is inhibiting and constraining in Peacham's emblem 132. Here, personified Matrimony is pictured in the stocks and carrying a yoke, visualizing the "want of libertie" that characterizes wedlock. The yoke is "an ensigne of servilitie" which is equally one of the conditions engendered by marriage (T4). An unhappy union is also the focus of Whitney's emblem 109, "Impar coniugium/An unequal marriage", which portrays marriage between unequal partners in the image of a living person bound closely to a corpse (197).[3] Whitney's emblem 165, "Post fata; uxor morosa, etiam discors/After death; a peevish and still contrary spouse", relates the story of a woman who drowns in a stream and her bereaved husband who searches upriver for her dead body because he suspects that she would continue to be as contrary in death as she was in life (Whitney 255).

As the desired consequence of conjugal relations, children are generally portrayed as a blessing in the Lord Mayor's Show. When London steps on the pageant stage not as a bride but as a venerable white-haired matron, mother to all within her metropolitan boundaries, the allegory emphasizes the loving bond which exists between her and her plentiful progeny, the majority of whom have turned out most satisfactory. Less well-adjusted offspring, on the other hand, is the topic of multiple emblems by Whitney and Peacham. Whitney's 161st emblem, for example, focuses on an indulgent mother and her criminal son: A convict on the way to his execution first embraces his mother, then bites off her nose. The moral to be gleaned from this scenario is that when "children steale, and come unto the rope: / it often is the parentes faulte, for giving them such scope" (Whitney 251). However, even progeny who seem promising in their infancy and not much in need of correction may still disappoint their parents at a later date, warns Peacham's emblem 159 (Z2).

In the streets of London, staged encounters between man and woman have much more beneficial consequences. Toward the end of Munday's *Metropolis Coronata* the new mayor encounters the Monument of London pageant where personified London and her

---

[3]   In *The Unfortunate Traveller,* Thomas Nashe employs the same horrific but fairly conventional image in his description of a battle: "as the tyrant Roman emperors used to tie condemned living caitiffs face to face to dead corses, so were the half-living here mixed with squeezed carcasses" (228).

twelve daughters, signifying the major livery companies, await the mayor's approach and it is here that the city, as woman, mother and spouse, acknowledges the mayor as her head and master. In Munday's *Chruso-thriambos*, the most spectacular and evocative of pageant sets is the Orferie in which the prime personage reflects the interests of the sponsoring company[4]: She is Vesta, rich and wealthy earth mother. It is the presence of Vesta and her daughters, personified Gold and Silver, which approves of and celebrates the inauguration of a member of the company of Goldsmiths. In Munday's *Triumphs of Reunited Britannia* the mayor meets a personification of Britannia at a pageant set referred to as Britain's Mount, where she is placed above her daughter kingdoms as well as personified London and diverse river personifications. Also present is Brute, the conquering and civilizing hero, whose function is to be a stand-in for James I and, to a lesser extent, for the mayor who is, after all, the monarch's substitute in the 'royal chamber' of London.[5] All of these encounters serve to confirm the new mayor's election as rightful and simultaneously imply the existence of a just universe in which the deserving will be rewarded – and not only in the hereafter.

In the course of Dekker's *Troia-Nova Triumphans*, the mayor meets Arete (signinfying virtue and the fulfillment of potential) in St Paul's Churchyard. Not only is she accompanied by the Liberal Arts and four Cupids, but Time, Mercury (Hermes), Desire, and Industry are seated astride the horses drawing the pageant stage. While all of them serve to highlight the destined nature of the mayor's inauguration, it is Arete whose blessing is the most powerful. In Middleton's *Triumphs of Truth* it is London's Triumphant Mount, set up near the Little Conduit, onto which the mayor is finally guided. Here, London and her illustrious companions are brought into contact with the mayor. In *The Triumphs of Honour and Industry* the mayor is climactically received at the Castle of Fame and Honor where he is promised to be given his own place in due course. Correspondingly, the Mount of Fame is the mayor's destination in Munday's *Siderothriambos*, while the Throne of Virtue awaits the mayor's approach in St Lawrence Lane in Middleton's *Triumphs of Honour and Virtue*. In all of these instances it is understood that the new incumbents richly deserve the mayorality and that they follow a foreordained route which reaches its climax in a meeting of mayor and eminent feminine personification.

In Dekker's *Brittannia's Honor* it is the eponymous Britannia who sanctions the mayor's new status from her Watch-Tower pageant set, while seven personified Virtues await the magistrate's approach at the Harbor of Health and Happiness in Heywood's *Londini Sinus Salutis*, the set from which the show derives its title. These Virtues, explains Heywood, are "necessary to bee imbraced by all such Majestrates, who after their stormy and tempestuous progresse through all judicature causes incident to their

---

[4] Hill notes that in 1611 (the year of *Chruso-thriambos*) James I had attended "the trial of the pyx", a ceremony gauging the purity of the silver and gold used for currency since "there was considerable concern from the crown that currency was being debased" (Pageantry 297). This would have loomed large in the Goldsmiths' year and found reflection in the Lord Mayor's Show.

[5] The equation of London with the king's *camera regia* or royal chamber is a concept that can be dated to at least the 1377-99 reign of Richard II (Bergeron, King James 218).

places, seeke to anchor in that safe and secure Port so styled" (296). The Gate of Piety recalls the title of Heywood's *Porta Pietatis* and it is here that Piety herself awaits her meeting with new mayor Maurice Abbot, accompanied by a multitude of subordinate Virtues, such as the Theological Virtues: Faith, Hope, and Charity (i.e. Love). Feminized Piety, rays of gold around her head, instructs the mayor that she is in fact a kind of limen, or gateway for him to pass, as it is she who "[p]oynts out the way to blisse, guirt with a ring / Of all those graces [accompanying her on the set] that may glory bring" (272). The pageant shrine unto which the mayor is led and from whence he receives his blessing in Heywood's *London's Ius Honorarium* is the Palace of Honor, set up in Cheapside and introduced by the Haberdashers' patroness St Katherine. Earlier, Mayor George Whitmore had already encountered the feminized personifications of London and a well-governed commonwealth on his triumphal route, both representing the city's flourishing under his masculine care and guidance. At the same time, the mayor may also be brought into communion with 'locations' that represent London and function as abstractions of the best aspects of the city. In Dekker's *Londons Tempe* it is 'Londons Tempe or the Field of Happiness' which figures as an impersonal yet material representation of London, as does the 'fair field' in Munday's eponymous *Camp-Bell, or, the Ironmongers Fair Feild*. The Fountain of Virtue meanwhile serves as a representation of the city in Heywood's *Londini Artium* while in *Londini Emporia* it is the Bower of Bliss[6] which takes on the function of an edenic location representing a perfect city of London, where the personified Cardinal Virtues, in their natural, prelapsarian habitat, confront the mayor.

The attitude that benevolent fate causes the preferment of worthy mayors and sheriffs runs through all shows. It is explicitly expressed in *Sidero-thriambos* by Munday who concludes in relation to the election of mayor Harvey and his two sheriffs that "the booke of *Fate* hath concluded of them, against which can be no contradiction" (C2). Neptune, in *The Triumphs of Re-united Britannia*, likewise tells the new mayor that "heauen hath cald thee to this dignity" (C4), whereas it is Father Time in Squire's *Triumphs of Peace* who "admits" the mayor to his new status (C2), and graces the festivities, intending "to show the loue, / I bare thee and thy Societie" (B4). Time, too, instructs the mayor that he "hath brought you hither (grave and great) / To inaugure you, in your Praetorium seate" in Heywood's *London's Ius Honorarium* (273). Confirmation of the mayor's fate is readable in cosmic signs in Munday's *Chruso-thriambos*: Leofstane recalls for the mayor's benefit that "at the very instant of your choyce, the Sunne did as readily thrust foorth his Golden beames, to guilde the instant of your Inauguaration" (C3).

Along these lines, ritual is understood by Van Gennep to establish relations between the mundane or man-made and the cosmic, "by a sort of pre-scientific divination" (94). Overall, the Lord Mayor's Show employed analogies relating the man-made and the cosmic with some success – while also displaying a degree of theatrical awareness of its own

---

6   In Spenser's *The Fairie Queene* the "bower of bliss" plays a negative part as a place of artificiality and indulgence. It is the lair of evil Acrasia, a "cursed land" (book 2, canto 1, stanza 51), though a "place pickt out by choice of best alive, / That natures worke by art can imitate: / In which what ever in this worldly state / Is sweet, and pleasing unto living sense, / Or that may dayntiest fantasie aggrate, / Was poured forth with plenifull dispence, / And made there to abound with lavish affluence" (book 2, canto 12, stanza 42).

means and effects. Finlayson, for instance, detects an "attempt to relate the terrestrial and temporal to the celestial and immortal" in the farewell speech in Heywood's *Londini Emporia* (856), concerning "the twelve celestiall Signes, which may aptly be applied vnto the twelve Moneths during the Lord Mayors gouernment" (C2). The constellations are invoked to benefit the mayor: Aries to enrich him, Taurus to give strength, the Twins to bring peace and increase, Cancer to abstain from bestowing negative influences, Leo to moderate his rage, Virgo to give advice, Libra to foster justice (ibid.). This rhetorical turn toward astrology presents the mayor's promotion as a cosmically ordained event and expresses the expectation that his term in office will unfold under benign stars.

2.2 *Various are the opinions of men*: Harmony and Conflict

The coming together of diverse London is celebrated in the Lord Mayor's Show: The pageant episodes suggest perfect social cohesion and hold out to spectators the option of identifying themselves with this vision. The Lord Mayor's Show audience, much like Elizabethan and Jacobean theatergoers, ranged "from the lowest social classes through to the middle classes, foreign visitors and ambassadors, and members of the aristocracy" (Lancashire, Comedy 7). The procession itself, notes Anne Lancashire, served the integration of "potentially conflicting social groups" (ibid. 10), and shared in the generally "celebratory and life-affirming" outlook of the festivities (ibid. 4). At the same time as the event facilitates a sense of community, it emphasizes the fact that the mayor is not isolated in his newly elevated place but has the trust, support and advice of his sheriffs and aldermen.[7] Chariots carrying mythical and historic forbears provide a secure sense for the civic dignitaries of taking their places as links in a long chain of venerable custodians of the city. Meanwhile, displays of humbler figures involved in various trades and crafts serve to create the image of an inclusive society that also allows for the incorporation of the less affluent majority of city dwellers into the fabric of civic society, at least on the level of Lord Mayor's Show ideology. Since the guild and the parish were the two most relevant communities to the average early modern Londoner (cf. Seaver 67), the company-sponsored Lord Mayor's Show was an appropriate platform for the formulation of an overarching sense of community into which a broad range of Londoners could be incorporated. The separate but overlapping levels of group identity that were addressed in the shows were the basic and inclusive level of the working populace of London, the level of company identity, as well as the exclusive levels of livery, high-ranking officials and former lord mayors.

Most Londoners, certainly, were people of limited status and means – the majority of them servants, apprentices, and people employed in one of the various branches of the cloth industry (Beier 213).[8] Most artisans, too, worked in small shops under masters and

---

[7] An exceedingly unusual exception to this rule is articulated in *Brittannia's Honor*: Here, personified Britannia advises the mayor to "trust none, For Officers Sell / Their Captaines Trust; let None but your owne Eyes, / Rule Chart and Compasse, There your safety lyes" (C2).

[8] Beier bases his claims on a study of three London parishes in the period between 1548 and 1652 (213).

alongside journeymen, apprentices, wage laborers, and servants (Seaver 64). It is precisely these Londoners of limited means whom the Lord Mayor's Show invites, on a wide and basic level, to share in a community of civic pride and mutual dependence in an effort to foster social cohesion and prevent discontent and disorder, the prospect of which was particularly fearsome in rapidly expanding city like London. Women, however, were by and large excluded from participation in the trades and their representation in pageant tableaux was therefore limited; reduced, for the most part, to the embodiment of abstract concepts which lent their support to the mayor and his company. In this respect the Lord Mayor's Show offers an ambivalent balance of inclusion and exclusion: While circa fifty percent of the population were predictably dismissed a priori, and social hierarchies were by no means abandoned, the aim of the show was nonetheless inclusive and it did, in fact, sympathetically represent an uncommonly broad range of social agents. Working man, mayor, and monarch alike were shown to play important parts in the wider community and to contribute to the peace and prosperity of the city.

The distribution of small gifts from some of the pageant sets, e.g. from the fishing boat in Munday's *Chrysanaleia*, also fostered bonds between the receiving spectators and the sponsoring city administrators, rendering tangible the theme of material inclusion in a harmonious community of industrious Londoners – the vision of London society favored by the companies. While the Fishmongers chose to distribute fish among spectators by the river bank in *Chrysanaleia*, the Grocers tended to opt for a range of spices and condiments to hand out to the multitudes. In 1617, for example, company records note that "50 sugar loaves, 36^{li} [li = libra = pound] of nuttmegge 14^{li} of dates and 114^{li} of ginger [...] were throwen about the streetes by those wch sate on the Griffyns and Camells" (Robertson and Gordon 92). At the same time, in a 'bread and cricuses' manner, witnessing spectacular displays together, irrespective of content, may have been another means of temporarily feeding a sense of affinity and kinship among spectators, joining them in a moment of shared awe. One such awe-inspiring moment during the 1609 show is hinted at in company records which refer to a mechanical whale which was "open for ffireworke at the mouth and water vented at the head" (Robertson and Gordon 73). Fireworks featured regularly in the shows and delivered visual stimulation while music and cannon shots stirred the emotions via the sense of hearing.

Scott Schofield has examined the shows' appeal to a sense of community and mutual responsibility and seized on London's mythic founder, the Trojan Brute, as "an important piece of cultural identity" (255). Schofield assesses the myth of Brute as "a celebration of story as well as of communities that embrace such tales in both oral and written traditions" (ibid.). Indeed, in the reign of James I the figure of Brute was drawn on in order to popularize and glorify the king's nominal unification of the kingdoms of England and Scotland by his adoption of the title "King of Great Britain", since under Brute, too, all of Britain had supposedly been one kingdom. In Munday's *Triumphs of Re-united Britannia* the character eulogizes the union of the English and Scottish crowns and at the same time epitomizes the city's ancient, myth-shrouded history. Brute certainly offered a point of identification for Londoners, residents of Brute's mythic 'Troynovant', or New Troy, who looked with fondness on the fanciful but gratifying origin story of Brute in Britain.

Other characters in the Lord Mayor's Shows serve functions similar to that of Brute, aiding the formation and perpetuation of urban community. Jason, for instance, is beloved of merchants. The golden fleece had great symbolic significance, not only for Drapers and Clothworkers. The characters of Henry fitz Ailwin and William Walworth, both famous historical mayors, are also co-opted to foster and celebrate company identity. The utility in pageantry of Brute and other semi- or entirely fictional characters was not significantly diminished by the circumstance that there was no agreement on whether or not these figures had, in fact, existed. While city chronicler John Stow fervently denied the truth of Brute's conquest of Britain, he nonetheless discussed the myth at some length, explaining that

> [a]s the Romane writers to glorifie the citie of *Rome* drew the originall thereof from Gods and demie Gods, by the Troian progenie: so *Giffrey* of Monmouth the Welsh Historian, deduceth the foundation of this famous Citie of *London*, for the greater glorie therof, and emulation of *Rome*, from the very same originall. For he reporteth that *Brute*, lineally descended from the demy god *Eneas*, the sonne of *Venus*, daughter of *Iupiter*, about the yeare of the world 2855. and 1108. before the nativitie of Christ, builded this city neare unto the river now called *Thames*, and named it *Troynouant* or *Trenouant*. (1)

Stow rejects this narrative of London's founding, however, and avers – after Livy – that whereas antiquity must be indulged, modern times do not warrant the same treatment.[9] Yet, whether or not pageant writers, company elites, or ordinary spectators actually believed that Brute had founded London "about the yeare of the world 2855" – and Erasmus had called out the self-absorbed folly of this belief a century earlier (The Praise 97) –, Brute remained an accessible symbol and a facilitator of community.

That social cohesion in the city was a pressing matter for the mayor, aldermen, and councilors is easily understood in view of the fact that fear of disease,[10] of economic difficulties and of resulting social unrest had been ubiquitous topics in the discourse of London since at least the reign of Elizabeth I. Already in the 1580s royal proclamations attempted to limit subsistence migration to London (Seaver 59), caused by a general fall

---

[9] Stow exhibits little patriotic pride in the nation's British and Saxon past, drawing a picture of incompetent Celts and vastly superior, long-suffering Romans in the following passage: "These Romaines at their departure, tolde the Britaines plaiynely, that it was not for their ease or leasure to take vpon them any more such long and laborious iourneys for their defence, and therefore bad them practice the vse of armour and weapons, and learne to withstand their enemies, whome nothing else did make so strong as their faint heart and cowardise." (6) Before their departure the Romans built a wall "of harde stone from the west sea to the east sea" for them. (6) Yet, this did not keep the Britons safe for long, who, eager for help against Picts and Scots, invited the Saxons into the country and were subsequently surprised by their refusal to leave again. Of these new invaders Stow has to say that, "[t]hese Saxons were likewise ignorant of building with stone, vntill the yeare 680" (7).

[10] With the plagues of 1603 and 1625 causing over 25,000 deaths on each occasion (Seaver 63), concern over the spread of infectious disease was justified. In between major, devastating outbreaks of plague, minor eruptions persisted, while various other infectious diseases also killed a considerable share of the population, including some ten percent of all Elizabethan apprentices (ibid. 60).

in living standards (Keene 58-59), and James I, too, worried about the capital's territorial expansion and the continual population increase through large-scale migration; in 1616 he drew the fearsome conclusion – still intermittently cause for alarm in the 21st century – that "with time England will only be London, and the whole country left waste" (qtd. in Seaver 63). A counter discourse to this alarming scenario was therefore needed; a discussion of the city which created and reflected a growing community of interdependent manufacturers and traders with good reason to contribute to their community. Not only were small-scale artisans and apprentices conceptualized as integral to the proper functioning of London society in this alternative discourse, held out to them also was the opportunity to increase their wealth and status by industry and virtue alone, which was no small incentive to identify with this outlook despite the fact that success, in real life, was far from guaranteed.[11]

That accomplishments in business were, if far from certain, certainly not impossible is demonstrated, for instance, by the progress of Maurice Abbot who became lord mayor in 1638. The son of an illiterate Clothworker, Abbot was fortunate enough to be allowed to attend grammar school (Thrush, Abbot n. pag.). Unlike his elder brothers (one of whom became Bishop of Canterbury, another Bishop of Salisbury), Maurice was unable to go on to university and was instead apprenticed to Draper William Garway (ibid.). Although Abbot did not set out on his life's journey as a pauper, his is nevertheless a genuine success story with the potential to encourage apprentices in similar positions.[12] Abbot's biography seems to corroborate the encouragement voiced by personified Honor in *Triumphs of Fame and Honour*, who promises apprentices that "[f]rom servitude growes

[11]   Ilana Krausman Ben-Amos has examined the fate of early modern apprentices in urban centers and has found that "[t]he drop-out rate of London apprentices throughout the sixteenth and seventeenth centuries was of the order of 50 per cent" (155). The rate of aborted apprenticeships in Bristol was even higher in the 16th and early to mid-17th centuries. Yet, it seems that chances of finishing an apprenticeship were neither significantly determined by the chosen trade nor by the social origin of the apprentice: the same drop-out rates existed for sons of husbandmen, merchants, and gentlemen, "[i]f anything, sons of husbandmen were somewhat more likely to become burgesses" (ibid. 160). Although Ben-Amos acknowledges that there were some economic challenges facing young men willing to set up their own shops in urban, competitive environments, the foremost among them "the cost of buying or renting a living place that could also accommodate a small shop" (164), she cautions against "ascribing too much misfortune, discontent or frustration to urban apprentices" (ibid. 171). She argues that "many apprentices did not remain in the town but migrated elsewhere" by choice (ibid. 157), sometimes before the termination date of their contracts, and often to set up businesses with the support of relatives (ibid. 166). A number of 17th century absentee apprentices, especially from port cities, would have also bought passage to America as indentured servants (ibid. 169).

[12]   Unlike Abbot, many of London's top merchants gained entry into companies by patrimony – so, for example, John Swinnerton (mayor in 1612-13), who was also educated at Merchant Taylors' School (Archer n. pag.), the largest of the humanist grammar schools (Hanson 420). William Cokayne (mayor in 1619-20) served an apprenticeship with his father before being made free of the Skinners by patrimony (Aldous n. pag.), and Christopher Clitherow (mayor in 1635-36) "followed his father into the Ironmongers' Company in 1601" (Thrush, Clitherow n. pag.). George Whitmore (mayor in 1631-32) was, instead, placed with his older brother, a Haberdasher (Hollis).

freedome, and from thence / (Through Industry) springs Worth and Eminence" (B). In the cities of early modern Europe, scholars insist, old bonds and values ceased to exist in the face of developing capitalism and other major transitions. However, some old bonds survived while simultaneously new bonds took shape, new communities sprang into being, and the Lord Mayor's Show contributed to the formation of a sense of identity in which most Londoners could share. In a social climate of change and friction, the shows articulated contemporary London as a place of stability and social cohesion, even as they did so by frequent reference to the past.

In contrast to the above, the popular emblems of the late 16th and early 17th centuries frequently point the finger sharply at instances where social life proves defective: at abuses of rank, friction, dissent, the dangers of misplaced trust, even the extreme case of civil war. In the woodcut print forming part of Whitney's seventh emblem an arsonist is setting fire to a building with a torch and another man is in the act of stabbing a victim who is already sprawled on the ground. The point of the emblem titled "Intestinae simultates/Internal dissenssions", the verse explains, is that in civil warfare "[n]one helpes to quenche, but rather blowes the flame" (96). Here no sense of community and communal responsibility can hold society together and prevent these random and heinous acts of violence and destruction. A small-scale outbreak of hostility is portrayed in the picture part of Whitney's emblem 17, "Ludus, luctus, luxus/Gaming, grief, gluttony", where a dispute has escalated and turned into a brawl. While no actual violence is depicted in emblem 46, "Varii hominum sensus/Various are the opinions of men", which shows a scattering of human skulls next to a chapel (Whitney 135), the verse articulates a dark understanding of the disparity of human wills and opinions that cannot come together, even in death. The image is paralleled, in less macabre form, in George Gascoigne's *The Adventures of Master F. J.* (1573) in which the narrator cites "the common proverb 'So many men, so many minds'" (27). Only a few pages further on in Whitney's tome, emblem 64, "Non dola sed vi/Not by deceit, but by force", displays the image of an ape in the act of forcing a dog's paw into a hearth fire. This illustrates that "when as ambition fowle doth prick, / The hartes of kinges, then there is no remorce, / But oftentimes, to aunswere their desire, / The subjectes feele, both famine, sworde, and fire" (Whitney 151). While the emblem text indicts the callous conduct of unpitying rulers, the woodcut simultaneously offers a depiction, in the form of a visual fable, of the casual, every-day violation of the defenseless by those in positions to abuse whatever kind of power they possess. An anecdote by the anonymous 17th-century pamphleteer 'N. D.' confirms the proverbial status of the fable. N. D. relates overhearing a conversation in a French inn among a group of travelers, who discuss the xenophobic insults they found themselves confronted with in England.[13] One of the group recalls "a fable of an Ape that had layd Chessenuts to roast in the embers, and when they were inough, the Cat sitting by the fire,

---

[13] One of the travelers – "[o]ne of *Cullen* in Germany" – relates how "being in *England*, and passing through a street of *London* [he] had an old shooe throwne by an Apprentice out of a shop ful in his face", having been mistaken for a Dutchman (12). The German reacts by throwing the offending boot back at his attacker which, in turn, results in a fierce counter attack by an entire group of London apprentices. Back in Cologne, he takes revenge on two entirely innocent English travelers by pushing them into the Rhine.

he caught her foote, and therewith raked then [sic!] out" (N. D. 20). He relates the fable of the ape and cat to fanatical Puritan preachers who would stir up young men in London to act against Catholic visitors to the city: "So these preaching-fellowes make the London-laddes the instruments of their intended endes" (ibid.). While in this anecdote the offense is initially verbal only – later, however, translated into physical violence by "London-laddes" under the influence of "preaching-fellowes" –, like the emblem it conveys human malice and social unrest.

Comparable to Whitney's censure of the exploitation of the vulnerable, Peacham's emblem 62 accuses those who use their might to "hazard first, the poore, weaker one" (K3). A glum tale, too, of the deliberate sacrifice of the weak is related in Peacham's emblem 148, in which two companions encounter "a great and ugly *Beare*" (X4), and while both men had earlier sworn to always protect each other, in this moment of crisis one abandons the other to his fate (see fig. 4). If even two close companions will soon turn on each other in a critical situation, as the emblem suggests, then what hope is there for the diversified population of a metropolis? A theme of fickle friends and the dangers of trusting too lightly also runs through Thomas Combe's *Theater of Fine Devices* and Whitney's emblem 146 explicitly warns against "[t]he perfidious friend" (235). Emblem 111 in Whitney's collection bears the motto "Animi scrinium servitus/Servitude, the cage of the soul" and combines the image of a caged bird with the textual elucidation that the songbird in its cage will still sing sweetly, even if sadly imprisoned, because servants are in no position to speak their minds to those they have to serve (199). Clearly, the world view underlying the emblem is not the same as that underlying the Lord Mayor's Show, i.e. a conception of social organization as organic and harmonious. Equally averse to an understanding of society as the seamless and happy cooperation of all is the message of individual gain and social strife expressed in Whitney's emblem 123, "Ex dammo alter-ius, alterius utilitas/One man's loss is another man's advantage", which is based on the familiar precept that when two fight, a third profits. In this case, a vulture profits from the quarrel between a lion and boar (211).

Animal imagery also helps express the deficits of man as a social creature in the motto of emblem 149, "Homo homini lupus/Man is a wolf to man". The emblem is concerned with the familiar story of mythical musician Arion but it carries much darker undertones here than it does in Lord Mayor's Show pageantry. The main moral of the emblem is the depravity of man toward his own kind: "No mortall foe so full of poysoned spite, / As man, to man, when mischiefe he pretendes" (Whitney 239).

TWO frendes there were that did their Iourney take,
And by the way, they made a vow to either,
What ere befell, they never would forsake,
But as sworne brethren, liue and die togeither:
Thus wandring thorough deserts, here and there,
By chance they met, a great and vgly *Beare*.

At whome, amazed with a deadly feare,
One leaues his frend, and climbeth vp a tree:
The other, falles downe flat before the *Beare*,
And keepes his breath, that seeming dead to be,
The *Beare* forsooke him, (for his nature's such,
A breathles bodie never once to touch.)

The beast departing, and the daunger past,
The dead arose, and kept along his waie:
His fellow leaping from the tree at last,
Askt what the *Beare*, in's eare did whispring say,
Quoth he, he bad me, evermore take heede,
Of such as thou, that failst in time of neede.

Ex Æsopi fabu.

Levitas

Fig. 4: A wanderer is abandoned to the mercy of "a great and ugly *Beare*" by his companion (sitting safely in the tree on the left) in Peacham's emblem 148 (X4). Image by courtesy of the David M. Rubenstein Rare Book & Manuscript Library, Duke University.

That Whitney does not shy away from depictions of unpleasant aspects of social coexistence is evident, too, in emblem 156, "Quod non capit Christus, rapit fiscus/What Christ does not take, the treasury snatches" (246). This refers to the contentious topic of taxation and, as Joan Larsen Klein notes, "the relationship of a rapacious king to his rapacious officers" (159). In the background of the picture a public execution is taking place: Three people are hanging from a gibbet while a group of onlookers is gathered at the foot of the structure.[14] Larsen Klein identifies them as equally moribund: "a crowd of other men [...] are tied by the neck to each other and [...] are apparently about to be hanged themselves" (ibid.). The picture displays a site of sanctioned violence in which convicts are irreversibly removed from society. While executions were certainly a part of life in early modern London, the subject is opposed to the inclusive and life-affirming bias of the Lord Mayor's Show and therefore (almost) entirely excluded from it.

A man raising one, wing-spouting arm toward the sky, while simultaneously weighted down by a stone tied to the other is the focus of Whitney's emblem 157, titled "Paupertattem summis ingeniis, obesse ne provehantur/Poverty hinders the greatest talents from advancing" (247). While here poverty is conceptualized as a damaging force that stands in the way of achievement despite great merit, in Lord Mayor's Shows a familiar theme is the potential for material self-improvement in a social environment that allows this, a proposition that also suited the Merchant Taylors' company motto: *concordia parvae res crescunt* (in harmony, small things grow). Correspondingly, in Middleton's *Triumphs of Integrity*, written for the Drapers, a speaker from the Mount Royal pageant set lists shepherd-born personages who ascended to the status of kings by virtue and industry alone. Contrary to this vision of ascent by merit, referred to by Hill as "civic meritocracy" (Pageantry 316), Whitney's emblem claims that adverse circumstances will defeat personal qualities and Peacham's emblem 24 bemoans that in this day and age "th' inglorious is / Allow'd the place sometimes in Honours chaire" (E4). The 50th emblem in the latter's collection warns that good and deserving men must often "give a farre inferior leave to thrive" in their place, or be persecuted and supplanted by the envious (I1). Not only are the deserving frequently hindered from advancement but those who do advance often do not merit this at all. A vision of society in which this is allowed to happen as a norm is a grim one indeed. The blameless may equally be harmed by "vaine *Opinion*: or vile envious spite" (Peacham, emblem 67, L2), which is one of the detrimental qualities that grows in the collective "infectious mind" of the multitude (Peacham, emblem 30, F3). The ideology of worldly self-improvement is also opposed

---

[14] Capital punishment in early modern England was generally reserved for repeat offenders or the perpetrators of particularly heinous crimes and of those committed by social inferiors against their superiors, known as "petit treason" (Perreault 75-76). Outsider status, too, was dangerous in judicial matters (ibid. 75). 'Outsiders' were more likely to be executed than other offenders for committing similar crimes because by their very status, defined by missing ties to a local community, they were deemed "the biggest threat to social stability" (ibid.). Similar to the scene in Whitney's emblem 156, an image in Otto Vaenius' *Q. Horatii Flacci Emblemata* – emblems based on the works of Horace – shows a corpse hanging from a scaffold in the background of a murder scene. Altogether, the pictorial elements accompany a proverbial statement on retribution that is slow but certain (qtd. in Manning 92-94).

in Francis Quarles' *Hieroglyphikes of the Life of Man* (1635), which promises a fall "[f]rom good, to bad; From bad, to worst of all" in matters of the world and of the flesh (qtd. in Freeman 123). For devout Quarles, the only improvement to aspire to is the purification of the soul and its ultimate union with god.

Another parameter for the corruption of society is introduced by Peacham in his emblem 74 which rebukes the poor treatment of the elderly: "Ingratefull times, and worthles age of ours, / That let's us pine, when it hath cropt our flowers." (M1) Peacham's emblem 89, bearing the motto "Sic vos non vobis", warns against spending "our time, to serve anothers turne", since nothing will be given in return (O1). Worse yet, people often "for good will render ill" (Peacham, emblem 176, Bb2). That royal courts are home to "monstrous harpie[s]" (R4), intent on furthering private ends without a thought spared for anyone or anything else is a warning issued by Peacham's emblem 115. While emblem 104, "Ex Avaritia Bellum", points out that it is the nature of avarice "to quarrell, or to kill" (Q2). Peacham ventures into the realm of fables with his emblem 92 (O2), the subject of which is an injured lion. As the carrion crows are shown pecking at the predator's bleeding wounds, so, explains the verse, one's enemies will seek out the most sensitive spots they can find in order to inflict most hurt. Inhumane military mores are the focus of Peacham's emblem 136 in which the author censures degenerate commanders, "[w]ho deeme it honour, and a soldiers guise, / To use on foes all villanous outrage: / Rapes, murders, rapines, burnings, robberies" (U2).

In Whitney's emblem 27, "Dolus in suos/Treachery towards one's own", the dangers of misplaced trust are expressed in bird imagery starkly alternative to the celebratory images of the pious pelican, the noble eagle – a symbol of royalty, longevity, and sharp eyesight (cf. Bath, Whitney's Concluding Emblem 295) –, or the pure turtle dove common in pageantry. The emblem picture shows ducks lured into a trap by a trained decoy duck. The fowl, "dowting not, her [the decoy's] traiterous harte at all, / Did flie with her, and downe with her did fall" (Whitney 116). The suggestion that both trusting too lightly and own's own mischievous thoughts in fact deserve the deceit this invites is made by Whitney in emblem 223, "Fraus meretur fraudem/Deceit deserves deceit". In an unflattering take on the head of the animal kingdom, the emblem depicts a lion in his den, a fox standing a little way off in front of the cave. Paw prints lead into the lion's den but not out of it. The verse explains that as the fox is astute enough to see through the lion's trick, it will not come any closer and so does not forfeit his life in naive trust. That "ravening wolves, in skinnes of lambes doe lurke," is the moral of Whitney's emblem 110, titled "Frontis nulla fides/No faith in appearance". While Peacham's emblem 47 presents personified Deceit in a golden coat (H4) – a possible loan from Ripa's *Iconologia* – which relates the commonplace that evil does not declare itself, or, as phrased by Shakespeare in *The Rape of Lucrece*, that "inward ill not outward harm express[es]" (l. 91). To recognize deception for what it is, even if it presents itself in its best clothes, seems therefore to be a hard if necessary task. This theme also runs through Peacham's emblem 198 (Ee1), which bemoans the fact that external appearances can easily belie inner reality, as illustrated by the pious hypocrisy of a sanctimonious Puritan. Blameworthy, too, is "the careless Pastor" who "teacheth well, but followes not the same" (Peacham, emblem 61, K3).

Rather than celebrate the virtues of office holders, their tendency toward self-service is indicted in Peacham's emblem 70 by way of a fable in which a fox is given the task to watch over a pack of hounds but keeps them starving, while enjoying the benefits of his position. Like the sly fox, there are those who, once "put in trust, / Doe robbe the Church, or Infantes of their dew, / Disposing of anothers as they lust: / Whome being bound, in Conscience to preserve, / They suffer oft, in open streete to starve" (L3). In general, emblems offer moral advice as "warnings presented by those who have gone too far or risen too high, and suffered the painful consequences" (Manning 269). As this suggests, methods of moral instruction are antithetically opposed in emblems and pageants: If any criticism at all is put forward in a Lord Mayor's Show concerning the magistrate's conduct in office, it is in the manner outlined in Francis Bacon's *Essay on Praise*: those who voice the praise, "by telling Men, what they are, [...] represent to them, what they should be" (qtd. in Wickham 80). In fact, poor relief and the support of religion are civic duties for whose fulfillment the newly inaugurated mayors as well as former dignitaries are almost always explicitly praised in the course of an inaugural show. While certain virtues are demanded of a good mayor, the commonly voiced assumption is that the mayor is already in possession of these. In *Londini Emporia* Heywood confronts the new mayor with qualities desirable in an officeholder, then immediately reassures him with the words: "All these things desireable being knowne to be eminent in your Lordship" (4). It is understood that the mayor has advanced to his position by virtue of his admirable qualities and that, as the king's substitute in the city of London, he will fulfill his duties well.

Just as the emblem of the fox put in trust illustrates the egotism of a tyrant, there are other emblems that are concerned with reprobate rulers. Peacham's emblem 85 points a finger at despots but nevertheless denies the subjects' right to rebel against them since "[s]uch wretches vile, [are sent] to be our punishment" (N3). Yet, while it posits their immunity, such a description of monarchs does little to aid their image. It is only after a tyrant's death that the victims of his terror will have their revenge (Peacham, emblem 144, X2). Rulers and subjects alike are painted in an unflattering light by Peacham when he mocks that "people, are like busie Apes inclin'd, / To imitate the Soveraignes manners still" (I2), whatever these may be. While monarchs and mayors are presented as thoroughly positive exemplars in Lord Mayor's Shows, emblems are more uninhibited in presenting those in power as ugly or frail. Van der Noot's emblem 16 presents kings, not in sumptuous royal style, but cowering naked behind a woman dressed in the classical apparel of war and identified in the verse as sister to Typhoeus, a Greek monster (23); Van der Noot's 19th emblem, based on Revelation 19:18, makes the gory prediction that the creatures of the Apocalypse will eventually "warre upon the kings, and eate their flesh" (26).

While the emblems of Whitney and his followers partake of a world view in which the social fabric is patchy and trust in peers and social superiors is often misplaced, the Lord Mayor's Show embraces a different ideology. Here, the mayor is part of a functioning community (diachronically as well as synchronically constituted) and can rely on the trustworthiness of his associates. Leofstane, in Munday's *Chruso-thriambos*, refers the mayor to these graue Senators your worthy Bretheren, who (in my time) were styled by the Name of *Domes-men*, *Elder-men*, or Iudges of the Kinges Courts, and were then assistant to me, in care, councell, and fatherly prouidence, for this Citties good, as these reuerend men haue bin to others, and now wil be the like to you. (B2)

In theory, the mayor can rest secure in the knowledge that he has the support of the alder-men. Jason, placed in the "Chariot of Honour" in Middleton's *The Sun in Aries* tells the mayor: "Thou hast th'assistance of grave senators here, / Thy worthy brethren, some of which have passed / All dangerous gulfs, and in their bright fames placed, / They can instruct and guide thee" (1589). In the chariot are placed characters from myth and clas-sical antiquity who are exemplars of "honour got by danger" (ibid.) and as such can instruct the mayor, in addition to the advice he may receive from his sheriffs, aldermen, and previous lord mayors. In his *Triumphs of Health and Prosperity*, Middleton refers new mayor Cuthbert Hacket to his sheriffs (and future lord mayors) Richard Fenn and Edward Brumfield whose turn it is to serve as "his lordship's grave assistants for the year" (1905). Especially if one or both sheriffs hailed from the same company as the mayor, i.e. the financing company, this very often served as an occasion to digress on the function of the office of sheriff and the personal merits of the office holders. In Heywood's *Londini Artium*, the Haberdashers' patron, St Katherine, points the mayor toward "the two Shrieues that his assistants are; / Chose by the publicke Voyce and Senats Doome, / As Censors, and the Tribunes were in Rome" (B3). The authority of historical precedent, however fabricated, serves to increase the esteem of the contemporary institution and, in the same manner, to confirm publically the importance of the sheriffs' contribution to city government. In Heywood's *Londini Emporia*, personified Cardinal Virtue Prudence, featured in the show's central pageant tableau, advises the mayor that he is expected to rule along with his "Censors, (Sheriffes elected, / And now in place)" (C).

The sense of a unified community engendered by the Lord Mayor's Show, its blocking out of potentially dissonant voices, was recognized and employed by the Crown in an effort to avert interest from another location of public interest in late October 1618. As spectators were awaiting the arrival of new mayor Sebastian Harvey south of St Paul's Cathedral, the execution of Sir Walter Ralegh was taking place at the Palace of Westminster, less than two miles upriver. While the former event was a celebration of social order and cohesion, the latter, punitive event displayed the physical destruction of a social agent who had allegedly acted in defiance of the sovereign's authority. As the execution itself posed a potential threat to order, the event was scheduled to coincide with the lord mayor's inauguration in an attempt to prevent large crowds from assembling in Westminster to collectively witness Ralegh's last moments. One public assembly – containing not only the seeds of powerful solidarity but also of upheaval – was played out against another.[15] Ultimately, however, the strategy of diverting interest from one

---

[15] The potential danger posed by any assembly of Londoners to "the unity of the city and to mag-isterial authority" had already been recorded by John Carpenter in the *Liber Albus* (James 28). K. J. Lindley notes that in London "[t]raditional holidays and festivals, and especially Shrove Tuesdays, were a regular source of anxiety as apprentices, and sometimes other unruly elements, engaged in acts of ritualised yet very real violence" (109), and that "[v]iolence was

matter to another failed since the proliferation of Ralegh's speech on the scaffold in printed form rendered the temporal coincidence of execution and Lord Mayor's Show an insufficient means to contain this particular force of disruption.[16] Ralegh had fallen in disgrace with James I upon the accession of the latter to the English throne and had spent time as a prisoner in the Tower of London early in the new monarch's reign. Following a conditional release in 1616 and a final, ill-fated trip to South America, Ralegh was imprisoned once more on the 28th of October 1618 (Beer 20-21). He was arraigned at the King's Bench and executed for high treason the following morning at approximately half past nine (ibid. 22).

Tracey Hill has speculated that the day's Lord Mayor's Show, Munday's *Siderothriambos*, featured personified Treason – whom Dekker imagined "with haires like Snakes" (The Seven Deadly Sinnes 15) – and Ambition shackled and subdued on the

---

generally directed at specific targets, particularly brothels and playhouses" (ibid. 110). B. L. Beer points out that although the uprisings in Norfolk and Cornwall of 1548 and 1549 were "the most serious" in England since the 15th century (London and the Rebellions 15), London's "City officials reacted to the crisis with a high sense of responsibility and determination" and therefore "London survived as a source of strength in a country badly shaken by rebellion" (ibid. 33). It is of interest that "[e]arly Tudor London was not the country's principal center of violence and discontent, for the problem of maintaining law and order was more acute in the countryside where the aristocracy and gentry had a long tradition of private warfare" (ibid. 15). In London, "the two most celebrated London riots prior to the 1640s were the pursuit and murder of Dr John Lambe, Buckingham's reputed magician, in 1628 [the city authorities were slow in taking action because of Lambe's unpopularity] and an exceptionally violent outrage in Fleet Street in 1629" (Lindley 114). Lindley finds it "a remarkable fact that so little blood was actually spilt" on these occasions (125), and believes this due, in part, to a system of poor relief implemented in the city – thus, generally preventing hunger riots – as well as a strategy of "appeasing rioters, and ostensibly removing the cause of grievance" employed by authorities who frequently lacked manpower and equipment to immediately, and violently, suppress outbursts (ibid. 121).

[16] Michel Foucault has argued that the tradition of circulating, as broadsheets, the 'last words' of criminals had ambiguous effects in 17th- and 18th-century France. Whether last words were faithfully transcribed or modified with poetic license after the fact, printed professions of repentance and moral exhortation could dissuade readers from a path of crime or they could turn a "convicted criminal [...] after his death [into] a sort of saint, his memory honoured" (67). Defiant words, presumably, could also be read in contradictory ways but their power would certainly be reinforced by the death of the (supposed) author. Thomas Nashe, in *The Unfortunate Traveller*, mocks and undermines the tradition of last words (spoken or printed). Wrongly imprisoned on a murder charge, protagonist Jack Wilton reports having "made a ballad for my farewell in a readiness called *Wilton's Wantonness* – and yet for all that scaped dancing in a hempen circle" (281). Later Jack witnesses the public execution of one Cutwolf (the second major torture and execution sequence of the narrative) who murdered the man who had previously killed his (Cutwolfe's) brother. Cutwolf is not repentant but cherishes his act of revenge when he addresses the spectators thus: "Men and people that have made holiday to behold my pained flesh toil on the wheel, expect not of me a whining penitent slave that shall do nothing but cry and say his prayers and so be crushed to pieces" (302).

Mount of Fame pageant set in direct response to Ralegh's trial and execution (159).[17] The possibility is intriguing and although the pageants would have already been designed by the time of Ralegh's arraignment, a deliberate reference can by no means be ruled out. The execution, in its relation to the Lord Mayor's Show bears closer scrutiny. Just like the scripted Lord Mayor's Show, its counter event, the public execution, unfolds theatrically with the traditional procession to the place of execution and the opportunity for the condemned to direct his last words at the assembled spectators. Ralegh made much of his last moments, interacting with his audience (Beer 25), moving from one side of the scaffold to the other – using his space effectively – and even embracing some of the lords in attendance (26). The scene is indeed reminiscent of Marvell's portrayal of Charles I as "royal actor" adorning the "tragic scaffold" (97) in his "Horatian Ode Upon Cromwell's Return from Ireland". Contrary to tradition, Ralegh did not confess his crimes prior to his beheading and equally refrained from uttering the traditional praise of the monarch (Beer 28). Since confession was "the act by which the accused accepted the charge and recognized its truth" (Foucault 38), and, simultaneously, the system of arriving at that truth, Ralegh's refusal to cooperate went beyond questions of personal guilt or innocence and denied the judicial system on which rested his charge.

His behavior established around himself a community of those affected by his words and actions, more specifically, a counter-community formed in opposition to the monarch at whose behest Ralegh had been put on trial. Simultaneously, between Paul's Wharf and the Guildhall, the city was celebrating a vision of itself as a unified, well-ordered and stable community centered around the lord mayor. The theme of obedience to superiors is the defining characteristic in the dialogue between the characters of master and mate, who are handling a cannon on one of the pageant stages in Munday's show. When the master asks for his mate's whereabouts, the boy answers promptly: "Here Sir, at hand, / To doe what ere the Maister shall command." (B3) The boy displays complete deference to his master, infused with a happy eagerness to fulfill what both characters understand as his duty. The master then tells his underling that, "[o]ur Gunners Arte, / In this Triumphall day must beare a part" (ibid.).[18] He includes his subordinate in their shared identity as gunners and this, in turn, invites spectators in similar relationships of dependence and tutelage, a not insignificant part of the London population, to enter into a shared sense of identity. Later in the show, Fame, on her pageant Mount, "seemeth to present the new sworne *Lord Maior* to Soueraigne Maiesty, whose Lieutenant and lawfull Deputy hee is now inuested for *London*" (B4). On the Mount of Fame Virtues ride in triumph and Vices are displayed in defeat, signifying the proper order of things and the thorough defeat of all threats to the unity of the city.

[17] Hill points out that "[n]o other Lord Mayor's Show cites 'treason' twice in this fashion" (Pageantry 300).

[18] After their serious neglect earlier in the century, "[t]he London trained bands [...] were reorganised in 1616 into four regiments commanded by colonels and under the generalship of the lord mayor" (Lindley 122). It is possible that the gunner pageant not only alludes to the Ironmongers – and possibly the necessity of securing the commonwealth against traitors – but also to the contemporary restructuring of London's armed forces.

In Westminster, meanwhile, the moribund Ralegh, by his refusal to acknowledge his crime, repent and subject himself entirely to the king's authority, did not fulfill a regime-stabilizing function by the spectacle of his death but rather chose to continue to pose a challenge to the same. The unintended effect (by the crown) of Ralegh's last moments conforms to notions formulated by Michel Foucault in *Discipline and Punish* on the necessarily equivocal nature of public torture and execution.[19] Although Foucault explores the development of the penal system in France, many of his findings can equally well be applied to other European settings. Even while "[t]he very excess of the violence" enacted on the body of an offender in the course of an execution was "one of the elements of its glory" (Foucault 34), the spectacle also "ran the risk of being rejected by the very people to whom it was addressed" (ibid. 63). Normally, a public audience at the scene of an execution was to bear testament to the justice of the sentence being carried out and to affirm the monarch's authority – which was inevitably called into question by any breach of the law. Yet, for a variety of reasons, spectators could conceivably withhold their support from the crown and instead sympathize with the alleged offender:

> In calling on the crowd to manifest its power, the sovereign tolerated for a moment acts of violence, which he accepted as a sign of allegiance, but which were strictly limited by the sovereign's own privileges. Now it was on this point that the people, drawn to the spectacle intended to terrorize it, could express its rejection of the punitive power and sometimes revolt. (59)

In some cases, previously established circumstances disposed the public to side with the condemned. On the other hand, "one finds many examples when the agitation was provoked directly by a verdict and an execution" (60).

In this context of crime and punishment, mention should perhaps be made of the most gruesome element in any of the early 17th-century Lord Mayor's Shows. In Munday's *Chrysanaleia*, a macabre prop is the (supposed) head of Wat Tyler, leading figure in the Peasants' Revolt of 1381 and reportedly killed by London mayor William Walworth in the reign of Richard II. In the course of the show, Walworth, "sometimes twise Lord Maior of London, and a famous Brother of the Fishmongers Company" (B3), is resurrected and joins the proceedings, accompanied by five knights on horseback – his former allies in the confrontation with the Kentish rebels (ibid.). Also present is "Londons Genius, a comely Youth, attired in the Shape of an Angell, with a golden Crowne on his head, golden Wings at his backe, bearing a golden Wand in his hand" (ibid.). In what amounts to an extreme aesthetic conflict for modern minds, this beautiful child "bear[s] the Rebels head on Walworth's Dagger" (B3).[20] Yet, what distinguishes this display of

---

[19] Already Ralegh's 1603 trial, where he stood accused – on flimsy evidence – of having participated in the plot to place Arbella Stuart on the throne, had not been an unmitigated success for James I and his Attorney General Edward Coke. On that occasion, too, the prosecution had failed to create public support for the verdict (Bliss 39; Hadfield 17).

[20] Pamela Nightingale deems it likely that "Walworth did not plan to kill Wat Tyler. However, in previous personal confrontations he had shown an impetuous streak, and Tyler's insolence roused him to lunge at him with his sword, either killing him outright or inflicting a mortal wound, before he rode off to fetch the militia [from the inner city]" (n. pag.).

punitive violence from the spectacle of Ralegh's decapitation, aside from the obvious difference between reality and make-believe re-enactment, is the fact that Tyler's execution is presented as a *fait accompli* and, thus, refuses the malcontent the opportunity to make his case and rouse potential sympathizers. There is no moment at which the ranks of Londoners are not already closed against Tyler, producing the suggestion of their approval of and complicity in his killing over two centuries ago. Typically, however, the Lord Mayor's Show finds less violent means to facilitate the incorporation of Londoners into one undivided community, as, for example, the evocation of a shared pride in the city and its culture.

2.3   *Ambition workes our shame*: Worldly Aspiration and Religious Renunciation

The perceived sins of ambition and pride are frequently castigated in the emblems of Whitney and Peacham, whereas no Lord Mayor's Show can do without showing these qualities in a good light. Pride in one's guild or company, in one's profession, in London, and, not least, in the office of lord mayor are necessary themes in mayoral pageantry. The moderate ambition of the busy and hard-working company man, too, is celebrated as work ethic rather than derided as vain, as misguided, or as aiming above one's station.

On the other hand, to "flee this faulte" is the unambiguous advice formulated in Whitney's emblem 92, "Ridicula ambitio/Ridiculous ambition", in which the verse further cautions that unless avoided "[a]mbition workes our shame" (180). The same warning is issued in emblem 86, "Noli altum supere/Do not aim at lofty things", by means of an archer shown in the act of aiming at a bird in the sky while on the ground, outside of his field of vision, a snake is attacking his exposed calf. The verse moralizes the visualized anecdote by the exhortation: "Let mortall men, that are but earthe and duste, / Not look to highe, with puffe of worldlie pride: / [...] / Leste when theire mindes, do mounte unto the skies, / Their fall is wrought, by thinges they doe dispise." That those who look to better themselves unduly will soon be humbled is a theme running through Whitney's emblem book as is the lure of wealth, its potential to bedazzle and corrupt. The emblem under the motto "In Astrologus/Against astrologers" rails against a surfeit of ambition in pursuit of knowledge, glory, or wealth by combining the image of Icarus falling from the sky with an admonition directed at the ambitious that they should reconsider their ways, "[l]east as they clime, they fall to theire decaye" (Whitney, emblem 28, 117). Both emblem 28 and, to a lesser extent, emblem 92 explore the theme of falling from a height that has been reached by wrongful means or is otherwise taboo. The same is expressed in emblem 229, "Qui se exaltat, humiliabitur/He who exalts himself will be humbled", in which the boiling contents of a pot are shown bubbling and spilling over the brim, above the moral that a "proud" broth "comes to naughte, with falling in the fire" (Whitney 319). The tenor of all these emblems is reminiscent of Francis Quarles' undifferentiated disparagement of secular advancement. In Peacham's fifth and sixth emblems pride is censured as shameful vanity (C3). Number five, "Philautia", refers to the vice of "Self-love" which is allegedly greatest in the proud and causes them to be blind to their own imperfections (fig. 2). The following emblem, "Humane traditiones", depicts a tree breaking apart as it can gain no grip on the castle wall where it grows, the moral being that those "puffed up with pride, and glory vaine; / Unto their shame, doe moulder downe, and fall". As "[n]o vice offendes the Lord, so much as pride" (emblem 64, K4), Peacham strictly advises to "meddle not, with thinges above thy reach" (emblem 109, R1) and chides "the proude vaine-glorious wight, / Who where he comes, will make a goodly show / Of wit, or wealth, when it is nothing so" (emblem 63, K4).

Even city scribes themselves can be critical of pride and ambition. Dekker takes London to task for being overly proud in *The Seven Deadly Sinnes of London*. While the anonymous voice of *Londons Lamentation* admonishes "Lovely London, the beauty of England, and admiration of the world, [to] leave off thy haughty pride, and ambition" (1). The Lord Mayor's Show, however, celebrates status elevation, the moment when an alderman experiences the climax of his civic career and the direction of movement it emphasizes is therefore clearly up, not humbly down. Furthermore, as a means to procure further funds, bachelors (also known as yeomen) in the new mayor's company had the opportunity to be translated into the livery of their company during mayoral years – another instance of supposedly well-deserved betterment. Status advancement, of course, generally goes hand in hand with a degree of ambition prior to advancement and with feelings of pride when said advancement is achieved, and both of these sentiments were welcomed by the Lord Mayor's Show. Pride is explicitly acknowledged as a positive quality, for example, in Heywood's *Londini Artium* when Arion addresses the river Thames with the words: "How I admire thy Glory, State, and Pride" (B). Palmer argues that Mayor William Walworth's part in putting down the Peasant Revolt, appropriated by Munday for his *Chruso-thriambos,* is used to distinguish for the audience between "malevolent ambition in distinct contrast to the mercantile ambition of the guilds, who embody the Christian practice of distribution" (381).[21] The pride and ambition of craftsmen and tradesmen are, thus, to be understood as positive qualities which ultimately serve the good of the entire community. While it is hard to argue with Palmer's convincing and well-phrased argument, it must be added that Lord Mayor's Shows did not generally present two distinctly separate categories of ambition but rather presented ambition in general in a positive light, as a trait that reflects strength of character and, at the same time, does not disavow communal responsibility.

Civic pride is, of course, one of the linchpins of the Lord Mayor's Show – pride in occupation, in citizenship, in company membership, in the city corporation as well as the city in general. All of these forms of pride are instilled in mayor, livery and spectators via key figures co-opted from the intersecting realms of history, mythology and moral allegory. Positive recognition of these figures is a means by which group membership is reinforced and pride, in turn, acts as a vital instrument of group cohesion. The chariots in which representations of civic and royal forbears, metaphorical 'ancestors', are presented

---

[21] In Thomas Nelson's 1590 Lord Mayor's Show "the figure representing Commonwealth reacts to personified Ambition by observing that the government will seek to banish ambition and to guarantee that 'this peace may neuer cease' and thus rid the country of vice" (Bergeron, The Elizabethan Lord Mayor's Show 278). Like Munday's *Chrysanaleia*, Nelson's show also dealt with the Tyler/Straw uprising of 1381 and Walworth's role in it (ibid.). Ambition is here attributed to Tyler and becomes synonymous with uproar and violence, which simultaneously, and conveniently, disconnects it from the context of mercantile enterprise.

to the mayor's entourage and to the crowds of spectators constitute focal points around which a proud sense of community coheres.[22] Displays which feature commoners enacting various crafts and trades, also elicit a communal sense of pride and make possible the integration of the non-liveried majority into a unified idea of London.

Pride in a merchant identity, specifically, is also conveyed by reference to heroic explorers of classical myth, primarily by reference to Jason – a conflation of mercantile enterprise and heroic questing that is ridiculed elsewhere. In Munday's *Metropolis Coronata* Jason, Medea and a crew of Argonauts open the day's festivities on the Thames and Jason is showcased as a proto-merchant. The golden fleece is invoked multiple times as the object of a heroic quest, in analogy to the valuable commodities imported by London merchants. In this manner Munday's *Triumphs of the Golden Fleece* appeal to the merchant ego by invoking "Prince *Jason*, and his valiant *Argonautes* of *Greece*," who "passed to *Colchos*, to fetch from thence the *Golden Fleece*, which is the Creast of the DRAPERS Armorie". Heywood creates another analogy between Greek heroes and London merchants by choosing the character of Ulysses (Odysseus to the Greeks) to open and bring to a close *London's Ius Honorarium*. In Heywood's *Londini Emporia* merchants are defined as

> those, by whose adventure and Industry unknowne Countries have beene discovered, Friendship with forreigne Princes contracted, barbarous Nations to humane gentlenesse and courtesie reduced, and all such usefull commodities in forreigne Climates abounding, and in their owne wanting, made conducible and frequent, nay, many of them have not beene onely the Erectors of brave and goodly structures, but the Founders of great and famous Cities. (A3)

Merchants are conceptualized as discoverers of foreign territories, as facilitators of diplomatic relations, benefactors of foreign peoples and, above all, as benefactors of the London populace and the entire realm. It is a "Noble Profession", indeed, which achieves all of the above, including the founding of great cities, as Heywood affirms in *Londini Artium* (A3).

One of Whitney's emblems (number 216) celebrates Francis Drake by favorable comparison to Jason, essentially positing Drake as a new and superior version of the old prototypical adventurer, but there is no further identification of Drake and London-based merchants.[23] Middleton creates this link in *Triumphs of Health and Prosperity*, in which an unidentified speaker at the Sanctuary of Prosperity pageant identifies Drake as "England's true Jason" (1904). The dramatist notes that "on the arch" of the 'Sanctuary'

---

[22] Bergeron notes that Thomas Nelson's "use of a former Lord Mayor and other historical figures is an important first [in 1590], for almost all mayoralty pageants of the early seventeenth century will include such personages both as compliments to the trade guild and as worthy examples to be imitated" (The Elizabethan Lord Mayor's Show 279).

[23] The emblem picture shows a globe surrounded by reigns and surmounted by a ship. While the globe itself is here part of a composition that celebrates the accomplishments of Drake, elsewhere it signifies the suffering that being in the world entails as well as earthly obstacles to salvation. Emblem 119 in Peacham's *Minerva Britanna*, for example, identifies a globe as representing one of the "humane miseries" (S2).

"hangs the Golden Fleece, which raises the worthy memory of that most famous and re-nowned brother of this company, Sir Francis Drake, who in two years and ten months did encompass the whole world" (ll. 83-88). A performer situated on the device refers to Drake as "England's true Jason, who did boldly make / So many rare adventures" (ll. 101-02). Drake is thereby identified by the sponsoring Drapers not only as kindred in spirit to London merchants in general but as a prodigy from their very own ranks. Similarly, in Webster's *Monuments of Honour*, famous navigators Drake, Hawkins, Frobisher, Humphrey Gilbert, Thomas Cavendish, Christopher Carlisle, and John Davis appear on a globe device, expressing the nation's pride in its seafaring men, a group according to speaker Oceanus, unique in the world (B). Here, too, the prestigious seafarers and navy reformers are affiliated with London merchants who bring prosperity to the realm by their ventures.

That "there is no subject upon earth received into the place of his government with the like state and magnificence", is Middleton's famous, yet, in its context by no means unusual boast (Triumphs of Truth 968), since pride in the uniqueness of the Lord Mayor's Show itself is routinely professed in the commemorative pamphlets. Further examples of this are Middleton's insistence, in his *Triumphs of Integrity* pamphlet, that of "all solem-nities by which the happy inauguration of a subject is celebrated, I find none that transcends the state and magnificence of that pomp prepared to receive his Majesty's great substitute into his honorable charge" (ll. 24-27), and the opening lines of Heywood's *Londini Artium* which remind the mayor of "the Dignity of your place, and Magnificence of your Inauguration" (A2).

That not even the pride of the gods can triumph over the pride of London merchants may be demonstrated by the example of Mercury. As patron of merchants and eloquence, the deity is always a positive asset to the Lord Mayor's Show, while for Whitney he serves as an incarnation of the random powers of fate against which mere mortals may struggle but never win. In his second emblem, "Qua dii voacent, eundum/Where the gods call, we must go", a severe Mercury points the way to a traveler on the road (Whitney 91). Although it is not unusual for the messenger god to act as a guide, here he serves to express the ominous circumstance that the human traveler has no option but to go where forces beyond his control point him, without the least assurance about his final destination. While Mercury more commonly plays a minor role in the pageants, as in Dekker's *Troia-Nova Triumphans* and Taylor's *Triumphs of Fame and Honour*, the deity with the caduceus is in the limelight in Heywood's *Londini Emporia*, where he is the speaker at the helm of a pageant ship placed in Cheapside. There, he praises the new mayor, "[w]hose winged ships all foreigne Seas have plow'd", for his trade ventures, his import of desirable wares in exchange for "some surplus ware", goods the city and the realm can spare without suffering any negative consequences (B3-B4). In the pamphlet commemorating *Londini Emporia* the messenger god is described as "the Leader of the Graces, the Inventer of Wrestling, the Deviser of Letters, the Patron of Eloquence [...] but he is also termed the god of Barter, buying, selling, and commerce in all Merchandise whatsoever" (ibid.). Yet, despite his manifold qualifications, Mercury is here placed in the service of the mayor, not the mayor reduced to bow to the will of the gods. A similar role reversal between gods and men touches Neptune in Dekker's *Troia-Nova Triumphans* and is described by Gordon Kipling as "the *triumphator* of the seas yield[ing]

66

to triumphant London and becom[ing] a mere henchman in the Lord Mayor's procession" (46).

2.4   *Do not trust prosperity too much*: Wealth as Boon and Burden

That the mayor, by means of his "winged ships" on "foreigne Seas", may acquire substantial fortunes is not a fact to his discredit, whereas the corrupting potential of wealth is a theme of some importance to Whitney and Peacham. The accumulation and distribution of wealth, understood as the result of merit, is celebrated in Lord Mayor's Shows for its beneficial effects on the London community and the entire realm. Meanwhile, the ignorance of the rich as much as the folly of their attendant fools and flatterers is a recurring motif on the pages of emblem books. Only a minority of the members of the great livery companies were themselves wealthy, of course, yet the mayor himself had to be a man of substantial means since the office constituted a great strain on the personal finances of its incumbent. Before Mansion House was erected in the 18th century, to own a large residence in the city, functioning as a representative space, was mandatory. Any mayor-to-be who was not already in possession of such a mansion (most were) had to accept the financial burden of acquiring one – as did James Pemberton for his term in office in 1611-12 (Lang 45). Furthermore, each mayor had to bear "the heavy responsibilities for entertainment and hospitality associated with the office" (Brenner 63-64).

The annual shows themselves were expensive projects (and this was certainly supposed to show) and the companies consequently took great pride in their communal ability to finance them. Kathleen McLuskie detects two opposing early modern discursive traditions concerning the moral implications of material wealth: on the one hand, the "complaint tradition" vilifies possession while, on the other hand, a 'celebratory tradition' glorifies wealth as contributing to the welfare of all (61). Adhering to the former tradition, Anthony Nixon finds in his 1616 work on *The Dignitie of Man* that there is much virtue in mediocrity (72), since riches "stirre us up to superfluitie, and pull us back from *Temperance*" (95), i.e. back from a cardinal virtue. Moreover, possession breeds pride, covetousness, and anxiety (ibid. 96). While emblems by Whitney and Peacham confirm Nixon's professed attitude and share in the complaint tradition, the Lord Mayor's Show takes the opposite position and celebrates affluence.

The idea that wealth is detrimental as it inevitably leads to a pathological compulsion to increase it indefinitely is anathema to the frequent celebration of material self-improvement in Lord Mayor's Shows. This is, however, the tenor of a considerable number of emblems in Whitney and Peacham's collections. The concept of greed as pathology is present in Whitney's emblem 213, "Animus, non res/Mind, not property", which combines the image of Diogenes in his barrel with the moral that "he is pore that covettes more and more. / Which proves: the man was ritcher in the tonne, / Then was the Kinge, that manie landes had wonne" (301). Covetousness is designated "that greedie Monster" in Peacham's third emblem (C2), and the insatiable desire to accumulate more and more is one of the two offenses indicted in Whitney's emblem twelve, bearing the motto "Frustra/In vain". The emblem picture shows a pierced and leaking barrel in reference to the Greek myth of Danaus' daughters. "No paine will serve, to fill it to the toppe," expounds the verse, "For, still at holes the same doth runne, and droppe." (101) The moral warns, firstly, against the "the blabbe" who cannot keep secrets and, secondly, against the "covetous man, thowghe he abounde with store / Is not suffusde, but covetts more and more." The well-known story of the punishment visited on the daughters of Danaus for the murder of their husbands (they had to carry water in perforated containers) is here applied to two foreign contexts in each of which the metaphor of the leaking vessel works in a slightly different way. Words leak from the mouth of the "blabbe" while, in the context of covetousness, the leaking barrel that can never be filled signifies the per-petual lack of satisfaction in a greedy man.

The vanity of possessions in the face of mortality finds expression in the emblem titled "Mortui divitiae/A dead man's riches" in Whitney's anthology. The brevity of human life and the fleetingness of worldly institutions are commonplaces in the emblem books of the 16th and early 17th centuries. Van der Noot, for instance, expresses these considera-tions by combining the picture of two obelisks, one standing, one broken on the ground, with the solemn message that "nought in this worlde but griefe endures" (emblem 8, 15). Another one of his emblems integrates the picture of a palace that is on fire and breaking apart with a condemnation of the pointless vanity pertaining to worldly things. As a "sodein earthquake loe, / Shaking the hill even from the bottome deepe, / Threwe downe this building to the lowest stone", so other buildings and objects crumble in time and are therefore not worthy of much regard (Van der Noot, emblem 7, 14). All the pillars, diamonds, marble, crystal, gold, and precious stones that are consumed in the fire or shattered into fragments are mere material vanities, not representative of immaterial worth, and transitory to boot. Confronted with the overpowering notion of complete extinction, it is not surprising that material possessions should lose their significance in the face of graver concerns. Whitney's emblem 65, "Nimium rebus ne fide secundis/Do not trust prosperity too much", offers a message similar to Van der Noot's, i.e. not to hold too dear "anie worldlie thinges, / For frowninge fate, throwes downe the mightie kinges" (152). Jupiter, in Whitney's emblem picture, far from lending his might in support of merchant London as he does in the Lord Mayor's Show, appears as a force of arbitrary destruction.

Plainly, the Lord Mayor's Show is not the place for meditation on transience and mortality but instead a framework for the celebration of the city, of its economic and political foundations, and the communal life that gives rise to and sustains these. This means that its orientation is firmly toward the material world and the growing community of Londoners which it attempts to ideologically integrate into a harmonious whole. The form that the celebration of the city and its community takes is not one that shies away from displays of splendor. Instead, it often makes use of these in order to impress and entertain as well as to show the potential rewards of a life spent dedicated to industry. In *Triumphs of Honour and Industry* personified India holds a block of gold which not only visualizes the lucrative nature of trade with the Far East but shows trade and prosperity in a positive light. In the same pageant Fortune's wheel is made of silver, Perfection wears "a crown of gold" and Wealth bears "a golden key where her heart lies" (ll. 91-95). Furthermore, the symbolic props of personified Merchandise – a globe – and Industry – a golden ball – associate the entire planet with wealth and the ways of procuring it.

An antithetical distrust of wealth lies at the heart of Whitney's emblem 215, "Aureae compedes/Golden shackles", which decries "fetters made of goulde" in combination with the picture of a courtier in leg stocks (305).[24] The 'poison' that is gold is also warned against in the emblem under the motto "Saepius in auro bibitur venenum/Poison is more often drunk in gold", number 87 in Whitney's *Choice of Emblems*. Discouraging social climbing, the moral of the emblem is to "make thy choise, amongste thy equalls still." (175) This opposes the idea of betterment by industry embraced by the Lord Mayor's Show. Echoing this precept, personified Industry holds a golden ball both in Middleton's *Triumphs of Honour and Industry* and in his *The Sun in Aries*. In the latter show, the ball is topped by "a Cupid, intimating that industry brings both wealth and love" (ll. 260-61). Here, too, wealth is construed as a beneficial force, achieved by industry and therefore well deserved. By the syntactic arrangement of "wealth and love" around a central conjunction, the former is also semantically enriched by the latter. The idea, unsurprisingly embraced by the Lord Mayor's Show, that wealth is not only a positive force in general but that merchants earn their wealth through industry and merit is opposed to the idea endorsed by Peacham's emblem 81 which compares a game of football with the distribution of wealth in the world. Like everything else in the material world, the distribution of "[t]his worldly wealth" is random since wealth, like a football, "is tossed to and fro" and as in a football game, all players, like "Brutes", fight for themselves "with might and maine" (N1).

While wealth itself is conceived of as constraining and as an accompaniment of a debauched existence in Whitney's emblems 215 and 87, number 80 does not condemn the possession of riches as such but rather indicts the failure to dispense with some of them in order to relieve privation, whether one's own or others'. The emblem titled "Avaritia/Avarice" shows Tantalus, shoulder-deep in water, while above him – just out of reach – the branches of a tree droop with appetizing fruit. The verse accuses the type of person who "dare[s] not touche his store, when he doth neede" (168). A reverse image of the tight-fisted Tantalus, equally unappealing in its own right, is the self-congratulatory samaritan attacked in Whitney's emblem 241, "Noli tuba canere Eleemosynam/Do not trumpet your charity". The emblem picture shows a sumptuously dressed man handing alms to a beggar while simultaneously holding a trumpet to his lips. The verse notes that it is better to give in secret, yet still in the sight of god, and not to proclaim one's charity, since "therby dost showe, / Thy chiefe desire is, that the world maie knowe" (330). A reminder that "best desert, still liveth out of view" (M3), is also the central argument of Peacham's emblem 78. The implication that philanthropic deeds may be born from selfish motives is certainly steered clear off in the Lord Mayor's Show. Instead, the charitable distribution of funds in support of building projects, education, religion, or poor relief is regularly praised and construed as benefiting not primarily the giver but the city and the realm. And, indeed, in this instance pride may not have been entirely misplaced as K. J. Lindley has credited "the existence of a system of poor relief in the City [of London], far in advance of the rest of England" (116). Whereas in the country food shortages and grain

---

[24] Distrust of appearances is also at the core of Peacham's emblem 79, the verse of which notes that while some trees overshadow others in might, the overshadowed may yet "in vertue [...] excell" (M4).

hording sporadically caused riots, so for example in 1607 in the Midlands (Greenblatt, Tyrant 156), this was not a common occurance in London.

Under the motto "Male parta male dilabuntur/Ill-gotten, ill-spent", Whitney's emblem 178 presents the image of an ape throwing coins out of an upper story window (fig. 5). The ape, notes the verse, represents a usurer's servant taking his revenge against an unkind master. The pleasant by-effect of the ape's revenge is that "[t]he sighte, righte well the passers by did please, / Who did reioyce to finde these goulden crommes" (268). This is not only an illustration of the trope that gains made by fraudulent means will not bring lasting satisfaction, but also constitutes an irreverent look at the charitable distribution of riches. The scenario posits the giver as an ape, the money as stolen – twice – and the profiteers as lucky rather than needy or deserving. The emblem not only contrasts with earnest accounts in praise of charitable civic dignitaries, it also offers an evocative antithesis to the distribution of 'crumbs' of 'gold' and 'silver' among the spectators in, for example, Munday's *Chrysanaleia*. A connection between apes and merchants, parallel to the association of apes and usurers, is drawn by Peacham in his emblem titled "Vane merces" (fig. 6) which satirizes merchant pride and suggests that the prototype of the modern merchant has more in common with an ape than with Greek Argonaut Jason, depleting national stores in exchange for foreign trifles (Aa2).[25] Usurers, predictably, do not feature in Lord Mayor's Shows and the unsavory term itself is only used to point out that the mayor's own wealth is certainly acquired "with an unusuring hand" (Middleton, *Triumphs of Honour and Virtue* 1720).

Corruption of the mind by accumulation is a theme taken up once more in Whitney's emblem 188, "Auri sacra fames quid non?/What does accursed greed for gold not drive men to do?", in which a man rather risks drowning than cease his hold on a sack filled with treasure (278).[26] The sentiment is echoed in Francis Quarles' emblematic rendering of the shipwreck of the human soul which finds no support whatsoever in worldly things but receives comfort only from divine love (qtd. in Freeman 127). Thus, the possession of riches is the cause of pathological behavior in Whitney's emblem 188, as well as in numbers twelve and 213, cited above, in which it causes a detrimental compulsion, addiction even, to continue to increase one's fortune without end. The harmful effect of wealth is echoed in Peacham's emblem 51 which warns that riches, though they may seem sweet at first, "breede our bane of care" or even "with their losse, bereave us of our wits" (I2). This seemingly poses a conundrum since wealth is noted to exert a negative influence irrespective of whether one actually has it or not, it is enough to have been infected with greed. All "worldly greed", regardless of particular consequences, is in fact "antithetical to Christ", goes the argument of Whitney's previously cited emblem (number 156), "Quod non capit Christus, rapit fiscus" (246).

---

[25] Merchant monkeys also featured in Flemish Baroque painting: In response to 'tulip mania' sweeping across the Netherlands, Jan Brueghel the Younger rendered tulip merchants and speculators involved in the craze as so many smartly dressed monkeys in a painting known as "A Satire on Tulip Mania".

[26] In Nashe's *The Unfortunate Traveller*, trickster protagonist Jack Wilton inverts the proverb. After having robbed and absconded from Lady Juliana's house with his courtesan Wilton muses: "*Quid non auri sacra fames*, what defame wil not gold salve?" (300)

70

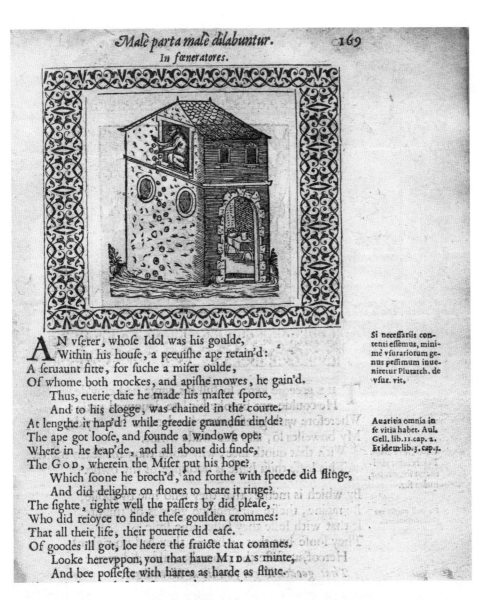

AN vſerer, whoſe Idol was his goulde,
Within his houſe, a peeuiſhe ape retain'd :
A ſeruaunt fitte, for ſuche a miſer oulde,
Of whome both mockes, and apiſhe mowes, he gain'd.
    Thus, euerie daie he made his maſter ſporte,
    And to his clogge, was chained in the courte.
At lengthe it hap'd? while greedie graundſir din'de?
The ape got looſe, and founde a windowe ope:
Where in he leap'de, and all about did finde,
The GOD, wherein the Miſer put his hope?
    Which ſoone he broch'd, and forthe with ſpeede did flinge,
    And did delighte on ſtones to heare it ringe?
The ſighte, righte well the paſſers by did pleaſe,
Who did reioyce to finde theſe goulden crommes:
That all their life, their pouertie did eaſe.
Of goodes ill got, loe heere the fruicte that commes.
    Looke herevppon, you that haue MIDAS minte,
    And bee poſſeſte with hartes as harde as flinte.

Si neceſſariis con-
tenti eſſemus, mini-
mè vſurariorum ge-
nus peſſimum inue-
niretur Plutarch. de
vſur. vit.

Auaritia omnia in
ſe vitia habet. Aul.
Gell. lib.11.cap. 2.
Et idem lib.3. cap.1.

Fig. 5: Whitney's 178th emblem castigates a usurer with a heart "as harde as flinte" who keeps a 'peevish ape' (268). Image by courtesy of the Penn State University Libraries.

R ICH *NAVPALVS*, hath secretly convaid,
  Our English fleece so long beyond the sea,
That not for wit, but for his wealth tis said,
Hee's thence return'd a worthy Knight awaie,
    And brought vs back, beades, Hobbie-horses, boxes,
    Fannes, Windmills, Ratles, Apes, and tailes of Foxes.

And now like *IASON*, vp and downe he goes,
As if he had th' *Hesperian Dragon* slaine,
And equaliz'd in worth, those old Heroe's,
That in the *ARGO* cut the Grecian maine:
    Honour thou didst, but doe his valour right,
    When of the fleece, thou dubbest him a Knight.

Vellera divendit Belgis laudata Britannûm,
  Sed nugas referens N A V P L V S inde domum:
Vellere factus eques, volitat novus alter I A S O N
  Vilescit (rides) velleris ordo nimis.

Basil: Doron.

Aa2.   *Haud*

Fig. 6: Under the motto "Vane merces", Peacham ridicules the pride of merchants in their own institutions and endeavors by identifying a merchant with a feebleminded monkey (Aa2). Image by courtesy of the David M. Rubenstein Rare Book & Manuscript Library, Duke University.

The contrast between emblem and Lord Mayor's Show pageantry culminates in Whitney's emblem 227, entitled "In divitem, indoctum/On the ignorant rich man", which inverts the symbol of the golden fleece to great effect. The emblem picture shows Phrixus crossing the Hellespont, named for his drowned twin sister, on the golden ram in grandiose pose: "On goulden fleece, did Phryxus passe the wave, / And landed safe, within the wished baie: / By which is ment, / the fooles that riches have, / Supported are, and borne through Lande, and Sea [...]." The fleece, still attached to the ovine beneath, is not connected to heroic endeavors (as it usually is) but becomes a means of luxurious transportation for spoiled and unworthy types. A triple analogy is established between, on the one hand, a common domestic sheep in a golden fleece, a leaden sword in a golden sheath, and, on the other hand, a wealthy individual of inferior mind. The verse admonishes that "if the minde the chiefest treasure lack, / [...] / Thoughe goulde wee weare, and purple on our backe, / Yet are wee poore, and none will us comende / But onlie fooles; and flatterers, for their gaine" (317). The golden fleece, appropriated in many a Lord Mayor's Show – especially those commissioned by the Drapers – as a symbol of mercantile merit and enterprise here becomes a symbol of vacuous grandeur and the pampered, undeserving rich.

In contrast to this notion, when John Squire expresses pride in the fact that he believes his pageant devices to appear "far more ritch then any, in regard no mettall was used to adorne it but gold and siluer" (C2), he voices a common sentiment. Lord Mayor's Shows could not do without impressive sights to please both the crowds and the sponsoring companies. Pageant dramatists, thus, aimed at creating rich and captivating displays confirming the authority of the great companies in whose hands lay the government of the city. That a certain grandeur was essential for achieving client satisfaction is borne out by the conception of the annual show as an incomparably lavish event. Since the beginning of the 17th century almost every commemorative pamphlet opened with the declaration that no mayor or magistrate, anywhere in the known world, receives an inaugural show as impressive, as full of pomp and splendor as does the lord mayor of London. Taylor's avowal that "no Kings Deputy, or Magistrate / Is with such pompous state inaugurate, / As Londons Mayor is", is representative of the general sentiment (qtd. in Williams 511). Although the Lord Mayor's Show had not existed in this elaborate form before the end of the 16th century, it was commonly accepted, within a very short time, that this was the form it deserved and should always have. It was even implied, despite evidence to the contrary, in the manner of an invented tradition, that this was how it had always been – an assessment that corresponds to Edward Muir's view that rituals (like the Lord Mayor's Show) are "'invented traditions' par excellence" for the reason that they "varied from one repetition to another but [...] attempted to mask variation by asserting their unchanging character" (131).

Aside from the splendor of the Lord Mayor's Show as a whole, the separate pageants also frequently referenced the rich rewards that may spring from the enterprise of merchants, as when Thetis, in Webster's *Monuments of Honour*, voices the following blessing for the benefit of the new mayor: "Rich Lading swell your Bottomes, a blest Gale, / Follow your ventures that they neuer faile" (B). Some of the profits thus gained were expected to go toward the funding of the arts and sciences.

The mayor's support of the arts is traditionally highlighted and celebrated in mayoral pageantry, whereas it is neglect of them that is pointed out in emblems by Whitney and Peacham. The claim that an urban, materially-minded environment is not conducive to the arts is made in Whitney's emblem 176, "Si nihil atuleris, ibis Homere foras/If, Homer, you do not bring anything, you will go outside" (266). The picture shows a poet who is identified as Homer and attended by the Nine Muses before an urban backdrop. The fact that the great poet finds himself sadly unwelcome in the city signifies that the intellectual climate is such that, without wealth or commodities to their name, even the best of poets and the muses themselves will find no favor. Correspondingly, Peacham's emblem 24 indicts contemporary times for their failure to uphold the arts. In his day and age, Peacham criticizes, "Armes, ill, but worser, Artes doe fare" (E4). In emblem 97 he regrets that "[s]uch is our age, where virtue's scarce regarded, / And artes with armes, must wander unrewarded" (P1). The same moral is expressed, coded in botanic terms, in Peacham's emblem 200: a laurel tree, representative of learning, has ceased to flourish. As the laurel is withering, so the arts and sciences are neglected by those who should be their patrons (Ee2).

Mayoral pageantry is kinder to the Muses. As such, they are not banned from but welcome in the city in Squire's *Triumphs of Peace*, lending their presence in tribute and gratitude to the mayor. A pageant device on the Thames presents Apollo on Mount Parnassasus along with Mercury, god of trade and eloquence, and the Nine Muses. The Muses make instrumental music as the floating pageant device accompanies the mayor's barge to Westminster, before returning to the city to await the return of newly sworn-in Francis Jones in St Paul's Churchyard (B). The Seven Liberal Arts [logic, grammar, rhetoric, arithmetic, geometry, music, and astronomy], "Mothers to all Trades, Professions, Mysteries and Societies" (B2), are among the entourage of Virtue in *Troia-Nova Triumphans*. Virtue's chariot is drawn by four horses: On the first couple of these ride Time and Mercury, on the second Desire and Industry, ("in the shape of an old Country-man, bearing on his shoulder a Spade"). They all "make men in Love with Arts, Trades, Sciences, and Knowledge" and only by recourse to the latter, explains Dekker, can anyone hope to ascend to the throne of Virtue (B3). Virtue herself remarks that even "the seed of Civill, Popular government, is sowne" by the Sciences, Trades, and Professions (ibid.). Already in 1602, the year that saw the last of the Elizabethan Lord Mayor's Shows and the first of Munday's contributions to the genre, Apollo and the Nine Muses, represented by ten scholars, came before the Lord Mayor in Cheapside (Bergeron, The Elizabethan Lord Mayor's Show 282).

In Heywood's *Londini Status Pacatus*, a personification of the river Nile compares his seven-forked scepter, representing the sources of the Nile, to the Seven Liberal Arts which the mayor supports. The state of the arts in London, under the care of the mayor, is understood as proof of the "Cities magnitude and worthinesse" (363). That it is not only the mayor in isolation but the citizens, too, who contribute to the city's "magnitude and worthiness" is a point made by Heywood in *London's Ius Honorarium*. The pageant author praises the citizens of London, who not only bear arms in public but also "neglect not the study of arts, and practice of literature in private" (280). In Webster's *Monuments of Honour* the "Monument of Charity and Learning, [...] fashioned like a beautifull Garden" (B4) celebrates the traditional sustenance of the arts by city magistrates. The garden set features an impersonation of Sir Thomas White, former mayor (1553-54) and founder of Oxford's St John's College, who is placed beside a model of the college he established (Hill, Pageantry 31).[27] Personifications of Charity and Learning are also in attendance as a visual eulogy to White's generous patronage.

The treatment of Apollo in emblem and Lord Mayor's Show also serves to illustrate the divergent perspectives adopted by the formats. While the god is frequently employed by pageant dramatists to honor the new mayor's actual or hoped for support of the arts, he appears in Whitney's emblem 13, "Superbiae ultio/Vengeance on pride", not as a paragon of learning but as a murderer. The emblem picture shows Apollo and Diana hovering in the sky, shooting and killing Niobe's children with their arrows in punishment of their mother's hubris. Niobe is bent forward in grief, caught in the process of her transformation into rock. One child is lying on its back, an arrow protruding from the stomach, another is crawling in the foreground with an arrow in its back. The children must die so "[t]hat mortall men, shoulde thinke from whence they came, / And not presume, nor puffe them up with pride" (Whitney 102). This violent tirade against pride is anathema to the Lord Mayor's Show – as noted above – which celebrates self-improvement, including material betterment, by means of mercantile enterprise. In pageantry the figure of Apollo is invoked for his associations with refinement and knowledge, flattering the mayor by implying his possession of these same qualities or by pointing out his generous support of them. Emblem books, too, featured Apollo in his function as paragon of knowledge and the arts, yet neither does Whitney shy away from presenting the god as the source of brutal violence against the innocent. Certainly, Niobe's punishment is the stuff of classical legend rather than an original story but the choice of material lies with Whitney as does the grim manner of its presentation. Conversely, Apollo is always depicted in a positive light in Lord Mayor's Shows. So, for example, in Dekker's *Londons Tempe* where Apollo's Palace constitutes the final pageant set of the show and carries, in addition to Apollo himself, all seven personified Liberal Arts. The Nine Muses are the god's companions in Squire's *Triumphs of Peace*, mentioned above, where they sing a song and play an archaic melody on their instruments, the lyrics and musical notations for which are included in the pamphlet (B2). Company funds were not only expected to subsidize poor relief, education and the arts, some resources were also redirected to finance appropriately sumptuous 'vehicles' to feature in mayoral pageantry.

The Chariot of Man's Life

The triumphal chariot is a ubiquitous element in Renaissance art and it is no wonder that chariots should have been an essential part of Lord Mayor's Show pageantry, whether horse-drawn or set on pageant stages to be carried by porters. They were generally decorated in thematic affiliation with the pageant set they formed a part of or they might constitute an entire pageant episode by themselves. Such is the case in Dekker's *Troia-*

---

[27] Hill points out that White had also been involved in preventing the succession of Lady Jane Grey to the English throne in 1553, following the death of Edward VI (Pageantry 31).

Nova Triumphans where the 'Throne of Virtue' pageant device is, in fact, a chariot. As sumptuous triumphal vehicles, chariots gave an air of dignity to their exclusive passengers, be they personified Virtues or historical monarchs, and lent their splendors to the shows themselves. A chariot fulfills a different purpose in Whitney's *Choice of Emblems*, where it signifies the dangers inherent in a lack of control over oneself. In the emblem picture a charioteer is evidently unable to control his horse and, thus, horse and runaway chariot "praunce, and yerke, and out of order flinge, / Till all they breake, and unto havocke bringe" (95). In conclusion, the anecdote of the charioteer's misadventure is applied to human character and constitutes a warning against impulsiveness. The wild runaway horse as a metaphor for inadequate affect control was a Renaissance commonplace, with a history reaching back to antiquity, that could be expressed either by inept charioteers or by riders unable to keep their horses in check.[28] The difference between the utilization of chariots as expressions of dignity and wealth, on the one hand, and their conception as objects of potentially negative import, on the other hand, is worth pointing out. It, too, reflects the ideological differences between the influential emblem books of the late Elizabethan and Jacobean periods and the Lord Mayor's Shows of the same era. One genre is always celebratory in outlook, the other is inward looking and, not infrequently, darkly sceptical of society and material possessions. In Van der Noot's emblem number nine a chariot is among the objects representing grandeur, one of the "faire thing[s]", against which the emblem writer warns: "Let me no more see faire thing under heaven, / Sith I have seene so faire a thing as this, / With sodaine falling broken all to dust." (16) Here, chariots are among the things to be renounced in the face of fickle fate and mortality.

Chariots not only featured as land-bound vehicles in Lord Mayor's Shows, they also served as marine vessels on the Thames and were sometimes even conveyed from river to land in the course of a show. Abram Booth, who spent 15 months in England as secretary to a delegation of the Dutch East India Company, witnessed Dekker's 1629 *Londons Tempe* and recorded his admiration for the waterborne chariot of Oceanus. This looked like "a shell, drawn by two horses of the sea, which swam through the sea, wrought in an artful way" (22). In 1612 Dekker opened his *Troia-Nova Triumphans* with a "[s]ea-Chariot artificially made, proper for a God of the sea to sit in", with "shippes dancing round about it" and "Dolphins and other great Fishes playing or lying at the foot of the same, [...] drawne by two Sea-horses" (A4). A further sea chariot, constructed like a sea creature, carried personified Fame and actors impersonating Henry fitz Ailwin and other renowned Drapers in Munday's 1615 *Metropolis Coronata*. The Chariot of Man's Life, carrying personified Time, makes appearances later in the same show along the processional route. In Middleton's *Triumphs of Health and Prosperity* the Chariot of Honor first appears on the Thames, then transfers to land, 'drawn' by lions who, in turn, support personified Power and Honor. While the chariot which carries as its preeminent passenger the Triumphing Angel is the final pageant device in Munday's *Chrysanaleia*, it still retains a connection to the Thames as representations of mermen and mermaids are attached to it. The chariot that carries Richard I, King John and attendant Virtues in

---

[28] In *The Blacke Rod and the White* (1630), a plague pamphlet attributed to Thomas Dekker, the point is put explicitly: "the Horses, that draw us, are our wilde passions" (212).

Munday's *Chruso-thriambos*, on the other hand, is drawn by heraldic leopards (quite possibly 'lions passant' and not leopards in the modern sense). However, means of transport even more significant in the context of the Lord Mayor's Show than the chariot, were certainly ships and boats.

2.5 The Progress of *wealthy bottoms* Contra the Shipwreck of the Soul

Seagoing sailing ships, fishing vessels, galleys, and barges are among the most frequent pageant devices in Lord Mayor's Shows, appearing both on the Thames and set on portable stages on land along the processional route. While the ship, along with the castle, appears to have gone out of fashion as an element in other types of open-air pageantry in the 16th century, it remained a crucial fixture in Lord Mayor's Shows well into the 17th century (Wickham 92). Ships here served as convenient visual representations of the endeavor and achievement of merchants, effectively becoming what Victor Turner calls "master symbols representative of structural order, and values and virtues on which that order depends" (93) – symbols which, according to Turner, are employed in ritual as a means of reinforcing social order. Other objects and characters – a golden fleece, a sheep or a shepherd, a hammer and anvil – also served to focus a sense of community based on recognizable symbols of trades and industries but none surpassed the signifying power of the ship as a "master symbol". As an exemplar of trade, the ship recalled the venturous, mercantile foundations on which the city was originally built and on which it continued to grow. By its evocation of the significant role of seafaring in the social and economic makeup of the city, the ship could generate a sense of community based on its generally recognized role in commerce. Not for nothing had city chronicler John Stow noted the location of London by the river Thames as essential from the inception of the city onward, since by it "all kind of Marchandise bee easily conueyed to *London*, the prinicpall store house, and Staple of all commodities within this Realme" (11-12). In the same vein, to wish somebody "good shipping to Wapping" – a maritime district just east of the City of London – was a proverbial way for Elizabethans of saying *bon voyage* (Nash 221, ann. 402). Taylor's *Triumphs of Fame and Honour* highlight the role of the river in commerce by presenting a flotilla of vessels on the Thames, supposedly laden "with Packs, dryfats, and divers other commodities, that marchants and others that are free of the Company of Cloth-workers, doe receive from foreign parts by Sea" (n. pag.). With reference to the display, water deity Thetis proclaims:

> I every twelve houres [with the tide], by this Child of mine [the Thames], / Do send you silks and velvets, oyle, and wine / Gold, silver, jewels, fish, salt, sundry spices / Fine and course linnen, druggs of divers prices: / What every Realme or climate can produce, / I see it safe transported to your use. (n. pag.)

In an appraisal of cartographic and other visual representations of Tudor and Stuart London, Lawrence Manley affirms the importance of the river, noting that: "Nearly all the London panoramas of the period [...] foreground[...] the Thames and its shipping, thus emphasizing a fundamental reciprocity between the powers of nature and culture."

(Matron to Monster 358) In emblems, however, ships not only symbolize human achievement, they are at least as likely to represent the fickleness and limits of that achievement. In Whitney's, Peacham's, and Quarles' books ships are presented rudderless and adrift on the ocean, directionless, storm-tossed, wrecked. To Joan Larsen Klein, in *A Choice of Emblems* the sea itself "iconographically represents a frightening, destructive, and evil world" (161). On the Thames and on the streets of London, on the other hand, in the course of a Lord Mayor's Show, merchant vessels are never adrift but steered firmly, and for the benefit of the commonwealth, toward their destination, either by the will and skill of their human crews or by the benevolent forces of fate. In either case, they make their way in a world that is well-disposed toward the industrious and worthy.

With the remodeling of the Elizabethan sea force under naval commanders Francis Drake and John Hawkins and the construction of new, leaner galleons for the royal fleet, seafaring had recently become a pursuit of wider national interest and prestige (Bindoff 268).[29] Accordingly, these newly constructed vessels were owned by and named after prominent personages of the day (ibid.). By the end of the 16th century the new English navy was in a position to compete successfully with the Spanish and Portuguese marine forces (Zeeden 94). Drake's successful circumnavigation in his *Pelican*, later rechristened *Golden Hind* (ibid. 259), also fueled pride and interest in maritime endeavors. Under Elizabeth I the military and commercial functions of seafaring began to overlap to a significant degree, as Drake organized his voyages – i.e. to Spain and the West Indies in 1585-86 as well as his attack on Cadiz in 1587 – "as semi-official joint-stock enterprises" (Bindoff 269). Even after peace with Spain had been negotiated under James I, rivalry on the seas continued and a general antagonism remained. The Lord Mayor's Show, on the other hand, tended to focus on peaceful economic cooperation on an 'international' plain, among European powers as well as between continents.

In the 1560s and 1570s, partly as a result of Spanish interference in the Netherlands, English merchants headed for new markets in Europe, Asia, and Africa (ibid. 284).[30] In the 1590s direct contact with the Far East was reestablished and the foundation of the East India Company by royal charter followed in late 1599 (ibid. 287-88). Staples among English exports of the period were cloth, hides, lead, tin, and metal wares (ibid. 285). Luxury foodstuffs, fine cloth, alum, timber, and marine supplies were imported (ibid.). Meanwhile, the overall organization of international trade was undergoing considerable

---

[29] Along with changes in the navy's material makeup, the strategies of naval warfare underwent changes, with engagements increasingly taking place far from British shores (Bindoff 267). The first conflict in which England depended crucially on its navy was the war against Spain in the final decades of the 16th century (ibid. 265). Merchant ships were actively involved in the encounter with the Spanish Armada and other sea skirmishes of the period (Finlayson, Jacobean Foreign Policy 605). John Watts (lord mayor in 1606) was the owner of a vessel called the "Margaret and John" which was sent by the City of London to engage the Spanish Armada in 1588 and Watts himself served as a volunteer aboard his ship (Appleby n. pag.).

[30] In the late 1560s English operators succeeded in gaining a profitable foothold in the triangular slave trade against Spanish opposition (Bindoff 254). Looking east, by 1620, the East India Company had established trading posts in Sumatra, Java, Borneo, Malacca, Celebes, Siam, Malabar, India, and Japan (Loomba 1717).

changes, partly due to the privateering enterprises undertook by Drake and those following his lead. These semi-legal operations could result in profits of up to 500 percent or fail spectacularly (Heinemann 7). Since the risk of falling victim to privateers prevented small enterprises from participating in overseas trade, monopoly companies thrived: between 1577 and 1588, to countenance the risks involved, numerous trading companies were founded, such as the Spanish, Barbary, Levant, French, and Eastland Companies (Bindoff 286). At the same time, the much older company of Merchant Adventurers, whose main business had been the export of undyed cloth, lost their supremacy to smaller 'interlopers' in the anarchy and disorder of war (ibid. 287). All of these developments were of primary concern for London merchants, many of whom held shares in these new trading companies.

While the Lord Mayor's Show attempted to cultivate a semi-mythic lineage of ocean-going adventurers – from heroes such as Jason and Ulysses via privateers such as Drake to contemporary London merchants – emblems tended to question this grand teleology more than affirm it.[31] Peacham's emblem 168, titled "Vane merces", mentioned above, satirizes the self-perception and self-representation of English merchants as contemporary Jasons, daring venturers and 'knights of the golden fleece', in mocking allusion to both the fabled Argonauts and the eponymous Catholic chivalric order (Aa2). The emblem picture suggests that a monkey dealing in toys and trinkets rather more aptly embodies the current merchant habitus than do those heros of old "[t]hat in the ARGO cut the Grecian maine", and whom Lord Mayor's Show authors liked to appropriate and cast in the roles of mythic forebears. Less satirical though as dark in outlook is Whitney's emblem eleven, headed "Res humanae in summo declinat/At their summit, human affairs decline", which presents a shipwreck as the symbol of the brevity and fickleness of good fortune in this life. The verse accompanying the image explains:

> The gallante Shipp, that cutts the azure Surge, / And hathe bothe tide, and wisshed windes, at will: / Her tackle sure, with shotte her foes to urge, / With Captaines boulde, and mariners of skill, / With streamers, flagges, topgallantes, pendantes brave, / When seas do rage, is swallowed in the wave. (Whitney 100)

Random forces can, thus, bring to destruction even the best of vessels and most expert crew. The loss of a merchant ship, the loss of lives and profits – in spite of the merit and work ethic of even the most zealous of self-made merchants – is certainly not a scenario ever explored in the Lord Mayor's Show. Here, plans come to fruition and ships reach their harbor. It is apt, therefore, that personified Success, in *The Triumphs of Honour and Industry*, should be identified by the painting of a ship moored securely inside a harbor.

In the manner of Whitney, the second emblem in Van der Noot's collection also presents a ship in peril, as does Peacham's emblem 158 (Z1) which compares the sea to the world and a burning sailing ship to fickle opinion. Meanwhile, Peacham's 80th emblem establishes seafaring as a metaphor for life since life, like a ship, "passeth on, though we

---

[31] Hill argues that the fact "[t]hat Drake was repeatedly juxtaposed to Jason and his argonauts as part of the treatment of the golden fleece trope points up the hybrid nature of the Shows' sources" (Pageantry 319-20).

do what we please" (M4), making men and women slaves to time and fortune. Emblems of this type use the shipwreck motif as a representation of the individual – often the individual soul – isolated from the fellowship of other humans or, more pressingly, from the presence of God and exposed to perilous forces. In this traditional vein Thomas Wyatt creates a troubled persona, alienated and defenseless, who finds himself in distress at sea, "despairing of the port" in his introspective sonnet "My Galley Charged". In the Lord Mayor's Show, contrarily, the vessel at sea does not invoke the individual's plight in a hostile world but a communal success story.

A negative association of seafaring and material wealth, which could not have pleased merchants, is established by Whitney's emblem 188, previously mentioned, bearing the motto "Auri sacra fames quid non?/What does accursed greed for gold not drive men to do?" (278) The emblem picture shows a man in the water weighted down by a sack on his back, identified by the verse as containing possessions saved from a shipwreck. Because the owner is too consumed by greed to consider surrendering his precious load, it threatens to pull him under and puts his life in peril. The conception of wealth in the Lord Mayor's Show is antithetically opposed to that offered in emblem 188. Fame and profit, as argued above, are here conceived of as the just rewards of mercantile endeavor, including trade by sea. In Middleton's *The Sun in Aries*, Jason presents himself as a proto-merchant in as far as he represents those who gain wealth and status by adventurous seafaring, i.e. commercial risk-takers. The hero introduces himself with the words: "I am he, / To all adventurous voyages a free / And bountiful well-wisher, by my name / Hight Jason, first adventurer for fame, / Which now rewards my danger" (1589). Pride in a spirit of commercial endeavor – a spirit that is willing to countenance risks in the expectation of substantial profits – is here formulated and, at the same time, embodied in the Argonaut. If one, for a moment, envisions Jason, not riding proudly above the waves, but drowning in the Grecian main, greedily clinging to a soaked golden fleece which is dragging him down into the depths, the differences in outlook between emblem and Lord Mayor's Show become plain. The former denounces material greed and implicitly posits that fate is capricious and often malignant and that, in any case, the material world is not to be trusted, while the latter celebrates accumulation and assumes that risk-taking will be compensated.

The opening of the Lord Mayor's Show lent itself exceptionally well to the display of ships, 'sea chariots', or pageant islands, since early in the morning the mayor was conveyed to Westminster by barge, accompanied by a flotilla of decorated vessels carrying selected representatives of the twelve great livery companies as well as the many minor guilds.[32] When Dutchman Abram Booth was present for the inaugural celebrations of

---

[32] Sir John Norman, according to civic legend, was the first mayor to travel to Westminster by barge in 1543 – "at his own cost and charge, and for the reliefe of poore Watermen, who were much distressed in those daies." In the pamphlet accompanying his *Himatia-Poleos*, Munday relates that Norman's was "a costly Barge, and the Oares are said to bee covered with silver" (B3). The same pamphlet records that the St Paul's choir boys honored the new mayor with a rendition of "a pleasant song called, Rowe thy Boate Norman", while carrying silver oars and dressed in "faire wrought wastcoates, and caps" (B3-4). Hill points out that Norman may not, in fact, have been the first mayor to travel by river to Westminster (Pageantry 32), but "[i]t does

1629, he witnessed "seventy barges of the 8 Companies and sixty Guilds, every one with its banners, decorated in an artful manner, and finally the barge of the Mayor himself with the Sheriffs and Aldermen of the city, decorated with the banners of the King and the City" (22). In Dekker's *Troia-Nova Triumphans* boats on the Thames surround the sea chariot of Neptune, drawn by pageant hippocamps, while personified Love ("the day's love, the city's general love") opens Middleton's *Triumphs of Love and Antiquity* from a ship on the Thames. In Munday's 1623 *Triumphs of the Golden Fleece* the mayor's barge is not only accompanied on its way to Westminster by music from "Drummes, Fifes, Trumpets, and other Iouiall Instruments", present, too, is an 'Argo' carrying Jason and Medea, built "after the old Grecian Antique manner, [...] for more quicke and agile passage on the Seas". Munday, who "was especially prone to use ships, in various guises, within the pageantry he devised" as Hill observes (Pageantry 159), had already presented Jason's Argo on the Thames in his 1615 *Metropolis Coronata*. In Heywood's *Londini Artium*, Arion comments with delight on the "Barges, strong, / And richly deckt" (B2) accompanying the mayor upriver. Pageant ships serve as triumphal vehicles for the multitude of characters who have supposedly come to London to pay tribute to the new mayor. Not infrequently, however, they carry meaning that goes beyond their function as a means of transportation.

A pageant vessel bearing the name *Royal Exchange* opens Munday's *Triumphs of Re-united Britannia*: on board are a master, a mate, and a boy. The ship, as the trio's workplace, becomes a site of communal solidarity which is further extended to the spectators. In Munday's *Himataia-poleos* "a Shippe, very artificially and workemanly framed, called the *Barke-Hayes*" after the new mayor opens the show. It is also occupied by a master, his mate, and a boy, and is "supposedly laden with woollen sloathes, to make exchaunge for other Countries best commodities" (B2). Trade and the community that exists around it, and lives by it, are also celebrated in Munday's *Metropolis Coronata* by means of a pageant ship: The "Ioell", like the "Barke-Hayes", also bears the name of the newly invested mayor and carries a master and his mate. Correspondingly, the first pageant device of Munday's *Chrysanaleia* is "a very goodly and beautifull fishing Busse, called the *Fishmongers Esperanza*, or Hope of *London*" and carries fishermen at work (B). As they talk among themselves, aboard their Spanish-named vessel, they distribute their 'catch' to the spectators surrounding the pageant set, establishing a tangible connection that stretches beyond the small group of actors and incorporates the audience into a circle of economically interdependent Londoners.

A glorification of the military and mercantile uses of sea power opens Munday's show *Chruso-thriambos*. A variety of decorated barges are assembled on the Thames, some enacting skirmishes to demonstrate naval skill, while in their midst a particular vessel carries the richly styled "Golden" royal couple, referred to as Chiorison and Tumanama. Their ship serves as triumphal vehicle at the same time as it emphasizes overseas trade as a source of great wealth for merchants and the metropolis. In his pamphlet, Munday invites readers to "[i]magine then, that from the rich and Golden *Indian* Mines, sundry Ships, Frigots, and Gallies, are returned home" (A4), bringing with them the acquired

seem to be the case that Norman's inauguration was the first time when a livery company (in the case, the Drapers) had its own barge built, rather than hiring one" (ibid. 33).

treasure of metals, minerals, and other commodities. The 'royal couple' also accompanies the mayor's procession on land, then seated astride golden leopards. The acquisition of precious metals, minerals, and 'exotic' goods made possible by seafaring is also celebrated in Squire's *Triumphs of Peace* (1620). A sailboat on the Thames carries feminized personifications of Asia, Africa, America, and Europe,[33] while Aeolus symbolically provides for the wind in the ship's sails. Marine deity Oceanus, moreover, promises: "My care shall be for euer to attend; / Your wealthy bottoms to your coasts apace; / And this my promise will I neuer end" (A2). Aeolus extends the promise, adding that, "with prosperous gales, / I will send home your ships, and take delight / To play with gentle murmures on your sailes" (B). As the keeper of the winds personally assures the new mayor that "both seas, and winds, themselues unite, / Vnto your good" (B), benevolent fate smiles on mercantile achievement.

A pageant device in Webster's *Monuments of Honour* (1624), referred to above, consists of a globe which showcases "seauen of our most famous Nauigators", namely Francis Drake, John Hawkins, Martin Frobisher, Humphrey Gilbert, Thomas Cavendish, Christopher Carlisle, and John Davis (A4).[34] In his speech, Oceanus identifies the navigators by name and adds that they, as worthy men, "neare dye" and that England is envied the world over for seamen such as these (B). The pageant episode is a clear expression of that lately found pride in England's newly competitive position on the seas and the resulting military and economic benefits. Later in the same show another pageant ship features. This, notes Webster, is "called the *Holy-Lambe*, which brings hanging in her Shrowdes the Golden-Fleece, the conceite of this being that God is the Guide and Protector of all Prosperous Ventures" (B4). Five years later, Dutchman Abram Booth set down his suspicion that that year's water entertainment on the Thames, consisting of Oceanus in his sea-shell chariot, indicated "that the English wanted to be Lords of the Ocean" (22). In Webster's and Dekker's pageants overseas trade is once more presented as an activity sanctioned from on high, while the myth of Jason as proto-merchant blurs into explicitly Christian territory in Webster's "*Holy-Lambe*". On the pages of many a contemporary emblem book, from Whitney to Quarles, man has to suffer shipwreck before God takes any interest in his distressed soul, while Webster, in a manner typical of the Lord Mayor's Show, expresses his firm belief in God as a "Protector of all Prosperous Ventures". The means by which seafarers may navigate waterways safely are the focus of the water entertainment in Heywood's *London's Ius Honorarium* (1631). Ulysses' passage between the threats of Scylla and Charibdis is enacted on the Thames where these monstrous sites are reproduced as pageant floats. While some wrecked vessels are suggested by the floating scenery, Ulysses offers valuable advice on how to

---

[33] Of all continental personifications, only Africa "was copied from Roman sources: her appearance on Hadrianic coins (dating about A.D. 138) was well known in the Renaissance and surely accounts to some degree for the popularity of the Continents as an iconological subject" (Le Corbeiller 217).

[34] Hill comments that resurfacing anxieties over relations with Spain in the 1620s, spurred on by news of the ill-fated Spanish match (between the future Charles I and the Infanta Maria Anna), led to a renewed cultural potency of the figure of Drake (Pageantry 300).

pass hazards like Scylla and Charibdis securely and avoid maritime misfortune.[35] The focus is therefore firmly on the means to prevent calamity rather than on its unavoidable occurrence and the attitude communicated is again one of confidence in benevolent fate that smiles on merchant vessels. The same outlook is confirmed in Dekker's *Brittannia's Honor* which presents a shipwright in the company of angels, personified Virtues, and former monarchs at 'Britannia's Watch-Tower'.

On land, too, pageant ships appear in celebration of seafaring, a circumstance that is not too surprising in the context of the Lord Mayor's Show since, as mentioned above, pageant devices could transit from water to land without need for a narrative explanation. A celebration of commerce and exotic splendor, as experienced by the senses, is staged for the Grocers by Middleton in his 1613 *Triumphs of Truth*, in which a royal couple of 'moorish' origin arrive by boat in St Paul's Churchyard. They are accompanied by attendants while around them five separate pageant islands display personifications of the senses of sight ("Visus"), hearing ("Auditus"), touch ("Tactus"), taste ("Gustus"), and smell ("Olfactus"). The senses are accompanied by their "proper" symbols: the eagle ("aquila"), deer ("cervus"), spider ("araneus"), ape ("simia"), and dog ("canis") (ll. 390-97).[36] The celebration of the senses reinforces the show's worldly orientation and commends transoceanic trade as an operation that is not only economically gainful but exerts an all-around beneficial influence.

Reminiscent of Webster's globe set in his *Monuments of Honour,* an intricate mechanical device referred to as the Globe of Honor features in Middleton's *The Triumphs of Honor and Vertue*. The outside of the apparatus is decorated with "ships that have been fortunate to this kingdom by their happy and successful voyages" (1721). In Munday's *Sidero-thriambos*, close to the Mount of Fame set "is figured a goodly Shippe, whereby she [Fame] conueighes all beatitudes of Kingdomes, Cities and Nations, to the furthest remote Countries" (B4-C). Both pageant episodes laud maritime enterprise as a source of pride and fame. The same qualities are also invoked in Heywood's *Londini Status Pacatus* which showcases as its fifth and penultimate pageant set a ship bearing the arms of the trading companies of which the new mayor was a member. Both mayor and companies, the image declares, derive their wealth and prestige from overseas trade. A celebration of seafaring in the service of trade is also incorporated into Heywood's *Porta Pietatis*, the fourth pageant episode of which consists of a pageant ship on dry land. From this vessel a young sailor informs the new mayor, Maurice Abbot, "Grave sir, the merchant's trade / Is that for which all shipping first was made" (271). Abbot himself was not only a prominent member of the East India Company, he had himself visited South Asia in the early 17th century. In his farewell speech directed at Abbot that night, an actor embodying changeable sea god Proteus once more refers to the pageant ship that, in his

---

[35] Similarly, personified London warns new mayor Thomas Myddleton in *The Triumphs of Truth* that "power's a dangerous sea, which must be sounded / with truth and justice, or man soon runs on / 'Gainst rocks and shelves to dissolution" (ll. 591-93). Her warning is softened, however, by the fact that she has already shown herself convinced of Myddleton's moral worth and his consequent ability to avoid all "rocks and shelves" in the navigation of his political life.

[36] The same animals embody the senses in Cesare Ripa's *Iconologia* (Robertson and Gordon xxxix).

estimation, "the merchant's honour loudly tells" (274). Not only do mercantile operations depend on the use of ships, ships were initially invented for the purpose of trade. A circular interdependence, therefore, associates trade and ocean travel and the glory that belongs to one also belongs to the other. In Heywood's *Londini Emporia* oceangoing enterprise is again associated with divine blessing. In Cheapside the mayor and his entourage encounter "a Ship most proper to the Trade of Merchant-adventurers" (B3), at the helm of which is Mercury, not imperiling trade by his 'mercurial' nature but, instead, lending celestial support.

Semi-divine support of the enterprise of merchants is also granted by the character of Medea. In Heywood's *Londini Status Pacatus* she rides in a chariot, signifying "*consilium*, or Counsell" (368), while she accompanies Jason and his Argonauts in the water pageant opening Munday's *Metropolis Coronata*. In *Triumphs of the Golden Fleece*, the water entertainment adjoined to Middleton's land entertainment for the 1623 Lord Mayor's Show, Medea, sitting in a vessel rowed by her "Tributary Indian Kings", is the center and focal point. Munday explains her presence in the following terms:

> We suppose this Argoe to be returned from *Colchos*, purposely to honor this Triumphall day, by the rare Arte of *Medea* the Enchantresse, that kept the Fleece there so long a time, and wherewith she was now the more willing to part; in regard of her affection to the DRAPERS Companie, to whom she gave it freely, for an honor and Ornament to their Armes. (n. pag.)

Medea, "Enchantresse" and Jason's helpmeet, is glorified as a benefactor of the company, even a kind of patroness, by her gift of the fleece. Through her commandeering of the vessel and the emphasis on the overseas origin of the fleece, she is also associated with mercantile seafaring ventures. The pageant set, including Medea, is transferred to land later in the day, joining the mayor's procession through the city "for adding the more splendor to the Triumphs Solemnitie". This is a presentation of the character that is altogether far from the theme of infanticide which is foregrounded in Whitney's presentation of the character.

Another character with maritime associations who appears in emblems as well as Lord Mayor's Shows is legendary Greek poet and musician Arion who, according to myth, was saved from drowning by a dolphin after having been robbed and thrown into the sea by pirates. In Whitney's previously mentioned emblem 149, titled "Homo homini lupus/Man is a wolf to man", Arion is depicted as a victim of the cruelty of humans toward their own kind. The verse moralizes that there is "[n]o mortall foe so full of poysoned spite, / As man, to man, when mischiefe he pretendes" (239).[37] In the context of the Lord Mayor's Show, Arion occasionally features as an ornament to the river entertainments and here the focus lies firmly on the poet's miraculous rescue rather than on his previous misfortune. In Munday's *Chrysanaleia* Arion is not presented as a victim but instead

---

[37] The animal that saved Arion's life itself becomes the victim of cruelty in Whitney's emblem 98, bearing the motto "On him who will perish from the harshness of his own" (187): A dolphin – with the long and curvy tail of a fish, a squashed face and wings or baleen plates at its sides – is cast from the sea by Neptune and must perish out of its own element.

strikes a dignified pose astride his dolphin. Both poet and dolphin also play a part in Munday's *Chrysanaleia*, where they follow the opening pageant of a fishing boat and crew. On their inclusion in the celebrations the character of Walworth has the following to say:

> The Embleme of the Dolphine is the Armorie / Belonging to our brethren, and beside / Speakes somewhat of that creatures qualitie, / By nature Musicall, as hath been tryde: / Poesie and Musique therefore thus do ride / Vpon his back, in sweete *Arions* shape, / Who, by a Dolphine, thus did death escape. (C3)

Not only does the dolphin reference London's Worshipful Company of Fishmongers, since cetaceans feature in the company arms, but the legend of Arion is linked to the sponsoring company in such a way that the musician's triumph reflects positively on them. In Heywood's *Londini Artium* Arion not only appears on the Thames in the morning, he also bids the mayor good night at the close of the day's ceremonies. In the commemorative pamphlet, Heywood ruminates extensively on the myth of Arion, emphasizing the poet musician's resourcefulness and his triumph over adverse circumstances. In Heywood's take on the myth, the musician is not thrown overboard by his would-be murderers but takes the initiative himself and jumps into the sea to escape danger, secure in the knowledge that he will be saved. Following his arrival on Italian shores, Arion is "graciously entertayned" by the local monarch, who proceeds to capture and punish the rogue sailors who were willing to take his life (B). This reinterpretation of Arion's fate as triumph rather than misfortune is echoed in the positive representation of the senses in the Lord Mayor's Show, which contrasts notably with their darker significance in contemporary emblem books. *Memento mori* motifs were among the regular stock-in-trade of emblematists and this tradition, so John Manning, can be traced back to Alciato himself, who "includ[ed] six emblems on the subject that were duly collected under the heading 'Mors', and these do not include the numerous depictions of murders, suicides, tombs and mourning in the rest of the volume" (286). He goes on to comment that there are dangers inherent in "creating such an overwhelming impression of mortal futility", namely, the promotion of "a despair that leads to the ultimate sin, the despair of salvation, for which there is no remedy" (ibid. 294).

It is within this framework of mortal futility that Whitney's emblem 248, "Ex maximo minimum/The least from the greatest", reflects on the inevitable decay of the senses as a result of the body's mortality (see fig. 7). The emblem combines the image of a human skull with the dire outlook that "[t]he head, I meane, that is so ritchly bleste, / With sighte, with smell, with hearinge, and with taste" must come to this: "a skull, both rotten, bare, and drye" (336). This demonstration of the inevitable decay of the rich blessings of sight, smell, hearing, and taste – the omission of touch probably due to its not being primarily situated in the head – offers a notable contrast to the celebration of the senses in Munday's *Chrysanaleia* or Heywood's *Londini Speculum*, where the conception of these rich blessings is not qualified by reminders of death and deterioration.[38] Likewise, the high

---

[38] In Spenser's *The Fairie Queene*, at the allegorically potent castle of virtuous Alma, the bulwarks of Sight, Hearing, Smell, and Taste come under attack by the enemies of temperance,

proportion of *memento mori* emblems contrasts with Bergeron's perception of a theme of immortality running through Lord Mayor's Show pageantry.

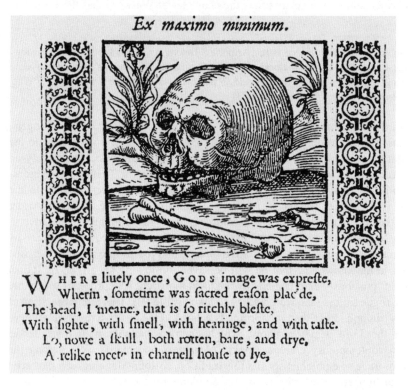

Ex maximo minimum.

W H E R E liuely once, G o D s image was expreſte,
Wherin, ſometime was ſacred reaſon plac'de,
The head, I meane, that is ſo ritchly bleſte,
With ſighte, with ſmell, with hearinge, and with taſte.
Lo, nowe a ſkull, both rotten, bare, and drye,
A relike meete in charnell houſe to lye,

Fig. 7: Whitney's emblem 248 depicts a "relike meete in charnell house to lye" (336). By this, the emblematist formulates a conventional message of worldly impermanence. Image courtesy of Penn State University Libraries.

Mortality, on the other hand, is the point in Peacham's emblem eight which presents a disembodied hand holding a human skull – an arrangement that calls to mind Hamlet's iconic mortuary musings. The verse explains that it was the (slightly inhospitable) custom of an Ethiopian princess to place skulls before her guests in order to drive home the lesson that even princes are "but clay" (C4). Skulls as reminders of mortality also feature in Whitney's emblem 46, "Varii hominum sensus/Various are the opinions of men" (135), while a shroud draped on a lance and crossbar signifies inevitable death in his emblem 94, "Mortui divitiae/A dead man's riches". The moral here, too, is that even he who "set in mightie CÆSARS chaire," is as mortal as the poor and obscure are and will certainly share their fate: "The Prince, the Poore, the Prisoner, and the slave, / They all at lengthe, are summonde to their grave." (Whitney 182) Target of both emblems is a perceived

while a fifth bulwark faces an onslaught of "sensual delight" (book 2, canto 11, stanza 9-13). The senses are here, too, pictured as corruptible and a threat to a virtuous existence.

overestimation of worldly things, of both material wealth and immaterial fame or glory, at the cost of proper religious devotion and preparation for the resurrection of the soul. This all-consuming embrace of the spiritual, set against the renunciation of the material world, is echoed in the popular emblems of Francis Quarles and his school of emblematists. Theirs was what John Manning calls a *"post mortem* consciousness", which comprehended the world as "transitory; its joys an evanescent, deluding dream, mere trivia when weighed against the considerations of eternity and the fate of one's eternal soul" (274). The distrust and disdain leveled at the senses is symptomatic of this general outlook of worldly scepticism.[39]

The point that the senses are not only perishable but that they can deceive, too, is emphasized in Peacham's emblem 67, in which the emblematist cautions that "soone the Sence deceiv'd, doth iudge amisse, / And fooles will blame, whereas none error is" (L2). In the advice of personified Thames in Heywood's *Londini Emporia*, on the other hand, which is concerned with the sense of sight, there is no implication that the sense is deceitful. It is rather the means by which deception can be prevented. Thames tells the newly elected mayor that "you must alwayes have an Eagles eye / To out gaze the Sun, and keepe that Aquilant sight / To see what's wrong, and to distinguish right" (B). In *Londini Speculum* personified Sight serves as the speaker at the show's main pageant set and Heywood explains that "the eyes are placed in the head as in a Citadel, to be watchtowers and Centinels for the safety, and guiders and conducters for the sollace of the body" (315).[40]

In Middleton's *Triumphs of Truth* the personified senses are stationed each on their own pageant island in St Paul's Churchyard, accompanying a fictitious royal couple from far away, exotic lands, while all five senses surround a lemon tree, punning on mayor John Leman's name, in Munday's *Chrysanaleia*. Lemon trees, explains Munday in the pamphlet, "both in fruit, flowers, rinde, pith, and iuyce, are admirable preseruers of the sences in man, restoring, comforting and relieuing any the least decay in them" (B3). What the pageant offers is in effect an antidote to the decay prophesied in Whitney's emblem, that sight, smell, hearing and taste must soon degenerate into "a skull, both rotten, bare, and drye". The personifications themselves are presented "in their best and liueliest representations, as fitly iumping with our Morall methode" (B3). The senses are gateways to the material world and, by celebrating them, the pageant implies that the material world should not, in fact, be denied but perceived and even enjoyed. Howard

---

[39] Rejection of the body and the material world was also extant in other contemporary publications, as for example in Francis Rous' *The Mysticall Marriage* (1631), in which the author dismisses "the bodily eyes" in favor of "two better eyes, the one of humane reason, and the other farre excelling that, [of] divine and heavenly light" (239).

[40] In the pamphlet commemorating *Londini Speculum* Heywood elucidates the show's title as referring to the ability of personified London, in her own self, to clearly "behold her owne vertues" and the desideratum that, by the example of London, other cities may see "how to correct their vices" (305). Personified Sight restates the sentiment, arguing that London "[s]hewes not alone what she is" but offers the rest of the world the opportunity to see "[i]n her, what their great Cities ought to be" (316). The sense of sight here, too, bears positive connotations, as offering true access to the world and as an incentive to growth and development.

Bloch has pointed out that in *On the Creation* [*De Opificio Mundi*], Philo of Alexandria formulates an "explicit analogy between woman and the sensible" (14). As "[t]he onto-logical status of woman is [...] analogous to that of the senses within the cognitive realm", so man is considered analogous to the rational mind (ibid.). Furthermore: "Man as mind and woman as sensory perception are, as Philo explains, mutually exclusive" (ibid.). The Lord Mayor's Show, then, – in its celebration of perception and heavy reliance on feminized personifications – overcomes the traditional co-denigration of the senses, the female and the feminine (between which contemporary discourse does not distinguish). At the same time, the ways in which personifications (including the personified city) serve the shows, and the ideological assumptions based on which they are created cannot be considered favorable to women in any straightforward sense. The shows certainly do not suggest equality between the sexes. Sensory perception and the material world, however, rate highly in the civic imagination.

In Chrysanaleia the character of William Walworth explains, with reference to the lemon tree pageant, that,

> as the Sences sit about the Tree, / And shewe you how their vertues are supplyed / Still with fresh vigor: So (no doubt) will be / Your busiest troubles sweetly qualified, / By those fiue helpes that hold vp dignitie, / Discretion, Policie, and Prouidence, / Courage, Correction, these barre all offence. (C3)

In a somewhat crooked analogy, the mayor is encouraged to gain moral sustenance from the virtues of discretion, policy, providence, courage, and correction, just as the lemon tree rejuvenates the senses. The medium of pageantry itself favored an affirmative attitude toward sensory perception: Multiple channels of cognition were simultaneously engaged by the proceedings. Not only sight but hearing, and touch (e.g. of other spectators or of costumed whifflers clearing the way ahead of the procession), as well as smell (e.g. of the crowds, of fireworks and cannon shots, of spices) influenced an observer's experience of the festivities. Moreover, the senses aided the operation of allegory since the bearers of allegorical meaning were "objects designed for particular settings and [...] images that represent abstract ideas in embodied form, [...which] operate in the physical world of the senses" (Baskins 1). Certainly, the presentation of an array of embodied – and gendered – Virtues and of personified London herself utilized allegorical strategies of this type as a way of rendering the idea of the city concrete, thus allowing city dwellers to more easily formulate their collective identity as Londoners, as craftsmen or traders united by their common connection to the metropolis.[41]

---

[41] Baskins affirms that allegory in the realm of politics tends to provide a graspable means for people to self-identify "as citizens and subjects" (1).

2.6 Can the Ethiopian change his skin, or the leopard his spots?
Representations of Ethnic Others in Lord Mayor's Show and Emblem Book

Ethnic 'others' referred to as blacks, Indians, Turks or "moors" appear with great regularity as characters in Jacobean and Caroline Lord Mayor's Shows and although their conversion to Christianity via English merchants is often lauded, they are nevertheless celebrated in their 'otherness'. Hill concurs that "the Shows undeniably do negotiate the 'otherness' of non-Europeans encountered on trading voyages" (Pageantry 292) and even discusses the "intriguing possibility" that black people, instead of white actors in blackface, may have sometimes played parts in the shows (ibid. 145). The Grocers, in particular, frequently staged pageants commemorating their involvement in the spice trade which included 'moors', but the representation of non-Europeans was by no means restricted to one company. Despite the occasional whiff of religious bigotry,[42] these visually marked others are never presented as inherently inferior types of human being. They are, in fact, acknowledged as a part of the seafaring merchant culture of London, with the city conceptualized as the richly diverse nexus of exploration and long-distance trade which brings into contact people and commodities from the farthest corners of the known world to their mutual benefit. That good international relations are a precondition for mutually beneficial trade is spelled out by Middleton in the pamphlet recording his *Triumphs of Honour and Industry*: Personified Merchandise is presented with a globe intended to convey a desire for "love and peace amongst all nations" (l. 88). In contemporary emblem books, however, the 'racially' defined inferiority of non-Europeans in general and Africans in particular is a prevalent theme.

The term "moor" was used indiscriminately in the 16th and into the 17th century to refer to persons of darker than European complexion, belonging to an unspecific 'exotic', non-European ethnicity or faith (Bartels 308). In travel narratives of the period the designation "negroe" was typically applied to West Africans while "moor" signified North African origin (ibid.). This is not a terminological differentiation employed with any consistency in the Lord Mayor's Shows of the period prior to the Civil Wars, however. Luciano García García convincingly propounds that the term's definition in contemporary discourse rested on tendential oppositions in "three main semic areas: /Europeannes [sic]/ vs. /Africanness/, /whiteness/ vs. /blackness/, and /Christianity/ vs. /Islam/" (149).[43] However, the term was by no means restricted to indicating black African Muslims. García's categories refer to dissimilarity from Northwestern European norms in (1) geographic origin, (2) religious belief,[44] and (3) skin color, and deviation

---

[42] In *Chrysanaleia* Munday praises the Fishmongers' involvement in the crusades against "*Saladine* and al his other heathen miscreants" (A). This is an exception, however, and is stated in the commemorative pamphlet only and not voiced by a character during the event. Furthermore, Munday's comment touches not on a recent or ongoing struggle (at least not directly) but on the distant past.

[43] Bergeron asserts: "Although Moors are not necessarily Turks, people often conflated them with Ottomans because of a shared Islamic religion." (Turks 260)

[44] García observes that "moors" in contemporary plays are sometimes rather associated with pagan or classical deities than monotheistic Islam (136).

from what was considered the norm in any combination of these categories was enough to warrant the designation "moor" or "blackamoor". Loomba confirms that natives of such outposts of the East India Company as Sumatra, Java, Borneo, Malacca, Celebes, Siam, Malabar, India, and Japan could also unproblematically be labeled 'moors' in contemporary conversations and publications (1717). The example of a young boy in *Londons Tempe*, described as a "a little Indian blackamoor" by Abram Booth (who also sketched the boy and pageant stage) further illustrates how the blurry category "moor" incorporated a heterogeneous collection of identities based on geographic origin, ethnicity, physical features, or religious affiliation. The boy is the central character of a pageant tableau that also contains actors representing a Turk and a Persian. He is seated atop an ostrich (an African bird, but here primarily referencing the sponsoring Ironmongers)[45] and holds "in one hand an arrow and in the other a long tobacco-pipe" (22). The choice of props for the boy, an arrow and a tobacco pipe, mark him as a young native American rather than a 'spice islander' or inhabitant of the Indian subcontinent, yet he is still identified as a "blackamoor".[46]

As regards the status of the Turkish in the cultural imagination, "an odd and unequal mixture of fear and admiration" prevailed (Bergeron, Turks 272). While the Levant Company, founded in 1581,[47] facilitated new, direct trade with the Ottoman Empire, Turkish pirates in the Mediterranean posed a danger to trade and Ottoman expansion remained a point of concern even after the defeat of the Turkish forces at the 1571 Battle of Lepanto (ibid. 263). Reflecting these matters, numerous dramatic works of the late 16th and early 17th century dealt with Islamic themes (ibid. 264).[48] At the same time a conflation of

---

[45] In his *Sidero-thriambos* pamphlet, Munday explains why ostriches are suitable birds to appear in pageants for the Ironmongers: "for naturally they digest both Steele and Iron as is avouched by many credible Authors" (B3). In Thomas Nashe's *The Unfortunate Traveller* the narrator reports that "the ostrich will eat iron, swallow any hard metal whatsoever" (263). An ostrich – "cut out of timber to the life" and biting a horseshoe – features in Dekker's *Londons Tempe*. In *The Unfortunate Traveller* another means of representing the sizable bird is suggested: The Earl of Surrey, who appears as a character in the narrative, has dressed up his horse in this manner: Its trappings are "bolstered out with rough-plumed silver plush in full proportion and shape of an ostrich. On the breast of the horse were the foreparts of this greedy bird advanced whence, as his manner is, he reached out his long neck to the reins of the bridle, thinking they had been iron" (262). Ostrich wings are fastened to the horse's sides and the horse's tail supports a bird's tail feathers.

[46] A native American, here designated as "that kind savage the Virginian", in an early forumulation of the 'noble savage' trope, is also invoked in Middleton's *The Triumphs of Love and Antiquity*. Orpheus claims to see the 'Virginian' in the crowds along with "the noble English, the fair-thriving Scot, Plain-hearted Welsh, the Frenchman bold and hot, the civilly instructed Irishman" (ll. 186-94).

[47] Turkey and Venice Company merchants came together in 1592 to form the Levant Company (Brenner 57); the Turkey Company had been founded in 1581 (ibid. 58). Cf. Brenner: "In much the same way as the Turkey Company took over the Levant-oriented commerce of the Russia Company, the East India Company was established in large measure to assume an important commercial role hitherto carried out by the Levant Company." (59)

[48] In his epic retelling of the battle of Lepanto, republished in 1603 along with his *Basilicon Doron*, James I represented "the Turks as worthy opponents" but made "clear that victory

southern European Catholics (generally Spanish) and non-European strangers in English discourse confused classification still further (Cuder 86). The associative fusion of identities was facilitated by the circumstance that Spanish Christians and Muslims had shared the Iberian peninsula during the Middle Ages and both groups were renowned for their military and commercial prowess (ibid. 88).[49] Yet, despite this "racialization of the Spanish" (García 131), in the 1580s conflicts between the Spanish and the English led to a significant temporary improvement in the relations between England and the Barbary States since they were now united by a common enemy (Alsop 135).[50] However, following the accession to the English throne of James I, peace was reestablished and pageantry reflected the changed political climate: In *The Triumphs of Honour and Industry* a Spaniard and a Frenchman speak in praise of London in their native tongues. They are a part of the "Pageant of Several Nations" which also includes personified Peace, Prosperity, Love, Unity, Plenty, and Fidelity (ll. 101-07). England's relationship with Spain and France, following the 1604 peace treaty between England and Spain, was twofold: Fear of "imminent invasion" and Catholicism co-existed with a boom in trade with both countries (Levin 1252).

The pageant is a testament to the priority of good economic relations over patriotic fervor and religious bigotry in the ideological orientation of the Lord Mayor's Show. Not only the French and Spanish are made to laud London, "a Russian Prince and Princesse; richly habited in Furres, to the custome of the Country" ride in a lynx-drawn chariot in *Brittannia's Honor* (B3). Along with them ride an old nobleman, a woman, a physician, a judge, and a skipper – all of them proudly sporting their fur cloaks, fur-trimmed robes or furred caps (B4). The presence of personified Fame further commends the Skinners' commercial association with Russia, whence furs were imported.

belongs to the Christian forces by divine intervention" (Bergeron, Turks 258). In *Lepanto*, James I had to balance sympathy for the Christian forces with a rejection of Catholicism. Turkish characters had also featured in the festivities in honor of Prince Henry's baptism in 1594 at Stirling: A mock battle was to pitch "three Turkes, three Christian Knights of Malta, three Amazones, and three Moores" against each other, impersonated by the king himself and his guests (ibid. 259). Interestingly, "in a new wrinkle on the myth of warfare between Christians and Turks, a Turk (Lennox) won" (ibid. 260). For Henry's investiture as Prince of Wales a sea battle against Turkish pirates was staged (ibid. 263), and in June 1613 the City of Bristol presented a similar entertainment to Henry's recently bereaved mother, Queen Anne. An influential work concerning the conception of Turks and the Ottoman Empire in Britain was Richard Knolles' 1603 *The Generall Historie of the Turkes*: "This masterful study, the first of its kind in English, had other editions in 1610, 1621, 1631, and 1638, all testifying to its importance and the interest that it created. Knolles solidifies the wary view of the Ottoman Empire, but he also acknowledges their considerable achievements." (ibid. 261) However, a negative attitude was proverbial: "turning Turk" was "a nightmare envisioned by Christians, a mark of contemptible behavior" (ibid. 267).

[49] In *Lust's Dominion* (a play probably written by Thomas Dekker), the character of Eleazar is identified as of North African origin but also associated with Spanish, sub-Saharan African and Indian identities (Cuder 90).

[50] As one result of the improved relations, a playing company from Algiers was given royal permission for a tour of England and received with enthusiasm (Alsop 135).

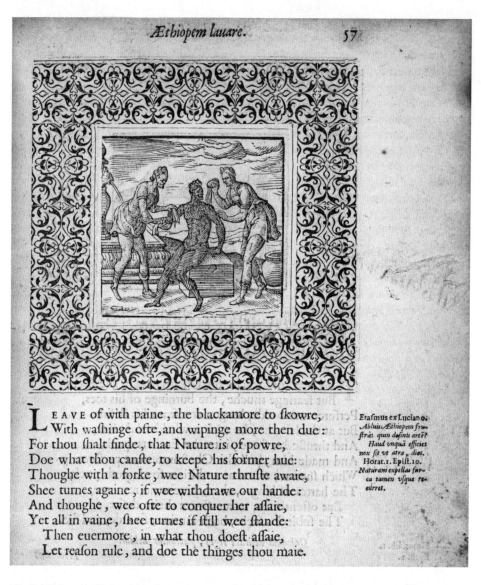

L EAVE of with paine, the blackamore to skowre,
With washinge ofte, and wipinge more then due:
For thou shalt finde, that Nature is of powre,
Doe what thou canste, to keepe his former hue:
Thoughe with a forke, wee Nature thruste awaie,
Shee turnes againe, if wee withdrawe our hande:
And thoughe, wee ofte to conquer her assaie,
Yet all in vaine, shee turnes if still wee stande:
　　Then euermore, in what thou doest assaie,
　　Let reason rule, and doe the thinges thou maie.

Erasmus ex Luciano.
Abluis Æthiopem fru-
strà: quin desinis artè?
Haud vnquà efficies
nox sit vt atra, dies.
Horat.1. Epist.10.
Naturam expellas fur-
ca tamen vsque re-
currei.

Fig. 8: Whitney's 63rd emblem bears the motto "Aethiopem lavare" and advises to "[l]eave of with paine, the blackamore to skowre" (150), i.e. not to attempt the impossible. Image courtesy of Penn State University Libraries.

In general, English attitudes toward Africans, Asians and the more recently encountered native Americans were ambiguous and unstable, irrespective of the terms used to designate them, with a tendency to deteriorate into hostility.[51] Letters written by Elizabeth I between 1596 and 1601, addressed to the lord mayor of London and other officials, refer to "divers blackmoores brought into this realme, of which kinde of people there are already here to manie", these are for the most part "infidels, having no understanding of Christ or his Gospel" (qtd. in Bartels 305). Elizabeth considers their presence in her realm a problem, not only because these foreigners are "infidels" and differ so markedly from Europeans in their cultural ways, but also – and here she voices a familiar argument – for the purported reason that many Englishmen "for want of service and meanes to sett them on worck fall to idlenesse and to great extremytie", a situation that could be remedied, the queen argues, if the "infidels" left their employment as servants and opened up these positions to the idle English (ibid. 308). Her solution is the deportation of "divers blackmoores" from England via the offices of a German merchant, a plan that would have benefited her own financial interests rather more than those of her English subjects living in "great extremytie".

While Elizabeth I advocated the deportation of "infidels" and "blackmoores" from England, Walter Ralegh's reports from South America (1584) lauded the physical beauty of the native tribes and their civility – which he did not find lacking in comparison to European conventions of conduct (qtd. in Montrose 7). Yet, Ralegh's own portrayal of native South Americans is ambiguous, at times sympathetic and equalizing, at times hostile and patronizing (Montrose 25). Relations between English settlers and native Americans in North America at the beginning of the 17th century were equally unstable, wavering in between tentative cooperation and outright warfare (Perreault 86-89).[52] At the same time as these momentous encounters were taking place, London experienced the constant in-flow of immigrants from Ireland, Scotland, Wales, the Low Countries and Germany, and although these constituted the majority of immigrants, some more 'exotic' aliens from as far afield as the Americas and Africa also arrived in the city (Seaver 61). Londoners, confronted with these various newcomers, reacted in multiple and conflicting ways:

> While they welcomed the opportunity to be viewed as a refuge for oppressed Europeans, immigrants were a convenient target upon which to blame the economic and social ills that seemed to plague the country. Anti-immigrant riots broke out in several areas, especially in

---

[51] The beginnings of skin color-based racism in Europe are difficult to determine with any certainty. Bartels notes that scholars of early modern culture tend to pinpoint its emergence at the end of the 16th century, while 18th century scholars rather place it in the final decades of that century (306).

[52] From 1609 to 1614 warfare characterized relations between natives and settlers in Virginia (Perreault 86). While the situation stabilized subsequently, it was permanently altered for the worse following a surprise attack on settlers in 1622 and the settlers' extreme use of violence in retribution. The incident also influenced relations between English immigrants and natives in New England (ibid. 89).

London, by the end of the century. Significantly, animosity toward immigrants seems to have increased with growing familiarity. (Perreault 77)[53]

It seems that this attitude to European 'others' was echoed on a grander scale in relation to non-Europeans and non-Christians. Yet, with its focus on community, the Lord Mayor's Show opted to advocate the incorporation of ethnic others into the life of the city rather than to promote conflict.

In contrast, one of the most widely distributed emblems of all combines the picture of a black man in the process of being washed by one or more white men with the proverbial explanation that it is a vain endeavor 'to wash an Ethiopian'. So predominant became this trope in European culture that it remained available over the centuries via paintings, engravings, satirical cartoons and other media, and even became the framework, in almost entirely unchanged form, for a number of racist soap adverts in the 19th and early 20th centuries. The motif seems to have originated as a *Greek Anthology* epigram by Lucian that was subsequently incorporated into lists of proverbs and added as a fable to the Aesopic corpus (Massing 182-83). Rhetorical questions raised in Jeremiah 13:23 are associated with the adage: "Can the Ethiopian change his skin, or the leopard his spots? Then may ye also do good that are accustomed to do evil?" (cf. Massing 181-82) From these sources the European Renaissance appropriated the trope and continued its perpetuation by means including the popular genre of the emblem book. Andrea Alciato was first to incorporate the proverb in emblematic form into his influential *Emblematum Liber* (fig. 9).[54] Notwithstanding the circumstance that Ethiopia was, in fact, a Christian country, other writers and emblematists followed suit, among them Cesare Ripa and Geffrey Whitney (see fig. 8), whose 63rd emblem advises to "[l]eave of with paine, the blackamore to skowre" (150). While some writers went on to voice the thought that, though the 'moor' could not change his skin, the inner self might after all undergo transformation (a highly problematic notion itself, of course), it was the simple, overtly racist moral of the original proverb that was encountered most frequently. In that tradition Dekker, faced with the impossibility of redeeming the wicked, exclaims in his *A Rod for Run-awayes* (1625): "I wash an Aethiope, who will never be the whiter for all this water I spend upon him" (151).

An entry in Peacham's manuscript emblem book *Basilikon Doron* – based on a treatise by James I and presented to Henry, Prince of Wales, in a bid for patronage – calls to mind Alciato's original emblem. Peacham's emblem depicts a black woman whose alleged baseness is determined by her 'race', her genealogical descent, since "virtue or vice

---

[53] Severe May Day riots against 'aliens' in the city erupted in 1517 (the context for Sir Thomas More's plea for humanity toward refugees – now attributed to Shakepeare – in the eponymous Elizabethan play) and continued to erupt occasionally throughout the Elizabethan, Jacobean, and Caroline periods. K. J. Lindley states: "Popular xenophobia, and especially hatred of Spain, combined in most cases with a virulent anti-catholicism, made foreign ambassadors and their servants liable to abuse and affronts as they passed along London streets and occasionally full-scale riots ensued. Ambassadors could feel particularly vulnerable when the traditional festivals came round" (111).

[54] Massing notes that "Alciati's verses in fact reproduce his Latin version of Lucian's epigram from the Greek Anthology, which was first published in Basle in 1529" (186).

follow breeding" (MS Royal 174). This attitude is echoed in emblem 49 in *Minerva Britanna* which puts forward the argument that there are "infected races" who live on a diet of poisonous creatures (I1). This notion was widespread. It is reflected, among other places, in Thomas Nashe's *The Unfortunate Traveller* which refers to the "Candians" who "live on serpents" (285), and "the Ethiopians inhabiting over against Meroe, [who] feed on nothing but scorpions" (287). To be sure, these turns of phrase are commonplaces, used frequently and without much, if any deliberation. Yet, their significance is not diminished by this widespread, unthinking use. On the contrary, the pervasiveness of the metaphor – however unconscious – reveals its cultural force.

The message of the typical Lord Mayor's Show is very different from the one propagated by emblems in the tradition of Alciato. The exotic others presented on pageant floats on the Thames or along the processional route are certainly styled as visual 'curiosities' to be appreciated by spectators. Yet, they are beautiful and impressive sights, adding to the mayor's glory in having such people come to him in tribute, and they are at home in the company of personified Virtues, former company worthies, patron saints and classical deities. Beauty and resplendent wealth aside, however, when they speak, Lord Mayor's Show 'moors' prove capable of profound intellectual insights and, at variance with the developing concept of the noble savage, they comport themselves as bearers of civilization in their own right, neither as brutish barbarians nor as uncorrupted innocents in a state of nature. As previously mentioned, Munday's *Chruso-thriambos* opens with a pageant vessel on the Thames, supposedly arrived from India, carrying the royal couple Chiorison and Tumanama who have been, explains the author, "(at their own entreaty) brought into England, with no meane quantity of Indian Gold" (A4).

Chruso-thriambos's Indian couple display their wealth and splendor – very much proverbial by this time[55] – in tribute to the new mayor and they simultaneously forge a connection with him as a member of the company of Goldsmiths by means of their imported "Indian Gold". A similar scenario had unfolded during the Lord Mayor's Show of 1591, in which a pageant vessel on the Thames had supposedly arrived from strange and prosperous, far-away lands, bringing with it "strangers lovingly inflamde" (qtd. in Lancashire, Comedy 10). Like Chiorison and Tumanama, these travelers would have been visually marked as strangers (ibid. 11). The mayor is told to continue on his way to Westminster "with these friendly strangers, man by man" (ibid.), conveying an attitude of respect and harmony between partners in trade no matter their origin or skin color. While the financial incentive underlying the partnership is certainly acknowledged, it is not constructed as its sole determinant.

---

[55] Cf. Dekker's facetious observation that "Gold's no Christian, but an Indian elfe" (Wonderfull Yeare 22).

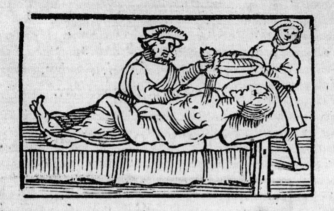

Abluis Aethiopem quid fruftra? ah define, noctis
Illuftrare nigræ nemo poteft tenebras.

AERE QVANDOQVE SA=
lutem redimendam.

E 3

Fig. 9: Andrea Alciato's emblem on the futility of washing an 'Ethiopian' depicts the latter under-
going a sponge bath. Yet, the illustration in the first edition (published by Heinrich Steiner in
Augsburg in 1531) does not in fact show a dark-skinned person on the receiving end of the bath.
Image by permission of the University of Glasgow Library, Special Collections.

The first pageant episode on land in Munday's *Chrysanaleia* is constituted by a "King of Moores, gallantly mounted on a golden Leopard" who is flanked by six "tributarie Kings on horse-backe, gorgeously attired in faire guilt Armours", and who is throwing "gold and silver euery way about him" (B2). These black kings are not only a rich and sumptuous spectacle to be admired, their distribution of gifts also establishes a direct material connection between them and the spectators. Furthermore, they appear as a source of wealth that directly profits the London populace with no European intermediaries represented or needed to facilitate a transaction. Later in the same show the character of William Walworth explains that the pageant episode was designed to express the special bond of friendship between Fishmongers and Goldsmiths and it may have done just that, yet it unquestionably also propagates a particular view of ethnic others. Walworth further explains that the king's "Indian treasure liberally is throwne: / To make his bounteous heart the better knowne" (C3). Significantly, even without recourse to conversion narratives, the Indian or "King of Moores" is here certified to be in possession of a "bounteous heart" that is not entirely reducible to an aspect of his financial prowess.

It is noteworthy that the Lord Mayor's Shows of this period present non-Europeans and non-Christians as autonomous partners in trade since elsewhere in contemporary discourse (and not only in discourse) ethnic others, Africans in particular, were themselves being turned into commodities. Queen Elizabeth's letters on the deportation of "blackmoores", mentioned above, partake in this discourse of dehumanization and commodification. The second of her letters commands that in exchange for services rendered by Lübeck merchant Casper van Senden – returning to England from Spain 89 English prisoners of war – 89 "blackamoores" in service in England were to be handed over to him (Bartels 313). As Van Senden's efforts could not have come to fruition "without great expence", Elizabeth deems it a reasonable request by the merchant "to transport so many blackamoores from hence" (qtd. in Bartels 312). While Emily C. Bartels interprets this as "part of a prisoner exchange with Spain" (313) in which Englishmen and "blackamoores" were given equal status, the black men and women were effectively downgraded to mere commodities, a type of currency to pay for the deliverance of Englishmen. In her third letter, Elizabeth again asserts that she wants "the said kind of people [...] out of this Her Majesty's dominions. And to that end and purpose hath appointed Caspar van Zenden, merchant of Lübeck, for their speedy transportation" (qtd. in Bartels 316). No reference is made in this letter to any prisoner exchange scheme, which threatens subjects who "are possessed of any such Blackamoors" and yet unwilling to part with them with her majesty's displeasure.[56] In Elizabeth's economic transaction

---

[56] Bartels interprets the letters as expressing a development toward color-based racism, "an important shift from a practical argument based on economic expediency to an ideological argument grounded on natural difference" (315), "from the contingent to the absolute, the practical to the ideological, the economic to the racial" (219). However, economic considerations and racism determined Elizabeth's stance in all three letters and to argue that there is development from "the economic to the racial" obscures the fact that they go hand in hand here. In all likelihood Elizabeth could benefit more from selling blacks to Van Senden than she could from their labor in England. Considerations of 'racial' or religious inferiority thus allow for the

with Van Senden, "blackamoores" are certainly commodified while the mercantile out-look shaping the Lord Mayor's Show still presented ethnic others – even if exoticized and sometimes made a pretty spectacle of – as partners in trade, not as commodities in them-selves. While the representation of strangers in dramatic and other texts echoed a social attitude which "moved between awe and rejection" (Cuder 85), the Lord Mayor's Show, in its treatment of the 'other', moved between awe and inclusion. Already in George Peele's 1585 show a child actor "appareled like a Moor" advised the mayor on his duties toward London, a "lovely lady" placed into his care by Queen Elizabeth (Chambers 563), demonstrating that interethnic dialogue could be imagined to take place on an equal or near-equal footing at this point in time by the company-men of London.

The perceived beauty of the exotic other is highlighted in Middleton's *Triumphs of Honour and Industry*, the first pageant episode of which features a "company of Indians, attired according to the true nature of their country, seeming for the most part naked". Middleton's description of the Indians resolves a contradiction pointed out by Hill between the authorial description of an Indian child in Dekker's *Londons Tempe* and Abram Booth's eyewitness account of the same child: "The Indian boy on the ostrich is said by Dekker to be wearing 'attire proper to the Country', whereas in Booth's drawing the boy does not appear to be wearing anything" (Pageantry 124). Clearly English conceptions of Indian dress tended toward the scanty.

Middleton's Indians in *Triumphs of Honour and Industry* are "active youths" working and dancing on a luxurious pageant island and in doing so they display the same cheerful industry as, for example, Mulciber's [Vulcan's] singing workforce of metalsmiths, or the dancing watermen in John Taylor's *Triumphs of Fame and Honour*. The dancing underscores the worldly, material thrust of the Lord Mayor's Show: Whereas John Lowin, in his *Brief Conclusions of Dancers and Dancing* (1609), deems dancing unacceptable when it is primarily intended as a "pleasure of our eyes" (D2), or aims "to please the world" instead of God (C3), the pageants unapologetically stage worldly dancers whose main concern is to please the eyes of Londoners.[57] It is to Lowin's chagrin that "now very often, in a great many places, among the Christians them-selves, [...] not only the Women, but also the Men" increasingly dance for their worldly pleasure and amusement (ibid.). At the same time, the pamphleteer insists that "the *Dances* do not seeme to become so well the lower set, as the higher" (D) and that, in general, the activity is "more becoming unto women, then unto men" (D). The Lord Mayor's Show, meanwhile, employs elements of dance not only in a celebration of the material world but also presents male dancers of the "lower set".

A chariot accompanies the Indian dancers' pageant island, inside of which ride personified Traffic or Merchandise, Industry, and a feminized personification of India,

---

commodification of human beings for the economic benefit of others. In turn, hoped-for economic advantages certainly encourage diagnoses of 'racial' inferiority.

[57] According to Lowin it is only virtuous to dance when the activity is either directly dedicated to God or, indirectly, in "celebration of some solemne feast consecrated unto God" (B3). In these cases "the forme of dancing ought to represent holinesse" (B4). It is still an acceptable, though not absolutely virtuous, pastime, Lowin concedes, when pursued as a chaste and "honest recreation" or as a means to preserve bodily health (Cii).

who is styled in the manner of "a triumphantly rich personage" (1256). The representation of a territory (city, country, or continent) morphed into a feminine body, ready for the adoration and exploitation by masculine factors was not a strategy limited to the representation of ethnic others but was widely applied in arts and pageantry and will be discussed in more detail in chapter three, in relation to its function in the Lord Mayor's Show as a celebration of the ritual marriage of mayor and metropolis. The gendered nature of personification in ancient Greek, Roman, and European medieval art will then be investigated in more detail, and the sufficiency of grammatical explanations challenged.

Briefly, the "ur-definition of personification" is given in the *Rhetorica ad Herennium* which states that an "*urbs invictissima*—an 'unconquerable city'" is to be embodied by a virginal woman, "implying semantically that a female body […] is that which may be penetrated through a violent, masculine invasion" (Paxson 152-53). This discursive strategy survived into the European Renaissance and was re-utilized in the age of discovery in order to describe new territories and legitimize their annexation and economic exploitation. In the final decades of the 16th century the image of personified America, in the guise of a nude woman awaiting Europeans to take possession of her uncivilized, passive body had achieved wide cultural circulation. The phenomenon, summed up by Louis Montrose as the "gendering of the New World as feminine, and sexualization of its exploration, conquest and settlement" (2), is echoed in Middleton's presentation of India and employed to exemplary effect by Sir Walter Ralegh in *The Discoverie of the large, rich, and beautifull Empire of Guiana* (1596). Herein, Ralegh famously concludes that,

> Guiana is a countrey that hath yet her maydenhead, never sackt, turned, nor wrought, the face of the earth hath not bene torne, nor the vertue and salt of the soyle spent by manurance […]. It hath never bene entred by any armie of strength, and never conquered or possessed by any christian Prince. (428)[58]

The strategy of sexualized territorial personification, exemplified above, merges with the presentation of an 'exotic' other in Middleton's *Triumphs of Honour and Virtue*, in which "a black personage" embodying India, "the Queen of Merchandise", is displayed on a bed of spices, while Indian attendants and European merchants (representing personified Commerce, Adventure, and Traffic) surround her. In the words of Phil Robinson, "the practices of trading and colonialism [are here] figured as what is close to becoming a polyamorous assault" (n. pag.). There may be some self-congratulatory missionary zeal detectable in the next gesture of Commerce, Adventure, and Traffic, who present to India "a bright figure, bearing the inscription of Knowledge" (ll. 47-49). Yet, whether that knowledge is supposed to be understood as purely religious awareness or whether 'carnal knowledge' may also be implied remains uncertain. The presentation of dark-skinned India is significantly qualified, however, by her self-assured words.[59] "Draw near", she

---

[58] Cf. Fallstaff in *The Merry Wives of Windsor*: "[S]he is a region in Guiana, all gold and bounty." (I.3.366-67)

[59] Loomba hypothesizes that this may be the first instance of a speaking part given to a black person in a civic pageant (1715). Her claim justly highlights the importance of character speech,

says, "this black is but my native dye, / But view me with an intellectual eye, / As wise men shoot their beams forth, you'll then find / A change in the complexion of the mind: / I'm beauteous in my blackness" (1719). India first notes the dichotomy between exterior and interior: While her 'black' body should indicate a sinful inner self,[60] conversion has changed "the complexion of the mind". However, her last line – a variation on 'black is beautiful' *avant la lettre* – returns to the exterior in a manner that slyly overcomes the conception that dark skin has 'dark' associations and cannot of itself ever be appealing, whether the person in question is a Christian or not, as India proudly proclaims that she may be black but she is nonetheless beautiful: "I'm beauteous in my blackness."[61]

In Middleton's *Triumphs of Truth* the mayor and entourage meet a black royal couple in St Paul's Churchyard.[62] What is notable about the black king, however, is not so much the fact of his conversion to Christianity but the patience and intelligence with which he confronts the spectators. In his long speech, he wonders initially, "does my complexion draw / So many Christian eyes that never saw / A king so black before?" Then there is a surprising development as the speaker realizes that the people's amazement is directed at the triumphs of the day, i.e. that he is not himself the object of wonder and perplexity at all. The king goes on to explain that his external appearance often leads people to make false value judgments about his beliefs and character, but that he is prepared to "forgive the judgings of th'unwise" (973). The image of 'blackness' broadcast to the spectators is not one of primitivism in any of its manifestations. Instead the black king displays neither less rationality nor less civility than a 'well-bred' Englishman may have been expected to. Heywood, in an unobtrusive manner, also makes a point of the common humanity of Europeans and non-Europeans in *Porta Pietatis*: An Indian character, seated on a pageant rhinoceros, gives a speech in which he points out how trade on land and sea makes all wares and valuables "by free transportage ours" which, in turn, brings fame to "*our* nation" (269) (emphasis mine).[63] Thus, Indian and Londoners are made to share one identity, as people who depend on trade to secure their livelihoods, to establish bonds with

---

although it is not quite correct. Nine years earlier, Middleton himself had given (thoughtful and sympathetic) lines to a black king in his *Triumphs of Truth* (1613).

[60] The popular association of black skin and the darkness of hell comes to the fore in the late Elizabethan or early Jacobean revenge tragedy *Lust's Dominion* (García 135). In the same vein, in act four, scene two of Shakespeare's *Titus Andronicus* a nurse refers to the new born son of "moor" Aaron as a "devil" – as well as a "loathsome [...] toad" and a "joyless, dismal, black, and sorrowful issue" – for his dark looks. Cuder notes that on the Renaissance stage, the "foreign Other" was frequently represented as an instigator of rebellion and in that role served "as an instrument to display a desirable subversive conduct" (87).

[61] Rebecca Ann Bach refers to personified India here as 'inarticulate', in *Colonial Transformations: The Cultural Production of the New Atlantic World, 1580-1640* (Basingstoke: Palgrave, 2000. 161.), but her reading, in my view, does little justice to the character's dignified self-assertion.

[62] Loomba notes that while some of the foreign rulers encountered by British merchants and explorers showed an interest in Christianity, religious conversion was not, in fact, a likely consequence of intellectual curiosity (1717).

[63] Incoming lord mayor Maurice Abbot was a well-traveled man and experienced in the arts of diplomacy and financial negotiation: "After joining the newly formed Levant Company in

others, and to thrive.[64] Already in 1585 foreign merchants had been represented in the festivities and been shown to congratulate the mayor on his new position (Lancashire, Comedy 5).[65] The effect, to Lancashire, is the invocation of a "kind of love – based on good economic relationships", which "is a key aspect of London's mercantile wealth and power" (ibid.). This theme of respect and harmony between trading partners from different countries and continents, evident in 16th-century Lord Mayor's Shows, continues to manifest in pageants into the mid-17th century.

2.7   O life, long to the wretched: Misery and Well-being

The communal identity referred to above is essentially a happy and contented one, whereas Jan van der Noot's emblem eight exemplifies an outlook, not infrequently found in emblem books, that conceives of the mortal's fundamental lot as an endless string of calamity and suffering. In contrast to Van der Noot's dictum that "nought in this worlde but griefe endures" (15), Lord Mayor's Shows are themselves joyful occasions and they perpetuate an ideology of positivity and purpose, which encompasses and aims at more than the resurrection of the soul: Life in the material world of London is full of opportunity for the industrious, full of reward for the deserving, and community for those who are willing to participate in it.[66] Less cheery – and more in line with Van der Noot's 'emblematic' position – is Whitney's emblem 81, titled "O vita, misero longa/O life, long to the wretched", which provides a graphic representation of Prometheus's never-ending torment (169). That it is not only those perpetually "wretched" by some inherent quality or fault of their own that suffer in life but that, in fact, human life itself is suffering is the message of Peacham's emblem 119 which lists the unavoidable "humane miseries [...], / That doe our life, unto the last amate": these are chiefly the rod, women, old age and

1588, he travelled to Aleppo, where, in 1592 [when he was in his 20s], he lent the English ambassador to Constantinople 4600 ducats, a sum which suggests that he had already begun to make his fortune." (Thrush, Abbot n. pag.)

[64] This applied to the majority of Londoners who were small-scale producers and traders, or servants and apprentices of the latter. Close to three-fifths of occupations followed by Londoners of Middleton's period were in the production of goods (Richardson 54).

[65] As early as 1521 a "King of Moors" figured in a Midsummer entertainment alongside "60 morians [moors] at 4d. Each for two nights and one [costlier] woman morian at 8d", as company records register (Robertson and Gordon xvii). Ana Elena González-Treviño has argued that the sums sponsors were willing to invest in the depiction of various strangers "suggests the City's considerable interest in representing all significant varieties of otherness despite the financial investment in creating these new characters" (111-12).

[66] Many scholars interpret the mayor's role in the Lord Mayor's Show as comparable to that of 'Everyman' in medieval morality plays, tempted by personified Virtues and Vices in the course of an inaugural show (e.g. Loomba 1714; Bergeron, Civic Pageantry 139). Manley describes this as a "primordial agon between the forces of creation and destruction" (308). Inherent in this approach, however, is a tendency to exaggerate the role of vice and destruction in an overwhelmingly celebratory and cheerful genre.

disease (S2). The picture of a woman holding a rod and urinal while leaning on a globe accompanies and completes the verse.

The pursuit of uplifting activities does not lighten the dismal mood in Whitney's emblem 15, "Voluptas aerumnosa/Sorrowful pleasure", in which Diana [the equivalent of Greek Artemis] watches Actaeon being attacked by hounds, accompanied by the moral that one should not "pursue [...] fancies fonde, and thinges unlawful crave" since regret and punishment will follow swiftly (Whitney 104). Hunting also provides the metaphorical means for representing human calamity in Van der Noot's first emblem which elucidates the picture of a deer – simultaneously pursued by dogs in the foreground and fallen prey to them in the background – with the statement that "[c]ruell death vanquishing so noble a beautie, / Oft makes me waile so harde a destinie" (8). The same metaphorical terrain is occupied by Peacham's fourth emblem – "Nusquam tuta" [nowhere is safe] – which showcases a deer, an arrow protruding from its side, vainly attempting to run to safety. Like the wounded animal, the verse explains, a human sinner suffers for his sins but finds no respite in the "shifting of his ground" (C2). Man's unshakable "guilt and sinne" (X3) is also the focus of Peacham's 146th emblem which expresses the sinner's plight aided by the picture of a naked young man tormented by snakes who cling to him and cover much of his body.

Peacham's emblem 28 declares how to noble thinkers, looking down as from a great height unto the little lives of lesser people, these must appear as a "multitude of Antes" involved "in their follies tragaedie" (F2). What is more, among the foolish multitudes some contribute nothing to the common good but instead waste their talents and become a "needeles burthen which the Earth did beare" (Peacham, emblem 100, P2). Dire as the human experience is, Peacham warns against attempts to alter one's state for the better: His emblem 155 claims that excising old evils merely invites new, worse ones to grow in their place. This is illustrated in word and picture by a "Lazar poore [...] full of sores, and loathsome ulcers", plagued by flesh-eating flies (Y4). When the flies are chased off his skin, no respite follows because more aggressive insects will immediately take the place of the old ones (see fig. 10). His situation will only be made worse by any attempt to better it.

WHEN as *TIBERIVS CÆSAR* paſt along
   The ſtreetes of *Rome*, by chaunce he did eſpie
A Lazar poore, who there amid the throng,
Did full of ſores, and loathſome vlcers lie,
About the which, ſo buſie was the flie:
   That moou'd with pittie, *CÆSAR* willed ſome,
   Stand by to kill them, as they ſaw them come.

Whereat the wretch, did ſuddainely replie,
Theſe flies are full, pray let them yet alone,
For being kill'd, a freſher companie,
More hunger pincht, would bite me to the bone:
So when the wealthy Iudge, is dead and gone:
   Some ſtarued one ſucceedes, who * biteth more,
   A thouſand times, then did the full before.

Vide Crocelli nomen habes

non du

i. quod Crocem maximè timent. Vnde (ſcilicet) inoculc Crocem inuenta Croceta. a ſe lauritum.

* *Caninum legis ſtudium dixit. Columella lib : 1.*

Quemadmodum vis morborum pretia medentibus, ſic fori tabes pecuniam advocatis fert. Tacitus Annal: 11.

Salentij

Fig. 10: Peacham's emblem 155 warns that one source of distress may soon be succeeded by a worse one (Y4). Image by courtesy of the David M. Rubenstein Rare Book & Manuscript Library, Duke University.

Not only are men and women presented as sinners, fools, and useless wretches, their bodies plagued by snakes, sores, and flesh-eating pests, "[c]haracters burp, fart, vomit, spew, shit, piss and spit their way through numerous emblem books" (Manning 271),[67] suggesting the corruption of both body and mind. Even when there is a bright side to existence, as in Whitney's 101st emblem, its glow is not radiant: Under the motto "Infortunia nostra, alienis collata, leviora/Our misfortunes, compared with those of others, become lighter", an ape and a monkey find some satisfaction in the knowledge that their lots are perhaps more easily borne than that of a sad blind mole (190). While Whitney's emblem 25 bears the motto "We are all consumed by cares" (114), it offers the, after all, hopeful advice that the companionship of a friend may stave off an early grave. Yet, the emblem renders this claim not as a message of hope but phrases and illustrates it as a warning. The focus is not on the pleasures of companionship but on the loneliness and misery that may mark the absence of it.

In the general melancholy of the emblem book even creatures as strong and imposing as elephants are not exempt from mischance. Co-referencing peace, fidelity, chastity, and wisdom (Bright and Bowen 17),[68] elephants are featured in a number of popular emblems in which these very virtues are under attack. In the Lord Mayor's Show, too, exotic animals such as elephants were not infrequently utilized by pageant writers and artisans to add observable interest to the celebrations, to reference company arms,[69] as well as to visualize the broadening effect of mercantile enterprise which brought London into contact with the fauna of distant continents.[70] While the verse of Willet's emblem 89 claims that God created the elephant in order to show his strength and magnitude, for Whitney, the animal served primarily as a purveyor of dispiriting ideas. In emblem 155, "Nusquam tuta fides/Nowhere is faith safe", the elephant figures as an embodiment of

---

[67] Manning believes that these scatological instances amount to "an element of satiric reprehension of vice in the works of Alciato and La Perrière and other early emblematists" (205), and that they are, in fact, precursors of the 18th-century satirical cartoon.

[68] A widespread belief – perpetuated by, among other sources, Horapollo's *Hieroglyphica* – maintained that elephants feared, above all, the squealing of pigs (Bright and Bowen 18-19). Sir Thomas Browne criticized emblem books for spreading similar superstitions, such as the notion that lions are afraid of roosters. Any protective strategy based on this belief, Browne wisely points out, would be an altogether "unsafe defensative" (qtd. in Praz 225).

[69] Abram Booth, eyewitness to the performance of Dekker's 1629 *Londons Tempe*, recognized lions as "representing the East Indian Company – whose coat of arms has been decorated with 2 suchlike lions" (22). A lion's head also appeared in the upper and lower left quarters of the Goldsmiths' shield which, in turn, was supported by a rearing unicorn. The Merchant Taylors' shield, supported by dromedaries, contained – above a tent and robes – a lion "passant", i.e. in side view, with one paw lifted (Burke 619-20). A lynx formed the crest of the Skinners' arms. The Drapers' crest was topped by a ram, and the Fishmongers' shield displayed dolphins. All of these creatures, and more beside, could be staged and referenced in pageants.

[70] In the margins of emblem 106 in his *Minerva Britanna*, Peacham recounts the story of the first rhinoceros to have arrived in Europe since Roman antiquity: In 1515 an Indian rhinoceros reached Lisbon – commemorated by Dürer's famous engraving – which Manuel I attempted to pitch in battle against one of his elephants. The elephant fled the scene, however, and the rhinoceros was subsequently drowned in a shipwreck on its way to Rome (Q3).

faith. The emblem picture shows the animal resting against a tree, while the verse explains that "[t]he Olephant so huge, and stronge to see, / No perill fear'd: but thought a sleepe to gaine / But foes before had undermin'de the tree, / And downe he falles, and so by them was slaine" (Whitney 245). Into a similarly gloomy category falls the fable adapted by Whitney for his 210th emblem, "Victoria cruenta/Bloody victory", which involves a tragic realization of the trope that sin never pays. The picture shows an elephant lying on its side, while in the background a man is falling backwards onto a sword. The verse explains that the elephant's demise was caused by a snake bite but that, when it fell, the elephant landed on top of the snake that had previously attacked it and so, in an instance of poetic justice or 'instant karma', the snake, too, was killed (Whitney 298). Thus, in both emblems the elephant exemplifies positive qualities but is nevertheless defeated, whether due to a lack of vigilance or for no detectable reason is left to the readers' discernment.

In Heywood's *Londini Artium* an elephant – chosen, so the author, to signify "incomparable strength and most pregnant understanding" (C) – features in the show's fifth pageant episode. The animal is led by an Indian boy and carries a model castle on its back. In the words of its young handler, this suits the elephant since there is no animal "[i]n this high nature, apter or more fit" to serve as an "Embleame or Symbole, for a Government" (ibid.). Here, the elephant stands for the moral and physical strength of the city of London and its civic administration. In Webster's *Monuments of Honour* personified Obedience, one of a group of personages commemorating the deceased Prince Henry Stuart, is accompanied by a representation of an elephant: "the strongest Beast, but most obseruant to man of any Creature" (C2). Henry had been expected to be in the audience for Dekker's *Troia-Nova Triumphans* in 1612, along with his sister's suitor, the 16-year-old Frederick V of the Electoral Palatinate, but the crown prince contracted a fatal illness and did not attend. Elegiac tributes to the prince were produced in large numbers in the aftermath of his unexpected death and the trend did no abate for many years. The elephant in Webster's 1624 homage to Henry is not only spectacular for its size, it is notable for the virtues it so impressively embodies. As demonstrated above, elephants are creatures of misfortune in Whitney's emblems: Where they deserve mercy and benevolence, they are crushed instead. Yet, the elephant's fate changes with medium and genre: in the context of the Lord Mayor's Show, the animal is not made to suffer defeat but exudes strength, reliability, and virtue. Where the elephant is vanquished in emblems, it triumphs in pageants.

From merchant monkeys to woebegone elephants, the preceding pages have amply illustrated the divergent thematic leanings of popular emblem books and Lord Mayor's Shows. Therefore, when scholars inevitably note the "emblematic" proclivities of Middleton's or Munday's city pageantry, a measure of wariness is advisable since the two cultural formats demonstrably varied in form, function, and, as argued above, in message. A further consideration that may cast some doubt on the accepted trajectory of influence from emblem to pageant is formulated by S. Schuman who raises the widely overlooked point that the influence between the genres was mutual (28). In support of his claim, Schuman argues that Thomas Combe may have been inspired by Shakespeare's *Love's Labour's Lost* when compiling an emblem titled "All those that love do fancie most, / But lose their labour and their cost" for his *Theatre of Fine Devices* (ibid.).

Rosemary Freeman confirms that influence was not unilateral by her assertion that Peacham probably derived personifications from the works of Edmund Spenser (109). These reciprocal relations between emblem books and other literary and cultural productions are a further testament to the broad variety of material incorporated into the works of Whitney, Peacham, and other emblematists of the period. At the same time, Freeman maintained, "the matter, if not the manner" of emblem books can be found in the work of almost all Elizabethan and early Jacobean poets (99), and Manning, who disagrees with Freeman on multiple counts, acknowledges that, from birth to death, from the constraints of poverty to the duties and privileges of kingship, almost every aspect of human existence was transformed into emblem form (15). Nevertheless, it bears repeating that the manner in which material was presented and interpreted differed between emblem book and Lord Mayor's Show.

3   The Lord Mayor's Show as Rite of Incorporation

The OED defines "ritual" as a "ritual act or ceremonial observance", or "in later use: an action or series of actions regularly or habitually repeated". For the near-synonymous "rite",[1] the first entry reads, "prescribed act or observance in a religious or other solemn ceremony". According to the sum of definitions and example listings provided by the OED ritual performances are primarily characterized by regular repetition, the invariable order of their elements, and the special significance attributed to ritual behavior and the occasions which demand it. In later uses of the term, the focus on a magico-religious framework lessens while the meaning-component of routine repetition is increasingly stressed.

According to anthropologist Arnold van Gennep the force of ritual revitalizes social activity – which spends and exhausts itself – at certain, recurring intervals (182). Van Gennep's classificatory model of rites distinguishes between eight distinct types, conceding that, in practice, exact categorization may prove difficult. "Sympathetic rites", for instance, assume reciprocal relations between entities, whereas "contagious rites" are based on the assumption that characteristics are transmitted from one entity onto another (ibid. 4-7). Further, "animistic rites" invoke a personalized power, while "dynamistic rites" refer to an impersonal force or power (ibid. 10). Rites may also be defined as either "direct" or "indirect", and "positive" or "negative", i.e. enacting volition or taboo (ibid. 8). Recalling the main tenets of the OED-definition, Victor Turner's "operationally useful" definition describes ritual more generally as meaningful, formalized behavior, performed on specific occasions and referencing higher beings or powers (Ritual 79). In contrast to Turner, other anthropologists would eliminate the religious element from their definitions (ibid.).[2] Suspending judgment on whether or not definitions of ritual must incorporate a supernatural dimension, the following chapter is informed by Turner's broad understanding of ritual as potent (though not necessarily practical or rational) behavior, enacted invariably on specific, important occasions and expressing communal values.

My understanding of "rites of passage" is based largely on Arnold van Gennep's eponymous publication *The Rites of Passage* (1908) in which he delineates how significant transitions in the lives of individuals or groups are accompanied by rites which aid transformation and avert the possibility of crisis sparked by change. Van Gennep argues for the near-universality of rites of passage – not contradicted by great contextual variation – and attests "a wide degree of general similarity among ceremonies of birth,

---

[1]   Arnold van Gennep uses "rite" and "ritual" interchangaebly (e.g. 4).

[2]   Theater scholar Richard Homan sees the desired 'efficacy' of ritual as its defining feature, separating ritual drama from other types of drama. If the purpose of a performance is primarily aesthetic then he classifies it as non-ritual theater, following the definitions of Richard C. Webb and Anthony Graham-White (304).

childhood, social puberty, betrothal, marriage, pregnancy, fatherhood, initiation into religious societies, and funerals" across societies separated by time and space (3). Not restricted to changes in the lives of individuals, rites of this type may also accompany recurring changes, e.g. of a seasonal nature, which affect a community as a whole (ibid.). All rites of passage, so Van Gennep, possess a tripartite structure in which rites of separation (preliminal phase) are followed by transition rites (liminal phase) and, finally, by rites of incorporation (postliminal phase) (ibid. 11). In the preliminal phase ritual subjects are detached from their previous positions. Subsequently, in the liminal period, the initiates pass through "a limbo of statuslessness" (Turner 97). Reincorporation into society follows in the third and final phase in which "the passage is consummated" (ibid. 94-95), and a new status or position is achieved. However, not all phases are equally pronounced in all rites of passage: marriage rites, for example, privilege rites of incorporation while transition is stressed in pregnancy rites and, unsurprisingly, funeral rites tend to focus on aspects of separation (Van Gennep 11).

In *The Ritual Process: Structure and Anti-Structure* (1969), Victor Turner has introduced the concepts of "communitas" and "structure". Turner defines structure broadly as the entire complex of rules, regulations, and hierarchies which constitutes social organization. Structure is not just "the set of chains in which men everywhere are, but the very cultural means that preserve the dignity and liberty, as well as the bodily existence, of every man, woman, and child" (140). Communitas, on the other hand, is a mode of personal interaction that is not based on structural differentiation but privileges the communion of individuals on an equal footing, allowing them to experience an "essential and generic human bond" (ibid. 96-97). Turner understands both structure and communitas as fundamental aspects of all societies and as concepts that mutually depend on each other (ibid. 130). Where "structure tends to be pragmatic and this-worldly", communitas tends toward the metaphysical, toward "imagery and philosophical ideas" (ibid. 133). This binary scheme is neither flawless nor universally applicable, but as a basic conceptual apparatus it offers advantages for the present chapter in which I attempt to examine the Lord Mayor's Show as a ritual process which stresses both social structure and mutual dependence – of an ideological and practical variety. Turner's interpretive approach is attractive to scholars of English religious and processional drama, possibly because Turner stresses the importance of the intermediate stage of the proceedings (drawing on Van Gennep's thoughts on liminality) and holds that this stage facilitates the experience of communitas (96).[3] This hermeneutic, it would seem, is especially pertinant to civic occasions which observe adjustments to the status quo and which hinge on the passage from one state to another (like inaugurations). Turner further argues that, in literature and in religion, often "normative and ideological communitas are symbolized by structurally inferior categories" (ibid. 133).[4] In the following chapter, one argument I will propound is that communitas is symbolized in the Lord Mayor's Show by the

---

[3]   Richard Homan, for example, refers to communitas and structure in his discussion of the York Cycle (315).

[4]   Communitas can be experienced in a number of settings: There are, according to Turner, spontaneous, normative, and ideological forms of communitas, with the latter two kinds already falling under the auspices of structure (132f.).

structurally inferior category of "woman" – via personifications who appear in the pageants. While Turner's model has been applied to processional drama and pageantry, it has not been applied to qestions of gender and personification.

The present chapter deals with representations of space but still I am not concerned with matters of the so-called 'spatial turn'. While I understand the significant role culture plays in cognition, and am fully aware of the fact that human endeavor affects space which, in turn, affects people, I deliberately dare to disregard poststructuralist spatial theory. Since I believe that my interpretation of the Lord Mayor's Show as rite of passage and ritual marriage festivity does not crucially depend on the terminological frameworks of Lefebvre et al. I have made the informed decision not to employ them. Neither Lefebvre's triad of spatial forms nor de Certeau's distinctions between strategies and tactics, maps and tours, let alone Deleuze and Guattari's 'rhizomatic' accounts of striated and smooth space would enrich the present study in any meaningful way. That is not to deny that concepts relating to the interface of social and natural space can be insightful in their own right, nor that they can be fruitfully employed as analytical tools. Still, in an academic climate that defines space with increasing exclusivity as the product of social forces (e.g. West-Pavlov 22), and which steers toward the abandonment of "the distinction between space and meaning" (ibid. 24), some counterbalancing is called for. The notion, postulated by poststructuralist theoreticians of space, that space and meaning cannot be differentiated, in its consequence, denies the existence of a knowable reality. This is a view which I emphatically do not share. Rather, in the words of Susan Sontag, it is my belief that "[t]here is still a reality that exists independent of the attempts to weaken its authority" (109). Indeed, Sontag's position gains more urgency in a world of 'alternative facts'. I will therefore proceed on the assumption that the Lord Mayor's Show occurred annually in a complex but ultimately real and knowable environment. This stance is neither invalidated by the fact that I examine personifications of places and spaces in the following pages nor by my discussion of the ways in which London is understood and portrayed – and to which purpose – since there is a difference, however complicated and contested, between the material city and its various representations and associations.

3.1   *To be her Husband for a yeere*: Marriage Ritual in the Lord Mayor's Show

As the newly sworn-in mayor progresses from the social position of alderman to that of lord mayor, his ritual passage through the streets of London serves not only as a spatial enactment of his rise in status but simultaneously confirms a metaphorical bond of marriage between mayor and city. While the territorial passage of the mayor and his liveried train – between the river bank, the Guildhall, and the mayor's personal residence – represents the political appropriation of the traversed territory, the mayor also takes on features of a groom penetrating the streets of the feminine-gendered city.[5] The Lord Mayor's Show, while officially honoring the mayor's inauguration, simultaneously

---

[5]   Tracey Hill confirms how "the passing of the Lord Mayor through the City worked as a literally visible assertion of his authority" (Pageantry 10).

becomes a wedding masque, accessible to all Londoners, that celebrates the symbolic 12-month-marriage of London and lord mayor. When the character of Pythagoras tells new mayor Richard Fenn in the final moments of Heywood's *Londini Speculum*, that "to a World of Care / You are ingag'd to morrow, which must last / Till the whole progresse of Your Yeere be past", he spells out quite plainly that he considers Fenn to be wedded to his new office (317). The mayor's dual union both with his office and, figuratively, with the city itself makes it necessary for him to undergo a rite of passage which moves him from one stage of his professional life to the next and which, at the same time, reconciles his constituents to a new phase in the government of the city. The ritual passage embarked upon by each new occupant of the mayor's office is structured so as to favor rites of incorporation into his new station, while the significance of separation from previous positions and of the liminal in-between state is somewhat downplayed.[6] A similar emphasis on rites of incorporation in combination with the relative negligence of rites of separation and transition is characteristic of actual (non-figurative) marriage rites (Van Gennep 117). The metaphor employed to frame the mayor's political preferment in terms of marriage not only eases administrative transformation; it also naturalizes the prerogative of the company elites to wield power by reference to supposedly 'natural' gender relations and the conventional correlation of the commonwealth and the family unit.[7] As Robert Cleaver explains in his *Godlie Forme of Householde Government* (London, 1600), a guide to proper conduct in the Christian home: While "Matrimonie maketh equall many differences" (149), still "by nature woman was made mans subiect" (ibid.).

Furthermore, just as rites of passage from bachelordom into matrimony tend to include rituals invoking fertility and material prosperity, a flourishing commonwealth is invoked in Lord Mayor's Shows as the happy product of the mayor's administrative care of the city. A case in point is Dekker's *Londons Tempe* (1629): a lush and leafy arbor expresses the fruitfulness of the civic territory under the care of Mayor James Campbell (whose father, Thomas, had been mayor some twenty years previously). Styled by Dekker "*Londons Tempe, or The Field of Happinesse*", the pageant arbor not only refers to the title of the eponymous show but also puns "vpun the name of *Campe-bell*, or *Le Beu Champe,* A faire and glorious field" (C). The set, a territory shaped by Campbell's beneficial influence, thus represents the flourishing state of affairs in the city, or, as eye witness Abram Booth put it, "the fertility of the country" under Campbell's government

---

[6] Cf. Edward Muir: "A procession was, in effect, a mobile and extended threshold between one social state and another" (131).

[7] According to Robert Cleaver's contemporary treatise on family life, the proper roles of husband and wife are the following: "1. The husband his dutie is, first to love his wife as his owne flesh. 2. Then to governe her in all duties; that properly concerne the state of mariage, in knowledge, in wisdome, iudgement, and iustice. Thirdly, to dwell with her. Fourthly, to use her in al due benevolence, honesty, soberly, and chastely. [...] 1. The wife, her dutie is, in all reverence and humilitie, to submit and subiect her selfe to her husband, in all such duties as properly belong to marriage. Secondly, therein to be an helpe unto him, according to Gods ordinance. Thirdly, to obey his commandements in all things [...]. Fourthly and lastly, to give him mutuall benevolence." (119)

(22). From the pageant stage, where he presides over the feminine shapes of Flora, Pomona, Ceres, and Ver, sun god Tytan identifies the "faire and glorious field" with Campbell's London and as the mayor acts favorably on the city, so the deity's rays of sunlight act on the feminine earth to produce plentiful increase. In Heywood's *Londini Emporia* a pageant tableau referred to as the "Bower of Bliss" assumes the function that is fulfilled by Campbell's "glorious field" in Dekker's show. Heywood's paradisal pageant may "aptly be titled FREEMANS Bower" (C), explains personified Prudence to newly sworn-in Mayor Freeman. Here, too, the new mayor's effect is to render London flourishing and productive. Likewise, the Imperial Fort – a non-anthropomorphic but sentient rendering of London – in Heywood's *Londini Speculum* derives "all her grace" from new mayor Richard Fenn (313-14).

Some scholars have picked up on the marriage allegory in the Lord Mayor's Show but have not pursued the subject very far. James Knowles has pointed out how the speech accompanying the water entertainment in *Triumphs of Love and Antiquity* (1619) depicts the mayor's year in office as a marriage of mayor and city and, further, how "marital imagery" is deployed in Webster's *Monuments of Honour* by comparing the Lord Mayor's Show to the Venetian Marriage of the Sea (166).[8] However, following this very brief, intriguing mention, Knowles refrains from paying any more attention to the phenomenon despite the fact that it suffuses all Lord Mayor's Shows of the period and, to my knowledge, has not been analyzed in any detail before. Tracey Hill records that "it had long been the tradition to refer to the individual being celebrated in a civic triumph – be they monarch or mayor – as London's bridegroom, an analogy Munday uses to rather peculiar effect in 1616" (Pageantry 167), but she does not examine the phenomenon further.[9] Bergeron, for his part, has noted that, in *The Triumphs of Truth*, Middleton "deliberately emphasizes the feminine gender" of personified London, "so that he may pursue the metaphor of the city as caring mother," and further link London to a female Truth (Bergeron, Annotation 966). The personification of London in the Lord Mayor's Show is effective because, as a collective body-metaphor, it serves to create a legitimate community out of wildly disparate elements (cf. Mazza 41).[10] At the same time, the

---

[8] Knowles also posits Corpus Christi processions as precursors to later civic pageantry of the type of the London Lord Mayor's Show (158-59). These civic rituals and displays seek to promote harmony and stability between guilds and among the urban populace as a whole (159). By reference to paternalistic magistracy, poor relief and a culture of charity in the city, the benefits of trade and the civilizing potential of urbanity, early modern civic pageantry also justifies city life in the face of antimetropolitan discourses (162, 167, 170-73).

[9] Hill also notes: "At a thematic level, as in the royal entry with the relative positions of monarch and people, the mayoral inauguration was sometimes likened to a marriage between the Lord Mayor and the City. Indeed, in terms of their gendering of the relationship between ruler and ruled there is little difference between the two genres." (Pageantry 17-18)

[10] In her introduction to *Der verfaßte Körper: Zum Projekt einer organischen Gemeinschaft in der Politischen Romantik* [The written/composed body: on the project of organic union in political Romanticism], Ethel Matala de Mazza cites the Pauline paradigm of a collective body [the church as the body of Christ] as the basis for construing a collective national body (Mazza 40). Cf.: "Erstens möchte sie [die vorliegende Arbeit] die Leitmetapher des sozialen Körpers

111

personified city was cast in multiple roles: as a bride to the mayor and as a mother to all Londoners (including the mayor), the feminine personification of London becomes integral to the family and household model of civic administration. The family model, as alluded to above, adds conceptions of 'natural' order and codes of behavior to the 'natural' community itself, embodied in anthropomorphic London.[11] As in any commonwealth, clarifies contemporary Londoner Robert Cleaver, "there are two sorts in everie perfect familie: 1 The Governours", and "2 Those that must be ruled" (15). In a proper household, a husband and wife rule over children and servants. They are responsible for seeing to it that all members of the household are clothed, fed, healthy, and put to diligent work (ibid. 61-62). Yet, at the same time as a wife shares in the responsibility for children and staff, ultimately she must always defer to her husband. After all, in Genesis God himself tells Eve that her "desire shall be to thy husband, and he shall rule over thee" (3:16, King James Bible). A wife's first duty is therefore to be her husband's helper, and, so Cleaver, "in her selfe to give example to her Household of all readie submission to all good and christian orders" (60). In 1615, Alexander Niccholes similarly instructs readers of his guidebook on how to choose a spouse that a wife is intended as "a helper meete" for her husband, "not a hinderer, [but] a companion for his comfort" (1). For a good husband this means that "[t]he best rule that a man may hold and practise with his wife to guard and governe her, is to admonish her often, and to give her good instructions, to reprehend her seldome, never to lay violent hands on her; but if she be good and dutifull to savour her" (ibid. 169).

On the topic of personified London William Hardin has argued that in order to curb unregulated urban growth and to affirm the traditional limits of the city, Heywood presents London in *Londini Speculum* as "a passive female figure" (20) and a "maternal embodiment" (32). Hardin's astute reading of Heywood's pageant is based heavily on contemporary notions of female submissiveness and familial codes of behavior – such as those outlined above – but it does not take into account that a strategy of personification is not necessarily restricted to promote constraint and segregation and that Heywood himself had explicitly included the 'unregulated' suburbs in his vision of London in the pamphlet commemorating *Porta Pietatis* (263).

Along lines similar to Hardin's, Lawrence Manley has analyzed London as "heroic matron" – though not as bride and mother – in an essay on the topography of Tudor and

---

aus der *semantischen Umbesetzung des christlichen Gedanken einer Leibeinheit* plausibel machen [...]" (ibid.).

[11] At the same time, the family was understood as a fit template for civic relations based on the enormous contemporary significance of the marriage bond. As the only sacrament dating back to before the fall of mankind, marriage was considered "the basic unit of human relations around which all society is built" (Ferrante 32). Robert Cleaver phrased his opinions on wedlock thus: "Matrimonie then being an indissoluble bond and knot, whereby the husband and wife are fastned (sic!) together by the ordinance of God, is farre straighter then any other coniunction in the societie of mankind. Insomuch that it is a lesse offence for a man to forsake father and mother [...] thé it is for him to do the like toward his lawfull maried wife." (99) According to Francis Parlett, recorder of King's Lynn in the 1630s, the "'first seed of government' sprang directly from the first marriage, between Adam and Eve, and the first family they generated" (qtd. in Patterson 161).

Stuart London. His London-as-matron also incorporates the quality of submission which is desirable in a good wife and is instrumental in disseminating notions of conservative, unchanging order. The topographical accounts under Manley's consideration, for example those of John Speed and William Camden, had this use of the feminized city as a unifying agent in common:

> The procedure to which they all contributed was the personification of the city as heroic matron, symbolically submissive intermediary between nature and the higher claims of political culture. This gender-based procedure, which dominated many of the major descriptions of Tudor-Stuart London, effectively suppressed the more dynamic aspects of urban life – especially the power of the metropolitan economy both to enfranchise and to enslave individual subjects without regard to the sovereign's intent. (Matron to Monster 348-49)[12]

As this demonstrates, the personified city could be encountered in a variety of contexts in early modern discourse. Moreover, the adaptation of marriage terminology and ritual for use in non-nuptial contexts was not unique to the Lord Mayor's Show. As Van Gennep notes, initiation into religious orders is frequently enacted along these lines (99), and in early modern England both Elizabeth I and James I freely employed matrimonial metaphors for political purposes.[13] Just as Elizabeth I had presented herself as chaste bride to Britain, so her successor was conceptualized as bridegroom to the realm – both in his 1604 royal entry through London and in the king's own parliamentary address in the wake of the entry. In his speech James I appropriated for himself the metaphorical roles of husband, head, and shepherd, while allocating to the realm those of wife, body, and flock respectively (Bergeron, King James 227). This gendering of roles and characteristics conforms to the received notion of passive and enduring womanhood, standing in complementary opposition to active and constructive masculinity. Just as it is implicit in

[12] According to Manley, "[b]y subordinating to a transhistorical, transindividual identity the viewpoint of observers historically situated in space and time, and by stretching this identity over millennia, the personification of London unified in one body the city's discontinuous spaces and naturalized the erratic development of is culture" (Matron to Monster 349-50). Stow, however, deviated from the above formula by inserting himself and, thus, the life span and perspective of an individual observer, into the narrative – an approach which would prove influential later in the 17th century (ibid. 364). Still, Stow also feminizes the city in his account. Looking at territorial personification in a modern context, McGraw and Dolan have examined "how different ways of embodying the state – as a leader, a political institution, or the nation's people – influence attitude formation processes" (300). They report that embodiment tended to lead to more strongly held attitudes (ibid. 314), and that "in the political realm, the personification of collectives (states, parties, institutions) as monolithic actors characterized by malevolent intent is often used strategically by political elites to mobilize public opinion and collective action against opponents" (ibid. 317).

[13] In the anonymous pamphlet *A Student's Lament*, Elizabeth I is rendered the "mother of all true English children". In the same pamphlet, feminized England asks of dissenters: "Why do yee devide your selves within me? Are yee not all mine? Shall the hand teare out the eye, the foote put the neck in jeopardy?" (B4) To personified England, the English are simultaneously her children and the parts of her body.

the crown's politically motivated discourse of marriage, this conception of gender also suffuses the contemporary Lord Mayor's Show, where it is, however, tempered by the attribution of mystical powers to feminine personages – such as personified Virtues or the City *herself*. As feminized personifications are deified in the classical tradition (Ferrante 37), so they are in the Lord Mayor's Show. Corresponding to Victor Turner's hypothesis that "the 'structural' or synchronic inferiority of certain personae, groups, and social categories in political, legal, and economic systems" is counterweighed by a type of mystical power attributed to the marginalized (99-100), woman's structural inferiority – the subordination of her property and person – is paradoxically the condition on which rests the ascription of metaphysical powers to feminine personages in the Lord Mayor's Show. Because women are structurally inferior they are endowed with mystical powers and can serve as semi-divine mediators between man and those heavenly or hellish spheres which are understood to deny and transcend direct human access.

At the same time, in the mayor's active passage through the passive streets of the feminized city echoes the gender binary of compliant, material femininity on the one hand and active, creative masculinity on the other. The mayor walks the city streets and inscribes them with his authority while London gratefully accepts this inscription, sometimes as obedient wife, sometimes as "blessed Mother and bountifull Nurse" (Heywood, Londini Artium A4), who now bows to the authority of her eldest son. While the mayor as bridegroom proceeds through the city on an established route with his entourage in rank and file, the diverse crowds who assemble to watch the show form a more disorderly and less visibly, purposefully dynamic mass and so demonstrate their allegiance to the urban bride. The crowds are, much like feminized London, full of potential but in need of a restraining and guiding force.

Catherine Patterson has examined the records left by one Francis Parlett who was recorder (i.e. legal advisor and Justice of the Peace) of the Norfolk town of King's Lynn in the 1630s. In particular, she has set out and commented on his notes relating to a speech he delivered at the inauguration of Bartholomew Wormell as mayor of King's Lynn in 1632 (159-60). In this speech Parlett "offers advice on good government cloaked in an extended metaphor of marriage: the mayor as husband and the town as wife" (Patterson 159). Parlett touches on many of the topoi manifest in the London Lord Mayor's Show and, thus, demonstrates the cultural pervasiveness of understanding a mayor's position as equivalent to a husband's. Initially Parlett addresses outgoing mayor John Wallis. Wallis, according to Parlett, was a good husband to the town, having treasured his wife's honor, peace, and profit (ibid. 160). Yet, these virtues do not solely belong to the wife/city. Effectively, "[t]hrough his good government, Wallis has made the town good" (ibid.). Introducing Wormell to his office, Parlett makes these observations: "The town, he says, cannot be considered a maid, as she has been so many times married – every year to a new mayor. But she also cannot be considered a widow, because the same instant her marriage to the outgoing mayor ends, her marriage to the new mayor begins." (ibid.) The same situation, the possibly troubling inclination of the city toward serial monogamy, is also addressed (in mostly humorous fashion) in the Lord Mayor's Show. Parlett notes, too, that the town is "an ancient Body, a body politic, whose head you [the mayor] are to be, as the husband is the head of the wife" (qtd. in ibid. 161). The mayor demands "obedience from and in turn protects and corrects his metaphorical spouse" (ibid. 167).

114

All of these notions – a husband as a head affixed to a potentially unruly spousal body, as a protector and corrector – are referenced in London's Lord Mayor's Show.

Patterson contends that "[o]n the surface, the extended metaphor of marriage seems to be simply a rhetorical device, and a somewhat hackneyed one at that" (169), and that it is notable that Parlett "portrays the mayor's relationship with the town not as a pater-familias ruling over children, but rather as a husband in partnership with a wife" (ibid. 170). Yet, the same scenario unfolds in the Lord Mayor's Show (though the mayor here also has a paternal role to fill), suggesting that the portrayal of a mayor as married to his (personified and feminized) city was a very common early modern conceit, related to similar strategies centered on monarch and realm.

The marriage metaphor serves a purpose, or multiple purposes, in London as presumably in King's Lynn. In the same way that marriage is not a bond entered into by groom and bride alone but a social and economic undertaking which affects "not only two individuals but above all the collectivities to whom the maintenance of cohesion is important" (Van Gennep 120), a new mayor's union with the city has consequences for his municipal constituents. The unprecedented size and diversity of London, moreover, made the maintenance of social cohesion a project of vital importance – a project to which the annual Lord Mayor's Show contributed. Like the potential disruptive force of a new marriage on a previously established familial order, a change in the highest office of a community harbors the possibility of discord. To soothe tensions and render the change as smooth as possible, the Lord Mayor's Show incorporates not only the mayor into his new office and joins him to the city, ordinary spectators, too, are integrated into an idea of the city and made partners in a reciprocal bond. Hill's observation that "[i]n the civic arena 'self-fashioning' was on the whole more collective than individual" (Pageantry 19), endorses the integrative orientation of the mayoral entertainments. Some of these strategies of the Lord Mayor's Show – personification and, above all, incorporation – are also strongly discernible in the liturgy and entertainments pertaining to the feast of Corpus Christi. There is an argument to be made that the latter may in some crucial ways be a precursor to the former.

3.2 Collective Body Imagery in Corpus Christi Observances and the Lord Mayor's Show

Not only were the formal elements of the Lord Mayor's Show inherited, as Glynne Wickham points out, from the 'emblematic' theater of the middle ages, the allegorical utilization of the female body in the Lord Mayor's Show has antecedents in the late medieval Corpus Christi celebrations. Hill supports the hypothesis that "chief among the enabling factors of the Shows proper was the extant dramatic tradition of 'the medieval cycle drama' usually sponsored by the guilds" (Pageantry 37), although she does not further specify moments of influence or correspondence. Both types of festivity served as ritual occasions on which to formulate civic identity by means of incorporation into a collective body.[14] As an entity intimately familiar to the human mind, both as subject and object of perception and sensation, the human body of course constantly plays a part in the visualization and conceptualization of states and processes. Since the healthy body is a highly efficient unified organism, it is not surprising that it should frequently signify the synthesis of diverse elements or functions into a superordinated collectivity. The metaphor of incorporation into a single organic entity signifies coherence, harmony, and purpose in community. One instance of this type of conceptual incorporation is the way Christians may conceive of their interconnectedness as sharing in the body of the Church. Often, the church was – and is – not only represented as a collective entity made up of all communicants but is feminized and anthropomorphed into the bride of Christ, who presides over clergy and common worshipers alike as God, head, and husband.

Members of the Christian Church may not only envision their communal identity as constituted by incorporation into the body of the feminized church, they may also immerse themselves in the body of Christ himself by the ritual consumption of his flesh and blood in the sacrament of the Eucharist.[15] Corroborating the unifying potential of the sacrament, the *Sermo de corpore Christi* explains that even though the bread that is Christ's body is fragmented it nevertheless remains whole like the image reflected by a fractured mirror (Rubin 217). Accordingly, all who share in the sacrament and receive the host become absorbed into the composite but undivided body of Christ. The same concept – the creation of a complete picture from the various reflections of separate, fragmented mirrors – is utilized by Heywood in *Londini Speculum*. The show's name-giving pageant not only features personified Sight but also incorporates innumerable mirrors in its design. In William Hardin's analysis this leads to an effective merging of ideology and reality. The pageant moves through the city and as it does so its surroundings become a part of the pageant insofar as crowds and buildings are reflected in the mirrors: "That is to say, the mirrors provide a sort of emblematic *tabula rasa* that the City – its buildings, its crowds – literally fill so that they become part of the display." (Hardin 26-27) At the same time, the effect is analogous to the one outlined in the *Sermo de corpore Christi*. A collective image or entity takes shape from a multitude of separate elements and the effect is not free of ideological implications.

The image of the church as the body of Christ – with Christ simultaneously presiding over it as head (e.g. Col. 2:19 and 1:18, King James Bible: "And he is the head of the body, the church") – is of special importance to St Paul, formerly Saul of Tarsus, who influentially utilized the analogy in his address to the Corinthians (cf. Hicks 32). These Corinthians, Ruth Ilsley Hicks points out, were residents of "a cosmopolitan city, including in its population people from all parts of the Roman Empire" (ibid.). Like

---

[14] Lancashire attests to the "ritualized civic context of moral, social, and political expectations" inside of which the Lord Mayor's Show is set (330).

[15] Christina von Braun argues that a collective body is constituted by both spiritual and bodily components. A community based on shared beliefs is bolstered by motifs which emphasize the bodily reality of the superordinate social body. The ritual of holy communion achieves this affirmation of bodily reality: Consumption of the wine and wafer which represent the flesh and blood of Christ allows believers to merge simultaneously with God and the other members of the congregation (qtd. in Mazza 41).

London, it was also a port city. The metaphorical incorporation of its population into the body of Christ might therefore have appealed to St Paul as a means of imposing a collective identity on those who may have been hard pressed to find other common denominators.[16]

Corpus Christi festivities in honor of the Eucharist were held annually in England since the early fourteenth century and included mass, processions, and plays. While Rome required the annual reception of the Eucharistic sacrament of all its constituents, most English synods required a minimum of three communions a year (Rubin 218). When the Eucharistic articulation of identity became increasingly contested as a consequence of reformatory disputes over the nature of transubstantiation,[17] the notion of the civic body began to fill the void. As congregants shared in the body of Christ in the ritual reenactment of the Last Supper – and as church members are incorporated into the body of the Church – so the inhabitants of London and other urban centers could now conceive of themselves as elements swallowed up in the civic body of the personified city. Thus, following the substitution of church membership for citizenship in the wake of the disintegration of the Roman empire (Arendt 34), the articulation of communal identity came full circle as participation in the body of the church was re-translated into participation in the body of the realm or the city.

The trend is epitomized in the Lord Mayor's Show: it celebrated the personified city in its relations to mayor and residents and allowed all Londoners to experience a measure of unity in diversity by incorporation into one civic body. In the same fashion as Christ was styled husband of beatific New Jerusalem, London's lord mayor is transformed, with his inauguration, into both head and husband of London. In the book of Revelation (also known as the Apocalypse of John), the narrator asserts that "I John saw the holy city, the new Jerusalem, coming down from God out of heaven, prepared as a bride adorned for her husband" (21:2, King James Bible). The premise also features in the medieval hymn *Urbs Beata Jerusalem* which refers to Jerusalem as a bridal chamber or *thalamo* (Kipling, Enter the King 18-19).

Munday makes the analogy between London and "the holy city" explicit in *Chrysanaleia*: London becomes "England's Jerusalem", while Norfolk-born Mayor John Leman is likened to Jesus by his identification with the pelican, a long-established symbol of Christ.[18] There are antecedents to this scheme in royal pageantry: Gordon Kipling has

---

[16] Following St Paul's example, other Christian writers employed the metaphor. It is utilized by Augustine in *De Civitate Dei/City of God* and Origen of Alexandria's *Contra Celsum/Against Celsus* (Hicks 34).

[17] Cf. Thomas Cranmer's ridicule of a belief in 'real presence': "They say, that in the sacrament, the corporall membres of Christe be not distant in place, one from another, but that wheresoever the head is, there be the feete, and wheresoever the armes be, there be the legges, so that in every parte of the bread and wyne, is altogither (sic!), whole head, whole feete, whole fleshe, whole bloud, whole heart, whole lunges, whole brest, whole backe, and altogither whole, confused, and mixte withoute distinction or diversitie. O what a foolishe and an abominable invencion is this, to make of the most pure and perfect body of Christe, suche a confuse and monstrous body?" (qutd. in Read 13)

[18] Leman (1544-1632), though based in London, remained in close contact with East Anglia throughout his life and established a near monopoly in the cheese and butter trade (Ashton).

demonstrated how late medieval cities "imagined themselves transformed into another Zion, a celestial Jerusalem, whenever a king [as a type of Christ] made his ceremonial entry" (Enter the King 15).[19] In less auspicious literary and social contexts, too, London was likened to Jerusalem. In Dekker's plague pamphlet *The Wonderfull Yeare*, for instance, relating to the 1603 outbreak of 'the sickness' in the city, Dekker argues that "she [London] saw herselfe in better state then *Ierusalem* [...]" (34). Yet even Jerusalem can suffer and fall. As London is both spouse and mother to the lord mayor, so Jerusalem was "the very Nursery where the Prince of Heaven was brought up" (Dekker, The Seven Deadly Sinnes A2). Christ, monarch, and mayor are all understood to relate to cities in corresponding ways (and all cities are potentially Jerusalem).

The mechanisms of personification and ritual marriage, in the inaugural show, both naturalize the city as a coherent entity and justify the mayor's position of authority. In comparable fashion, the Eucharist became an important symbol in the political life of communities: Not only did it serve to naturalize communities by the notion of incorporation, it also legitimized powerful authorities: "Those using it wished to imply that the very same will which made God institute the eucharist and ordain its celebration also placed the monarch in his God-given position." (Rubin 259) Both, Lord Mayor's Show and Corpus Christi celebration, thus affirmed a well ordered universe, be it Christian or civic, in which a multiplicity of constituents held a share.

The feast of Corpus Christi initially spread from Liège to Rome and, via Avignon, developed into a universally accepted occasion in the Christian world in the early fourteenth century (Rubin 10). In 1316 Pope John XXII instituted the festival under Canon Law, calling for a mass as well as a procession to be enacted on the date (Craig 594-95). Corpus Christi plays, accompanying the festivities, were instituted in the late 14th and early 15th centuries all over England (ibid. 596). Elaborate cycle plays, however, seem to have originated in the north and east of England and to have been centered there (ibid. 590; Rubin 271).[20] Broadly speaking, Corpus Christi drama – staged between late May and late June – consisted of the open-air performance of biblical episodes in the vernacular, infused with local characteristics (ibid.). Craig sums up the nature of Corpus Christi plays thus:

> Corpus Christi plays were characterized, in the first place, by completeness of cyclical content. They extended from the Creation to Doomsday, and they included plays of the

---

[19] For example, in 1392 the reconciliation of Richard II with London (after the city had denied a loan to the monarch) was celebrated by means of a civic triumph (Kipling, Enter the King 12). The triumph saw "London progressively take[...] the form of the New Jerusalem" while Richard was "revealed as a type of Christ – the Anointed One, heavenly spouse, savior, and lord" (ibid. 17).

[20] Elaborate cycles survive from York, Chester, Wakefield, fragments from Coventry, Norwich, and Newcastle, as well as the East Anglian "N-town play" (Rubin 271). Cf. Craig: "What seems to have been done was to transfer to Corpus Christi day and to arrange, in the extensive cyclic form, plays already of considerable development." (598) Bergeron has argued that "[t]he Biblical influence [in the early Lord Mayor's Shows] probably reflects the continuing influence of the medieval dramatic forms, especially the cycle plays" (The Elizabethan Lord Mayor's Show 272).

Nativity, as well as of the Passion and Resurrection. They seem all to have been acted by craft guilds [...] and to have been [...] under municipal control. (594)

Specialized Corpus Christi societies existed but these did not commandeer complete control of the celebrations around the feast. In York, "the Corpus Christi guild gained the most coveted ceremonial role of carrying the shrine housing the host" in the procession but the cycle drama was in the hands of the manufacturing and mercantile guilds and even the "the procession continued to be a local civic affair, controlled by the mayor and city council of York, who most importantly decided the marching order of the participating crafts" (Rice and Pappano 48-49). Expenses for processions, pageants, and drama were levied from members of the organizing craft guilds (Rubin 241), which constituted "the most substantial administrative, economic and political unit[s] of late-medieval towns" (ibid. 238). These episodic performances of Christian history, from Genesis to Apocalypse, were still considered Corpus Christi drama even when they were moved to new dates – as happened in Chester, where the ceremonial calender was rescheduled so that the plays were staged on Whitsun/Pentecost (Craig 591).

The Last Supper was conceived of as the founding event of the sacrament of the Eucharist and, thus, of all Corpus Christi celebrations. Christ's declaration at the Last Supper that "[t]his is my body" is related in four canonical books of the Bible (Read 3).[21] As was the case for the Lord Mayor's Show, the "curious recent foundation" of the festivity had to be grounded "in a larger scheme of things" (Rubin 227).[22] The new occasion had to establish and defend its place in a Christian calender and within Christian narratives of sin and salvation. It did so by establishing itself in a long tradition of commemorating the Last Supper and by retroactively claiming a prestigious share in its own founding moment. Moreover, the feast was considered "a living eucharistic affirmation, not merely [...] a memorial" (ibid. 216), and the sacrament itself promised the salvation of the soul, provided one had not neglected to "prepare, repent and confess" in anticipation (ibid. 220). The processions and plays which became a part of Corpus Christi transformed the feast into a popular occasion: The festivities soon not only attracted townspeople but those living beyond the city walls and even further afield (ibid.

---

[21] Cf. Matt 26:26: "And as they were eating, Jesus took bread, and blessed it, and brake it, and gave it to the disciples, and said, Take, eat; this is my body." (King James Version); Mrk 14:22: "And as they did eat, Jesus took bread, and blessed, and brake it, and gave to them, and said, Take, eat: this is my body." (KJV); Luk 22:19: "And he took bread, and gave thanks, and brake it, and gave unto them, saying, This is my body which is given for you: this do in remembrance of me." (KJV); 1 Cor 11:24: "And when he had given thanks, he brake it, and said, Take, eat: this is my body, which is broken for you: this do in remembrance of me." (KJV) Rice and Pappano note that "for all of its history, the York cycle was, unlike the Chester cycle, a Corpus Christi performance, and thus the mythography of the Eucharist was central to its narrative and production." (ibid. 119) By "placing Christ's body at the very center of the Corpus Christi enterprise, the [York] guilds maintain that all members of the community partake in the sacred body that transcends base commercialism" (ibid. 132).

[22] The only processional model in England on which the Corpus Christi procession could draw was the Anglo-Norman Palm Sunday procession which ritually reenacted Christ's entering into Jerusalem (Rubin 244).

263-64). One consequence of the increased popularity of Corpus Christi and of the Eucharist itself – combined with the notion that even laying eyes on the sanctified wafer was beneficial – was a growing demand in the populace to be allowed to view the Eucharist (ibid. 289). Congregants began articulating their feeling that they, in fact, had a right to see the host and Walter Doget of Eastcheap, London, took matters into his own hand: In 1370 he tore a hole into the wall of his abode adjacent to the parish church of St Leonard's to be able to view the Eucharist itself and the Lord's Supper, as the *London Assize of Nuisance* reports (qtd. in Rubin 290). To Doget, his move would have seemed reasonable enough since, according to theories of vision current in his day – the theory of extromission and Roger Bacon's account of the "multiplication of species", – visual perception depended on emanations from objects themselves which entered the eye (Muir 137-38). Thus, seeing a sacred object was considered to have a genuinely beneficent impact on viewers. It was this understanding of sight which underlay "the reputed capacity of public processions to create social harmony" by means of "the radiation of beneficial species [...] throughout the troubled atmosphere of the community" (ibid. 130).

In a frequently quoted article on the function of Corpus Christi, Mervyn James argues for the unifying potential of the festivity, particularly by its utilization of body imagery and its focus on incorporation. To James, the late medieval and early modern Corpus Christi festivities allowed townspeople to view urban society as one organic whole comprised of multiple parts (4).[23] Not only the Corpus Christi procession itself enacted this type of social conciliation, the traditional cycle plays were also suitable vehicles for the expression of social cohesion since they represented the whole of history, beginning at the very beginning with Adam and Eve, in an episodic structure which ultimately cohered into one narrative (ibid. 15-16). Moreover, the material conditions of production – each affluent guild sponsored one pageant out of the total number – contributed to a theme of wholeness made up from a variety of parts. Precisely because the social ties of rural feudalism were of little importance in towns, the festival of Corpus Christi was most "elaborate" and "developed" there, as an alternative means of fostering communal solidarity (ibid. 4-5). With the Eucharist as the body of Christ, in which the faithful may share, and the mayor representing the head of the secular civic body, Corpus Christi utilized metaphors of body to uphold social bonds in an urban environment in which numerous self-interested social agents had to be accommodated (ibid. 11). In the wake of the Reformation the civic body steadily takes the place of the body of the church and the body of Christ: "under Protestantism, the Corpus Christi becomes the [secular] Body of the Realm; and urban rituals, like religious rituals, tend to become progressively secularized, privatized and monopolized by the magistracy" (ibid. 23). With the mayor still conceptualized as head, the body to be governed eventually became that of the personified City.

[23] Rice and Pappano confirm that "the York cycle has been subject to a range of critical interpretations drawn from the discipline of anthropology, models of ritual from Victor Turner and models of bodily organization from Mary Douglas, to connect the plays to the symbolism of Christ's body" (32), and that Mervyn James' article is "perhaps the most influential of these" (ibid.).

120

While there has been criticism of James's stance for being "overly rosy" (Clopper 100),[24] i.e. focusing too much on the unifying effects of the religious occasion, critical voices have so far failed to offer convincing alternative perspectives on Corpus Christi processions and drama in their relation to urban communities. Certainly, beyond the poles of civic harmony and civic strife from which Corpus Christi is frequently approached, there is no contradiction between the ritual enactment of urban harmony and the simultaneous existence of social conflicts. The latter, in fact, may necessitate the former. Rubin, too, disagrees with James's conception of Corpus Christi as a community-building event. She argues instead that performances reinforced hierarchies and social divisions and she rejects the community-affirming function of religious ritual in more general terms (2). At the same time, however, and somewhat contradicting her critical stance, she discusses the body as a unifying concept and states that Corpus Christi can be understood as "an integrative civic event" (269). James Knowles, on the other hand, emphatically approves of James's views on the processional unification of the body politic and the festivity's "symbolic resolution of the tensions between the guilds themselves and other sections of society" (158). Knowles does not mention Victor Turner but he does make the point – corresponding to Turner's communitas and structure dichotomy – that the Corpus Christi procession expressed both hierarchy and communal solidarity and that it did so by invoking the image of the human body, a unified organism in which different members and organs fulfill differentiated functions (ibid.). Knowles also regards the Corpus Christi procession as the legitimate forerunner of the Lord Mayor's Show (ibid.). Michael Berlin, too, achnowledges the integrative function of Corpus Christi and describes the festivities at Coventry as "bringing together social groups which might otherwise be divided and potentially in conflict with each other" (15).

The focal point of every Corpus Christi procession was, naturally, the Eucharist itself, inside a monstrance and surrounded by clerical and civic dignitaries (Rubin 251). It served as a heart and center around which different segments of society could both physically assemble and by reference to which they could ideologically cohere (ibid. 245-46). As the representative substitute of Christ himself and, therefore, the essence of the festivities, the Eucharist inside its display case was covered by a canopy. On the one hand, this highlighted the dignity and ritual potency of the Eucharist. On the other, the canopy transmitted some of the prestige associated with it to those urban dignitaries positioned beneath it and, thus, close to the vessel (ibid. 252). By the late 14th century most urban processions had come under the control of secular civic administrations (ibid. 248). Citizens marched "by crafts and in livery" (Craig 600), seeking thereby to express communal guild identity (Rubin 275). In the service of both self-identification and the assertion of their place inside a larger framework, some guilds additionally carried statues of their patron saints. While for lack of rank, lack of years, or lack of maleness not all congregants took part in the processions themselves (ibid. 266), they were nevertheless significant occasions for the showcasing of urban identity and order and, for many, to visibly claim a stake in this order. Like the Lord Mayor's Show procession, Corpus

---

[24] Sarah Beckwith, for example, criticizes Mervyn James for his interpretation of the plays as unifying. She believes they are indicative of various conflicts, primarily that between merchant and manufacturing guilds (qtd. in Clopper 100).

Christi parades were usually so structured as to end back in the place of setting out (Craig 600). Both also emphasized community – gathering members into one body – as well as hierarchy, arranging paraders in strict order of precedence and group affiliation. Children also participated in both Lord Mayor's Show and Corpus Christi parade, as actors and singers in pageants and simultaneously as "pre-political" beings who "symbolised that which was virtuous within the community" (Rubin 250-51). As the monstrance was carried out of the church and along the processional route, bells were rung, spectators gathered, and flags and garlands were displayed (ibid. 248-49). Bell ringers were sometimes given breakfast for their trouble (ibid.), a provision that was also frequently made for child actors participating in the Lord Mayor's Show.

One way in which the Corpus Christi procession was expected to be efficacious was in the host's favorable effect on the places it was brought into contact with, conforming to the theory of extromission. When the host was carried out of the sacred space of the church, its presence in the secular sphere was assumed to bring the sacredness connected to Christ's body into the city streets or, occasionally, even out onto the fields beyond the city walls (Rubin 247; Clermont-Ferrand 1161). A further function of the procession, albeit one less dependent on otherworldly agents, was the interconnection of various dissimilar locations. The paraders sewed "with a processional thread the periphery to the centre, the parishes to the cathedral, the suburbs to the market place" and centers of religious power to those of secular authority (Rubin 268). Processional routes were variable from city to city but never arbitrarily chosen. In York and Coventry, they followed the trajectory of the royal entry (Rubin 267), while in Chester the route linked the centers of sovereign, clerical, and civic power, weaving past castle, church, abbey, and administrative headquarters (Christie 143).[25] No elaborate cycles were developed in London but Corpus Christi was still celebrated in a variety of ways and places. The Corpus Christi fraternity of St Botolph's, Aldgate, probably staged pageants on the occasion of the feast (Rubin 238), and the Company of Skinners arranged the largest procession in the capital in the afternoon of Corpus Christi day from the mid-14th century until late into the 15th century (Craig 595). The paraders met at the company hall in Dungate Hill and proceeded to St Antholin's Church in Watling Street (Rubin 229-30). The procession, famously recorded by John Lydgate, focused on biblical providence and the prefiguration of current events in biblical episodes and featured numerous tableaux vivants (ibid. 229, 275). Although James argues that due to diminishing control over urban life by the guilds, the celebration of Corpus Christi ceased early in London, the Lord Mayor's Show actually took over many of the features and continued to fulfill many of the functions of Corpus Christi.[26] The Lord Mayor's Show is therefore heir to Corpus

---

[25] Cf. Christie: "The new route's performances in the city's major streets more firmly connected the plays to the city, emphasizing them as a reflection of civic identity." (143)

[26] Gordon Kipling regards the status of the civic triumph in London as equivalent to that of Corpus Christi cycles elsewhere (Triumphal Drama 37). He also asserts that royal entries "share a common dramatic heritage with the great religious dramas – the Continental Passion plays and the English Corpus Christi cycles – which sprang up throughout northern Europe at precisely the same period" (Enter the King 6-7), and that "[j]ust as late medieval Christians, as members of the Body of Christ, declared their devotion to their Lord in a Corpus Christi procession, so the

Christi ritual as much as it succeeded the Midsummer Watch, its immediate forerunner, which flourished in London until the mid-16th century.[27]

In cities like Chester and York, in the final decades of the 14th century, guild-produced cycle plays were becoming a part of the Corpus Christi celebrations alongside processions (ibid. 261). Like the church service, the plays, too, aimed at demonstrating Christian cosmology by referencing the creed's total teleology, from creation to revelation (Craig 599). In Chester, between ten and fourteen companies were involved in staging the plays (Christie 142). For congregants, service, procession, and plays all contributed to the feast of Corpus Christi and all aided in rendering their urban environment meaningful as a local expression of the divine plan. With the cycle plays, so Rice and Pappano, "local artisans not only displayed but also performed their status in the community" (18) and they did so by "embedd[ing] the biblical narrative in local culture" (ibid. 20).

The purpose of the cycle in York, argues Richard Homan, "(allowing that the historian can infer implicit purpose) was to preserve the balance of structure and communitas" (315).[28] Like the processions, the plays invoked a communal identity in which most city dwellers could share as Christians, without this negating established hierarchies. The cycle plays, realized by a communal organizational effort, and especially influenced by the Eucharist in York, sought to resolve social tensions not to amplify them. The engagement of all who made up the plays' diverse audience was actively solicited by music, song, or by evocative references to plebeian employments and more skilled labor (Rubin 284). Christie contends that non-specific allusions to labor in the Chester cycle served "as a generic sign of civic identity" (152), accessible to most audience members, and that they helped transform the stage action into a mirror for city and citizens (ibid. 152, 155). Rubin additionally mentions "dramatic techniques which broke down the distance between stage and spectator" as strategies to commit the audience to the proceedings (ibid.).[29] In Chester gifts, too, seem to have been distributed from the pageant stage during the Last Supper-episode put on by the Bakers, who had been instructed previously to "caste godes loues abroade with accustomed cherefull harte" (Late Banns qtd. in Christie 153).

---

same men received their newly crowned king as feudal lord" (ibid. 46-47). Medieval chroniclers confirm that the canopy held in place over the king parallels the baldachin sheltering the Eucharist/Christ in the Corpus Christi processions (ibid. 27).

[27] Cf. Berlin: "Midsummer had been the occasion for the structural integration of the different parts of the urban community." (18)

[28] In the second part of his essay Homan considers Turner's argument that ritual aims to resolve tensions, i.e. between incompatible principles that exist uneasily side by side in a given society (309). In York, Homan notes, the "distribution of political power among the guilds and groups of guilds is balanced to suggest representation of all, but in fact to concentrate power in the hands of the Mercers" (311). This dominance of the Mercers clashes with the principle of equal representation aspired to. Thus, the more democratic management of the cycle plays was an appeal to the commonality and a gesture of reconciliation designed to soothe tensions (Homan 311).

[29] Jane Oakshott confirms, from personal experience in reinacting episodic, processional drama, the format's potential to draw in an audience and to facilitate close contact with individual spectators (370).

One guild was normally appointed to prepare one pageant which would represent its members in the cycle but collaborations between guilds also occurred. Pageants and guilds were frequently matched by thematic correspondences between biblical episodes and the professions organized in a particular company (Rubin 278, Christie 144). In Coventry, the Pinners and Needlers presented the crucifixion and burial of Christ (Rubin 278), while in 1422 the Chester town council ordered the Ironmongers to nail Christ to the cross (ibid. 282). In York and Newcastle the Shipwrights produced the story of Noah, while the York Fishermen were tasked with staging the flood specifically (ibid.). In Beverley and Chester, it was the Watermen who furnished Noah's Ark (Craig 598). The Last Supper, with its breaking of bread, was re-enacted by the Bakers in York, Chester, and Beverley (Rubin 278, Craig 598). Whereas the Harrowing of Hell was assigned to the Cooks because, muses Craig, "we may suppose, they could handle fire" (598). Occasionally, companies were also co-opted to stage episodes which in some manner involved their patron saint (Craig 598). There was, thus, considerable intermingling of bible lore and present day, i.e. late medieval, narratives and circumstances.

The conception of "cycle plays as mirrors of contemporary life" is shared by V. A. Kolve, who argues that anachronisms in the plays helped the audience to envision themselves in the biblical episodes that were being presented to them (Christie 147-48). Yet, while according to Kolve these anachronisms themselves – the use of medieval technology, of fashion, or references to contemporary customs – were of secondary significance, Christie attributes central importance to them (ibid.). Homan, too, interprets them as meaningful, based on their effect: Not only do contemporary references compensate audiences for the comparative insignificance of their own status but they also prefigure their salvation (306). It is this which turns the plays into efficacious ritual (ibid.). Just as Old Testament events prefigure New Testament developments, episodes enacted in the cycle prefigure current and future events in the contemporary world. Thus, audiences were not only assured of their salvation but the act of watching the play actively contributed to achieving that salvation (Homan 305; 309). Practical reasons must also be considered, of course, for the proliferation of anachronistic elements but Homan makes a compelling argument nevertheless. In any case, the organization and content of the plays facilitated social cohesion in an urban, guild-dominated environment.

Corpus Christi festivities were certainly as much opportunities for the affirmation of civic identity as they were religious occasions – a core concern shared by the Lord Mayor's Show. In this vein, Anne Lancashire describes the function of street theater in general as "not only entertainment but also [as] a participatory ritual of civic affirmation, and/or of national politics" (323).[30] Both Lord Mayor's Show and Corpus Christi ceremonial and entertainment attempt to achieve social cohesion by envisioning urban society in terms of body: Central to the eponymous Corpus Christi celebrations was, of

---

[30] Lancashire defines the function of the Lord Mayor's Show as "the bringing together of civic London [...] in a communal act of honoring, celebrating, and promoting itself and its long-continuing civic institutions" (332). The attempt "to bring London into a harmonious whole, at least aesthetically and theatrically, and at least for the Show's duration" is strengthened by presenting "a model of the cohesiveness to which – at least from its rulers' viewpoint – the city should aspire" (ibid.).

course, the sacramental body of Christ while, in the Lord Mayor's Show, the body of the city becomes a protagonist, as it enters into a union of marriage with the lord mayor who is expected to care for and control his urban wife. The marriage of mayor and anthropomorphic city could be effortlessly superimposed on the template of Christ and his church since that relationship was commonly understood as an ideal model of spousal relations: "The Sonne of God so loved the soules of men, that hee would make them a wife, and marry them" (10-11), notes Francis Rous, while commenting on the *The Mysticall Marriage* (1631). In his "godlie" household guide Robert Cleaver admonishes husbands among his readership: "thy wife shall be unto thee as the Church, and though unto her as Christ: therefore thou shouldest shew they selfe unto her, as christ shewed himselfe unto his Church. The love of Christ unto his Church is incredible, and thy love also to thy wife ought to be most effectuall." (154) Elsewhere in his tome, Cleaver observes that a husband's duties toward his wife include discretion, absence of cruelty, and "that he love, cherish, and nourish his wife, even as his owne bodie, and as Christ loved the Church, and gave himself for it" (97).[31] The conception of the mayoralty as a (temporarily restricted) marriage universalized and justified London's civic administration. At the same time, just as the Corpus Christi processions and plays had facilitated symbolic integration into an urban and spiritual whole, the concept of the feminized City continued to do so by designating all city dwellers siblings and children of one mother.

3.3   The Unconquerable City and Female Matter

Transmitted via medieval literature and art to the European Renaissance, the tradition of gendered personification derives from the conventions of classical antiquity. In Demetrius' *On Style*, compiled around the first century AD, it is unambiguously announced that abstract concepts should be embodied in female figures (Paxson 152). Along the same lines, the first century BC *Rhetorica ad Herennium* had cited "the speaking female city" as the prime example of personification (ibid.).[32] This personified city, or "urbs invictissima," writes James Paxson, "is an impenetrated female body, one implying semantically that a female body, also by definition, is that which may be penetrated through a violent, masculine invasion" (ibid. 153). The early modern viability of the trope is demonstrated by Shakespeare, among others, who has Tarquin – in *The Rape of Lucrece* – formulate his assault on Lucrece as the conquest of a "never-conquer'd fort" by the "ram" of his hand against the "ivory wall" of her breast. His self-confessed plan "[t]o make the breach, and enter this sweet city", is a euphemism for violent sexual penetration. Supporting the importance of boundaries – and the threat of their breach – in

---

[31] George Webbe explains in *The Bride Royall, or, the Spiritual Marriage Between Christ and his Church* (1613): "The Churches marriage with Christ her Lord, is to the ioy and gladness of her heart begunne heere in this life, but perfected and consummated to her endlesse glory in the life to come." (64)

[32] There is not much information on the rhetoric of urban description in classical sources but Quintilian, for example, suggests to praise cities in the same way individuals are praised (Manley, Matron to Monster 354).

the definition of the city, Hannah Arendt has pointed out the original meaning of "urbs" as encirclement as well as the etymological affinity of "town" and German "Zaun", i.e. fence (431). The metaphorical embodiment of city or state, Arendt argues, was initially employed in the First Epistle to the Corinthians (Paul, 1 Cor. 12:12-27) and developed into a commonplace from there (54).[33] The Old Testament, meanwhile, presents an early instance of city personification: In the Book of Lamentations a voice asks of Jerusalem, defeated by Babylon: "How doth the city sit solitary that was full of people, how is she come as a widow, she that was great among the nations?" A city in a state of desolation is equated with a widow who has been deprived of the guidance and protection of a husband. Without protection the boundaries of the city will be breached. Without guidance no city can be "great among the nations". London, however, in the guiding hands of the annually installed mayor, is presented as a model of urban greatness. London's mirror, in *Londini Speculum*, shows "not alone what she [London] is, or once was, / But that the spacious Vniverse might see / In her, what their great Cities ought to be" (316). The urban splendor of feminized London can be directly attributed to the influence of the lord mayor, whose role as husband to the city requires him to act circumspectly, with all due "understanding and wisedome" toward the "weaker vessel", i.e. his wife (Cleaver 162).

This conception of territory as a feminine entity which needs to be protected and regulated in a manner comparable to the female body in patriarchal societies is echoed in Jacobean and Caroline Lord Mayor's Shows, as, for instance, when London – the "speaking female city" – notes in *The Triumphs of Truth*: "[W]ith what care and fear / Ought I to be o'erseen, to be kept clear?" (970) Feminized London herself acknowledges her need to be "kept" and overseen by the mayor, whose duty not only includes supervising and controlling the city's internal affairs but also extends to protecting her boundaries from hostile invasion. That it is necessary for the mayor to do so in order to avoid infiltration by unwanted forces of his walled city is confirmed in Heywood's *Londini Sinus Salutis* pamphlet, in which the author explains that "[i]t is one of Erasmus his undeniable Apothegms, that there is no Citie can bee so strongly immur'd or Defenc'd, but may bee either by Engins defaced, by Enemies invaded, or by Treason surprized; but the Counsells and Decrees of a wise Magistrate, are in-expugnable." (285) What is at stake is the body of the city. The civic, urban corpus has to be protected from the machines of war, from invasion, and treason but is incapable of protecting itself. The defense of the

---

[33] Arendt argues that "[t]he term *corpus rei publicae* is current in pre-Christian Latin, but has the connotation of the population inhabiting a *res publica*" while Greek "soma" is never used in a political sense (53). Ruth Ilsley Hicks, however, attributes to Plato "the earliest extant equation of state and human body" (30). She references *The Republic*. Here, Socrates argues that that city is the best "whose state is most like that of an individual man" (5.462c). Hicks aims to show in her paper that both the concept of the church as body of Christ and that of the state as collective body derive from a fable attributed to Aesop on "The Belly and the Members" which centers on "a quarrel between the stomach and the feet concerning their relative importance" (29).

urban body falls to Heywood's "wise Magistrate", i.e. to the lord mayor – a masculine governor in charge of a feminized city.[34]

The narrating voice of Munday explains in *Himatia-poleos* (written for the Drapers) that walls defend the city in a manner comparable to the protective function of clothes for the human body (B), while the city wall even becomes implicative of a 'chastity belt' in Middleton's *The Sun in Aries* in which the voice of the pamphlet narrator affirms, with reference to the Tower of Virtue pageant, that virtue (very much including chastity) is "as a brazen wall to a city or commonwealth" (1590).[35] Virtue safeguards the city but it is the mayor's duty to ensure that virtuous conduct prevails. Meanwhile, the actual city wall, while still "the strongest visual marker of the City" in the early 1600s (Hardin 18), had already lost its ability to demarcate absolute and definitive city boundaries (ibid.).[36] Not only the fact that houses were built up against the wall and, thus, obscured it from view, nor the rapid expansion of the suburbs were causing confusion, but so were conflicts over jurisdiction and over privileges previously exclusive to the inner sanctum of the City of London (ibid. 18, 23).[37] This 17th-century disorientation about the exact structure and shape of London is ingeniously reflected in cartographer William Morgan's choice to simply title his own map of inner city and extramural conglomerates "London Etc." (1681/2) (Glanville 82). Already in the first decade of the 17th century Dekker had personified London and Westminster voice the opinion that "wee are growne so like and everie day doe more and more so resemble each other that many who neuer knew us before, woulde sweare that we were all One" (The Dead Tearme F3). The cities not only appear like one urban area. They are also increasingly indistinguishable with regard to the vices practiced within them.

Complementary to – and interwoven with – the conception of a feminized city flourishing under the watchful eye of its "wise Magistrate", are the equations of the female with passive matter and of the male with form and motion, expressed in Plato's *Timaeus* and Aritotle's *De Generatione Animalium* (Teskey 297).[38] Plato's influential

---

[34]   In the "Epistle dedicatory" attached to his *Triumphs of Fame and Honour*, John Taylor confirms the mayor's function in keeping "[t]his citie (the Kings Chamber) [...] Cleane for his use, from foule pollution" (A4).

[35]   In Thomas Nashe's *The Unfortunate Traveller* narrator and protagonist Jack Wilton utilizes the same image when he asserts that the French city of "Turwin lost her maidenhead and opened her gates to more than Jane Tross did" when the English laid siege to it (210). Later in the narrative a rape is described using the same metaphor. The perpetrator, so Wilton, "used his knee as an iron ram to beat ope the two-leaved gate of her chastity" (ibid. 278).

[36]   In the words of Steven Mullaney, "[m]anifesting the authority of the city, London's ancient wall defined the community and proclaimed it, in a language of mortar and stone, to be an integral and coherent whole" (38). Beyond the walls, on the fringes of legitimate society, so Mullaney, all manner of liminal phenomena occur.

[37]   In particular, the New Incorporation of 1636 by which the freedom to trade freely in the suburbs could be bought against a fine to the crown irritated the city administration (Hardin 23).

[38]   Charlotte Witt and Lisa Shapiro emphasize that "matter and form are not equal partners in Aristotle's metaphysics; form is better than matter. And since hylomorphism [the belief that all objects are composed of matter and form] is the conceptual framework that underlies most of Aristotelian theory from metaphysics and philosophy of mind to biology and literary theory, it

127

mind/body distinction and his somatophobia are at the root of his misogyny in the *Dialogues* – since women are thought to be determined by their bodies –, while they also explain his more egalitarian stance in the *Republic* which invokes the equality of non-embodied souls (Spelman 117, 119).[39] The European Renaissance inherited this conception of woman as body and matter, man as spirit and form via Calcidius' translation of and commentary on the first part of the *Timaeus*[40] and Bernard Silvestris' 12th-century *Cosmographia* (also known as *De Mundi Universitate*), "which describes matter as a crude ancient mass which longs, against herself, to be united with form" (Teskey 302-03).[41] In Bernard's tome, Silva, matter, longs for form and for transformation into a better state by means of a masculine reagent (Ferrante 56-57). Yet, all the while she retains an obstinate "tendency to return to chaos" (ibid.). What prevents the universe from falling back into a state of confusion and darkness is only a continuous cycle of reproduction (ibid. 54-55), in which the tendential instability of matter is counterbalanced by the form-giving male principle. This gendered dichotomy of matter and form – and its relation to reproduction – was not only discussed on the pages of philosophical and religious tracts but was "built into medieval language, hence into medieval thought" (ibid. 6). Ferrante points out the significance of the fact that "the word mother, *mater*, contains in it the root of matter, *materia*" (ibid.). While women are associated with matter because they give birth, men are etymologically affiliated with virtue and strength: "The word virtue, *virtus*, is connected not only with *vis*, strength, but with *vir*, man" (ibid.). Thus, language itself bears testimony to the contrasting conceptions of what constitutes manhood and womanhood. The 17th century also retained a fluctuating degree of somatophobia: In 1631, Francis Rous writes of "gross and bodily Creatures" (4), gross because bodily, and asserts that, due to its obvious inferiority, "the bodie it selfe is to serve the soule" (4-5).

---

looks as if his supposedly universal and objective theories are gendered, and it looks as if his negative characterization of women tarnishes his philosophical theories." (n. pag.)

[39] On the constitution of soul and body, Anthony Nixon asserts that "the one is light, the other heavie. The one is a coelestiall fyre, the other colde and earthie: the one invisible, the other palpable [...]" (Dignitie 2). Value judgments are not far behind: "By the *Spirit*, wee tread the path to immortal happines. [...] By the *flesh* wee stray into the way of death, and misery" (ibid. 4). In Spenser's *The Fairie Queene* Alma's castle, representative of humankind, contains two types of 'proportion': "The one imperfect, mortall, foeminine" (circular) and "th' other immortall, perfect, masculine" (triangular) (book 2, canto 9, stanza 22). Furthermore, day is gendered male while night is assigned the female gender (book 3, canto 4, stanza 59-60).

[40] In neo-platonism, an on-going project was the conjunction of the *Timaeus* and the account of creation offered in Genesis (Ferrante 40). In a neo-platonic understanding, the process of creation consisted of the union of opposite elements (Ferrante 2). This allowed at least a more positive account of women than did biblical exegesis (ibid.).

[41] Cf. *The Fairie Queene*: "For in the wide wombe of the world there lyes, / In hatefull darknesse and in deepe horrore, / An huge eternall *Chaos*, which supplyes / The substances of natures fruitfull progenyes. // All things from thence doe their first being fetch, / And borrow matter, whereof they are made, / Which when as forme and feature it does ketch, / Becomes a bodie, and doth then invade / The state of life, out of the griesly shade." (book 3, canto 6, stanza 36-37)

128

An evocative illustration of the survival into Renaissance culture of the gendered matter/form binary is Theodor Galle's well-known engraving of Amerigo Vespucci's first encounter with personified America.[42] In Galle's vision America is a naked woman, reclining in a hammock, and thus expressing not only the alleged leisure of the pre-civilized human being but specifically the heavy passivity of her female state. Yet she reaches out toward the European discoverer as if, inspite of her heavy, material self, she longs "to be united with form" and to offer the landmass of her body to the masculine bearer of civilization. A discursive feminization of the continent was certainly opportune for those with vested interests in its exploration for resources and in establishing settlements since feminization equaled subordination and, further, denied the civilizations of native peoples.[43] Visual representations of personified countries or entire continents – in the guise of young women, generally full-bosomed, and well-proportioned – had circulated in Europe from at least the early 16th century.[44] Cesare Ripa's widely influential *Iconologia* (1603), for example, presented on its pages Asia, Africa, America, and Europe (as the foremost among them) – all costumed differently, but all physically attractive young women. Feminization and sexualization of territory is a discursive strategy also employed by Sir Walter Ralegh in *The Discoverie of the large, rich, and beautifull Empire of Guiana* (1596), in which he famously concludes that "Guiana is a countrey that hath yet her maydenhead". Ralegh's lieutenant, Laurence Keymis, shows himself equally eager to exhaust the graphic potential of the metaphor in *A Relation of the Second Voyage to Guiana*. Of the South American territory visited he has to say that "here whole shires of fruitfull rich grounds, lying now waste for want of people, do prostitute themselves unto us, like a faire and beautifull woman, in the pride and floure of desired yeeres" (qtd. in Montrose 18). Alexander Niccholes, in a 1615 treatise on marriage, plucks the metaphor from its colonial context and proves its relevance closer to home. On the choice of marrying a widow, which is generally to be advised against, Niccholes (flippantly misogynistic) notes: "The best is, though the worse for thee, they are navigable without difficulty, more passable than Virginia" (25).

---

[42] Certeau reads the engraving as the beginning of "a colonization of the body by the discourse of power" (232).

[43] An effort was made to discursively classify natives as dependents, justifying acts of violence against them as 'for their own good', just as the head of a family would be justified and even obligated to affirm his authority with violence if necessary (Perreault 74).

[44] Only personified Asia began to be portrayed as a (male) sultan from the second half of the 18th century onwards (Le Corbeiller 222).

Fig. 11: Amerigo Vespucci's discovery of America (engraving by Theodor Galle, ca. 1600, after Jan van der Straet), described by Michel de Certeau in *The Writing of History* as "an *inaugural* scene: after a moment of stupor, on this threshold dotted with colonnades of trees, the conqueror will write the body of the other and trace there his own history" (xxv) (emphasis mine). Image by courtesy of the Metropolitan Museum of Art (CC0).

As in the Guianas and elsewhere in the 'New World', so in Europe the equation of femininity and subordination was put to ideological use. In the words of William Hardin: "The 'feminization' of civic space was conducive to building ideologies of social domination and control [...]." (32) Neither was feminized territorial personification limited to the rhetoric of discovery and colonization.

The Ditchley Portrait of Queen Elizabeth I by Marcus Gheeraerts the Younger (ca. 1592) applies the metaphor strikingly to the Queen – but there are some snags. Commissioned by Sir Henry Lee to showcase his reconciliation with the monarch and her visit to his Oxfordshire estate – following an estrangement over Lee's open relationship with his mistress Anne Vavasour –, the painting shows Elizabeth standing on a map of Britain, her feet in Oxfordshire, with most of the island invisible under the sovereign's skirts (Weidle 44). The image confirms the queen's power over her territory and "suggests a mystical identification of the inviolate female body of the monarch [the 'virgin queen'] with the unbreached body of her land, at the same time that it affirms her distinctive role as the motherly protectress of her people" (Montrose 14).[45] Tensions and uncertainties accruing around the fact that a woman was, for the time being, head of the kingdom and thus fulfilling a traditionally masculine role echo in the Ditchley Portrait: in the painting, Elizabeth, a woman, becomes not only expressive of feminine matter but simultaneously of masculine form. The inviolate city of the *Rhetorica ad Herennium* is transformed into the inviolate realm in the queen's portrait and the queen becomes both the bodily matter of the realm and the authoritative figure protecting and shaping it. However, as elsewhere gender dichotomies were not swept away by a female sovereign, so the feminization of places and spaces and the gender conceptions inherent in the process accompanied and outlasted the Virgin Queen's reign.

Grammatical gender is identified as the principle reason for feminized personifications in Roman literature since most Latin and Greek abstract nouns are grammatically classified as feminine. Consequently, the advent of male personifications in the allegorical texts of medieval Europe is commonly understood as a result of "the decay of rigid gender structure" in the vernaculars (Paxson 159). James Paxson singles out *The Romance of the Rose*, the 13th-century French dream vision, as "the poem which seemed to open the floodgates for masculine personifications in later texts" (151), – a notable claim considering that French never lost its gender-based categorization of nouns. A grammatical explanation of the phenomenon is indeed insufficient according to Paxson (161), who cites the rhetorical figure of *antimeria*, – "whereby one can deform correct syntax or grammar in order to produce a solecism or creative 'error'" (ibid. 163) – as a stylistic possibility whereby the translation of grammatical gender into biological sex could have been easily circumvented. In further support of his argument Paxson points out that "personification already involves the radical suspension of fixed ontic categories such as bodily/abstract, human/non-human or living/non-living" (164). The opinion that the grammatical femininity of a class of nouns does not necessarily lead to their assumption of a female body when personified is shared by Joan Ferrante[46] and Gordon Teskey, the latter of whom believes that a grammatical explanation of the gender of personification is "at best a partial one" (Teskey 306).[47]

An association of femininity and (linguistic) ambiguity is connected to developments in the first century AD, when the assumption solidified that rhetoric finesse was by nature duplicitous since it involved a masking or embellishing of fact: "[P]lain speech gets 'dressed up' or 'mantled,' often to the detriment of the direct, the normal, the masculine, the healthy" (Paxson 166). At about the same time, Alexandrian Jewish philosopher Philo equated man with the rational mind, woman – the "unavoidable" origin of corruption –

---

[45] A depiction of London by Francis Delaram, dating from circa 1610, bears some slight resemblance to the Ditchley Portrait. It shows the city placed between the legs of a rearing horse astride of which sits James I (Manley, Matron to Monster 361).

[46] Ferrante argues that some words have masculine as well as feminine forms, as for example "animus" and "anima". In these cases, "the choice [of the gender of personification] may be determined by the qualities attributed to them" (37).

[47] Put forward as alternative models of explanation are the twin phenomena of misogyny and the supposed (pro)creative potential of women (Paxson 154-59), which could itself easily be integrated into sexist narratives.

with dream states and unreliable sensory perception (Bloch 14; Lévy n. pag.). Similarly, the *Glossa Ordinaria* – a high medieval commentary on scripture – defined man as "spiritus", i.e. the rational soul, woman as "anima", i.e. the lower soul and carnality (qtd. in Ferrante 17). Thus, the rationality of the conscious mind was vehemently gendered as masculine while its supposed opposite, the untamed irrationality of the unconscious mind, was firmly marked as feminine. Along the same lines, the classical trivium of language arts – grammar, logic, and rhetoric (the top three of the Seven Liberal Arts) – was split into the 'masculine' disciplines of grammar and logic (also *logos*), i.e. "the sciences of the true, respectively of rectitude of expression and of correct propositions", and the dubious 'feminine' discipline of rhetoric, an art increasingly laden down with associations of fancy and deceit (Bloch 17). The connotation of femininity and rhetoric, both always suspected of harboring and disseminating half-truths and lies, was perpetuated by later church fathers. That personified Truth could simultaneously assume the physical shape of a woman is partly explicable when considering idealization as the obverse side of medieval misogyny.[48] Hatred of women in combination with this type of idealization is detectable in Gregory's late 6th-century *Magna Moralia* where Wisdom assumes the shape of a woman (Ferrante 21), as does Philosophy in Boethius' sixth-century *De Consolatione Philosophiae*. Yet, Wisdom-the-woman can only communicate with men since her fellow women are not receptive to her excellent qualities (qtd. in Ferrante 21). The duplicity and inconstancy of womankind are topics of a famous diatribe by Andreas Capellanus. Whether his words are inflected with irony or not, Capellanus voices common tropes in his 12th-century *The Art of Courtly Love* (*De amore*), written at the behest of Marie of Champagne:

> No woman can make you such a firm promise that she will not change her mind about the matter in a few minutes [...]. Woman is by nature a slanderer of other women, greedy, a slave to her belly, inconstant, fickle in her speech [...] a liar, a drunkard, a babbler, no keeper of secrets. [...] Even for a trifle a woman will swear falsely. [...] Every woman is also loud-mouthed [...] (204, 201, 207; qtd. in Bloch 18).

Capellanus disparages the alleged duplicity of woman but also her lack of self-control, which he sees as the result of the degree to which she is determined by her body – "a slave to her belly". Control must therefore be supplied by an outside source: a source that is necessarily masculine. Gregory's *Moralia*, too, posited that women were weak and changeable, possessed of fickle minds (qtd. in Ferrante 20-21). The masculine mind, on the other hand, was thought stout and steady (ibid.). Akin to Capellanus' stance on the bodily contamination of woman, Thomas Aquinas made the claim that women were related to matter because their sole purpose was to bear children, whereas men also had other functions in the world (qtd. in Ferrante 104).[49]

---

[48] This misogyny took a turn for the worse, argues Simone de Beauvoir, in the 11th century after Pope Gregory VII made celibacy mandatory for priests (126).

[49] The claim is taken up by Beauvoir who argues that motherhood ties a woman to her body like an animal while men are able to transcend their bodies (e.g. 91). Despite arguing against simplistic biological arguments that seek to subordinate women, Beauvoir still affirms that biology plays a significant role in determining gender relations. She sees woman as bound and

This understanding of women as defined by body, of men as defined by superior rationality, is discernible in Middleton's *Triumphs of Health and Prosperity*, in which personified Government equates London with the heart in the 'body' of the realm (1905). Opposite the feminized heart of Britain, the monarch is identified as the head of the state. On a superordinate plain, the monarch is responsible for guiding and controlling the body of the realm according to the masculine qualities of sense and rationality. In London that function is fulfilled by the mayor. The heart, Government tells the mayor, is the "fountain of the body's heat" (ibid.) and an important source of material sustenance for the entire body. Thus, the mayor must take good care of the city and guide it well for the benefit of the body of the realm. He must do so as a husband vis-a-vis his wife since, as Robert Cleaver explains in his household manual, women must accept their husbands "for heads and governours" (235).

Articulating a similar conception of London's essential role in the wider kingdom, John Stow describes London in his *Survey* as dispersing "forraine Wares, (as the stomacke doth meat) to all the members most commodiously" (2: 212).[50] Both heart and stomach sustain life but a rational head still needs to guide the living body. At the same time, heart and stomach are organs which feature regularly in metaphors conveying emotional states across a variety of cultures. A dichotomy of metaphors involving head and heart and describing conceptually opposite states is certainly deeply rooted in the English language: The head has signified rationality and the capacity for insight and thought since the 1300s (Swan 46), while the heart has developed from communicating the love of god and generosity in Old English to signifying all emotion, including romantic love (ibid. 46, 69). It is no surprise, therefore, that London – personified as a woman – is identified with the heart or, more generally, those organs associated with emotional states, while the head stands for mayor and monarch.

The analogy of the roles of mayor and monarch vis-a-vis their personified domains, as husbands and as heads presiding over bodies, becomes apparent in a song penned by Dekker for recital at the Nova Felix Arabia arch which James I encountered on his coronation entry into and through the City of London. The song described the city as a summer arbor and a bridal chamber for the newly wed king and his bridal kingdom (McLuskie 76-77).[51] Akin to the marriage of mayor and city in the Lord Mayor's Show,

---

determined by her body to a much stronger degree than her male counterpart (e.g. 91). Man is at liberty to define himself as a free individual while woman, due to her biology, cannot conceive of herself as a free agent in the world, capable of making autonomous decisions. Moreover, the female organism is allegedly more prone to physical and psychological disturbances due to menstruation (Beauvoir 56; 59).

[50]   In Shakespeare's *Coriolanus,* Menenius Agrippa applies "a pretty tale" (I.1.74), i.e. a version of the fable of the belly and the members, to the citizens' rebellion against the senators. In Menenius's story the stomach (representative of the senators) tells the discontented body parts that, "I am the storehouse and the shop / Of the whole body. But, if you do remember / I send it through the rivers of your blood" to the other body parts in 'fair' proportion (I.1.116-18). What Erasmus calls "a silly, ridiculous story", to its ambiguous credit, (The Praise 52), Stephen Greenblatt describes as a "fanciful apologia for elite consumption" (Tyrant 161).

[51]   That the roles of sovereign and mayor are hierarchically ranked but analogous is implied, too, by the character of Pythogoras in *Londini Speculum*: Addressing the new mayor in St Paul's

the king's procession is referred to by Dekker as the celebration of his union with the country, while London becomes the location of these nuptials. As husbands to their respective realms, both monarch and mayor assume the function of heads guiding bodies. Robert Cleaver expresses the accepted correlation between head and husband in his manual on household morals: A good husband should oversee his wife and the rest of the household "even as the government and conduct of everything resteth in the head, not in the bodie" (225). Elsewhere Cleaver declares: "For like as the head seeth and heareth for the whole bodie, and giveth it strength of life: or as Christ doth defend, teach and preserve his Church, and is the Saviour, comfort, eye, heart, wisedome, and guide thereof: even so must the husband bee head unto his wife" (174).[52] Cleaver not only equates the husband's role opposite his wife with that of the head opposite the body but also with that of Christ in relation to the church, traditionally envisioned as woman and bride.[53]

In his description of the city as a bridal chamber Dekker may have been inspired by the title of 'king's chamber' supposedly borne by London since 'time immemorial', before legal memory, i.e. any time prior to 1189 according to the 1275 Statute of Westminster. During his coronation entry into London, James I had not only been confronted with an interpretation of the city as a bridal chamber, at the triumphal arch titled Nova Felix Arabia,[54] he had also encountered the motto "Londinium, Camera Regia" (London, chamber of the king), inscribed onto the triumphal arch at Fenchurch Street (Liddy 327). The chamber as a concept to articulate and influence relations between town and crown, regarding finance and privilege, emerged in late medieval London and was subsequently also employed in York and Coventry. In courtly terms, the phrase "king's chamber" could refer both to the sovereign's bedchamber as well as to his personal finances (Liddy 326). Thus, the appropriation of the phrase by city magistrates had a dimension of privilege as well as one of duty. The physical proximity to the monarch implied by access to his chamber could be translated into civic prerogatives, whereas the financial implication of the expression hinted at the duties of the city toward the monarch. Although "king's chamber" or "cameria regia" was never actually a formalized title, it was assumed to be such by many, including historian William Camden and playwright Ben Jonson (Liddy 324, 327). The label of proximity to the king, constituted

---

Churchyard, Pythagoras refers to the monarch's power, "[a]nd yours [the mayor's] benath Him" (312).

[52] Cleaver takes the analogy up again to express the duty of both husband and wife to stay loyal to one another, even in unfavorable circumstances: "Let not the bodie complaine of the head, albeit it have but one eye: neither the head of the body, albeit it be crooked or mishapen" (192).

[53] Personified London, acting as the prologue to Robert Wilson's *The Pleasant and Stately Morall of the three Lordes and three Ladies of London* notes that "thus the Lord [God] dooth London guard, / Not for my sake, but for his owne Delight: / for all in vaine the Centonels watch and ward, / Except he keepe the Citie day and night" (A3). God's function is here formulated in a manner akin to that of the mayor: to watch over the city and patrol its limits.

[54] In 1392 Richard II entered into London to be reconciled with the city following disputes over financial aids to the crown and disorder among residents. In this royal entry the citizens of London were portrayed collectively as a chastened bride while the monarch became the relenting bridegroom (Liddy 333). London itself was presented as bridal chamber on this occasion, too (ibid.).

by the phrase, was also regularly utilized in the Lord Mayor's Shows and the corresponding pamphlets. Here, too, it expressed a relationship characterized by special intimacy, privilege and duty. At the same time, the use of the phrase assisted the conception of mayor and monarch as equivalent in their respective spheres by the related formulation of the mayor's function as the king's substitute in the latter's royal chamber of London.

Having considered classical antecedents, grammatical explanations and the gendering of matter and form as bases for the gender of personification, an examination of the historical connection that European culture has established between metaphor and woman may shed some additional light on the phenomenon. It is woman's attributed "otherness and her relational and mediational importance in men's lives" which forge an association with metaphor since "otherness, mediation, and relation characterize the role of metaphor in language and thought" (Kittay 63). In the beginning, Genesis gives an account of the creation of mankind which equals the creation of man, while woman's entrance into existence is a secondary one – secondary both in time, as well as in function and worth. Initially Adam presides over all animals and it falls to him to name them. When Eve is created out of his rib, she is created as his subordinate, his helpmate and, like one of the animals, he names her too (like the Trojan Brute names Britain, like Amerigo Vespucci's name is imprinted on America). Language and woman are thus deeply entangled from the onset of history, as outlined in the Bible:

> woman, created from man, is conceived from the beginning to be secondary, a supplement. Here the act of naming takes on added significance. For the imposition of names and the creation of woman are not only simultaneous but analogous gestures thoroughly implicated in each other. (Bloch 10)

Language and woman co-occur in the Old Testament and just as signs are secondary to their referents, woman is secondary to man: "Woman's supervenient nature is, above all, indistinguishable from that of all signs in relation to the signified and of representation." (Bloch 11) After the fall, Adam and Eve are "exiled into a world of indirect knowledge" (Jager 232), where language and the ambiguities of representation – removed from God and direct knowledge and communication – are now their lot. This is a "result of the primal transgression and [...] a sign of exile from God's presence in the Garden" (Jager 229), which also makes it a consequence of Eve's very existence.[55]

---

[55] Jager notes that "the writing of history and the history of writing both begin with the Fall" (249): "Sin [...] generates writing." (ibid. 233) Although Eve is sometimes associated with writing, more commonly medieval thought construed writing (stable and authoritative) as masculine and speech (unstable and fleeting) as feminine (ibid. 239). In a brief piece on the practicability of a universal language classics scholar Graves Hayden Thompson discusses the association of language and women in droll terms that betray the casual misogyny of his time. Thomson asserts that "[u]ntil Eve was created, there was no language problem. In fact, there was no problem at all." (215) Language became necessary once Eve entered into existence: "This is not because, where there are two people, there must be language. It is because, where there is a woman and one other person, there must be language. [...] The woman took to the language business quite readily, and soon was engaged in interesting conversation with a serpent, undoubtedly a Progressive Educationist." (ibid. 215-16)

In Christian discourse, woman, then, relates to man as signs relate to referents and as metaphor relates to the literal – notwithstanding the metaphorical propensity of all language. By the mode of her creation, subordinate to Adam and born in a way that is not literally feasible, Eve signifies allegory and metaphor (irrespective of the feasibility of Adam's arrival on the scene). Bloch words it thus: "the creation of woman is synonymous with the creation of metaphor, the relation between Adam and Eve is the relation of the proper to the figural, which implies always derivation, deflection, denaturing" (Bloch 11). With Adam identified with the "proper" and Eve classified as unnatural, authenticity becomes a masculine quality whereas its antonym, inauthenticity, is feminized. The alleged inauthenticity of women, evident not only in the depth of their being but also in their surface appearance, is further considered by Bloch:

> This link between the derivative nature of the female and that of figural representation itself explains why the great misogynistic writers of the first centuries of Christianity – Paul, Tertullian, John Chrysostom, Philo, Jerome – were so obsessed by the relation of women to decoration, why they themselves were so fascinated by veils, jewels, makeup, hair style and color – in short, by anything having to do with the cosmetic. (11)

Decoration, as a state of being and as a practice, is assigned the feminine gender because decoration, woman, and metaphor are categorized alike: as secondary, derivative, inauthentic. In the words of Tertullian, "[w]hatever is born is the work of God," while "[w]hatever is plastered on is the devil's work" (qtd. in Bloch 13). The second-century theologian is open in his distaste for decoration and his hostility toward "the devil's work" easily extends to reflect negatively on the nature of women. Thomas Aquinas echoes this rejection of ornamentation intermixed with earnest misogyny, alleging that women "like to adorn themselves outside because they lack inner, spiritual beauty, and they lack inner beauty because that comes only when all things are ordered and disposed by reason, in which women are defective" (1 Tim., ch. II, lect. Ii, qtd. in Ferrante 101-02).[56] In Thomas Dekker's *The Seven Deadly Sinnes* of London it is women and fools who are enthralled by apish and superifical fashion (32).

While the gender of most personifications had long been feminine, now, the personification of personification also became a woman: "Personification as a concept (and itself personified) could be thought of as having the gendered qualities of the feminine" (Paxson 157). Eve, as mentioned above, was discursively interwoven with metaphor and second-century Christian scholar Tertullian described Eve explicitly as *janua*, a threshold or gateway: "This turns out to be a tacit way of signifying the *limen* or margin of that which is inside and that which is outside; *janua* means the very idea of insides versus outsides. Like Janus Bifrons, the old Roman *genius* of the threshold who faces two opposite ways" (ibid. 170). Eve can serve as metaphor and threshold because both concepts hinge on a discrepancy, the former between what is stated on the surface and what is referred to, or source and target of the metaphor, the latter between insides and outsides. Because ambiguity is attributed to woman, she can be turned into a "figural

---

[56] Beauvoir contends that ornamentation, while a diverse phenomenon, often assists the transformation of a woman into an idol (214).

or semiotic proxy" or "the figure for figure" (ibid. 171). In Beauvoir's opinion, personifications are traditionally feminized because woman has historically been perceived as a visible symbol of alterity (237). That belief, too, emphasizes 'difference' which associates women with gateways, the antithesis of inside versus outside, familiar versus other, and the possibility of passage between the two. In the same spirit, in folk tales and literature, a person undertaking a journey – a passenger – frequently obtains the key to an alien territory from a woman (Beauvoir 236).

The function of woman in Christian mysticism was also explicitly that of gateway or of mediator between disparate spheres.[57] The ideal woman, Mary, virgin and mother of God, was conceived of as an intercessor on behalf of man, a mediator through whom the worldly and divine spheres could communicate (Ferrante 100). In *De Assuntione* (BVM, VI, ix) 13th-century Franciscan theologian Bonaventure affirms his belief that it is only through Mary that any human being can reach Christ (qtd. in Ferrante 107-08). Moreover, he argues that part of man is inherently feminine and that it is this part which is most receptive to God. Underlining the function of woman as limen, Bonaventure also characterizes the soul as bride, daughter, sister, or beloved of God in *Vitis Mystica* (III, 5) and *Itinerarium Mentis in Deum* (IV, 8) (qtd. in Ferrante 106). The Virgin Mary also served as mediator between God and his human substitute on earth in a pageant in York in 1486, coming down from heaven for the sake of Henry VII and presenting the monarch with God's blessings (Kipling 47). In Lord Mayor's Shows, too, one finds two-faced geniuses of the threshold residing on pageant stages, feminized mediators between the spheres. These constitute the feminized limen of physical reality and transcendental civic ideology. The main pageant set in *Porta Pietatis*, for example, is the eponymous Gate of Piety; the goddess of the gate is personified Piety herself. At the climax of the show, the mayor is brought into communion with Piety and through her person he has access to transcendental qualities which sanction his position and justify the social order in the city. Ritual portals or thresholds frequently have to be passed by the itinerants in rites of passage (Van Gennep 21),[58] and, in time, the 'guardians' of these thresholds may come to overshadow the actual portals and the itinerant's passage through them: "The act of passing no longer accomplishes the passage; a personified power insures it through spiritual means" (ibid. 22). Correspondingly, London's lord mayor achieves a new status not by passing through a physical portal but by being brought into communion with a character who has incorporated the 'portal', a guardian of the threshold who has become the threshold. In this way, the actual passage through a portal is substituted by a metaphorical union or even marriage.

Marriage symbolism already had a place in 16th-century Lord Mayor's Shows, as when personified London, in the guise of a "lovely Lady", played by a child actor, was entrusted to the mayor's care in George Peele's 1585 production (qtd. in Lancashire, Comedy 4-5; Chambers 563), which not only "marks the beginning of a long and fruitful association of well-known dramatists with the mayoralty shows" but is also the first show

---

[57] See also Beauvoir's comments on this major tenet of medieval mysticism in *The Second Sex* (131).

[58] A threshold rite, according to Van Gennep, would also have been the original basis for the construction of Roman triumphal arches (21).

for which a textual record survives (Bergeron, The Elizabethan Lord Mayor's Show 269).[59] Anne Lancashire detects a "continuing thematic preoccupation" with love in these early shows (Lancashire, Comedy 4), and elsewhere argues that Shakespeare's romances and the Lord Mayor's Show "had a goal in common: the achievement of reconciliation and integration, in part through the magic of ceremonial spectacle and ritual" (335). This preoccupation with love not only serves the Lord Mayor's Show as an inclusive civic celebration, it also interlinks with the marriage metaphor that is so dominant in a majority of later shows. The "sociopolitical love" (ibid.) of Lancashire's description is easily translated into matrimonial love and back again. In the first decades of the 17th century the most explicit formulation of the marriage metaphor suffuses Munday's *Chrysanaleia*, which takes advantage of incoming mayor John Leman's status as a bachelor in the company of Fishmongers. Leman's bachelorhood is punningly translated, in the course of the festivities, into a matrimonial union with the personified City. Early in the show Leman's transitional experience from company bachelor to a husband of the city is voiced by the character of William Walworth, who has been resurrected on the spot by the genius of the city in honor of the occasion.[60] Walworth addresses Leman in the following way:

> The Genius speaks you in mine eare, / A Mayden-man, a Batcheler. / You being the second, let me say, / This is a blessed marriage day / Of you to that great dignity [...] / No doubt, but your chaste thoughts and life / Will be as chaste to such a wife. / All happy blessings crowne (I pray,) / Londons and Lemans wedding day. (C)

Walworth highlights Leman's position as company bachelor and alludes to the fact – further expounded in the margin of Munday's pamphlet – that Leman was only the second person in recorded history who had not been admitted to the livery of a company at the time of his election to the office of mayor. He goes on to liken Leman's inauguration to a marital union with his new office – "This is a blessed marriage day / Of you to that great dignity" –, before explicitly equating the mayor's rite of passage with his marriage to personified London: "All happy blessings crowne (I pray,) / Londons and Lemans wedding day". The Lord Mayor's Show, in turn, is transformed into the wedding celebrations for London, the bride, and John Leman, the groom. Later in the day Walworth is presented to the new mayor and his entourage again. Stationed near the Little Conduit, the former mayor calls Leman a "blessed Bacheler" and links his own life to Leman's by declaring: "As Walworth then, so Leman now may saye / Neuer had Man a happier Wedding day." (C4) The day's pageants and processions are here again presented as wedding festivities while Walworth establishes himself as a previous husband to the city. By Walworth's own admission – "As Walworth then, so Leman now", – it is not

---

[59] Bergeron notes that the pamphlet, titled plainly *The Device of the Pageant Borne before Wolstan Dixi*, "contains only the speeches, no type of description as became common in the Stuart era. The entertainment includes characters impersonating London (The Elizabethan Lord Mayor's Show 275-76).

[60] Unlike the city personification, the genius of the place is represented as a masculine personage. Parallel to this gendering, in 12th-century theologian Alanus de Insulis' *De Planctu*, Genius features as Nature's son and her alter ego, who gives form to matter (qtd. in Ferrante 61).

138

only 'bachelors' who enter into a nuptial arrangement with the city upon their inauguration but each lord mayor in the history of the venerable office, in his turn, is betrothed to London, and the feminized city is placed into his care. At the end of the day, Walworth addresses Leman – "Our Mayden Bridegroome" (C4) – one final time:

> Your marriage Rites solemnized / Bequeathes you to the Bridall bed: / Where you and your chaste wife must rest. / London (it seemes) did like you best, / (Although you are a Bacheler,) / To be her Husband for a yeere; / Loue her, delight her. Shee's a Bride, / Nere slept by such a Husbands side / But once before. She hath had many. / And you may proue as good as any / Haue gone before you in this place. (C4)

Walworth refers to the day's proceedings as Leman's "marriage Rites". Specifically, the oath of office lends itself to being interpreted in terms of a wedding vow, as a promise elicited from the mayor to care for but also to control the city now officially entrusted to him. For Francis Parlett, too, the mayoral oath is a "sacrament of matrimony without which you and the town cannot be joined together in marriage", as he explains in his 1632 speech in honor of the mayor of King's Lynn (qtd. in Patterson 169).[61]

The pageantry, banquet, and church service which follow the oath-taking all constitute a part of the metaphorical wedding celebrations. These take place in view of the public in the streets, among a select group of dignitaries in the Guildhall, and before the eyes of God in St Paul's Cathedral respectively. Walworth informs Leman in his farewell speech that, with the festivities past, the mayor now has leave to retire to his "Bridall bed" in which London awaits her "Husband for a yeere", there to be loved and delighted by him. Relishing the sexual innuendo, Walworth makes a point of referring to the personified City as a "chaste wife" in the "Bridall bed", which establishes London as a direct descendant of the *Rhetorica ad Herennium's* unconquerable city. According to Walworth it is the City herself who chose Leman as her husband for a year, despite the fact that Leman had not yet ascended to the livery of the Fishmongers. London is thereby given a mystical agency which is somehow at odds with the ordinary passivity of the feminized city. Nevertheless, once chosen, Leman is not only the City's "Virgin Husband", he is also "Londons Lord" (C4) and, as such, he takes his place in a chain of previous 'husbands'.

Middleton's *Triumphs of Love and Antiquity* opens with anthropomorphic Love – i.e. a personification of "the love of the city to his lordship" – who salutes Mayor William Cokayne and proclaims: "Desert and love will be well matched today. / And herein the great'st pity will appear, / This match can last no longer than a year" (1399). Personified Love declares that the mayor's credentials are such that he is truly deserving of "the love of the city" and goes on to lament the temporal restriction placed on the union of mayor

---

[61] Patterson stresses the early modern significance of oath-taking: "Not just mayors and aldermen, but all freemen – in some towns, a fair portion of the male population – entered a relationship with the town through oath-taking." (170) This also lend oath-taking to satirical undermining. The celebration of the mayor's oath in the Lord Mayor's Show is a far cry from, for example, Dekker's satirical conclusion that "Oathes are Crutches, upon which Lyes (like lame soldiers) go" (The Seven Deadly Sinnes 15).

and city. Just as Munday explicitly couples London and John Leman, Middleton is un-ambiguous in his use of the marriage metaphor: Mayor and city enter into a love match predetermined to last twelve months. In his brief introduction to *Triumphs of Love and Antiquity*, Lawrence Manley points out "[t]he pageant's underlying spousal tropes" (1397) but does not examine these and their possible implications any further. The show, certainly, thrives on these tropes and Middleton playfully draws on the associated semantic fields when he notes that, early on the day of the show, expectation is "big with the joy of the day" (1399). By invoking an image of pregnancy, Middleton alludes to the desirability of increase from any matrimonial match, including that of mayor and city. The pregnant city, the city giving birth, the city as mother to its many and varied population: All of these images of personified London are encountered in 17th-century Lord Mayor's Shows. All of them, too, create a link between a thriving civic community and physical fecundity, the profitable ability of a body – even the feminized civic body – to produce more bodies.[62] Love's parting words to Cokayne are the following: "You are by this the city's bridegroom proved, / And she stands wedded to her best beloved: / Then be, according to your morning vows, / A careful husband to a loving spouse" (1403). One final time the marriage of mayor and city is explicitly referenced as personified Love not only concludes that Cokayne is "the city's bridegroom" but also equates his oath of office, i.e. his "morning vows", with wedding vows. The mayor now has twelve months ahead of him in which to exercise his duty of care toward the City while his "loving spouse" is expected to answer to that care. The same duties awaited James Pemberton in 1611. In Munday's *Chruso-thriambos*, written that year for the Goldsmiths, resurrected mayor Nicholas Faringdon tells the incoming mayor to "[h]onour London with your care, / Study still for her welfare" (C). In exchange for Pemberton's efforts, London is bound to feel honored to be the recipient of his care and to respond appropriately. In the commemorative pamphlet for the show, Munday-the-narrator feminizes the city by speaking of "*her* worthy Consuls and Magistrates" (emphasis mine) (A3).

Similar to William Cokayne's "morning vows" in *Triumphs of Love and Antiquity*, the mayor's oath of office in Middleton's *Triumphs of Truth* is translated into a wedding vow by the Angel of Truth, who refers to the oath as "a marriage before heaven and men, / Thy faith being wed to honour" (970).[63] The celebrations that follow the oath-taking are then turned into wedding celebrations for both Cokayne and the new mayor of 1613, Thomas Myddleton (no relation to the playwright and pageant author). Thus, when Sheila Williams takes notice of Munday's own comparison between the candle-lit part of the Lord Mayor's Show and a wedding masque (504), in his *Metropolis Coronata* pamphlet, she comes close to the essence of the Lord Mayor's Show. Indeed, the concept of a special union is intrinsic to the Lord Mayor's Show: the city as a woman is joined to the mayor as her husband. The analogy bolsters the mayor's authority by reference to the sanctity of

---

62   In the prologue to Robert Wilson's *The Pleasant and Stately Morall of the three Lordes and three Ladies of London* (1590) personified London refers to the eponymous lords and ladies as her "increase" and "fruit" (A3).

63   Further drawing on the semantic field of matrimony, personified London tells the mayor at the end of the day that, having been present in the morning and joined in the celebrations, she also wants to be with the mayor at night: "Marrying to one joy both thy day and night".

married life and the hierarchical reciprocity of the masculine and feminine spheres. In *Monuments of Honour* London appears as a resplendent bride, although initially confused with Venice by Thetis, who marvels: "Sure this is Venice, and the day Saint Marke / In which the Duke and Senats their course hold / To wed our Empire with a Ring of Gold."

In *Triumphs of Truth*, Myddleton encounters personified London, too, but it is anthropomorphic Truth who shares in the spousal trope to a significant degree and exhibits many qualities of a spiritual bride. She tells Myddleton that, unbeknownst to him, she has long been by his side and that she hopes that he will remain devoted to her for as long as he is in office and even beyond (972). Truth is soon assured of the mayor's loyalty by "a blessed yielding" (ibid.) in his eyes, which leads her to affirm: "Thou'rt mine; lead on, thy name shall never die" (ibid.). Her mystic power asserts itself by her use of the possessive but while Truth claims Myddleton as her own, it is the mayor who is to "lead on", both metaphorically and literally in the festive parade. The immortality Truth promises to Myddleton is the reputation that comes from having served as lord mayor of London and which connects Myddleton to a long line of previous civic dignitaries – all, in their turn, betrothed to the City. In *The Triumphs of Truth*, Truth is an important aspect of the City: a virtuous concept which is supposed to dominate life under the jurisdiction of the Court of Aldermen and Common Council. While anthropomorphic London is not always personally present, a union between the new mayor and a feminized, anthropomorphous concept – which bridges the gap between real and ideal city life – constitutes the core of each show between the beginning of the 17th century and the onset of the Civil War.

Alongside personified Truth, London herself is present in *Triumphs of Truth* and dressed in "her habit crimson silk, near to the honourable garment of the city" (969), she imitates the sartorial style of a lord mayor's wife. With her white hair and red robe she also echoes the colors in the city's coat of arms. In her left hand she carries the golden key to the city, an accessory which not only alludes to her locked, walled, and unconquerable state but also turns London herself into a gateway. London as limen calls attention to herself as semantic proxy, to the rift between the concept she personifies, on the one hand, and her corporeality on the other hand. In Squire's 1620 *Triumphs of Peace*, new mayor Francis Jones encounters personified London in similar attire: "presented in a scarlet gowne garded with blacke Veluet, like a Lady *Maiores*; and in her hand two golden *keyes*" (B3). Here, too, the personified City visually substantiates her status as "Lady *Maiores*", i.e. as bride to Francis Jones, while simultaneously calling attention to herself as material as well as semantic gateway. Traditionally, in all large-scale pageantry, color was essential in allowing spectators to order and understand performances from a distance. Wickham emphasizes the symbolic and practical value of color in his discussion of costume in tournament entertainments and notes that "[c]olour was the simplest method of assisting recognition" (45). Hill confirms that "another way in which meanings were conveyed to the mayoral procession and to the onlookers was through the use of particular kinds of fabric and colour" (Pageantry 186). By the same simple method of color matching, personified London and the new mayor, in their stately robes, are designated a couple in the eyes of the spectators. "[Y]our beauty is your robe, your strength the sword [of office]" (271), a young sailor, stationed on a pageant ship, tells the mayor in Heywood's *Porta Pietatis*.

Fig. 12: Sir John Leman (1544-1632) dressed in conspicuous red robes and wearing the mayoral chain, ca. 1616. The Fishmongers' coat of arms, topped by a pious pelican and eponymous lemon tree, is visible behind Leman's right shoulder. Royal Collection Trust / © Her Majesty Queen Elizabeth II 2018.

Fig. 13: Sir Christopher Clitherow (1578-1641) is pictured in his red mayoral robes with the chain of office before his halved personal coat of arms. Clitherow was elected sheriff in 1625, a major plague year with high mortality also among city officials. In 1636, a 'minor' plague year, Benjamin Clitherow (probably Christopher's cousin) profited from his familial relationship with the mayor when he was made keeper of the New Churchyard (Hartle 25). © Christ's Hospital Foundation.

Meanwhile, Taylor, in *Triumphs of Fame and Honour*, references London's "civill grave robe", a fashion choice which matches the mayor's robes and which she complements "with her haire long hanging downe" (qtd. in Williams 521). In Taylor's pageant the personified city presides over a model of London – "sitting in one of the Gates of the Citie" – and states: "[...] I doe see this day, and now am seene / The Queene of Cities, Empresse of content, / And Princesse of unmatched government." (ibid.) London is presented as mother figure and spouse simultaneously, while her "civill grave robe" once more identifies her as the mayor's venerable partner. Mayors in office and those who had 'passed the chair' generally sought to be depicted in their mayoral apparel, confirming the symbolic importance of the stately red garment (see mayors Leman and Clitherow in their robes in figures 12 and 13). Dekker points out that Elizabeth I (herself a kind of mother to the maternal city) is to be revered especially since her "chaste hand clothed thy [London's] Rulers in Scarlet" (A3), a task passed to James I after her death.

3.4   The Womb of the City

The link between a prosperous community and physical procreation, mentioned previously, is made manifest in the frequently encountered pageant tableaux which feature gardens or arbors in bloom. The fountain, too, was an ideal symbol of fertility since, as Glynne Wickham put it, "[i]n an age devoid of taps and water mains, the fountain was literally the source of life and indispensable to hygiene. It was not difficult in consequence to attach to it the significance of fertility, abundance or purity" (1: 43). In Heywood's *Londini Artium*, personified Virtue – in the shape of a woman – gives a "Speech upon the Fountaine", in which she calls London "the Mother and the Fountaine" and refers to the mayor "as of all her Sonnes now eldest Child" (C2).[64] That the mayor is here referred to as the city's eldest son, when elsewhere he is designated her spouse, is due, at least in part, to the fact that first-born son and pater familias share a degree of authority denied to other members of the household. Cleaver justifies the preferment of the oldest son within the family with "the order of a familie, wich is an imitation of a state civil, or bodie-politike", and which therefore necessitates "that there be one before the rest as chiefe" (338-39).[65] Just as the first-born son has precedence before his younger siblings, so the mayor's legitimate authority extends that of his fellow Londoners, his brothers and sisters in London, for whom he bears responsibility. At the same time, the depiction of mayor as son in this context reinforces the motif of London as caring mother.

As mother and fountain, London allows natives of the city and strangers alike to "sucke the Milke of her brests" (B). Within her bounds "they are fed, here cherished by this excellent City, and therefore neither impertinently, nor unproperly may shee be stiled:

---

[64] Cf. Richard Niccols' 1616 verse encomium *Londons Artillerie*: "This Queene of citties, Lady of this Ile, ... / Upon her lap did nourse those sonnes of Fame, / Whose deeds do now nobilitate her name" (qtd. in Manley, Matron to Monster 360).

[65] Only if this order is intact "may be conserved that beauty of unitie and harmonie of concord, which the Almighty in his creation so wonderfully and diversly teacheth" (Cleaver 339).

Artium & Scientiarum inundans Scaturigo" (B).[66] London is presented as a charitable and generous mother whose gifts are visualized as the physical products of her body. The association of fountains and breasts speficically, as an aspect of the wider 'Mother Earth' metaphor, is laid out by Philo of Alexandria. According to Philo,

> Nature has bestowed on every mother as a most essential endowment teeming breasts, thus preparing in advance food for the child that is to be born. The earth also, as we all know, is a mother, for which reason the earliest men thought fit to call her 'Demeter', combining the name of 'mother' with that of 'earth'; for, as Plato says, earth does not imitate woman, but woman earth. [...] Fitly therefore on earth also, most fertile and most ancient of mothers, did Nature bestow, by way of breasts, streams of rivers and springs, to the end that both the plants might be watered and all animals might have abundance to drink. (chapter XLV, 106-07)

Philo's descriptions of the nurturing earth mother are appreciative. They are also commensurate with the positive assessment of nurturing London – feeding her offspring with the milk of her breasts – by a merchant and artisan culture that embraced the 'virtues' of breastfeeding. While the image of lactating London may have suggested vulgarity in courtly circles, where breastfeeding was a chore relegated to those of inferior standing, it highlights the good qualities of London to an urban audience who would, on the whole, have tended to agree with Cleaver's view that "it becommeth naturall mothers to nourish their children with their owne milke" (236). Later in Heywood's *Londini Artium*, the identities of London and mayor are fused when, in the final speech of the day, Arion tells the mayor "that you are the Spring and Fountaine made / To water every Science, Art, and Trade" (C2). This dedication desired of the mayor, to care for his constituents as a mother might for her children, was expressed in similar terms in Munday's 1616 *Chrysanaleia*, in which new mayor Leman was represented as a pelican, feeding the young with his heart's blood.[67]

A merging of the identities of mayor and city, like that in *Londini Artium*, is also suggested in Heywood's *Londini Speculum* by personified Sight, who informs the mayor that "she in you; you her shall live for ever" (317).[68] This absorption of two separate entities into one echoes the contemporary marital ideal according to which God "gave one to one, that two (not three or foure) may be one flesh" (Rous 19), and together form "one perfect bodie" (Cleaver 213), as ordained in Genesis (2:24). However, mayor and city also fulfill separate roles. While London-the-fountain may offer material support to her population, it takes the mayor to distribute what she offers and to make it usable in all areas of civilized society. Dependence on outside forces for the achievement of prosperity is also suggested in other pageants. A "woman of beautiful aspect", inhabiting a

---

[66] In a similar manner, the city of Pisa was commonly, from the 14th to the 18th century, personified in the shape of a "lactating Charity" (Baskins 96).

[67] Munday himself secured his will with the image of "the pelican in her piety" impressed on its wax seal (Hotson 4). Bergeron speculates that the author may have recalled his use of the pelican in the pageant of 1616 (Munday n. pag.).

[68] Hardin interprets this as an internalization of the metropolis by the mayor, "as a vision of the Mayor's civic conscience" (32).

pastoral setting, and attended by Faith, Hope, Charity, and Time, appears in Heywood's *London's Ius Honorarium*. She personifies a well-governed commonwealth, expressed by her beauty and by the flourishing of nature around her. The scene is, thus, strongly reminiscent of a pageant episode which featured in the coronation entry of Elizabeth I into London in 1559, which contrasted a verdant landscape with a barren one, representing, on the one hand, a well-governed state and, on the other, one that is poorly managed. The commonwealth as garden, with or without accompanying nymph, is not by itself capable of attaining an attractive form nor of bearing delectable fruit but depends on the care of gardeners, i.e. magistrates like the lord mayor and his subordinates. The scenario has biblical provenance: in the Song of Songs the male lover calls his beloved a "garden inclosed […], a spring shut up, a fountain sealed" (4:12; Landy 516); this beloved, too, depends on her male lover: "its fruit ripens and its spices become redolent only for the sake of the Lover […]: paradoxically the garden fulfills itself through self-surrender" (Landy 520). The locked state of the garden, closed off from its less paradisal surroundings, "may mean among other things that she is chaste" (Landy 519); this idea also works when, later in the Song, the female lover assumes the roles of city and palanquin, "and parts of her body are compared with parts of cities" (Landy 521). The potential affinity of the garden and marriage motifs (and the idea of the personified, marriageable city) was made especially evident in the 1532 reception of the Dauphin into Rouen, examined by Gordon Kipling, in which a "lady representing the city stood in the midst of a lavish garden calling to her *sponsus*, 'Let my beloved come into his garden' (Cant. 5:1)" (Enter the King 45). The same tropes still circulate in 17th-century London. Taking up matrimonial, horticultural, and aquatic metaphors, Dekker describes the church (like the city, a favorite subject of personification) as a garden to be pruned, a fountain to be kept clear, as well as a beloved wife to be kept chaste (The Seven Deadly Sinnes 29).

From the 'fertility pageants' in the Lord Mayor's Show which associate the city and 'fruitfulness' – by means of garden and fountain imagery – it is only a small step to conceptualize the personified City as capable of giving birth herself.[69] Munday, in his *Metropolis Coronata*, styles London "the ancient Mother of the whole Land" (B3), while in the opening paragraph of his *Himatia-poleos* pamphlet, he refers to "this famous Cittie of *London*, whose continuall teeming wombe (from time to time) brought forth many seuerall Mysteries or Professions" (A3-4). In Dekker's *Brittannia's Honor* Britannia – who functions as a superordinate version of London (see also page 153) – tells the mayor that she "bred you [Skinner Richard Deane] in her Wombe" and bids him to "Heare then a Mothers Counsell". In concrete terms, the City becomes a mother to all guilds established within her walls but that is not all. Her "continuall teemning wombe" goes on to breed still more people and professions as the city continues to change and grow. The ability to give birth not only makes a mother of the City but, consequently, makes a father of the mayor. In the pamphlet commemorating his *Chrysanaleia*, Munday not only presents new mayor John Leman as a self-sacrificing pelican, he also pronounces that with his inauguration Leman "becommeth a nursing father of the Family: which, though

---

[69] Thus, Hill's argument that, in making London the mayor's mother in his *Triumphs of Truth*, Middleton "takes his own idiosyncratic approach" is not quite true (Pageantry 18).

hee bred not, yet, by his best endeuour, hee must labour to bring vp" (B2). As London's husband, Leman becomes a father to the extended family of Londoners.[70]

The same principle of paternity is suggested in Heywood's *London's Ius Honorarium* in which Janus tells new mayor George Whitmore: "You for one yeare are made the Cities Father; These foure succeeding Seasons [Janus' daughters], I resigne / Unto your charge" (365). As head of the family, Whitmore assumes responsibility for his dependents, the feminized City and her plentiful offspring.[71] The character of Ulysses tells him that London, "[i]nto whose charge this day doth you invest, / Shall her in you, and you in her make blest" (272). In the particular union of Whitmore and London, as in the union of mayor and city every year, the masculine and feminine domains are combined and achieve completion, as they would in any good marriage. In this alliance of forces, the masculine principle is dominant, i.e. the mayor is in charge of the city and this is in her best interest. At night, Ulysses tells Whitmore that "[t]his Ancient Citty in her pristine Youth, / Your sword may reestablish: and so bring / Her still to flourish; like that lasting Spring" (280). The comparison of London to "lasting Spring" suggests the fertility pageant that opened the show, in which a "greene and pleasant Hill" bore a "variety faire and pleasant fruite" (272). As Ulysses declares, it is Whitmore who rejuvenates London and so enables her to bear "pleasant fruite". This feat is accomplished by means of the mayor's sword of office: a potent symbol not only of his official authority but of physical strength and masculinity, including obvious phallic associations.[72] The return of ancient London to childbearing age and ability, facilitated by Whitmore, brings together conceptions of the city as young woman and old woman, as spouse and mother, and also relates to the fertility pageants of Heywood's *Londini Artium* and *London's Ius Honorarium*, both of which confirm that the city's well-being and productivity depend on the mayor's assistance.

To conceive of London equally as wife and mother is not so extremely unusual considering, firstly, medieval conceptions of the virgin Mary as both mother of Christ and beloved of God and, secondly, the early modern equation of Christ and husband in the

---

[70] True to his position as a civic father figure, the terms of Leman's will contain benefactions to the city and its poor and is exemplary of the bequests made by London's wealthy merchants: "Among the beneficiaries of Leman's will, dated 8 July 1631, was Christ's Hospital, of which he had been president since 1618, and which gained lands in Whitechapel valued at £2000. There were smaller legacies (£150 in all) to St Bartholomew's Hospital and Bridewell, and provision for the poor of several parishes and for sea coal for the needy inhabitants of the alms-houses of his livery company." (Ashton n. pag.) Leman also left left instructions and means for the founding of a school in Beccles, Suffolk (ibid). Although it has moved from its old premises, Sir John Leman High School is still active as a coeducational secondary school. It was common for the city's rich merchants to found and fund schools, especially in their home towns outside of London.

[71] In his personal life, London-born George Whitmore was also blessed with 'plentiful offspring', i.e. "at least three sons and four daughters" (Hollis n. pag.).

[72] During his mayoralty Haberdasher Nicholas Rainton entered a dispute with the bishop of London, "when the latter challenged the traditional practice of lord mayors having their sword of office carried before them into St Paul's Cathedral" (Lindley n. pag.), confirming the sword as a potent symbol of power and not merely an irrelevant accessory.

147

microcosm of the household. A wife who relates to her husband as Mary does to God, appreciates him as son and beloved. In his 12th-century treatise on the Song of Songs, *Elucidatio in Cantica Canticorum*, Alanus de Insulis had described Mary as "properly mother as well as beloved for her breasts nourish the faithful with the two exemplars of good living, chastity and humility [...] her breasts are two arms of charity, one loves Christ as God, the other as son" (qtd. in Ferrante 29-30). A similar relationship model is embraced by London and the lord mayor, who is envisaged as a son of the personified city but also enters into a relationship with 'her' and assumes lordship over her;[73] and while the mother of god provides chastity and humility (as Alanus explains), in London's "Armes lie the sonnes of England to suck wealth" and even a measure of "wisedome" (The Dead Tearme B, A3).

We find London as "chiefe Mother and matrone" in Munday's *Himatia-poleos* (B2). In the show which honored Thomas Hayes of the Drapers, London-as-mother shared her maternal role with Himatia, personified Clothing or Drapery, who assumed the status of "Mother, Lady and commandresse" of all professions affiliated with the production of and trade in cloth (ibid.). The fact that Himatia represents 'Old Drapery' may simultaneously be read, so Hill, as a counterargument to "the attempted monopoly of 'new' drapery in the putative Cockayne Project" (Pageantry 295). Meanwhile, Middleton's *Triumphs of Truth* present London as "a grave feminine shape, [...] attired like a reverend mother, a long white hair naturally flowing on either side of her" (969). Here the City presents her ancient face but she is spouse too: As mentioned above, her dress signifies her status as lady mayoress. Complementing a headdress of model edifices[74] – reminiscent of Phrygian goddess Cybele, a precursor of city personifications, – London is wrapped in a robe of "crimson silk, near to the honourable garment of the city; her left hand holding a key of gold" (ibid.). While the miniature buildings aid in the metaphorical translation of city into woman, the garments clearly indicate that London is a wife to the

---

[73] Beauvoir has also pointed out that while Jerusalem and Babylon are envisioned as sexual partners – one legitimate, one sinful – cities are traditionally compared to mothers because they shelter inhabitants within their walls, a fact also noted by Carl Jung (Beauvoir 235). This, argues Beauvoir, is the reason for the representation of the Phrygian goddess Cybele as crowned with towers or turrets and for the home country to be known as "motherland" (ibid. 235). See also footnote 74 below.

[74] Originally a Phrygian goddess and subsequently adopted into the Greek and Roman pantheons, Cybele is associated with towns and city walls in Greek culture and became known as 'Great Mother' in her Roman incarnation. Typically, one of her attributes was a mural crown – a feature that also characterizes later city and state personifications such as, for example, *Italia Turrita*. Cf. Manley: "The personification of the city is a very old tradition that originates in the myths of the Cretan and Asian goddess Cybele. [...] Typically represented with a towering turretlike crown and cloaked with the fruits and gems of the earth, Cybele rides a chariot drawn by yoked lions" (Matron to Monster 354-55). In his 1556 *Imagine dei Dei*, Vincenzo Cartari explains that Roman goddess Terra, also known as Magna Mater, is recognizable by her "towered headdress". Cartari includes an illustration in his publication of a Syrian goddess corresponding to Terra who is seated in a lion-drawn chariot and wears a headdress of steeples (qtd. Bath 233).

mayor notwithstanding her status as "reverend mother". She addresses the mayor and advises him not to regard her words less because

> I a woman speak, / A woman's counsel is not always weak. / I am thy mother ; […] / I know that at this instant all the works / Of motherly love in me, shown to thy youth, / When it was soft and helpless, are summed up / In thy most grateful mind: thou well rememb'rest / All my dear pains and care; with what affection / I cherish thee in my bosom, watchfull still / Over thy ways; (969)

London positions herself as Mayor Myddleton's mother and voices her hope that her son will not forget her formative influence on his youth in the moment of his triumph. Nevertheless, now that Myddleton is no longer a "helpless" infant, London is happy to subordinate herself to his care and judgment, and she ends her speech on this theme. When she asks rhetorically, "with what care and fear / Ought I to be o'erseen, to be kept clear?" (970) London returns to passivity and compliance by appointing Myddleton the overseer and keeper of her body.

Both the ancient face of the city and her continuing fertility are referenced in Heywood's 1637 *Londini Speculum*. From the show's main pageant set, called London's Mirror, anthropomorphic Sight marvels:

> For Londons selfe, if they shall first begin / To examine her without, and then within, / What Architectures, Palaces, what Bowers, / What Citadels, what turrets, and what towers? / Who in her age, grew pregnant, brought a bed / Of a New Towne, and late delivered / Of such a burthen, as in few yeares space, / Can almost speake all tongues, (to her more grace.) (216)

Sight endows London with the shape of a woman but at the same time stresses the importance of citadels, turrets and towers as her physicals attributes. She wears these features on her person, as formulated explicitly by Dekker in his 1606 prose tract on *The Seven Deadly Sinnes of London*. Herein Dekker tells London that "thy Towers, thy Temples, and thy Pinnacles stand upon thy head like borders of fine gold, thy waters like fringes of silver hang at the hemmes of thy garment" (A3). Two years later, Dekker once again presents 'reverend' and 'aged' London crowned with "a heape of lofty Temples and Pynnacles" (The Dead Tearme C4). In the passage above, Sight presents London as an aged mother but simultaneously as still young and fertile enough to give birth to the diversified population of the ever-growing extramural wards and liberties. The City is here rendered in the same strokes as in *London's Ius Honorarium*. An "[a]ncient Citty in her pristine Youth", she is both mother and bride, combining different aspects of womanhood. Hardin reads the quoted passage from *Londini Speculum* as expressing highly ambiguous attitudes toward the physical shape of London and, in particular, toward the extramural territories. He argues that it "mystifies" the relationship between city and suburbs and interprets the birth scenario as "symbolically expelling the troubling polyglot suburban space" (34). However, Heywood praises linguistic diversity and the 'maternalization' of London is integrative in that it creates a shared identity for Londoners by rendering them siblings. The body of the city, thus, not only delimits, it also incorporates and, in fact, it is this function of embodiment that predominates in the Lord Mayor's Shows of Heywood and in those of his predecessors. Sight's defiantly positive account of the diversity of London's rapidly growing population is very much notable. In a climate in which the capital's rapid expansion was predominantly seen as a threat to social order and public health, this rhetorical embrace of the diverse multitudes of the metropolis is unusual and it confirms the above-mentioned integrating function essential to the Lord Mayor's Show. Certainly the city had long been a hub of international trade, as is attested by William Fitzstephen's eulogizing twelfth-century testimony that

> [a]t this Citie Marchant straungers of all nations had their keyes and wharfes: the Arabians sent golde: the Sabians spice and frankensence: the Scithian armour, Babylon oyle, India purple garments, Egypt precious stones, Norway and Russia Ambergreece and sables, and the French men wine. (qtd. in Stow 1: 80)

However, the close of the 16th century and the first decades of the 17th century saw an increase in the numbers of migrants arriving in London. Not only 'foreigners' from rural England, Wales, and Ireland but also 'strangers' from continental Europe and even a small contingent of Asians, Africans, and native Americans made their home in the city. With falling wages in the 1620s, newly evictable rural tenants flocked to the capital in ever larger numbers in the hope of gaining access to non-skilled work and charity there (Heinemann 6, 134). The response to this from native Londoners was not always peaceful. Stow reports on the Evil May Day of 1517, "an insurrection of youthes against Aliens on may day" (1: 99).[1] Riots against non-British migrants were also common in the 1590s and Bergeron attests to a "strong feeling against foreigners among London citizens at the time" (Munday n. pag.).[2] The depiction of all Londoners, dyed-in-the-wool merchants from the intramural wards and new arrivals alike, as children of one mother served as a mild antidote to the frictions and tensions generated by a growing population in constant flux. The use of the trope aimed at harmonizing and integrating all city dwellers, these disparate 'siblings', into a social whole. In Heywood's *Porta Pietatis*, London is deemed superior to her "twin-sister" Westminster – despite the presence of the royal court there – for "her antiquity, in the second for her ability, in the third, for her numerous progeny" (263). It is not only the dignity of age that renders London unique, nor the fact that she is a "breeder of great magistrates" (ibid.), but the talent, versatility and sheer number of her offspring – magistracy included – confirm her status as the most excellent city in the kingdom. Population increase as a blessing instead of a curse is a theme also present in *London's Ius Honorarium*. London appears alongside equally personified and feminized

---

1   B. L. Beer notes: "The Evil May Day riots of 1517 were the most striking example of discontent in London during the reign of Henry VIII. Grievances were directed against foreign merchants and artisans and as such were primarily economic although the privileges granted to foreigners represented Crown policy. Military forces led by the Earls of Shrewsbury and Surrey [Thomas Howard, Henry's father] quickly restored order. Over 400 persons were arrested and fourteen executed" (London and the Rebellions 16).

2   With the breakout of approximately 13 riots, the year 1595, and especially the month of June, was an unusually tumultuous period in the history of London (Bliss 24).

150

Westminster, York, Bristol, Oxford, Lincoln, Exeter as well as yet more unnamed cities. Registering amazement on their faces, London asks her companions:

> Is it to see my numerous Children round / Incompasse me? So that no place is found / In all my large streets empty? My yssue spred / In number more then stones whereon they tread. / To see my Temples, Houses, even all places, / With people covered, as if Tyl'd with faces? / Will you know whence proceedes this faire increase, / This ioy? The fruits of a continued peace. (275)

London's offspring is so numerous that the city appears tiled with faces. Yet, this is no cause for worry, assures the speaking city, but for joy. The civic pride in numbers formulated here stands in stark contrast to the notion put forward by Thomas Dekker in his 1604 plague pamphlet *Newes from Graves-end* that there are far too many idlers "living, / And wanting living" in the city, who give "Themselves to wast, deface and spoyle" and must therefore be decimated by contagious diseases (103). In *London's Ius Honorarium*, on the other hand, the city prides herself on her population density and accordingly creates a scene in which unity among the many and the various is not only a desirable state of affairs but has already been achieved, for without "continued peace" the city could not have grown so much nor continue to expand as it irrefutably does. Ingeniously, spectators are persuaded to believe in the possibility of harmonious coexistence of diverse groups in the city by the suggestion that this state has already been achieved.[3]

The portrayal of the city as spouse and mother, meant to placate and ideologically integrate, has a reverse side too, however. A reverend vision of the city as "chiefe Mother and matrone" has the potential to be transformed into a foul and fleshly spectacle, as, for example, Ben Jonson demonstrates in his scatological mock epic "On the Famous Voyage". The poem describes a boating trip up London's polluted Fleet River as an expedition deep into the monstrous innards of the humanoid City. Jonson's daring explorers make their way "thorough her [London's] womb [...] / Between two walls, where on one side, to scar men / Were seen your ugly centaurs ye call car-men", going about their excremental business. The teeming womb of the personified City is not a life-giving boon in Jonson's scenario. Instead, it is a stinking, dirty hellhole. It is simultaneously uterus and intestine: The processes of giving birth and excreting waste merge and form a single, repulsive image. In consequence, the feminized City encountered in "On the Famous Voyage" is not the reverend mother of *The Triumphs of Truth* but her distorted twin or mirror image, a gross, disease-ridden prostitute.[4]

---

[3] Cf. Patterson: It is "as if acting and speaking as though harmony exists [...] will help bring it about in reality".

[4] Peter M. Medine has called attention to the way in which Jonson satirically alludes to the mayoral festivities: "Jonson alludes to the annual procession here by identifying the reeking ship with the Mayor's colorful barge: in spite of the ship's present malodorous condition, during 'one day in the yeere, for sweet 'tis voyc't / And that is when it is the Lord Maiors foist' (11. 119-120)." (106) The word "foist" not only refers to the barge, and especially the traditional galley foist, but "suggests feast [... and] plays on its meaning as an emission of flatulent gas, and so indicates the essential vulgarity of the Feast [...]" and the people prominently involved (ibid.).

Certainly the function of one type of portrayal is very different from that of the other. As a ritual that celebrates city life and the status quo, the community-affirming Lord Mayor's Show could hardly present London with scorn and disgust, whereas Jonson-the-satirist exposes perceived flaws by unflattering exaggeration, using the available template of the feminized city. The association or even identification of female reproductive and excretory organs in the service of causing disgust is not original to Jonson's poem but had been tried and tested in medieval theology to misogynistic effect, so for example by Augustine of Hippo (cf. Beauvoir 225). Manley, too, has noted that "the history of personification is also a history of sexual ambivalence" (Matron to Monster 355). This is true, too, of city personification. Whereas Jerusalem is the chaste bride of Christ, irredeemable degeneracy is embodied in the Whore of Babylon in the Book of Revelation. Civic ideology not only creates in London a "once-againe New-reard-Troy" (The Seven Deadly Sinnes 41), but also a second Jerusalem, prepared for the second coming of Christ. Yet, the comparison with Jerusalem also evokes images of Babylon.

Royal entries into the late medieval capitol had already glorified the city as an incarnation of Jerusalem: in processions constructed around the liturgy of advent, London stood in for Jerusalem while the entering monarch acted as Christ's substitute on earth (Liddy 333). Yet, because the concepts of good city and bad city were too neatly intertwined, Jerusalem could never be thought without Babylon, thus offering a rich pallet of alternate images that could be utilized in order to subvert the image of the good city and the good wife.[5] In satire, with its stress on individual experience over and above community and transhistorical stability, these reverse images are most commonly found (Manley, Matron to Monster 356). As an example of the phenomenon, Manley cites Donald Lupton's *London and the Country Carbonadoed* (1632), in which personified London is described as a "pregnant glutton", no longer attractive to anybody because she has grown so large (ibid.). In times of plague, the sickened city could be envisioned as delivering "none but Still-borne Children" (The Runawayes Answer n. pag.). Indeed, whether in sickness or in health, in the early decades of the 17th century numerous Londoners may have imagined their city not as celibate and contained but as "an unmanageable body, open to passage, and enveloped by its vast suburban population" (Hardin 32). Jonson's mock epic shares in this scornful tradition. While babylonic London is a prostitute, the depiction of London as a New Jerusalem goes hand in hand with the conception of the personified city as an ideal wife – absolutely chaste outside of her matrimonial duties. In Dekker's *The Seven Deadly Sinnes*, London is 'goodly' but proud, wealthy but wanton (A3). There is potential for greatness as much as depravity. Dekker addresses the city thus: "Though hast all things in thee to make thee fairest, and all things in thee to make thee foulest: for thou art attir'de like a Bride, drawing all that look upon thee, to be in love with thee, but there is much harlot in thine eyes." (ibid.) London is a potential good wife and a potential prostitute. The city may support multitudes, including Dekker himself – who notes that from London's "womb received I my being, from thy brests my nourishment" – but all the same the city also "nourishes seven Serpents at thy brests" (ibid. A3v). Should London decide to kneel in front of the

---

[5]   Beauvoir, too, notes that there are virgin cities, such as Jerusalem, and unchaste, 'whore' cities, such as Babylon and Tyre (235). These are also simultaneously mothers and spouses (ibid.).

beast of Revelation, with the harlot on its back, its fall "will be greater then that of Babylon" (ibid. 45).

Contemporary notions of human nature and familial relations also align with the antithetical conception of Jerusalem, the wife, and Babylon, the whore. One of the reasons for the institution of marriage, explains Robert Cleaver to his early modern readership, is "that the wife might bee a lawfull remedie to avoid whoredome, fornication, and all filthie uncleane lusts" (158). In the Lord Mayor's Show, the ritual union of lord mayor and London, thus, prevents London from falling into Babylonian ways and gives the mayor a realm over which he can legitimately rule. In the same vein Francis Parlett instructs the new mayor of King's Lynn, in a 1632 speech, not to let his wife – the city – "be sordid or sluttish" but to see to it that she is "neat, cleanly, and sweetly kept" (qtd. in Patterson 166). The metaphor of the city as a woman – of the growing city as a pregnant and childbearing woman – had not lost its efficacy after the restoration of the monarchy, as is illustrated by Andrew Marvell who posits that "virgin buildings oft brought forth" in stanza eleven of his country house poem "Upon Appleton House" (219).[6] While the poem generically favors rural landscapes, the image of a female virgin giving birth to a settlement still evokes the chaste, i.e. unconquerable, she-city of Roman origin. Marvell's friend John Milton, meanwhile, connected the conception of state in terms of body with moral statecraft in his pamphlet "Of Reformation" and employs the image in repudiation of amoral Machiavellianism. He declares: "Alas Sir! A Commonwealth ought to be but as one huge Christian personage, one mighty growth, and stature of an honest man, as big, and compact in virtue as in body" (11).

London, in any case, is still represented as woman and mother, albeit a bereft one, as recently as the mid-20th century. In Dylan Thomas' "A Refusal to Mourn the Death, by Fire, of a Child in London", a reflection on civilian casualties of the Second World War, the final stanza laments: "Deep with the first dead lies London's daughter, / Robed in the long friends, / The grains beyond age, the dark veins of her mother, / Secret by the unmourning water / Of the riding Thames."

Mother Matter

Ideas on the gendered nature of matter and form familiar from the *Timaeus* find poignant expression in Munday's *Chruso-thriambos*. In the principle pageant set of the show matter is feminized in the womanly shape of 'earth mother' Terra, an amalgamation of Cybele, the Goldsmiths' métier, and the personified city. Terra is seated at the top level of a pageant set called the Orferie. This set consists of an artificial rock or mountain "with clifts, crannies, and passable places" (A4). At the lower stratum of the pageant rock, miners are employed at extracting valuable ores, while other workers further process the raw materials. On top of the structure are placed Terra, also referred to as Chthoon or Vesta, and her daughters Chrusos/Gold, the elder, and Argurion/Silver, the younger.

---

6   In a similar vein, in "On the Victory Obtained by Blake" Marvell evokes "the womb of wealthy kingdoms" (425). In *The Fairie Queene* Spenser had described the action of digging a double grave in these words: "The great earthes wombe they open to the sky" (book 2, canto 1, stanza 60), figuring death as a return to the womb of the earth.

Munday describes Terra as the "Queene of all other Vertues" as well as "the breeding and teeming Mother of all Gold, Silver, Minerall, and other Mettals" (B). Terra's fundamental worth and virtue is her vast materiality and the substantial riches which men possessed of a spirit of industry can extract from her – such men as are organized in the company of London Goldsmiths, it is implied, and their current head, new mayor James Pemberton. Chrusos and Argurion are themselves aspects of the maternal earth goddess Terra. As personifications of precious metals, they are precisely those riches which Terra can be made to yield to the labors of active manhood. Both Chrusos and Argurion have had to embark upon a "long and tedious iourney," notes Munday, "thorough their Mothers large limits and Rocky kingdome, leauing in euery Vaine, Sinnew, & Artery, the rich and valuable vertue of their splendour", in order to be present for Pemberton's inaugural festivities (B). This account of the travels of Silver and Gold offers a striking image that also allegorically accounts for the presence of metal ores in the crust of the earth – precious traces left behind by daughters in the veins of their vast mother. As a measure for their own protection, remarks Munday, the sisters sit chained to the pageant set.

The body of Terra – incorporating her daughters – is as that of personified America in Theodor Galle's engraving, poised toward the conquering Amerigo Vespucci, or as that of Ralegh's and Keymis' promiscuous Guyana: a territorial offering to be explored and exploited (and it resonates in terms like "motherload" and even the much more recent "motherboard"). A similar premise is also strikingly rendered in Francis Quarles' popular anthology of *Emblemes* (1635), a work based on and inspired by the influential Jesuit emblem books *Pia Desideria* and *Typus Mundi*. Quarles' emblem twelve in book one (the work being divided into five books of 15 emblems each) bears the motto, "Yee may suck, but not be satisfied with the brest of her Consolations" (48-49). The engraving accompanying motto and verse shows a globe from which protrude two substantial breasts. Two earthly fools – one fat, the other thin – are engaged in milking these. A cornucopia floats before the globe, at a point between the breasts, reinforcing its material, life-giving and sustaining potential and purpose. The image shares in and perpetuates the metaphorical feminization of matter but the tone of the accompanying text, in its denigration of worldly pursuits, is unlike that of the Lord Mayor's Show: The fools know no moderation (they represent foolish extremes) and suck both "food and poyson", "milk and death" from "th'earths full breast" (ibid. 49). Certainly, the mayoral entertainments also praise the golden mean, but for Quarles "[t]he meane's a vertue, and the world has none" (51).

Munday's all-encompassing earth mother, on the other hand, is "vncorruptible in her rich bounty to the world" (B), and offers her substantial gifts to masculine industry. Terra not only presented the London Goldsmiths, "her golden Sonnes", with an impartial touchstone to test the worth of metals but even surrendered her eldest daughter Chrusos (Gold) to them, to figure in their coat of arms. Here, holding a balance and a touchstone, Chrusos also represents Justice, in accordance with the company motto: "Iustitia Virtutum Regina" (B). The equation of gold with the cardinal virtue of justice speaks to the high ideological regard in which merchant London held the material commodities on which rested its prosperity as well as to the mystical power invested in the persona of humanoid Gold.

154

John Donne utilizes the association of gold ore (and precious gem stones) with femininity and the female in a comparable manner in his "Epithalamion made at Lincoln's Inn", in which the poet identifies the "[d]aughters of London" (l. 15) with "[o]ur golden mines" (l. 16) as well as in "To his Mistress Going to Bed" in which the speaker's beloved becomes his "Mine of precious stones, My Empirie" (l. 29); in the same poem Donne also refers to the woman as "America! my new-found-land, / My kingdom, safeliest when with one man mann'd" (ll. 27-28) and muses "How blest am I in this discovering thee!" (l. 30). In *A Midsummer Night's Dream* fairy queen Titania recalls how her Indian acolyte and mother to her young warden – currently sought after by fairy king Oberon – would imitate merchant vessels on the sea: a suitable role since, as merchant ships are often "rich with merchandise" (2.1.134), so "her womb [was] then rich with my young squire" (2.1.131). The formulation echoes the words of Thetis in Webster's *Monuments of Honour*, who hopes that "Rich Lading" will "swell" the mayor's vessels (B).

The feminized territorial entities of Terra, America, and Guyana all owe their being to the Aristotelian notion of passive feminine matter. They are anthropomorphic humus-soil: fertile – life-giving – and impressionable; they obtain form and higher purpose only through the intercession of masculine forces.[7] These forces come in the guise of London Goldsmiths and 'New World' discoverers who render their material potential usable by the extraction of resources and by 'civilizing' endeavors. The connotations of profit and reproduction borne by territorial personifications (such as India, Guyana, or London) bring to mind the etymological kinship between "mater" and "material", previously mentioned. It suggests that the cognitive feminization of matter is deeply embroiled in the language of Rome and, in consequence, the tongues and cultures influenced by it, reflecting and reinforcing the link. When matter is endowed with the perceived attributes of the female sex, it follows logically that it should be able to conceive, shelter, and birth new life – as demonstrated by Terra, America, Guyana, and London herself. Simone de Beauvoir has attempted to elucidate the phenomenon by recourse to a phase in prehistory when nomadic tribes settled down (92-94). At this time, Beauvoir notes, women were concerned with cultivating the land and with home-based crafts such as pottery and weaving, while men left the immediate home territory to hunt and fish (95). Women were then mystically identified with the life-giving earth which they worked, and the emergence of female fertility goddesses testified to their new prestige (ibid. 94-95). However, not only were these goddesses subsequently 'dethroned' and subjected to all-powerful male gods; political power, Beauvoir hypothesizes, generally remained in male hands even at this time of women worship (ibid. 97, 102) – when women delved and Adam did not (yet).

---

[7]   In *A light Bondell of iuly discourses calld Churchyardes Charge* (1580) Thomas Churchyard made the following statement about London, linking feminine city and fertile soil: "the Maiden toune, that keepes her selfe so cleane, / [...] Here is the soil and seat of Kyngs, and place of precious price" (qtd. in Manley, Matron to Monster 361).

Fig. 14: Fools milking the breasts of the world in book one, emblem twelve, of Francis Quarles' *Emblemes, Divine and Moral* (48). The title and verse completing the composition were placed on the opposite page. Image by courtesy of Penn State University Libraries.

The deep-rooted mental connection between the material world and woman lived on in a variety of discourses in early modern London, not least that of matrimony and family life. Robert Cleaver admonishes his readership to choose a wife wisely, just "[a]s hee that will plant anything doth first consider the nature of the ground, in the which he mindeth to plant: even so much more ought a man to have respect to the condition of the woman, out of whom he desireth to plant children, the fruites of honestie and welfare" (101).[8] Cleaver's analogy equates the condition of the ground with the qualities of a woman and compares the process of selecting and cultivating a plot of land to selecting a wife, dealing with her, and impregnating her. The alleged passivity of women is also reflected in Cleaver's guide to appropriate conduct in the household. "The dutie of the husband is, to be entermedling", he insists, "and of the wife, to be solitarie and withdrawne" (170). It is her duty to be a home keeper, to stay in the home at all times, unless to attend church, to tend to those in need, or to carry out household chores on her husband's orders (ibid. 95, 230). The husband, meanwhile, is in command of the entire household but above all, he should concern himself with life outside the home: He must "rule all household, especially outward affaires" (ibid. 88). If he fails to do this because of an interfering wife, "the house will come to ruine: for God will not blesse where his ordinance is not obeyed" (ibid.). Docility is therefore a desired trait in wives. The good wife is not only bound to the place of her home, she is also, ideally, a mute presence within that home: "Now silence is the best ornament of a woman, and therefore the law was given to the man, rather then to the woman, to shew that hee should be the teacher, and she the hearer", informs Cleaver (106).[9]

In a tribute to Princess Elizabeth Stuart on the occasion of her wedding to Frederick, Elector Palatine, in February 1613, Anthony Nixon, too, utilizes the metaphorical association of earthly matter and women, casually noting that "Elizaes Brest is that same hill, / Where Vertue dwels, and sacred skill" (B). Neither was the semantic tie lost on Shakespeare, who, in act five, scene three of *Richard III*, has the eponymous monarch declare that his countrymen have both "lands" and "beauteous wives". The two categories of ownership are interchangeable to the point of being synonymous and so are threats against both lands and women: To 'enjoy' the former and to 'ravish' the latter are the alleged goals of the king's enemies across the Channel.

---

[8] The analogy between a plot of land and a wife is employed once more by Cleaver when he argues that a husband should not attempt to rid himself quickly of an unsatisfactory spouse. Rather, he should work on his partner's improvement: "For like as the Husbandman doth with great labour and diligence till that ground, which he hath once taken to farme, although it be never so full of faultes: as if it be drie, if it bring forth weedes, brambles, or briers; or though it cannot beare much wette; yet through good husbandry he winneth fruite thereof: even so in like manner, hee that hath maried a wife that is irreligious or froward, if he diligently and courteously apply himselfe to weede away by litle and litle the noysome weeds out of her minde, both by holesome and godly preceptes, and by Christian conversation; it can not be but in time he shall feele the pleasant fruit thereof, to both their comforts: for as it is commonly said, a good Iacke maketh a good Gill." (102)

[9] Cf. Arendt: "The privation of privacy lies in the absence of others; as far as they are concerned, private man does not appear, and therefore it is as though he did not exist." (58) And because woman is always private, she never exists.

This gender conception also frequently suffuses narratives of civilization: Culture and sophistication are added to feral spaces, in the gendered terms of allegory, in Middleton's *Triumphs of Love and Antiquity*. From his wilderness-set, the character of Orpheus declares:

> Just such a wilderness is a commonwealth / That is undressed, unpruned, wild in her health; / And the rude multitude the beasts o'th' wood, / That know no laws, but only will and blood; / And yet, by fair example, musical grace, / Harmonious government of the man in place, / Of fair integrity and wisdom framed, / They stand as mine do, ravished, charmed, and tamed: / Every wise magistrate that governs thus, / May well be called a powerful Orpheus. (1401)[10]

Orpheus is straightforward in his conjuring of a feminized landscape which is rightly presided over by a masculine force of order and civility. His commonwealth-wilderness is a 'she' – "undressed, unpruned, wild" – while "fair integrity and wisdom" belong, once more, to the semantic field of masculinity. The pageant suggests an analogy between Orpheus and the mayor: as Orpheus is "the man in place" in his wilderness, so the lord mayor is "the man in place" in London: both are conceptualized as civilizing forces or rational minds, bringing immaterial culture to a material territory. The strategy is consistent with Manley's persuasive claim that dramatists often saw an opportunity in the mayor's return to the city from Westminster to stage "narratives of arrival" or journeys from chaos to civilization (308). Yet, this spin on the proceedings was not as a rule limited to one particular phase of the festivities. The metaphor of civilization so easily transfers from wilderness to city because place remains a woman, whether uncultivated and empty or densely populated, and it is always man's lot to 'ravish, charm, and tame' the feminized territory. The proper and desirable relationship between conqueror and territory is, thus, like that between man and woman. For the mayor this means that his relationship with the city of London can easily be conceptualized in terms of a marriage because the same principles apply in both cases. Bluntly put, man dominates and woman's obedience affirms his authority, while her passive contribution to procreation assures the continued existence of his line.

Both Munday's earth goddess Terra and the wilderness tamed by Orpheus in *Triumphs of Love and Antiquity* are examples of the Platonic gender formula vividly realized; matter is feminized vis-a-vis the masculine sphere of thought and form. Although they have material presence on their own, the wilderness-commonwealth and the vast anatomy of Terra depend on men like Orpheus or on the industry of Ironmongers to acculturate that material presence and to make it serviceable. The words of Andreas Capellanus – "[a] woman is like melting wax, which is always ready to take a new form and to receive the impress of anyone's seal" (qtd. in Bloch 19) – echo in both pageants.

---

[10] Orpheus also appears in Whitney's *Choice of Emblemes*. Emblem 97 shows him playing a harp, seated in the midst of a circle of animals. The accompanying epigram explains that the poet, "with his harpe, that savage kinde did tame: [...] But if wee thinke his playe so wroughte, our selves wee doe delude. / For why? Besides his skill, hee learned was, and wise" (287). Thus, it is not only the quality of his music but his wisdom that allowed Orpheus to influence birds, beasts, and gods alike.

Physical matter is feminized and rendered passive, whether that matter is wax, a territorially limited wilderness or all terra firma. To the point, in *A Midsummer Night's Dream* Duke Theseus tells Hermia that to her god-like father (Egeus) she is "but as a form in wax, / By him imprinted, and within his power / To leave the figure or disfigure it" (I.i.49-51); while the poet speaker in Donne's "To his Mistress Going to Bed" proclaims of his female lover's body that "where my hand is set, my seal shall be" (l. 32). The shaping of matter is left to masculine agents also in Clifford Geertz's discussion of royal progress entertainments. Geertz interprets royal pageantry as the "stamping [of] a territory with ritual signs of dominance" (Local Knowledge 125).[11] His pivotal European example is the coronation entry of Elizabeth I which, once more, demonstrates the manifold epistemological problems the reign of a queen in a patriarchal society entailed. Once again, Elizabeth is both matter and form, both feminine and masculine: Matter because she is a woman and associated with the realm she rules over, form because she is simultaneously enacting the masculine roles of chief commander and custodian. In the Lord Mayor's Show as much as in the royal coronation entry, the new dignitaries – male under normal circumstances – imprinted their authority onto a territory by ritually traversing it and forming matter according to their will. In the Lord Mayor's Show the mayor forms matter not only by traversing it but also by entering into a figurative marital union with it.

Thematically Munday's *Chruso-thriambos* is closely related to his *Sidero-thriambos*. In the show, the ages of the world are personified as "foure beautifull *Nymphes* or *Graces*; being named *Chrusos*, *Argurion*, *Calcos*, and *Sideros*" (B2). Of the four, Sideros, iron or the iron age, is

> sole Commandresse, in Mettals of most vsuall imployment; [She] affordeth out her bounteous *Myne*, all kinds of Martiall and Military weapons, honouring with them Armes and Souldiers. Likewise, for Tillage and Husbandry, those instruments best agreeing therewith: because it is the sustentation of life, and supporters of all other manuary Trades. Being not vnmindfull also, of Nauigation & Comerce with forraigne Nations, which can haue no consistence, but by her helpe. (B2)

Once again, one of Terra's daughters is the focus of a show. In *Sidero-thriambos*, written for the Ironmongers, it is naturally personified Iron and not Gold who takes precedence. At the core of the show is once more the motif of feminine matter, embodied in Terra's fair daughters, which yields material rewards to the industrious.[12] The gifts Sideros "affordeth out her bounteous *Myne*" profit everybody but they do crucially depend on the work of Ironmongers and affiliated specialists to be rendered usable. The metal ore must be extracted, smelted and worked in order to be transformed into weapons, agricultural tools, and implements used in transportation by land and sea. It is, thus, a combination of the raw materials offered by Terra and the efforts of various professionals which leads to successful enterprise, allowing London to remain a center of commerce and culture as

---

[11] Geertz examines instances of royal pageantry and parades from North Africa, Asia, and Europe (Local Knowledge 125).

[12] Cf. Francis Parlett's belief, expressed in his 1632 speech in honor of the mayor of King's Lynn, "that a town, like a wife, is only as good as she is used" (Patterson 169).

well as the "Nurse of our Nauie" (2: 213), as Stow proudly noted. The principle of feminine materiality molded by a masculine spirit of industry is embodied in Munday's show
by Sideros, on the one hand, and new mayor Sebastian Harvey, on the other. As the first
among the Ironmongers, he is symbolically the one whose efforts can bring forth all of
the above from the ample body of Terra.

A further civilization narrative and an example of the feminization of territory in a
Lord Mayor's Show is presented in Munday's *Triumphs of Re-united Britannia* in which
personified Britannia plays a significant part. Before her conquest by mythical Brute, the
needed "man in place" of Orpheus' description, Britannia's physique is equivalent to an
uncivilized wilderness. Only through Brute's efforts is she transformed into a civilized
space.[13] In Munday's recapitulation of history – a blend of biblical, mythical, and
historical elements – that opens the pamphlet, the creation of the world inevitably leads
to the founding of London: After the biblical flood, Noah's third son Iaphet was given
Europe and he, in turn, passed on to his own sixth son, Samothes, that part of Europe
containing Britain, not then known by that name. Samothes' descendants reigned until
the giant Albion, son of Neptune, conquered the land and called it Albion after himself.
The giants' hold over the territory was broken by the Trojan Brute, however, who arrived
in Britain following the destruction of Troy: "*Brute*, being directed by a vision in his
sleepe, to finde out a country scituated in the *West* with the remaines of his *Troyan*
folowers, arriued and Landed [...], the yeare of the world, 2850. after the destruction of
Troy, 66. before the building of *Rome* 368. and 1116. before Christs natiuity." (A3)[14] The
end of the race of giants meant the beginning of civilization in Britain, imported by Brute
and implanted by him in this new, wild place. Following his own reign, Brute divided
Britain among his sons into the kingdoms of Logria/England, Cambria/Wales, and
Albania/Scotland (A4) and only the recent arrival of James I, as a latter day Brute, carries
the hope that this division may be revoked and that Britain may be reunited once more,
as it ought to be.

The show's main pageant set displays personified Britannia along with her divided
kingdoms, "in the like female representations, *Loegria*, *Cambria*, and *Albania*" (B2).
Present also is "*Brute* her Conquerer" (B2). In a sexualization of the land that echoes
Ralegh's and Keymis' comments on the Guianas, Munday calls Brute's takeover of
Britain "his conquest of her virgine honour, which since it was by heauen so appointed,
she reckons it to be the very best of fortunes". Britannia herself affirms for the benefit of
Brute that he has "Crownd me thy virgin Queene *Britania*" (B3), making her not only
realm but sexual partner. The same paradox that applies to the unconquerable city,
discussed above, also applies to the whole of Britain: like the walled city, the sexualized
realm has to be kept 'intact' as a virgin, while it is simultaneously subjected to the

---

[13] Correspondingly, Stow interprets the history of the city as a history of civilization (2: 196-99).
[14] Bergeron claims that Munday "remains the only pageant writer to focus on this myth [of Brute's
conquest of Britain]" (Munday n. pag.). It is true that Munday's *Triumphs of Re-united
Britannia* is the only show in which Brute physically appears but other pageant authors, such
as Webster and Heywood, certainly draw on the myth. In *The Seven Deadly Sinnes* of London,
Dekker refers to London not as Brute's bride but as his "fairest-faced daughter" (41).

penetrating force of her subduer.[15] Yet, the process of subjugation is welcomed by Britain. Previously "a vast Wildernes, inhabited by Giantes, and a meere den of Monsters", Britannia is improved by Brute and his "ciuill followers, [who] first taught her modest manners, and the meanes how to raigne as an Imperial lady" (B2). On the pageant set, Brute himself instills the humbling knowledge in his personified realm "that [she] before my honord victorie, / Wert as a base and oregrowne wildernes" (B3).

With Brute's conquest, however, Britannia is civilized and as a testament to that feat, Brute names her after himself. In dialogue with her conqueror, Britannia acknowledges her transformation into "thy virgin Queene *Britania*" (B3). This baptism echoes Adam's naming of Eve in the Old Testament and the inscription of Amerigo Vespucci's name on the 'new world'. The notion of male priority before and command over signs was present, too, in contemporary discourse and related to the proper conduct of husband and wife toward each other. Robert Cleaver declares that as Adam named the animals under his command, "so he did name the woman also, in token that she should bee subiect to him" (235).

Brute, too, brands his territory with his name as well as with his force. Recollecting his complete appropriation of Britannia, he tells her that "not one withstood / My quiet prograce ouer all thy land" (B3). The activity he recalls, the imprinting of authority onto a territory by means of a progress across that territory, is relived on the day of the Lord Mayor's Show with the new mayor's parade through his city. In this ritual enactment of dominance, London assumes the role of Britannia while the incoming lord mayor becomes a conquering Brute. Although the role of the Trojan hero had earlier been assigned to James I, the mayor clearly shares in it here. Just as Brute made Britannia his "virgin Queene", mayor and city are joined in a marital union in which the husband is the source of form, of government and administration.

3.5   Naming and Punning

Naming as a strategy of marking ownership and authority over a territory is also reflected in London's alias of New Troy, a name given to the city by its mythic founder Brute. In his *Londini Speculum*, Heywood declares that London derives her "Antiquity" from Brute and was "first cald by him *Trinovantum*, or *Troy-novant*, *New Troy*" (305).[16] The name

---

[15] This paradox recalls the biblical virgin birth and is remarked upon by Alanus de Insulis in the *Anticlaudian* (qtd. in Ferrante 58).

[16] In his narrative poem *Troia Britannica* (1609), Heywood had outlined all of history, from creation – via the fall of Troy and Brute's founding of London – to the reign of James I (Kathman, Heywood n. pag.). Thomas Nashe habitually invoked the myth of Brute in Britain in a more tongue-in-cheek fashion, whether by mocking reference to his compatriots as "the generation of Brute" in *The Unfortunate Traveller* (227), or by dubbing London the "Great Grandmother of Corporations, Madame Troynovant" in *Pierce Penniless* (qtd. in Manley, Matron to Monster 356). To Dekker London is an "ancient and reverend Grandam of Citties" (The Seven Deadly Sinnes 37), and "Grandam almost to this whole Kingdome" (The Dead Tearme A3). Active at the same time as Nashe, Edmund Spenser was more deferential. In *The*

161

"New Troy" and the fabulous legacy it implied retained significance in contexts of civic pageantry and on occasions of civic pride in the 17ᵗʰ century. Heywood's allusion to London under her name of New Troy shows pride in the city's involvement with Britain's mythical founding father Brute who was, after all, thought to be a descendant of Aeneas himself. In all her ancient glory, the pageant poets agree, the capital is worthy of the attention of venerable authors like Geoffrey Chaucer, John Gower, John Lydgate, Thomas More, and Philip Sidney – poets "who do eternize brave acts" (B) –, as New Troy herself declares in Webster's *Monuments of Honour* (ibid.). In Webster's show the new mayor is met on his route by "a Person representing *Troynouant* or the City, in throned in rich Habilaments" (B). Beneath New Troy, i.e. London by its mythic name, sit personified Antwerp, Paris, Rome, Venice and Constantinople, admiring the English capital's "peace and felicity" (B).[17]

While London's founding myth and the city's associated alias of New Troy was a commonplace in contemporary discourse, its historical accuracy was nevertheless widely questioned by sceptic minds. Stow sums up Geoffrey of Monmouth's account of the myth in his *Survey*:

> As the Romane writers to glorifie the citie of *Rome* drew the originall thereof from Gods and demie Gods, by the Troian progenie: so *Giffrey* of Monmouth the Welsh Historian, deduceth the foundation of this famous Citie of *London*, for the greater glorie therof, and emulation of *Rome*, from the very same originall. For he reporteth that *Brute*, lineally descended from the demy god *Eneas*, the sonne of *Venus*, daughter of *Iupiter*, about the yeare of the world 2855. and 1108. before the nativitie of Christ, builded this city neare unto the river now called *Thames*, and named it *Troynouant* or *Trenouant*. (1: 1)

Stow himself dismisses this version of events, however, and voices the opinion, based on assertions by the Roman historian Livy, that modern minds should be less beguiled by ancient legends than the ancients themselves might have (understandably) been. At the same time as he denies the modern validity of the myth of Brute, Stow exhibits scepticism about Britain's Roman heritage as a case of the fated translation of empires. Wryly, he notes "that before the ariuall of the Romans, the Brytons had no towns, but called that a town which had a thicke intangled wood, defended as I saide with a ditch and banke, the like whereof the Irishmen our next neighbors doe at this day call *Fastnes*" (1: 4). In consequence of a certain cultural 'backwardness', so Stow, the Roman retreat left the British helpless in the face of new invasions. Philip Robinson stresses that, in fact, the post-Trojan founding myth of Britain in general and London in particular was recognized

Fairie Queene her declared: "For noble Britons sprong from Troians bold, / And Troynovant was built of old Troyes ashes cold." (book 3, canto 9, stanza 38)

[17] In Nashe's *Unfortunate Traveller* narrator Jack Wilton refers to "Rome, the queen of the world and metropolitan mistress of all other cities" (268), and "so old a triumphing city" (ibid. 269). Later, Jewish character Zadok, following his banishment, rails on "Rome, this whore of Babylon" (ibid. 294).

162

as fictitious by many contemporary scholars and historians (such as William Camden)[18] but that it still held significant potency. Not infrequently the same scholars who denied the truth of the myth in one place would strategically embrace it in another. As possible explanations for the ambiguity, Robinson cites "cultural lag" as well as the theory that the value of the myth – even if recognized as such – lay in its potential to create civic loyalty (223-25).[19] Thus Thomas Wyatt poetically envisioned his homecoming from antagonistic Spain to London – "the town which Brutus sought by dreams" – as a deeply patriotic journey echoing Brute's own peregrination.

In the cause of civic loyalty, the Lord Mayor's Shows not only alluded to the myth of Brute-in-Britain, pageant poets were also uninhibited about drawing parallels between the civic cultures of London and Rome and about alluding to the city's venerable history and traditions in general. In *Londini Speculum* Heywood affirms London's origin as New Troy, a settlement which subsequently became "*Caier Lud*, that is, *Luds Towne*, of King *Lud*, [...] and so from *Luds Towne*, [...] it came since to be called *London*" (306). This series of name changes, Manley attests, reflects the city's "loyal submission to a series of royal masters" (Matron to Monster 356), all of whom inscribe themselves onto the city, either directly by their own names or by aspects intimately connected to them. Dekker's London herself, in his prose pamphlet *The Dead Tearme,* links this process of submission to marriage and notes how "women married to great persons, loose their old names, so did I mine being wedded to that king [Lud]" (F4).[20] Lud, London recalls, "set a Corronet of Towers uppon my heade, and although it were not beautifull for Ornament, yet made he for me a Gyrdle, strong for defence, which being made of Turffe and other such stuffe, trenched rounde about, served in the Nature of a Wall" (ibid.). The defensive and architectural work is then continued by subsequent rulers.

By implanting speculative fiction in less contested history and by phrasing it in sober and seemingly disinterested language, Heywood manages to present civic myth in an authentic light. He establishes parallels between the censors and tribunes of Rome and elected office bearers in contemporary London in "The Epistle" preceding his *London's Ius Honorarium*, which takes as its premise the prerogative of some Roman magistrates to adjust or alter existing law. Heywood then goes on to declare that "[t]he first Sheriffes that bore the name and office in this Citty, were Peter Duke, and Thomas Neale, Anno 1209. The nouissimi, now in present Samuell Cranmer and Henry Pratt. Anno 1631" (268). The comparisons between London and Roman public offices – alluded to in the title – as well as the listing of London's first and most recent sheriffs establish a venerable

---

18 Already Polydore Vergil's 1534 *Anglica Historia*, commissioned by Henry VII, had denied British descent from Brutus and Troy (Wickham 2: 27), leading to charges of nationalistic bias against the Italian Vergil.

19 Robinson's own explanation is that the myth of Trojan descent was used by pageant writers to exploit its "multivocal ambiguity" (226).

20 In *The Fairie Queene* King Lud is referenced – in a list of Brute's descendants – as the monarch who reconstructed "[t]he ruin'd wals [...] / Of Troynovant, gainst force of enimy" and built Ludgate, "that gate, which of his name is hight, / By which he lyes entombed solemnly" (book 2, canto 10, stanza 46). In *The Seven Deadly Sinnes of London*, Dekker makes London not wife but "good daughter to King Lud, who gave her her name" (41).

tradition, legitimizing both the office of sheriff and its incumbents, both past and present. In the same vein, Heywood goes on to explain in the pamphlet text proper, that in ancient Rome the authority of some elected magistrates (praetors) grew

> to that height, that whatsoever he decreed or censured in publique, was cald *Ius Honorarium*, the first on whome this dignity was conferd in *Rome*, was *spur: furius Camillus*, the sonne of *Marcus*: And the first *Praetor* or Lord Maior appointed to the Gouernment of the Honorable Citty of *London*, was *Henry Fitz Allwin*, aduanced to that Dignity, by King *Iohn*, *Anno*. 1210. (270)

By reinforcing a parallel between praetor and lord mayor, Heywood relies on the legitimizing powers of history. So does Munday, who opens his pamphlet commemorating *Chruso-thriambos* with the following passage:

> The ancient *Romaines*, who were the first Creators of Consuls and Senators for publike rule and honorable gouernment, vsed yearlie triumphall shows and deuises, to grace their seuerall Inauguration. From which famous and commendable Custome, *London* (as well as other Magnificent Citties of the World) hath (from time to time) both deuised and continued the like loue and carefull respect, at the Creation of her worthy Consuls and Magistrates. (A3)

It is not only the Roman offices that are perpetuated in London, although this notion is important. To Dekker the aldermen "represent[...] the dignity of Romaine Senatours" and the two London sheriffs "personate (in theyr Offices and places) the Romane Consuls" (The Dead Tearme G). Importantly, the Lord Mayor's Show is established as heir to ancient Roman triumphs in celebration of "honorable gouernment" – a claim of successorship which is reflected in the titles of many shows ('triumphs'). Taylor's *Triumphs of Fame and Honour,* in which the author stresses the 500-year history of the office of lord mayor and its ceremonies (516), is just one example among many of this titular allusion to Roman heritage. In the passage quoted above, Munday explains that the ancient and venerable tradition of the triumphal parade was adopted by Londoners as well as by citizens of other European metropoles. However, the claim made by Middleton in *Triumphs of Integrity*, that of "all solemnities by which the happy inauguration of a subject is celebrated" (ll. 24-27) none could compete with the magnificence of the Lord Mayor's Show, was often repeated and showcases the self-understanding of Londoners as the true heirs of Roman civilization. However, despite these claims of ancient provenance, the grandeur of the pre-Civil War Lord Mayor's Show was a relatively recent phenomenon and the distinct format of the celebrations had not in fact existed before the second half of the 16th century. Still, pageant authors revel in the ancient dignity of London government and its customs while profiting from the validating and legitimizing aura of age – a process which is part of the allure of the "invented tradition". Demonstrating a like concern with age and historical precedent, members of the major livery companies enjoyed claiming seniority over one another: Hill confirms that "[b]eing able to claim first place in the historical chronology of the livery companies was a prized honour, and one which pageant writers naturally engaged with" (Pageantry 303).

In his *Triumphs of Truth* Midddleton writes of "those yearly ceremonial rites which ancient and grave order hath determined" that the mayor should undergo at St Paul's (975), while Munday praises his pageant chariot in *Himatia-poleos* for taking after "the triumphall Chariots of the Romaine Emperours" (B2). Meanwhile Heywood, in his printed record of *Londini Speculum*, confidently breaks up into its two main components the term "*Elder-man*, or *Alder-man*", and directly refers to the priority of age. At the same time, he points out that "the name of *Maior* [...] implyeth as much as *the greater*". The semantic digression, Heywood believes, "may serve for the Antiquity of London, and the Titles". In the same show Heywood also validates the current system of annual mayoral elections by referral to (multiple) ancient precedent(s): "I read that the *Athenians* elected theirs *Annually*; and for no longer continuance: [...] And the *Roman* Senate held, that continued *Magistracy* was in some respects unprofitable to the *Weale-publicke*" (304). Likewise, in a bid to affirm "the *Antiquity* of your [London's] yearely *Government*" (ibid), Heywood draws on the etymology of the term sheriff which, he explains, "implyeth as much as the Reeue and Gouernour of a Sheire, for Reeue: is Graue Count or Earle" (267). The meaning so added to the term increases the prestige and authority of both office and officeholders. Heywood's comparison of London sheriffs to Roman censors and tribunes, of London mayors to praetors (267-68), is followed by his confident conclusion that "the Dignities of this Citty [London], come neere to these in Rome, when it was most flourishing" (London's Ius Honorarium 268).

What has been demonstrated above is not only that naming strategies and creative etymologies are historically intertwined with gender conceptions but also that these strategies were applied in Lord Mayor's Shows in order to affirm and celebrate the current distribution of authority in the city and as a tool to shape ideas about civic life and politics. These phenomena also have a strong bearing on the discussion of punning.

"Serious Punning"

Closely connected to the idea that the Lord Mayor's Show is the modern incarnation of an ancient tradition and that London itself is the inheritor of Roman civic culture is another process, highly typical of the Lord Mayor's Show, which also utilizes the power of the past to validate present-day arrangements. This process may be described as "a kind of serious punning", based on Victor Turner's analyses of Central African ritual procedures (64). Turner describes how words used in ritual contexts are subjected to explanatory etymologizing, an activity that is here often based on "similarity of sound [homophony] rather than derivation from a common source" (ibid. 11). Whether the proposed etymology of a word is right or wrong, "for the people themselves it constitutes part of the 'explanation' of a ritual symbol" (ibid.), and as such it assumes a genuine worth and function within the ritual itself. A similar process – that may also be referred to as serious punning – is at work in the Lord Mayor's Show. The printed pamphlets in particular are full of sweeping etymologies dealing with official titles and the names of mayors and, sometimes, sheriffs (who were likely to be future mayors). At the same time, serious punning is by no means restricted to the pamphlets. This hitherto neglected aspect of the show-as-ritual puts etymology and semantics in the service of creating and maintaining social order. Notwithstanding an element of humor with regard to forced puns, the linguistic derivations naturalize and so justify the political arrangements and ideologically integrate officeholders into their new positions. The strategy fit in seamlessly with a culture that valued devices and clever (often polyglot) slogans which sometimes also made use of personal names.

With reference to the Shakespearean corpus both Kenneth Muir and Molly M. Mahood have corroborated that "[w]ordplay was a game the Elizabethans played seriously" (Mahood 9), and that puns had legitimacy not only in comic but also "in uncomic contexts" (Muir 42). Anne Lancashire has made a tentative move toward analyzing the importance of punning in the Lord Mayor's Show in her astute examination of George Peele's 1591 *Descensus Astraeae*. The show, celebrating the inauguration of Salter William Webbe, puns on the new mayor's name in a pageant featuring personified Nature, Fortune, and Time (Comedy 13). This trio is a version of the Greek Morai or the Fates. Nature (the equivalent of Clotho) is shown in the act of winding a web which she then passes on to Fortune (i.e. Lachesis) and Time (Atropos), implying that the mayor's election into office is both rightful and seasonable, notwithstanding the temporary limits placed on his term in office. The pun on Webbe's name, argues Lancashire, is not merely a comic and inconsequential interlude as is generally the consensus among scholars. "[T]he pun is a serious one", she echoes Turner's wording. Through it "the newly sworn mayor is both referred to and seen, in his office, as transitory" (ibid. 13-14). Lancashire's point is notable and accurate with reference to Peel's *Descensus Astraeae* but she does not go on to note the ubiquity of serious punning in the pre-Civil War Lord Mayor's Show. Beyond the meaning of each specific pun, the strategy not only creates "semantic enrichment" (Turner 64), but facilitates the semantic integration of people and concepts into a conceptual whole.

William Webbe was not the first of London's lord mayors to become the object of a serious pun in the course of his inaugural show. As early as 1431, according to John Lydgate, the entertainments for John Wells had been "devised notably indede / For to accordyne with the Maiers name" (qtd. in Hill, Pageantry 163). In 1554 Grocer John Lyon met with a pageant lion (qtd. in Lancashire, Comedy 22), while in 1568 Richard Mulcaster compared mayor Thomas Rowe (or Roe) to a swift and sharp-sighted deer (ibid. 21). In Mulcaster's show,

> three boys [...] talk[...] about the swiftness and attentiveness of the roe (pun on the mayor's name) which hearkens to the voice of the prophet. The third boy notes, for example: 'Our Roe by sighte in governement / Wee truste shall Rule so well / That by his doinges suche may Learne as covet to excell' (Bergeron, The Elizabethan Lord Mayor's Show 274).

Rowe, indeed, demonstrated some foresight by ordering the conversion of land to the west of old Bethlem Hospital into the New Churchyard, a non-parochial burial ground, to relieve the intra-mural parishes (Hartle 15). The project was swiftly realized and the new cemetery received its first burials in 1569. Some years earlier, in 1561, Mayor William Harper had been presented with a pageant of historical and mythological harpers (Lancashire 328), establishing a connection between Harper and a set of mythological heroes: Chief among them are David, Orpheus, and Amphion. David calls for Londoners to "reioyce [...] and hope well of yor mayre ffor neu' did a mylder man sitt in yor chiefest chaire", while Orpheus points out the power of the harp, and Amphion observes that even stones relent to the sound of music. Arion and Topas echo these sentiments in their brief speeches (Bergeron, The Elizabethan Lord Mayor's Show 272). Harper's inaugural show also references psalm 150 which bids worshipers to praise God "with the sound of the trumpet: praise him with the psaltery and harp" (ibid. 271-72). Occupational names such as Webbe – deriving from "weaver" – and Harper were of course highly suitable for visual representation but, while the puns exploited this suitability, they also went beyond the mere representation of a given occupation. In Webbe's pageant, weaving or at least the product of weaving is represented but the web that passes from Nature to Fortune and then from Fortune to Time is no ordinary fabric. By it, Webbe is shown as predestined to play his distinguished part in the political life of the city. William Harper's pageant also does more than display persons following an occupation, i.e. playing the harp. Ultimately, the display of mythological harpers identifies Harper not as an instrumentalist but as one who shares the company of civilizing heroes and has therefore rightly been elected lord mayor. In his account of the 1575 Lord Mayor's Show, William Smith, too, mentions a pageant bearing "certayne fygures and wrytinges, (partly towchinge the name of the mayor)" (qtd. in Hill, Pageantry 162); no pamphlet commemorating the 1606 show survives but "there was evidently some limited pageantry ordered for this occasion, including 'beasts' such as a seahorse and 'seawatte' (a play on the Lord Mayor's name, John Watts, who was a ship owner)" (Hill, Pageantry 73-74).

Punning was clearly integral to the proceedings. A theme of punning on new mayor Leonard Holliday's name runs through Munday's *The Triumphs of Re-united Britannia*, which opens with a pageant ship called "Royall Exchange". From aboard the ship its crew, consisting of master, mate, and boy, "liberally bestow" spices on the surrounding spectators in honor of this "cheerefull Holi-day" (B). Once more, the incoming mayor's surname is ideally suited for visual expression and once more the pun takes advantage of this circumstance but does more than just reference festivity. Instead, the whole history of Britain is linked to Holliday as the character of Albanact – legendary Brute's son – notes that the 'reunification' of Britain under James I and VI is truly a "happy Holi-day" (B4). Neptune, too, offers a variation on the theme of holidays:

> Bethink thee how on that high *Holyday*, / Which beares Gods Champion, th' Arch-angels name, / When conquering Sathan in a glorious fray, / *Michaell* Hels-monster nobly ouercame, / And now a sacred Saboath being the same, / A free and full election on all parts, / Made choise of thee, both with their hands and harts. / Albeit this day is vsuall euery yeare, / For new election of a Magistrate, / Yet, now to me some instance doth appeare, / Worth note, which to my selfe I thus relate, / *Holyday*, cald on *Holyday* to state, / Requiers methinks a yeare of *Holydayes*, / To be disposd in good and vertuous wayes. (C4)

Neptune calls up the context of the mayoral elections and notes both the annual recurrence of the event and the purported uniqueness of Holliday's mayoralty. By establishing a link between the holiday of St Michael, city politics, and Leonard Holliday's last name, Neptune's achievement is twofold: He glorifies London politics by the connection to St Michael and, at the same time, naturalizes Holliday's principal involvement in them.

Only fragments of Munday's *Camp-Bell, or, The Ironmongers Fair Feild* (1609) survive but the show's very title is a serious pun on new mayor Thomas Campbell's name. Hill cites Campbell's show as an example of the frequent titular allusions to "central thematic concerns, [...] the name of the Lord Mayor (*Camp-bell*, for instance), or to the name or trade of his livery company" (Pageantry 216). While there is no detailed description of the pageant in question, the character of St Andrew, whose speech has been preserved, explains to the mayor that it "derives its owne best conceit from the borrowed caracter of your name, *Faire Feild*, and your name being *Campbell*, dooth argue and expresse the very same" (B3). In addition to "goodly Trees, Fruites, and faire Fountaine that only gives it ornament" (ibid.), personifications of the seven virtues, cardinal and theological, reside on the pageant stage and promise seven years of future happiness for the city. Thus, Campbell shares in the identity of the city – and vice versa – while his name predestines him to have a beneficial effect on the metropolis, like a good gardener.

In his 1611 *Chruso-thriambos* Munday has the character of Leofstane etymologize the surname of new mayor James Pemberton, though not without mentioning the family names of his rivals in that year's mayoral election, Swynnerton and Myddleton (who were to be elected in 1612 and 1613 respectively):

> Next, three Names, all of equal sillable and sound, to happen in the immediate choice is a matter deseruing regard, and (from the Maioralities first beginning) never was the like. *Pemberton, Swynnerton,* and *Middleton,* Names of three most worthy Gentlemen, but of much greater worth in sence and significancie, as your own (my Lord, for breuitie) may yeilde an instance. Pemberton deriues it selfe from the auncient Brittish, Saxon, and eldest English, each Sillable suted with his apt meaning. *Pem,* implyeth the Head, cheefe or most eminent part of any thing; *Bert,* beareth the Character of bright shining and radiant splendour; and *Tun,* hath continued the long knowne Word for any Towne or Citty. (C3)

Initially, Leofstane's etymological explanation of the name's opening syllable "Pem-" as "Head, cheefe or most eminent part" naturalizes the new mayor's elevated position and his role as husband to the city, while the "bright shining and radiant splendour" allegedly inherent in the middle syllable, "-bert-", adds an element of glory. The final "-ton", of course, links Pemberton to the city of London and in combination with the preceding syllables he is firmly established in his office: the "bright head of this famous Citty" (C3). Personified Time acknowledges this etymological argument and adds that "such a goodly name, / Requires bright actions" (C4).[21] Thus, Pemberton is asked to live up to a destiny of greatness which Leofstane's etymological exegesis has only just produced. At the end of the show Father Time speaks up once more and this time uses Pemberton's given name to establish his authority, pointing out that "Iames thy gracious King, / Sets Iames (his Subiect) heere his Deputy" (ibid.), which, to Hill, amounts to a "somewhat forced comparison" (Pageantry 128). That although the new mayor's surname derives from a location, this location does not in fact have any tangible connection to London but may more probably originally refer to the Lancashire district of Pemberton is irrelevant. As is

---

[21] Hill has argued about this drawn-out excursus in etymology that although "one might be tempted to regard this is [sic] a banal observation when taken literally" (Anthony Munday 157), by the emphasis on the morpheme "-ton" the importance of London is heightened.

the more prosaic, alternate translation of the name from Old English as "barley farm on the hill". Here, as in Turner's study, whether an etymological analysis is founded or unfounded is inconsequential in terms of its ritual worth.

The precise etymology behind the surname of John Leman, incoming mayor in 1616, is uncertain, too. This, however, does not prevent Munday, in his *Chrysanaleia*, from employing serious punning in order to establish Leman in his office as well as at the heart of the city. Wickham's unfavorable comment that "[t]he lemon tree was used somewhat pedestrianly by Anthony Munday to figure a Lord Mayor of that name in 1616" (2: 216), fails to do justice to the function of the word play and may even have contributed to the critical silence on the topic of punning in the Lord Mayor's Show. Hill refers to the episode as an "opportunistic use of the image of the lemon tree to celebrate John Leman" (see fig. 15) (Pageantry 162). The pageant set in question – which survives in a rare conceptual drawing – features a lemon tree at its center. By using the tree to indicate Mayor Leman, it does take advantage of the concrete referent of homophonic "lemon". At the same time, however, it posits Leman as London's central pillar of strength and source of well-being by situating the health-giving tree at the center of the stage, with the personified Senses and a pious pelican-cum-offspring placed around and beneath it.

Caitlin Finlayson's assessment that the "lemon tree device in reference to mayor John Leman in *Chrysanaleia*" is nothing but a "facile pun[...]" does no justice to the significance of the episode and the prevalence of punning in general (Jacobean Foreign Policy 586). Furthermore, the potency of the tree as a signifier is supported by many instances of sententious trees and tree lists in medieval and early modern literature, for example in book one, canto one of *The Faerie Queene*. The lemon tree, explains Munday, is "a singular Embleme, corresponding with the Creast and Cognizance of the Lord Maior, and bearing an especiall Morality beside" (B2). Moreover, the tree's properties act on the senses in a way that is "restoring, comforting and relieuing" (B3). Citrus fruits are displayed in the tree's leafy crown and some are placed on the grass at its feet among the personified Senses (to whose well-being they contribute). Fairly often, particularly meaningful or spectacular contraptions were preserved after the celebrations. In this manner, and attesting to its popularity, the lemon tree device was kept in the Fishmongers' Hall during Leman's term in office (Chambers 563). It does not matter in the context of this pageant, as it did not above, that the surname in question probably does not derive from the citrus plant of Munday's choice but possibly from the French "le moin", i.e. "the monk", or even from the anglicized version of Irish "Leannáin", meaning "lover". The sobriquet "leman" was commonly used in this sense, so – to cite just one example – in Nashe's *Unfortunate Traveller* (296).

The motif of the pious and self-sacrificing pelican which presents Leman as an extremely giving and nurturing figure had also been incorporated into medieval celebrations of the Eucharist (Rubin 310-12), in which the bird's alleged parental devotion and martyrdom expressed Christ's self-sacrifice for the salvation of mankind. Lord Mayor Leman is, thus, not only depicted as a nurturing father to his Londoners – and encouraged to act accordingly – but also closely associated with Christ himself.[22] It

---

[22] A tree with special properties, watched over by a Christ-like figure, also features in passus 16 of William Langland's *Piers Plowman*. Here protagonist Will is told that charity "is a tree of

is important in this context not to mistake instances of *imitatio Christi* for mere self-aggrandizement or even blasphemy, as Gordon Kipling has stressed. Rather, they are often serious spiritual performances (cf. Enter the King 43).

Fig. 15: The lemon tree pageant from Munday's *Chrysanaleia*, featuring the pelican in her piety. © The British Library Board.

This vocabulary of Christian sacrifice and zealous parenthood, with a maternal tinge, as it is applied to Leman, is compatible with contemporary notions of ideal family life, as

> great excellence. / Mercy is the master root; the main trunk is pity, / The leaves are lawful words, the law of Holy Church; / The blossoms are obedient speech and benevolent looks" (180-81). Piers Plowman watches over the tree and protects it from harm (which also represents the trinity as well as the hierarchy of matrimony, widowhood, and virginity) (ibid. 181-83).

170

demonstrated by Robert Cleaver who argues that husbands and fathers ought to care for the bodies and, even more so, for the souls of all members of their households and to "kindle them in the zeale of God, [...] as a Nurse to emptie her breasts" (372). The association of the mayoralty with the duties of fatherhood is not unique to Munday's *Chrysanaleia* but is also expressed in other shows. In Heywood's *Londini Speculum* booklet, for instance, the narrating voice of Heywood addresses the mayor, in the second person, with these words: "You [mayors] are also cald *Fathers*, *Patrons* of the *Afflicted*, and *Procurators of the Publicke good*" (303).

In Munday's *Sidero-thriambos*, a 'British bard', whose speech is set off from the rest of the pamphlet by the use of gothic (black letter) script, "findeth, that in this yeare of 1618. the letter H. shall haue predominance in three distinct persons" (C2). By a 'magic trick' he proceeds to bring forth "three seuerall letters of H" and present them to his audience (C2). The letters refer to new lord mayor Sebastian Harvey and his two newly appointed sheriffs, Herne and Hamarsley. The bard predicts that Harvey, Herne, and Hamarsley will bring "Honor, Heale, and Happinesse" to the city and its population and that their work together will be so harmonious and beneficent as to "maken ey pleasing Symphony" (C3). This semantic enrichment of the names of the mayor and his sheriffs, based on a similarity of sounds, ascribes positive attributes to all three of them, which bodes well for their conduct in office, and creates the sense that this trio is peculiarly well suited to be working together. Although the origins of Harvey's family name, also carried by the Breton patron saint of the blind, cannot be established without doubt,[23] the association of Harvey and "Honor" makes the point that he will discharge his duties conscientiously. The same is true for the pairing of Hamarsley and "Heale" as well as Herne and "Happinesse", irrespective of the Old English origins of the names.[24]

In Middleton's *Triumphs of Love and Antiquity* the serious pun welcoming new mayor William Cokayne into office consists of "an artificial cock, often made to crow and flutter with his wings" (1400), which is fixed into position above the head of Orpheus.[25] From his pageant stage the mythical musician explains the presence of the bird to Cokayne in the following words:

How fitly does it match your name and power, / Fixed in that name now by this glorious hour, / At your just voice to shake the bold'st offence / And sturdiest sin that e'er had

---

[23] The name may derive from Breton words meaning "battle worthy", or it may be of Irish origin (Internet Surname Database n. pag.).

[24] The name, more commonly spelled Hammersley or Hammerslie, derives from the Old English terms for "an area cleared for agriculture on a (hamm) hill" (Internet Surname Database n. pag.). The name Herne may derive from Old English "hyrne" and Middle English "herne", referring to "someone residing in a nook or corner of land, or a bend in a river". There may also be a connection with the heron via Middle English "hern" (ibid.).

[25] Orpheus had appeared in Lord Mayor's Shows as early as 1561, as a representative of the civilizing powers of poetry (Manley 1398). As "the archetypal figure of the civic poet", Orpheus was well-suited to greet Cokayne on his arrival back in the city in Middleton's *The Triumphs of Love and Antiquity* (ibid. 1399).

residence / In secure man, yet, with an equal eye, / Matching grave justice with fair clemency, / It being the property he chiefly shows, / To give wing-warning still before he strike. (1401)

Orpheus insists that Cokayne's name and destiny match: Both the qualities of the man himself and the meaning of his name foretell greatness. This renders his recent promotion to the office of lord mayor only natural and expected, despite the fact that the economic ill-effects of the Cokayne Project (a forcible reordering of the cloth trade resulting in a major economic crisis) would have caused goodwill toward Cokayne among producers and traders to be still far from unanimous.[26] The alertness and boldness of the cock (a bird that frequently denotes incest in emblems) are qualities attributed to Cokayne. These supposedly allow him to recognize wrongdoing quickly and surely and to measure out justice in fair proportion to a crime. This is an important skill, too, for the head of a household – a role which Cokayne is about to assume for the commonwealth of London. It is necessary sometimes – if "there be contempt, or willing negligence" (Cleaver 51) – for the pater familias to punish a member of his household and so "reclaim[..] the offender from evil" (ibid. 50), for the sake of the entire household and for the offender's own good. At the same time, the alleged skill of Cokayne, to temper punishment with forewarning and mercy, is important in the head of a household, since whoever is punished unjustly will only be "hardened against just correction" (ibid. 51).[27] The authority thus established for Cokayne is unaffected by the untold circumstance that his surname might have easily (and more aptly) been explained etymologically as pertaining to a resident of the outlandish "pays de cocaigne" – a kind of cloud-cuckoo-land. The 19th-century application of the epithet "Cockaigne" to London – though not at all related to Mayor William Cokayne – is perhaps more pertinent.

Another quality possibly implied in the transference of the cock's fine qualities to Cokayne is of a Christian nature: On the title page of Jesuit Jeremias Drechsel's *Opera Omnia* (1643), his complete works, for instance, a cock or rooster sits on the head of personified Divinity, not only fulfilling his role as "herald of the morn" but also signifying

---

[26] The aim of Cokayne's project was "to transform the Merchant Adventurers' sole privilege of the exportation of undyed and undressed cloths into an exportation of the finished product" (Aldous n. pag.). Opposition by the old Merchant Adventurers was ignored and suppressed and the "New Company of Merchant Adventurers was established in its place and received its letters patent on 29 August 1615; Cokayne became its first governor. [...] All licenses for the exportation of undyed and undressed cloth were withdrawn, which annoyed the Dutch, the principal buyers. The project, and the new company, failed, and gave rise to one of the most severe trade crises ever to devastate England" (ibid.). Cokayne had made his fortune by exporting cloth to the Baltic and his willingness and financial ability to provide loans to James I had gained him the monarch's preferment (ibid.). Cokayne's funeral sermon was preached by John Donne (ibid.), and his tomb was a notable feature of St Paul's before its loss in the Great Fire of London.

[27] Cf. Nashe on the same topic: "Seldom do they prove patient martyrs who are punished unjustly." (The Unfortunate Traveller 255)

"the Father/Creator, whose voice called light out of darkness" (Manning 128).[28] Thus, by means of a symbolically charged male chicken, Cokayne – who has already been likened to Orpheus – is placed in a position analogous to that of Christ whose divine light mirrors the mayor's own duties in supplying and safeguarding the light of civilization.[29]

Fig. 16: William Cokayne's father, also called William, bequeathed a sum of money to the Skinners' Company for the production of gilded silver cups in the shape of cocks. The cups materialize and perpetuate the pun on the family name. They are still in the possession of the company and remain in use. In celebration of the election of new company officials, "the heads are removed and the bodies filled with wine to drink the health of the new Master and Wardens" (theskinnerscompany.org.uk).

[28] The rooster was also associated with Asclepius, the Greek god of medicine (Mannning 129). In Whitney's emblem "Medici Icon" Asclepius is represented with a rooster as well as a a scepter, a dragon, and a dog. Another emblem by Whitney bears the motto "Vigilante et Custodia" and deploys the rooster as a signifier of alertness (Freeman 61).

[29] Light itself begets a child on an unsuspecting woman in *The Fairie Queene*; as an explanation the narrator offers that, "Great father he of generation / Is rightly cald, the' author of life and light; / And his fair sister for creation / Ministreth matter fit, which tempred right / With heate and humour, breedes the living wight" (book 3, canto 6, stanza 9). Matter is here once more feminized while the male factor brings not only form but also light to the equation.

A particular area of the new mayor's real-life involvement in 'civilizing' endeavors is alluded to by Orpheus who claims to see a "civilly instructed Irishman" in the assembled crowds (ll. 186-94). Ten years previously, in 1609, following the Flight of the Earls, the Ulster Plantation project had been "foisted on a reluctant [city] corporation" by James I (Aldous n. pag.). During John Swinnerton's mayoralty (1612-13) the project came to a head as "serious building work at Londonderry commenced, and the fledgling city received its charter" (Archer n. pag.), but it was Cokayne who became the first governor of Londonderry and of the Irish Society, founded in 1613 to develop and defend Londonderry and Coleraine and expedite English colonization (Aldous n. pag; Beaven n. pag.).

Middleton's *The Sun in Aries*, celebrating the inauguration of Edward Barkham (a Draper and former Leatherseller), plays with the fact that the opening syllable of the mayor's name is a homonym of the nautical "bark" (Beaven n. pag.). Early in the show Argonaut Jason (who shares a love of hides and fleeces with the new mayor) expands on the pun, stating that "the bark is under sail / For a year's voyage", and voices the hope that "a blessèd gale / Be ever with it" (1589). Although the name's Old English roots actually connect it to a rural rather than a coastal location, the sea metaphor turns Barkham's life into a voyage and a success story that culminates in his mayoralty. The pun not only takes advantage of the boat as a concrete object but creates a wider narrative which produces in Barkham a daring man of action whose endeavors are cosmically rewarded and who can consequently be expected to serve a successful term in office.

From William Webbe – who is nominally sewn into his esteemed place in the fabric of society – to Edward Barkham – whose life is shaped as a journey that culminates in a successful mayoralty –, the mayors' achievements (culminating in the mayoralty) are explained and justified by the 'semantic enrichment' of their names. The family names of Webbe, Barkham et. al. no longer only identify them as individuals but define them in their contexts and naturalize their claims to leadership.

A cognitive phenomenon referred to as "fluency heuristic" may have had some bearing on the effect of serious punning. This refers to the circumstance that the form of a statement, and its familiarity, have an effect on the ease with which it is mentally processed. Perhaps unsurprisingly, easy to process information is more often taken to be accurate than difficult to process information. Matthew S. McGlone and Jessica Tofighbakhsh have analyzed the so-called "'rhyme as reason' effect" (425), i.e. the influence which form and aesthetic value – particularly rhyme – have on the perceived truth value of statements. In an experiment they confronted participants with aphorisms and found that rhyming or in some other way formally pleasing aphorisms were more likely to be judged as true than non-rhyming or otherwise less sonorous ones.[30] Norbert Schwarz concurs with the findings of McGlone and Tofigbakhsh, asserting that "beauty has often been offered as a heuristic for assessing truth" even though "beautiful theories" frequently prove wrong (136). He adds that, unsurprisingly, "this fluency-familiarity-

---

[30] Yet, participants were not conscious of this basis of their preferences: The researchers report that when asked directly whether they felt rhyming aphorisms to be more likely to be true than non-rhyming aphorisms, "all participants [...] responded 'no' (and many gave us quizzical looks)" (ibid.).

truth link has many undesirable consequences" (ibid. 137). For the lord mayor, however, consequences were largely desirable: Although not exactly equivalent, rhymes – the "identity or near-identity in stretches of sound" (Encyclopedia of Language n. pag.) – homophones and homonyms are comparable phenomena insofar as they all depend on identity of sound. The treatment undergone by names like Webbe, Harper, or Leman, therefore, may have increased the likelihood that spectators would have accepted a (non-verifiable) correlation between a mayor's name and his character or fate. While Londoners might not have been convinced that their new mayor John Leman had much in common with a citrus plant, it is possible that they would have intuitively found Leman's affinity with an invigorating lemon tree more believable.

Serious punning was not the sole preserve of the incoming mayors but was also applied to characters who appear in the shows, to professions and titles. In the pamphlet commemorating his *London's Ius Honorarium*, Heywood etymologizes the name of St Katherine, patron saint of the Haberdashers: "the name it selfe imports in the Originall, *Omnis ruina*, which as some interpret it is as much as to say, the fall and ruin of all the workes of the Diuell: Others deriue the word from *Catena*, a Chaine wherein all cheife Vertues and Graces are concatinated and link't together" (277). This seemingly thorough connection between praiseworthy Katherine and "all cheife Vertues" extends to the Company of Haberdashers, though Katherine was omitted from the company charter in 1578 in recognition of the changed religious climate (Rowland 318).[31] In *Londini Emporia*, also by Heywood and sponsored by the Company of Clothworkers, the narrator's voice defines "merchandise" as: "Mercatura, I. Merchandise, the Greekes call Emporia, and Emporos a Merchant, the Hebrewes Meker. From hence (it seemes) the Poets call Hermes [...] Mercury, making him the God of Merchants and Merchandise" (A3). The result of the etymological aside is a semantic web in which merchants and mercantile pursuits are inextricably linked with classical gods and notions of empire. This increases the prestige of the lord mayor and all merchants, not only by fostering an association with the classical pantheon but, more importantly, by suggesting that – ab origine – merchants have ever furthered the imperial interests of their own realm. Finlayson has argued that "[i]n connecting 'Mercatura' with classical mythology, and with the origins of 'mistery' [...], he [Heywood] elevates and romanticizes the origins of the livery companies, and specifically of the Clothworkers' Company" (845). Finlayson recognizes the importance of Heywood's etymology but errs in claiming that it is unique to *Londini Emporia*.[32]

---

[31] The Drapers, too, removed the Virgin Mary from their company insignia in the 1570s (ibid. 345), and the Merchant Taylors followed suit in 1586 when their coat of arms was "denuded of its religious imagery of Our Lady and Child with St John, [... and] replaced, incongruously, by the camels that were to feature shortly in the pageantry of the Shows" (Hill, Pageantry 31).

[32] Finlayson argues that Heywood's show is particularly "innovative and distinctive" (Londini Emporia 838), due in no small part to the "radically original way" in which Heywood digresses on the etymology of "merchandise" and thereby "expands [...] [his] performance material" in the printed pamphlet (ibid. 839). This, so Finlayson, renders *Londini Emporia* "unlike conventional titles which do not usually define their terms" (845).

In the same show, Heywood pays homage to sheep as the basic source of the livery company's wealth. Heywood produces an etymological link between shepherds and kings which proves that working with sheep, whether in close proximity (as shepherds, shearers etc.) or indirectly (as weavers and ultimately as cloth merchants), is noble work. In the pamphlet, he explains: "Pastor or Opilio in the Roman tongue, and in ours a Shepheard: the Hebrues call Roheh, from which some are of opinion Rex and Roy are derived, the Greekes call him Poimin, which properly implyes Ouium pastor or a feeder of Sheepe" (B2). Certainly the association, once made explicit, serves to reinforce the nobility and importance of trades which depend on sheep's wool and, most of all, of the producers and traders organized in the Worshipful Company of Clothworkers.

Generally speaking, serious puns in the Lord Mayor's Show are a means of naturalizing the system of political administration in London. At the same time, they serve to integrate office holders into their new positions and so legitimate both office and official. The example of James Pemberton is paradigmatic: Entering the office of mayor in 1611, Pemberton is defined as an individual destined to assume a top (pem) position in the city (ton), and to be a shining (bert) examplar in whatever capacity he fulfills – as is appropriate for a Goldsmith. When pageant writers expand on, and thereby expand, the meanings of mayors' names, they do more than engage in inconsequential punning. Pageant authors – by way of their semantic and etymological enhancement of names – attempt to shape the ways in which spectators perceive their social and political world. Both serious punning of the kind just outlined and the marriage metaphor, with its invocation of the family unit, serve to create and project the image of an ordered civic universe which aims to incorporate every city dweller. In Munday's *Chrysanaleia*, for instance, John Leman is both translated from a bachelor in the Fishmongers' Company into a husband to the city of London, and instituted as a central source of good for the city by means of the lemon tree pageant float. Both methods celebrate Leman while simultaneously binding him to the city and to his duties toward its residents. Similarly, in Middleton's *Triumphs of Love and Antiquity*, the pun on the observant cock establishes William Cokayne as a just and observant mayor while the marriage metaphor transforms him, too, into one of London's conjugal partners or, in the words of personified Love, into "[a] careful husband to a loving spouse" (1403). Twice over, Cokayne is set up as an authority figure, both caring and castigating, for the Londoners under his jurisdiction.

The integrating functions of punning and marriage symbolism are augmented by forces which may be rendered more intelligible by recourse to Victor Turner's concept of communitas. First, Turner's concept sheds some light on the transcendental powers with which feminine personages in the shows are endowed. Secondly, it also illuminates those pageant episodes that include representations of ordinary craftsmen and laborers and which allow spectators from different walks of life to experience a measure of solidarity and social cohesion during the celebrations.

3.6   Communitas: Inclusive Representations of the City?

Personified Virtue, one of the protagonists in Middleton's *Triumphs of Honour and Virtue*, tells the new mayor that it is neither wrong nor demeaning for "Great power to come to Virtue to be strong" (1721). This is so because, says Virtue, even though she is "but a woman, merciful and mild: / Therein is Heaven with greater glory styled / That makes weak things, as clemency and right, / Sway power, which would else rule all be might" (ibid.). Great power is here linked with masculinity while weakness is conceived of as a feminine quality.[33] The semiotic connection between women and "weak things" extends, however, to include the 'heavenly' qualities of mercy and justice which may sometimes, with peaceful persuasion, "[s]way power". Virtue concludes: "So power and virtue, when they fill one seat, / The city's blessed, the magistrate complete." (ibid.) To his own betterment, the mayor – masculine and strong – is asked to join with Virtue – weak, mild, a woman. By means of this metaphorical union of mayor and corporeal, feminine Virtue, the new lord mayor is given a divine commission to conduct himself virtuously in office. The implication is fostered that, with the personification as mediator, he can access a realm of qualities and sacred ideas otherwise denied to him. Edward Muir has registered the same notion in an Italian 14th-century fresco panel by Ambrogio Lorenzetti, titled *Allegory of the Good Government,* in which female personifications of virtues are ranked above a procession of male dignitaries. Muir holds that, "[t]heir location in the upper register of the picture corresponds to a conventional set of displacements whereby the exclusion of real women from political life enables them to be represented as icons of higher values" (144-45).

In London the voice of Virtue issues from a woman and her 'bid for power' succinctly expresses a central paradox of the early modern Lord Mayor's Show: On the one hand, women are subjected to men and the fact of this subjection is the reason why abstract concepts colonize the female body in the rhetorical figure of personification. On the other hand, these personifications are endowed with special powers which allow them to enter into a union with the lord mayor, a union that is sometimes explicitly, sometimes implicitly conjugal in nature – as when Virtue in *Triumphs of Honour and Virtue* asks the mayor to "have his splendours mixed / With these of mine" (1721). The desired state is achieved when the mayor fuses his own identity onto that of Virtue and tempers his strength with her mercy. Much as personifications embody "concepts which are essential to man's moral well-being" in the Western rhetorical tradition (Ferrante 2), feminized personifications in the Lord Mayor's Show frequently signify indispensable qualities to be taken on by the mayor for his betterment or already attributed to him.

Certainly, the power inherent in these very qualities is partly responsible for the mystic aura of personifications like Virtue above, who also claims, however, that "the essence of my deity" (l. 206) is "power raised by me" (l. 207) and not the other way around. In other words, personified Virtue is potent because virtue is itself a powerful concept but it depends on the body of the personification to take shape and receive a

---

[33] Hill confirms the use of "gendered figures" in the Lord Mayor's Show, whose significance is "inflected by the standard misogyny that underlies so much early modern culture" (Pageantry 18).

voice. Teskey argues that when concepts are projected onto female bodies, women become "the agents, not the receptacles of paternal inscription" (306). Although this potential is largely left unexplored in the Lord Mayor's Show, personification certainly creates an opportunity for the subversion of the very assumptions on which it rests.

Victor Turner offers a compelling take on notions of power, real and imagined: mystic powers, in the absence of practical ones, are ascribed to marginalized groups. "[W]eak things", like Middleton's Virtue, possess mysterious powers precisely because they are weak under normal circumstances. They possess "the permanently or transiently sacred attributes of low status or position" (Turner 109). It follows logically that this endowment with ritual power should also extend to women in general, whom the social structure of early modern London clearly placed at an enormous disadvantage, forcing them to work in unregulated and underpaid areas of production and trade (Korda 464). Married women were placed firmly under the authority of their husbands and only widowhood brought some degree of self-determination. Those 20 to 30 percent of adult women in 17th-century England who were unmarried yet not widowed had to contend with extremely discriminatory conditions in securing their livelihoods (ibid.).[34] Guilds involved in the cloth trade, for example, in spite of styling themselves as benefactors of the working population as a whole, attempted to prevent women from working as seamstresses (Rowland 363).

In concurrence with Turner and reflecting the lot of early modern women, Simone de Beauvoir has argued in *The Second Sex* that women have been 'others' within a collective they could not – and cannot – as a sex, escape (16). At the same time, she holds that "mystery" is a quality frequently ascribed by men to women and that this, as a process, is not unique, but that the quality of mystery is ascribed to any "slave" or person of low and marginal status.[35] Affirming the historical association of women and slaves as well as the connotation of femininity and physicality, Hannah Arendt has pointed out that "[w]omen and slaves belonged to the same category [in ancient Greece] and were hidden away not only because they were somebody else's property but because their life was 'laborious,' devoted to bodily functions" (72).[36] Women, thus, fulfill all the conditions required by Turner's definition to be the bearers of mysterious power, counterbalancing and obscuring their real-life lack of agency and influence. Bloch, too, points out the binary

[34] Women could be bound apprentice in a handful of trades, mainly those which were too unprofitable for men to undertake, such as lace-making (Seaver 66). Widows had the right to continue the business of a predeceased husband and keep on any apprentices bound to him at the time of his death (ibid.).

[35] In an article on the philosophical distinction between mind and body and the denigrating association of woman and body, Elizabeth V. Spelman argues: "In the history of political philosophy, the grounds given for the inferiority of women to men often are quite similar to those given for the inferiority of slaves to masters, children to fathers, animals to humans." (127)

[36] Mystical power – in the absence of actual power – and femininity are also linked phenomena in a very dfifferent cultural context. Turner analyzes the relationship between the chief of the Central African Ndembu, known as the Kanongesha, and the structurally inferior leader of the conquered Mbwela people, the Kafwana. The subordination of the Kafwana was accompanied by his investment with ceremonial powers and his symbolical feminization opposite the Kanongesha, endowed with the attributes of cultural manhood (99).

conception of femininity out of which grow the traditional roles of "seducer and redeemer" assigned to women, typified in biblical Eve and Mary. These opposing character molds for women – previously discussed – also express the paradox touched upon above: "that the periods of greatest misogynistic activity can also be periods of intense woman worship, as in the example of twelfth- and thirteenth-century mariolatry" (Bloch 8). Bloch's paradox parallels Turner's thesis: Both describe scenarios in which disenfranchisement on the one hand (and vilification) is coupled with idealization on the other.

Periods characterized by the twin phenomena of misogyny and women worship have also produced narratives of the union of man and woman as harmonious completion. In the courtly literature of the Middle Ages a hero may be rewarded for overcoming frailties and shortcomings by being (re)united with his beloved, signifying the personal achievement of a better state (Ferrante 3, 74). Here women are simultaneously congratulatory trophies and bearers of divine sanction. Harmonious unification is also a central topic in the Lord Mayor's Show. If the paradox described by Turner et al. is considered in conjunction with the motif of marriage – as it infuses the Lord Mayor's Show – we should encounter brides possessed of mysterious powers, despite the fact that they willingly subordinate themselves under new husbands. This is indeed the case and almost all feminine personages encountered in 17th-century Lord Mayor's Shows are at once powerful and meek.

In agreement with this phenomenon, Bradbrook argues that in late Elizabethan shows "the metamorphosis of the Lord Mayor was accompanied by something like the descent of a goddess" (60-61).[37] In a similar fashion, the descent of "angels, saints, and the Virgin Mary [...] from heavenly pageants" had also "mark[ed] the epiphanies of medieval kings" (Kipling, Enter the King 32). Certainly, the mayor's ritual ascendance to his new position co-occurs with and is affirmed by the appearance of a feminine personality of great and seemingly transcendent powers. With her speculation on "the descent of a goddess", Bradbrook puts a finger on the thematic crux of the shows: the metaphorical marriage of mayor and city. She even goes on to argue that the motif of marriage of mayor and city "not only echoed the royal image of the monarch being married to the kingdom – Elizabeth spoke of her coronation ring as her wedding ring – it also implied that, like Peleus or Anchises, he [the mayor] had married an immortal" (63). She therefore suggests that a goddess not only descends but is also wedded to the mayor, confirming his authority. However, after linking these phenomena – the appearance of a goddess and the mayor's marriage to his territory – Bradbrook abruptly leaves the topic, after only a brief paragraph, and does not return to it. Yet, all of these aspects constitute the ritual core of the early modern Lord Mayor's Show: Each new mayor enters a metaphorical bond of

[37] Finlayson, too, recognizes the principle but does not explicitly formulate the liminal role of the feminine personification: "Typically, the Lord Mayor's shows take as a title an abstract concept or virtue that is, to varying degrees, both the focal element of each show and related in two or three devices and/or speeches to either the mayor or the merchant class [...]. The invocation of a universal value is clearly intended to associate the immediate ceremony with the supernal, and the connection with the mayor is rarely tied to any contemporary event or personal quality." (Jacobean Foreign Policy 586)

marriage with the city in his charge, who becomes a woman, structurally inferior to him and men in general. This inferiority is at the same time counterbalanced by a type of mysterious authority, which allows personified London in *Triumphs of Truth* to tell the mayor not to regard her words any less because "I a woman speak, / [since] A woman's counsel is not always weak" (969). The function of this ritual marriage is the mayor's reintegration into society following status elevation and the naturalization of his new position in front of a multitude of witnesses. The fact that the mayor's bride, whether she be personified London or an anthropomorphic Virtue (an aspect of the ideal city), has mystical powers further affirms the mayor's authority and that of his administration, giving it a quasi-divine blessing.

In Middleton's *Triumphs of Integrity,* Virtue, who is here cast in a motherly role, possesses the power to raise shepherds to kings – kings who will then be able to exert physical, tangible control over their dominions. In demonstration of this, her pageant stage, first encountered in St Paul's Churchyard and identified as the Mount Royal, contains "certain kings and great commanders, which ancient history produces, that were originally sprung from shepherds and humble beginnings" (ll. 45-47). A speaker on the stage explains that the mayor's advancement is, in fact, due to Virtue's preferment: "Her favour hath reflected most and best / Upon that son whom we of honour call; / And may't successively reflect on all." (ll. 101-03) The speech not only characterizes Virtue as a mother and establishes a mutual bond between her and the mayor, it also creates a sense of community among Londoners and their mayor, by the implication that an experience similar to the mayor's may be within the reach of every Londoner. The mysterious power of Virtue which has raised him to his current position may, after all, "successively reflect on all". With the help of personified Virtue, the mayor – "that son whom we of honour call" – and all Londoners can once more be envisioned as siblings and so be encouraged to live accordingly, i.e. in familial harmony.

In the same show, Integrity, a feminine personage, inhabits the pageant set called the Crystal Sanctuary. This is a luxurious structure with golden pillars and silver battlements. It is even "for the night triumph adorned and beautified with many lights, dispersing their glorious radiances on all sides through the crystal" (ll. 199-102). The pageant set is constructed to reflect the personification's "immaculate" (l. 192) character and poise and at the same time lends her an aura of sovereignty. From amid her palatial surroundings, Integrity declares: "The temple of an upright magistrate / Is my fair sanctuary, throne, and state" (ll. 223-24). Following her speech, Integrity's mobile Sanctuary joins the mayor's procession and accompanies it for the rest of the day. Like Virtue before her, the character of Integrity is infused with a mysterious power, and she offers to align that power with the mayor's own by equating her "fair sanctuary" with the mayor's temple. This posits her also as the goddess of Bradbrook's description, who descends from heavenly spheres for the sake of the mayor and proceeds to join with him – an acknowledgment and approval of his person and power. Similar to Virtue's king-making ability and Integrity's hold over the mayor, the Triumphing Angel in Munday's *Chrysanaleia* is seated above the character of King Richard I and holds his crown in place

(B4), sustaining his authority.[38] Meanwhile, in Dekker's *Troia-Nova Triumphans*, personified Fame and Virtue choose to yield to and support new mayor John Swinnerton, and Mayor Robert Parkhurst is aided by Fame and Truth in Taylor's *Triumphs of Fame and Honour*. A pageant set-up represents the "Island and Tower of soveraigne *Maiestie*" in *Camp-Bell, or, The Ironmongers Fair Feild* (B2). On a throne on the island "sitteth a beautifull Nymph, attyred aptly to her high state and dignity, in whome we presuppose the person of *Maiestie*" (B). The scene suggests a "fortunate and happy Island", with Majesty and her companions embodying aspects of Mayor Thomas Campbell's government.

In Munday's *Himatia-poleos*, a mysterious power is Himatia's, a feminine personage who incorporates all aspects of the Drapers' business. She presides over her own pageant set which depicts the various trades associated with the sponsoring company: "In the supreame and most eminent seate, sitteth Himatia, or Cloathing, as Mother, Lady and commandresse of all the rest" (B2). Beneath her, others are engaged in various specialized professions. Later in the day, following the Guildhall feast, the actor impersonating former mayor Sir John Norman identifies them as Himatia's "Daughters and attendants placed about her" (C2). Himatia, too, is one of those feminine entities, discussed above, who command enigmatic powers and pay tribute to the new mayor. The working people at the base of the set, meanwhile, allow the working population of London to see an idealized representation of themselves on stage – confirming Lancashire's estimation of the "thoroughly inclusive" nature of the "entertainment display[s]" and the "political aims" of early modern London street theater" (323).

A scene similar to that described above, an exalted personage benevolently presiding over her laboring dependents, is encountered in Squire's *Triumphs of Peace*. Here, the patron saint of the Haberdashers, St Katherine, presides over a pageant mount, while beneath her, twelve "maydes of honor" represent the twelve major livery companies – a number also infused with significance by, for instance, the twelve apostles, tribes of Israel, and city gates of the New Jerusalem. On the base of the stage, diverse craftsmen are shown working (it is unlikely but not impossible that women were among them): "carding *Wooll*; some *Spinning*; others *Knitting capps*; with her *Feltmakers*; one *Bowed*; one *Basoned*; and another *Blockt*" (B3). Carding and spinning were "the two first steps in the lengthy process of creating cloth" and jobs often "performed by poor and middling women in the household" (Rice and Pappano 170).[39] Some of the workers on the pageant mountain may therefore have been played by women or young men personating women, though this is far from certain.

Behind the pageant mountain, a shepherd watches his small flock (ibid.). In this scenario, not only is there a descending deity who lends her presence to the festivities and

---

[38] Although once referred to as "hee", the two other pronouns which designate the angel – "her" and "she" (B4) – suggest that the angel was indeed a feminine personage.

[39] In medieval representations of the character, Eve sometimes carries out the 'feminine' task of spinning, leaving to Adam more 'masculine', agricultural chores, and Thomas Nashe, in *The Unfortunate Traveller*, associates chamber maids with the spindle and distaff (220). These representations were the basis for John Ball's Peasants' Revolt slogan which asked: "When Adam delved and Eve span, who was then the gentleman?" (Greenblatt, The Rise and Fall 189)

displays deference to the mayor, i.e. St Katherine, but those characters who are placed in her close vicinity play a significant role in their own right. These exemplary cloth workers were designed to allow small crafts- and tradesmen, maybe even wage laborers, to feel represented and included in the official ideology of merchant London. The pageant breaches boundaries between the higher and lower strata of London society as all may, for the moment, perceive of themselves as essential to the urban economy, no matter how far apart they normally find themselves in the socioeconomic hierarchies of everyday life. Still, whatever the potentially beneficial consequences of strategic 'communitas', it is also unquestionably problematic. Not only does it draw on and perpetuate an ambiguous image of women (and others marginalized by dominant social groups), it also appropriates the voices of the disenfranchised ("I a woman speak") and makes them say what may be convenient for socially superior agents.

Overall, the Lord Mayor's Show incorporates representations of strict hierarchy – e.g. in the formalized procession of the company officials in ceremonial dress – but also makes the promise of an inclusive and harmonious community in which the mayor is merely the first among equals. That this is also the case in the earlier Corpus Christi celebrations, i.e. that both structure and communitas co-occur, has been propounded by Mervyn James. As a festivity which strongly references the human (and divine) body, Corpus Christi was ideally suited to employ an image of the body as an organic and inclusive avatar for society. Thus, the stage was "set for the kind of social experience which Victor Turner in *The Ritual Process* calls 'communitas', in which, as he puts it, the structural aspects of society are reversed [...]" (James 11). However, the reverse of communitas was expressed in the Corpus Christi parade too: "the opposite emphasis, that of social differentiation, with its stress on the segmented occupational roles in the urban community, and its vertical structure of status and authority, is if anything even more emphatically spelt out, as the guilds file past in the due order and precedence" (ibid.).

This dual effect of making social structure visible (thereby reinforcing it) and, secondly, generating communitas as a mode of interpersonal relations is also characteristic of the Lord Mayor's Show, in which both the former and the latter was achieved by representations of menial workers and craftsmen in harmonious and productive coexistence with social superiors. Figures of average or low standing in the social hierarchy such as shepherds, sailors, weavers, or smiths are represented on pageant sets alongside those eminent personifications just discussed, deities, former company worthies, or representations of royalty. These lowborn characters humbly acknowledge the new mayor in his function but they are simultaneously bearers of a special kind of authority themselves. Beyond the bond of common humanity that connects them with their social superiors, these people share to a significant degree in the economic system on which London society is founded.[40] To acknowledge their major contribution, i.e. the degree to which urban society depended on workers like them for its continuation, was at once necessary and remarkable: necessary because of its integrative function; remarkable because the wider discourse of the London poor was overwhelmingly characterized by

---

[40]   Coleman points out the significant economic factor that was labor: "Not only in food production but in the all-important cloth industry, labour was the most important item in direct production costs." (122)

fear of uncontrollable population increase, sedition and disease. The debate outside of London rested on the tenets that the laboring poor are numerous, that they should be kept employed and, finally, that they should be kept poor (Coleman 112). Yet the London Lord Mayor's Show continuously framed its presentation of the poor in a positive and inclusive manner: The poorer sort, if not the most down-and-out types, are shown working, in exaggerated bliss, alongside the middling sort of professionals, under the aegis of some Deity, Virtue, or London herself, and poor men supported by the companies walked in the mayor's procession every year (Hill, Pageantry 192). In the pamphlet commemorating his *Londini Speculum*, Heywood argues that the Company of Merchant Adventurers, of which the new mayor was a member, "were first trusted with the sole venting of the man-ufacture of Cloth out of this kingdome," and that by this enormous undertaking "the poore in all Countries are plentifully maintained" (307-08). The contribution of the Merchant Adventurers to securing the livelihoods of the poor is presented and understood as a major positive feat.[41]

At the same time, the suggestion is raised in a number of shows that it is far from impossible for any virtuous and industrious man, no matter his social origin, to improve his material lot in the world. Furthermore, the system of poor relief implemented in London was alluded to in the shows with pride, and not as a necessary price to be paid for the maintenance of social order. In London, says personified Sight in *Londini Speculum*, "th' Orphants cause, / And Widowes plea finde helpe" (317). Stow, too, voiced his appreciation in his defense of London (countering fears against the city's expansion), arguing that the capitol "releeueth plentifullie, and with good pollicie, not onely her owne poore people [...] but also the poore that from each quarter of the Realme do flocke vnto it" (2: 213).[42]

---

[41] The integrating work these pageants do might also be understood in the terms put forward by Snow et al. in "Frame Alignment Processes, Micromobilization, and Movement Participation". Frame alignment processes are described as lining up individuals' values or beliefs with those embraced by a given social movement organization (Snow et al. 464). That is, they bring "to-gether social psychological and structural/organizational factors and perspectives" (ibid.). Snow et al. examine four related frame alignment processes, which they call: frame bridging, frame amplification, frame extension, and frame transformation. The term "frame" is adopted from Erving Goffman and can be defined as "schemata of interpretation" (Snow et al. 464). Frame alignment practices have also been described as actions aimed at preserving community in groups which contain heterogeneous social actors and which are therefore likely to experience tensions (Chalmers Thomas, Price and Schau 1024-25).

[42] The Poor Law of 1598, amended in 1601, "codified and extended throughout the country" practices which were already generally established in urban centers such as London: "[t]he statutes required that every parish henceforth provide basic food, shelter, and clothing for the legitimately needy who lived within it, financed by compulsory taxation of wealthier local residents" (McIntosh 458) and, in practice, by the charity of private benefactors and institutions. Yet, "details about who was to receive assistance and how it was to be administered were left entirely in the hands of individual parish officials" (ibid). Furthermore, most communities coupled their distribution of benefits with "attempts to discipline or expel idle, ill-behaved, or nonresident poor people" (ibid. 459).

In *Himatia-poleos* the main pageant set not only displays eminent Himatia but, as briefly mentioned above, also presents a variety of workers – who Munday-the-narrator refers to as the personified professions of "Carding, Spinning, Weauing, Rowing, Fulling, Shearing, Dressing, Dying, Tentering and performing all other seruices to woollen Cloathes" (B2).[43] At the Little Conduit, a speech that is given from the pageant stage by an unidentified speaker recognizes the people fulfilling these jobs as the reason for such "happy blessings" as peace, plenty and bounty, and as the cause of a flourishing commonwealth (C3). Praise of this type for what are essentially menial laborers allows small craftsmen and wage laborers in the audience to feel incorporated into the structure of the well-working commonwealth. Meanwhile, the third pageant in Taylor's *Triumphs of Fame and Honour* features a model of the city of London which depicts "shops and men at worke upon cloth, as Cloth-workers, fullers, shermen, and others" (qtd. in Williams 520). The representation of the skilled workforce is a metaphorical hand extended to the working population of London, giving them reason to feel included in the social, economic, and spiritual community of the capital. From nearby the model city, personified London encourages the spectators with the words: "Worke on my Lads, and you in time may be, / Good members of this Honour's Company" (qtd. in Williams 521). Williams argues sensibly that the couplet would have been delivered in a loud voice or even as a shout, to be audible to as many people in the vicinity as possible, including those in less privileged positions who would have been out of earshot otherwise (524).[44] Both via the manner of their delivery and through their content, the lines function as a gesture of inclusiveness which explicitly links the represented workers and professionals in the model with the assembled spectators in the streets of the actual city. At the same time, the opportunity of material improvement through diligent industry is held out to them – as members of the company of Drapers.

The same incentive to share in this particular vision of London is offered to apprentices, who are reminded by personified Honor in Taylor's fourth pageant that "from th' apprentice seven yeares servitude / Proceeds the grave gowne, and the Livery-Hood" (B). By pairing an apprentice with personified Obedience (ibid.), Taylor suggests that novices in any given trade should embrace their duties and, for their own good, obey their masters.[45] Young men are urged to finish their apprenticeships with the vision that their work will be rewarded and a prosperous future as members of any one of the London guilds – and, thus, as freemen and citizens – awaits them. Customarily, the minimum age

---

[43] Hill points out that "[i]n *Himatia-Poleos* Munday also anachronistically elides the functions of manufacture and retail which for the Drapers, as for most Companies in this period, had long since become separated" (Pageantry 295).

[44] To Taylor only the industrious are real citizens. On the other hand, "[a]n idle Citizen is like a Moth" (n. pag.). Williams sums up Taylor's stance in this way: "Lazy people are not real citizens; there is room only for the industrious. But to the industrious, however lowly, no door is closed." (524) Equally, to Williams, Taylor's fourth pageant serves as "an ingenious expression of the view that the individual can and should try to rise in the world by the exercise of the virtue most suited to his calling" (525).

[45] Personified Honor also insists that "[l]ow steps begin to mount the highest hills" (Triumphs of Fame and Honour B).

at which London apprentices could be bound to their masters was 14 (Kathman 415). While contracts spanning a period of less than seven years were available for youngsters – demanding harder, less skilled work but offering the benefit of wages –, these placements were much less prestigious and did not, with their fulfillment, result in the freedom of a company (ibid.). Thus, the completion of a seven-year apprenticeship, at a minimum age of 21, was indeed the route young men had to embark on if they were looking for "a higher social status at the end of the term" (ibid.). 'Waterpoet' and one-time Lord Mayor's Show scribe John Taylor humorously confirms in his "Navy of Landships" that apprenticeship is undeniably a ship "very slow of sayle", as it makes its way "in our *Troynovantine* Ocean, within the sound of *Bowbell*" (83). Yet, he grants that those who ride in it for the stipulated period, "(in time) they sayle in the Lordship, Courtship, Surety-ship, or some other bottome of Honour or eminency" (ibid.). Abraham Jackson stays within the confines of the same metaphor as he phrases the aim of his guide book for apprentices as directing "the ship of their behaviour" toward the official completion of their schooling (34).[46]

A belief in upward mobility by means of apprenticeship is also embraced by the anonymous author, only identified as D. N., of an Elizabethan pamphlet titled *A Student's Lament that Hath Sometime Been in London an Apprentice*. D. N. urges: "Remember, remember your selves, you young men of London" (C2), and warns against the dangers of disobedience and sedition. Yet, the apprentice-turned-student reminds his fellow young men that "servants know how to obey, that being masters they may be obeyed" (C). Discipline and obedience are, thus, not merely ends in their own right but stepping stones on the way to better things. To D. N., London's apprentices are the city's future "Magistrates, [...] Chiefs of Companyes, and Office-bearers" (4). It was even conceivable that apprenticeship might, in due course, lead to the mayoralty itself, as is attested by Edmund Bolton who cites the examples of Sir Godfrey Bullen and Sir Martin Calthorpe, both of whom "ascended by due degrees from the condition of Apprentises to the greatest annuall honor" (4).[47] Even for experienced magistrates, however, dutiful submission remains an important virtue. As Dekker notes, the aldermen themselves share in the

---

[46] Jackson also informs his readers that Greek painter Apelles allegedly represented 'the good servant' with the following attributes: the ears of a donkey to signify obedience to his master's commands, a pig's nose to signify "quicke sent, to smell out what may conduce to his masters profit" (31), arms full of tools and instruments to signify his readiness to carry out any task, broad shoulders to signify his willingness to shoulder burdens, an empty belly to signify sobriety, a hind's hooves to signify promptness, and, finally, a pair of padlocks on his lips to signify his willingness to keep the secrets of his master's house (32-33).

[47] Bolton discusses the contentious question whether apprenticeship invalidates gentry, as was the common assumption. He comes to the emphatic conclusion that apprenticeship is no form of bondage but rather a contract entered into by free men and, thus, does not affect social rank bestowed by birth (31). Moreover, he argues that freemen of the city were asked to swear only to take on as apprentices the sons of freemen – a proposition that, he believes, countermands the status of an apprentice as a bondsman (ibid.). Yet, this does not make apprentices infallible, many of whom have, in fact, "drunke and sacrificed too deeply to their new Goddesse, Saint *Fashion*" (ibid. 40), leading them, for example, to abandon their traditional caps.

government of the city but "submit[...] themselves to the authority onely of One [the mayor], thereby teaching examples of Obedience" (The Dead Tearme E).

Londoners occupying the lower ranks of the ladder of success are depicted in the main pageant of *Chruso-thriambos* which consists of Terra's mine and workshop: here laborers and craftsmen are shown performing a wide variety of tasks associated with metalworking (A4-B). A similar scene is depicted in Munday's *Sidero-thriambos*, an offering for the Ironmongers' Company. Here the worthwhile and productive labor of ironsmiths and associated professionals is showcased. The workers represented on the pageant stage, Munday affirms, "doe out-were their worke merrily, as accounting no toyle tedious, thus bestowed in the Societies seruice" (B). An equally jovial scene is encountered in *Londons Tempe*, in which cyclopes happily sing a song as they work together in Vulcan's workshop. Northway has speculated that the song, which "embraces the vernacular" (180), creates an aura of harmony around the work being done which engulfs the audience (ibid. 181), and that this may reflect the company's attempt to motivate their members to increase production (ibid. 174). Whether or not this is true, the musical interlude celebrates hard physical work and the people who do it – involving them in the guilds' dominant vision of itself and the city. At the same time, this cheerful idealization of labor also forges a positive connection between the working poor and the highest ranks of London society. Northway has argued that the "vernacular [of the song] operates here as a worker's echo of the exalted, a version of work in the shop that replicates the work of the Lord Mayor" (180). The established parallels support the ideological assumption that all Londoners are children of the city and, thus, effectively siblings. At the same time, the opportunity for self-improvement is implicit in the correlation between lord mayor and common laborer, which also results in an alignment of their aims and values in life: As the mayor reaches the pinnacle of success in the city through industry and devotion to the virtues of emergent capitalism, so his less fortunate brothers may similarly better their lots by adherence to the same principles.[48] This corresponds to the more general outlook embraced by the show writers that one's own efforts and character are enough to warrant social and material improvement.

The narrative of apprenticeship embraced in the Lord Mayor's Show follows the same trajectory as that of middle class self-improvement. It is an equally inclusive narrative that offers a disproportionately large section of the London population a reason to identify with the companies' conceptions of themselves and of London. In the discourse of middle class household protocol, the virtue of obedience also features heavily. It is to be embraced by all those dependent on the head of the family: servants, apprentices, and children alike. Robert Cleaver explains in his familial conduct book how "[t]he householder is called Pater familias: that is, a father of a familie, because hee should have a fatherly care over servants, as if they were his children" (364). In the microcosm of the household, the head of the family effectively occupies the place God holds in the

---

[48] Northway, too, has voiced the assumption "that the liveries used pageant speeches as an opportunity to keep alive the possibility for this attainment of an elite position" (186), despite obstacles to advancement and the differentiated hierarchies of the livery companies. She also argues that some speeches were geared specifically toward apprentices, encouraging them to fulfill their contracts (ibid. 184).

macrocosm (ibid. 342). Children, servants, and apprentices, thus, must obey all commands from their father or master unless these contradict God's word as interpreted by the Anglican Church. However, while humble service and loyalty are ideally their own rewards, a more compelling incentive to obedience is the prospect of an improved social and economic position. An apprentice at the beck and call of his master may not unreasonably envision his future self as the head of his own household of subordinates. Based on his conception of the ideal household as a harmonious and organic unit, Cleaver declares: "Masters ought not as Tyrants, to use their servants as their Horses or Asses: but to deale with them lovingly & christianly, because they are all members of one bodie, whereof Christ Iesus is head." (366) Cleaver likens the well-functioning household to a human body, the most familiar of organic units.[49] The integral household of his description is characterized by mutual respect among its members and by its members' consciousness of their particular roles within it. Analogous to Cleaver's ideal household, London, as has been shown, was conceptualized as either family unit or single unified body, sometimes both at the same time.[50] In both household and city, the virtue of obedience was deemed crucial. Correspondingly, the anonymous author of the *Student's Lament* links the deference owed to the head of a household, to that owed to city and sovereign. He identifies himself proudly as a former "Apprentice of London, that famous Citie, the mother Citie of this royall kindome. To which Citie & patria & parente, I am beholding" (B3). The pamphleteer calls London his mother and confirms his loyalty to city and country. An obedient subject himself, he warns that it is "hatefull ambition, even of folly itselfe to bee derided: when the scholler shall attempt to correct his master, the childe the father" (ibid.). According to this former London apprentice, disobedience is as problematic in the political realm as it is in the more intimate realm of the household.

Munday offers a positive representation of the relationship between master and subordinate, based on obedience as well as mutual respect, in *Sidero-thriambos*: a master gunner and his mate mind a cannon together which has been mounted on a movable pageant stage and which serves as an example of what metal ore may be transformed into in skilled hands. The staged interaction of the two men is a variation on the idealized dynamics of a master/apprentice relationship, so important to London merchants and craftsmen. The following exchange between them emphasizes the desired qualities of obedience and diligence in the mate, while the master is presented as a good-natured and instructive superior:

---

[49] Hannah Arendt has proposed that, in fact, with the onset of modernity, every communal arrangement is understood in terms of family, i.e. as a collective household. Problematically, according to Arendt, the social realm that emerges together with this conception of the state-as-family is neither properly private nor public (33).

[50] Cleaver's tract opens: "A Householde is as it were a little common wealth, by the good Government whereof, Gods glorie may be advaunced, the Common wealth which standeth of severall families, benefited, and all that live in that familie receive much comfort and commoditie" (13). Cleaver also argues that "the household, when their master and mistresse, or dame, are of debate, can no other wise bee in quiet, and at rest, then a citie, whose Rulers agree not" (177). Only a good husband "is reckoned worthie to rule a common wealth, that with such wisedome, discretion & iudgement, doth rule and governe his owne house" (ibid. 178).

Maist. Where are you Mate? / Mate. Here Sir, at hand, / To doe what ere the Maister shall command. / Maist. [...] Now Mate, thou seest, this is a Iouiall day, / And every Trade triumphes as best it may, / (By yearly custome) gladly to expresse, / Their free affection, in full chearfulnesse. (B3)

The master's explanation of the Lord Mayor's Show focuses on the voluntary involvement of all trades and associated guilds rather than on the mayor himself. Along with the evident participation of master and mate themselves in the festivities, the master's lines speak to diverse interest groups. The frame of perception adopted by the custodians of the cannon is extended toward "every Trade" by the physical presence of representatives of the diverse minor and major guilds marching in the procession and by the master's emphasis on the importance of their attendance.

Given that apprentices were a numerous and socially highly significant group of Londoners, it is not surprising that they should have been represented and engaged in Lord Mayor's Show. Margaret Pelling confirms the system of apprenticeship to have been one of the most significant "forms of interdependency in society which bridged the gap between the family and 'the State', and connected families one with another" (33). The notion is only reinforced by the fact that in the 17th century only a small minority of apprentices and servants were placed in the households of relatives (ibid. 41), making the newly forged occupational bonds all the more vital in the absence of familial ones. Dependants like servants and apprentices, Dekker explains to householders, "are your adopted children, they are naturalized into your bloud" (The Seven Deadly Sinnes 41). The discourse of master/servant relationships in the Lord Mayor's Show, too, implies that apprentices have their fixed place in the household of London, under a paternal (and fraternal) mayor and that, while their obedience is imperative, they may themselves one day ascend to positions of authority. Thus, the "Lordship, Courtship" and "Surety-ship" are held out as promises to the apprentices of London. In the meantime, some of them were allowed to board more literal ships and accompany the mayor's barge upriver to Westminster, as observed by eye witness Leopold von Wedel in 1629 (Northway 183).

As in *Sidero-thriambos*, in Heywood's *Londini Sinus Salutis* the benefits that iron working bestows on society are invoked in tribute to the company of Ironmongers. The show's fourth pageant device, the pamphlet notes, "is a Castle munified with sundry Peeces of Ordnance; and Accomodated with such Persons as are needfull for the defence of such a Citadell" (292). From this device, Mars pronounces the civilizing potential of metal working, without which "[i]n Denns and Caves wee should be forc'd to dwell", since "no Art, Craft, Faculty, or Trade, / Without it, can subsist" (295). Everybody, thus, gains directly as well as indirectly from metal working and the specialized vocations concerned with it. The characters on the pageant stage, "needfull for the defence of such a Citadell", not only demonstrate some of the uses of transformed metal but also represent the working population of London, while the fortress – a bounded, secure space – stands in for the city of London, once more an *urbs invictissima*. Representation is here, as in the pageant featuring master and mate, the precondition for social integration.

A team of master and mate not only appears in Munday's *Sidero-thriambos* but also in his *Triumphs of Re-united Britannia*. Yet, the scene shifts away from cannon and castle

188

toward a maritime scenario. The show's first pageant episode is centered on a ship called "Royall Exchange", on board of which and engaged in discussion are a master, his mate, and a boy. As the conversation among the trio reveals, the ship's owner is supposedly the lord mayor himself, a fact which the mate relates to his foreman: "Maister, good newes, our Owner, as I heare, / Is this day sworne in London's Maioralty" (B). The boy, third in the hierarchy, cheerfully confirms this, pointing out the parading liverymen and the sounds of drums and brass instruments. The master, thus informed of the situation, proves to be as happy about it as his subordinates. He proceeds to instruct his two eager helpers to "[t]ake of our *Pepper*, of our *Cloues* and *Mace*, / And liberally bestow them round about" (B). The assembled spectators receive these gifts from the pageant ship and a tangible connection is thereby forged between them. The master voices the hope, in the form of a previously discussed pun on the mayor's name (Leonard Holliday), that this contribution might still enhance the "cheerefull Holi-day" (B). The distribution of small giveaways, what Hill refers to as "souvenirs, of a kind" (Pageantry 233), from pageant sets was common practice: In *Chruso-thriambos* personified Gold and Silver "bountifully hurle abroad their Mothers treasure" (C2), for the benefit of those Londoners near enough to catch some of Terra's cache. This renders physical the metaphor, discussed earlier, of the material gifts which 'mother earth' brings forth and bestows on the people when she is cultivated and managed properly. Meanwhile, it is neither glittering pageant rock nor coins but a different commodity entirely which is distributed "bountifully among the people" (B2) in Munday's *Chrysanaleia*: Fishermen – labeled "painfull and industrious" (B) – generously hand out their fresh catch to spectators assembled at the river bank. This strategy of handing out gifts not only resulted in increased engagement and enjoyment for the crowd, it also implicitly demanded loyalty to the mayor and his administration from those who received gifts. Whether spices, fish, coins or other commodities, the little gifts came with little hooks attached: show planners and sponsors counted on recipients to subscribe to their own civic beliefs in response to them.

The fishermen in *Chrysanaleia* are presented in the act of "drawing vp their Nets, laden with liuing fish" (B2), before they go on to distribute their perishable goods. In a speech delivered some time later at the Little Conduit the character of William Walworth explains the meaning behind the fishermen pageant to the mayor and his entourage:

> The Fishing Busse instructs you first to know / The toylsome trauell of poore Fisher-men, / Subiected to all weathers, where and when. / In stormy tempests they omit no paine, / To blesse all lands with the Seas bounteous store: / Their labour doth returne rich golden gaine, / Whereof themselues taste least by Sea or shore, / But (like good soules) contented euermore / With any benefit their toyle can bring; / The Fisher well is term'd Contents true King. (C3)

Walworth's speech encourages the mayor to identify with the hard-working fishermen who may be far from affluent but who are nevertheless content with their lot in life, contributing as they do to the well-being of the commonwealth as a whole – a sufficient reason to hold them in high esteem. The representation of fishermen in a pageant episode as well as Walworth's charitable explanation of the pageant elevate the status of middling professionals and common laborers in general and inspire them to take pride in their trades and crafts and in their place in urban society. In *Chrysanaleia* a reference to St Peter, himself a fisherman before "his best Master [...] made him a Fisher of men" (B2), demonstrates the distinguished company of which London's Fishmongers are worthy and serves to inculcate a sense of self-worth in them. Similar occupational groups are also afforded positive representation in Heywood's *Porta Pietatis*, in which a young sailor speaks from a pageant set that represents a sailing ship. Although neither wealthy nor high-born, he, too, is represented as sharing in the economic infrastructure that supports the city and, as such, recognized as a legitimate part of London. The sailor's role is his simultaneous engagement of the attention of sailors, watermen, and Londoners of low standing in general, on the one hand, as well as his invitation to those of higher standing to identify with the lowly but virtuous despite differences in rank and means.

Sailors and watermen are also shown to gain contentment from their river- and seafaring work in Taylor's *Triumphs of Fame and Honour*. The opening water entertainment consists of a barge, carrying aquatic goddess Thetis and personified Thamesis (another name for the Thames, common in pageantry, based on the river's Latin epithet of "Tamesis" and/or the confluence of Thame and Isis at Dorchester), which is rowed along by two sailors and two Thames watermen. Following a speech by Thetis, the rowers "ouer-joyed, pike their oares, and every one of them drinks his Kan as a health, tossing them up, and presently falling into a Rugged friskin daunce" (qtd. in Williams 514). The episode not only entertains with a choreographed dance but simultaneously offers up Thetis as a mother figure – the river Thames is identified as one of the deity's daughters – who helps merchants procure commodities like "silks and velvets, oyle, and wine, / Gold, silver, Jewels, fish, salt, sundry spices" and more (ibid. 513). The positive representation of a section of the city's working population, i.e. sailors and watermen, integrates these also into a unified vision of the city. Pageant episodes of this sort all share in the show's perpetual function: cohering diverse London into one harmonious conception of urban life. In *Londini Artium*, Heywood asks rhetorically: "What City in Europe yeeldeth more plenty? More variety?" (B) No city, in his estimation, is a conglomerate of more disparate components than London, but the city still achieves unity out of this diversity and is better for it. Early in the show, Arion is proud to declare that the Thames effectively connects London to all parts of the ever-increasing known world. Heywood-as-narrator explains how this affects the climate of enterprise in the city: "The populous Streets rather appeare an open Mart, then an ordinary Market; shee not savouring and fostering her owne Natives onely, but Strangers, and of all forraigne Nations whatsoever" (B). All of London's merchants, small tradesmen and craftsmen, whether born in the city, migrants to the city, or on a visit from overseas, share in the feminine personage that is London and profit from her generosity, as temporary or permanent siblings. That community in variety is achievable is also imparted by Orpheus – perhaps ominously – in Heywood's *Londini Status Pacatus*, who praises the peacefulness of "unanimous hearts" around the central figure of the mayor (367).

Orpheus had previously appeared in Middleton's *Triumphs of Love and Antiquity*, where he had also emphasized the harmonious coexistence of multiple ethnicities in London. Then, the musician had declared that he could see in attendance "several countries, in those faces plain, / All owing fealty to one sovereign; / The noble English, the fair-thriving Scot, / Plain-hearted Welsh, the Frenchman bold and hot, / The civilly instructed Irishman, / And that kind savage the Virginian, / All lovingly assembled, e'en by fate" (1401).[51] Orpheus's reference to his audience, while in praise of the sovereign's sphere of influence, is a signal to them that they are a part of the city as the sponsoring company conceives of it, be they English, Scottish, Welsh, French, or even of a background commonly, and often strategically, considered 'primitive', such as Irish or native American. Notwithstanding the hostile testimony of Orazio Busino, a priest in the Venetian ambassador's retinue, that a Spanish character in *The Triumphs of Honour and Industry* (1617) made antics toward the Spanish ambassador and his more general profession that foreigners are "little liked, not to say hated" in London, their representation is routinely sympathetic in the Lord Mayor's Show. Busino's perspective and that embraced by the Lord Mayor's Show are certainly not irreconcilable, as the tensions Busino detects go some way toward explaining the necessity of the integrating approach taken by the show planners. The 'Pageant of Several Nations', also in *Triumphs of Love and Antiquity*, presents a Frenchman who addresses the crowd in French as well as a Spaniard who does the like in Spanish – both characters delivering praise for the new mayor. Also represented on the same stage are an Englishman, an Irishman, a Russian, a Turk, a Jew, a Dane, a Pole, and a so-called "Barbarian", possibly indicating a North African from the Barbary Coast. While the set-up might have been used for ridiculing foreigners, the evidence suggests that this was not the case. Not only was an Englishman presented among the other nationals, the fact that the non-English characters spoke in their own native languages instead of accented English implies that French and Spanish speaking guests or residents were actually spoken to by the pageant characters and so pulled into a vision of a diverse but still harmoniously unified London. It is certainly plausible that the residents of Petty France, for instance, an area to the south of old Bethlem Hospital would have felt addressed (Hartle 20). At the same time, tensions and prejudices manifested in other areas of literary and cultural production. In *The Seven Deadly Sinnes of London*, Dekker – who sounds a harmonious note in the Lord Mayor's Show – writes of "Irish beggers" (13), and "Irish rebell[s]" (5) repeatedly, refers to the cruelty of "Turkes and Tartars" (37), the conspirative and cruel Spanish and French (21, 41), and admonishes Barrabas Bankruptism, "the rich Jew of London" who emerges from "the Sinfull Synagogue" (12). Elsewhere he refers to the "wild Irish" (The Dead Tearme G), taking his cue from John Stow, and announces "the Irish mans disease, (Lazynes:)", "the Dutchmans weakenesse (in not Bearing drinke:)" and "the Italians evill spirit that haunts him, (Lust)" (ibid. C2).

In his *Triumphs of Honour and Industry*, Munday included a pageant explicitly celebrating international cooperation, which Levin speculates, "must have appealed to the [sponsoring] Grocers in their capacity as traders working to encourage and even protect commerce with 'strangers'" (Introduction 1253). In the show anthropomorphic Industry rides in a chariot alongside personified India. Industry holds a ball on top of which is

---

[51] Brenner notes that the Virginia Company had received its initial charter in 1609 but that, "[a]s a result of its financial impotence, the Company was soon forced to give up direct control of colonial development. Between 1614 and 1619, colonial entrepreneurship was taken over by private individuals" (66). Confirming these de facto developments, the official dissolution of the company followed in 1624 (ibid.).

placed a golden Cupid, as mentioned in chapter two. As an accessory this device is intended to convey the power of industry to get "both wealth and love, which overflows / With such a stream of amity and peace, / Not only to itself adding increase, / But several nations where commérce abounds / Taste the harmonious peace" (1256-57). Commerce is here defined by personified Industry as an activity that profits everybody involved in it and creates bonds between partners, as opposed to one that is based on exploitation and inequality.

Another integrative concept which simultaneously elevates the poor and humble is that of shepherd and flock. Predominantly employed in shows sponsored by the Drapers, it served both as a reference to the economically significant cloth trade and as a unifying image which implied an analogy between mayor and shepherd. As a metaphor of biblical provenance, and one employed by the monarch, its realization in pageant form functioned to highlight "the spiritual [...] importance" of the mayor (Finlayson 850), by correlation to Christ, as much as his political eminence, conceived of as analogous to the sovereign's.[52] Meanwhile, the equation of Londoners with the shepherd's flock suggests the mayor's ability to keep his dependents together and to protect them from any outside threats. Accordingly, a shepherd in Heywood's *Londini Emporia* explains to the mayor: "The numerous throng, which you this day behold / Are your owne Sheep, this Citty is their fold" (B2). The numerous residents of the metropolis all cohere into one flock under the guardianship of a paternal mayor. It is certainly not difficult to envision the mayor's livery-clad followers as his loyal flock when Time, in Heywood's *London's Ius Honorarium*, urges the mayor to see and acknowledge "all this goodly band / Now in their City Liveries", prepared to "follow, where your Colours fly" (273). Later on in the same show, personified London herself reflects on the company motto – "Serve and Obey" – and the potential of obedience to incorporate "many into one" (275).[53]

In Heywood's *Londini Emporia* a shepherd emphasizes the great benefits of the cloth trade for the population of the realm: "Give due respect on this in general: / For since the Trade of Cloathing first begun, / Both from the scorching of the sommers Sun, / And blustering North Winds, Rich, Poore, Young and Old / Have beene defenc'd" (B2-B3). From the beginning, the herdsman suggests, the trade has been nothing but beneficent, clothing and sustaining rich, poor, young, and old alike. The fifth pageant of Taylor's *Triumphs of Fame and Honour* also features a shepherd, bearing the pastoral name of Endimion, who notes that mighty and noble men have started out on their life journeys as humble shepherds (qtd. in Williams 526). The same claim is made by Arion in

---

[52] Cf. Kipling: "Pageant shepherds serve also as emblems of peace and as allegorical types of Christian pastors." (Enter the King 29)

[53] The example of Mayor Nicholas Rainton (1569-1646) illustrates that the idealization of sheep herding and its metaphorical connotations could certainly be contradicted by real-life circumstances. Rainton traded "in satin and taffeta imported from Florence and velvet from Genoa [...]. His 1636 enclosure of a considerable area of common land in Enfield encountered great local resentment, and a legal challenge by dispossessed commoners, and after his death there was anti-enclosure rioting" (Lindley n. pag.). For these reasons, it is no surprise that his 1632 Lord Mayor's Show, Thomas Heywood's *Londini Artium & Scientiarum Scaturigo*, contained no shepherding pageants.

Midddleton's *The Sun in Aries*. With reference to a pastoral pageant, featuring Phoebus among a set of "fine woolly creatures", the mythic musician explains that "kings and rulers are in holy writ / With shepherds paralleled, nay, from shepherds reared, / And people and the flock as oft cohered" (1591). In a reversal of Peacham's satiric claim that would-be Jasons only deal in inessential toys and trifles and overestimate their own importance, Taylor's Endimion argues that the raw commodity of wool generates profits far beyond even the value of Jason's golden fleece: "Wooll [is] turn'd to Cloth; and Cloth by transformation, / [...] turn'd to gold, that you may say with joy, / That *Iasons* fleece (to yours) was but a toy" (ibid.). Like the shepherd in *Londini Emporia*, Taylor's specimen points out the economic advantages that derive from the rearing of sheep:

> By picking wooll, thousands releife doe gaine, / As many carding, spinning doth maintaine: / Wooll-men, a great and wealthy trade doe drive, / Weavers, in great abundance worke and live, / The Clothiers, Fullers, Tuckers, Shermen, Dyers, / From the sheepes fleece have feeding and attires. (ibid.)

With that in mind, it is clearly no overstatement that, "(under heaven) the Ram's the Instrument" (ibid.). Finally, a dance of shepherds in celebration of both the animal and the company of Clothworkers – whose coat of arms featured the ram as a crest – concludes the pageant episode.[54]

In Heywood's *Londini Status Pacatus*, Medea, too, praises the role of sheep in supporting various trades and industries such as "Carding, Spinning, Weaving, Fulling, Shearing" (369). Poverty-stricken commoners who find employment in any one of these areas gain a means of economic support, yet without employment "might starve for want of lively-hood" (ibid.). In the same manner, the first pageant on land in *Porta Pietatis* is a shepherd plus dog and flock who praises sheep as the best of animals and as the economic foundation of the Drapers. These points, however unsubtly made, would have resonated with an audience well aware of the importance of trade in wool and cloth, "the principall and noblest *Staplewares* of all these Ilands" (Bolton 53-54).

"[A]re poore plaine meaning Sheepheards woondred at, like Comets or blazing Starres?" (B4), challenges a shepherd in Munday's *Himatia-poleos*. Accompanied by "a goodly Ramme or Golden Fleece", this pastor is brought face to face with the new mayor and, as previously mentioned, proceeds to deliver a speech on the topic of Cotswolds shepherds. These, so the pageant-pastor, traditionally celebrate the election of a member of the Drapers' company to the office of lord mayor of London with the gift of a superior ram. In celebration of the animal, he rhymes: "From the Ramme / we have the Lambe / From both our finest / woolles are shorne / Wooll had thus from / the Ramme and Lambe / Makes the best Cloath / that can be worne. / Thanke then the Draper / that began: / To make such Cloathing, / meete for man" (B4-C).[55]

---

[54] Williams argues that these shepherd pageants "probably owe their popularity to the continued success of the pastoral" as a literary genre (527).

[55] He recapitulates: "For, if wee haue no Ramme, wee are sure to haue no Lambe: no Lambe, no Wooll: no wooll, no Cloth: no Cloth, no Draper." (C)

However unsubtle his approach, the shepherd's chain of causality nevertheless makes a point of the humble foundation (to be respected) of a vast and important industry. Furthermore, the figure of the shepherd has the potential to connect heterogeneous groups because it resonates with high ranking individuals, including the lord mayor himself, as well as individuals of modest means and status – reflecting both the shepherd's role as a leader and nascent sovereign as well as his proverbially humble nature.

4   Conclusion

The years following Henry Garway's mayoralty, which had been launched with genre-appropriate positivity in November 1639 with Heywood's *Londini Status Pacatus*, were altogether less peaceful than hoped for, in London as, of course, elsewhere in the British Isles. Merchant Taylor William Acton succeeded Garway as lord mayor but was removed from office for his royalist leanings before the end of his term. He was succeeded by Grocer Edmund Wright, whose inauguration was not accompanied by pageantry of any sort (Hill, Pageantry 281-82). In a continuing back and forth, in 1641 Royalist Richard Gurney assumed the mayoralty but was stripped of it in 1642 and replaced by Puritan Isaac Penington (Seaver, Review 1589).[1] The winter of 1641-42 was to be an overall turning point in city politics (Brenner 72): London became a Parliamentarian bastion as Royalists were forced from political life for the time being (ibid. 86).

The political struggle in London largely hinged on "whether or not the City constitution, and the structure of power and privilege which it sanctioned, was to be maintained" (ibid. 72). Those in favor of the status quo (by 1640, a majority of Levant-East India merchants) sided with the Crown in the attempt to protect the established order (ibid.). Colonial merchants, in league with "colonizing aristocrats", took a stance in favor of Parliament, against the Crown and the aldermanic elite (ibid. 69). However, Mayor John Adams (voted into office in 1645) had strong Royalist sympathies and in late 1646, at the end of the first Civil War, the tide had turned once more and London was on the verge of entering into a crown-city alliance again (ibid. 88): "a new coalition of conservatives in the city rallied behind the so-called Presbyterian party [opposing the Independents], anxious for peace with the king" (Seaver, Review 1589). Since London had no professional military defense of its own, the New Model Army encountered no serious opposition when it entered London in August 1647 and brought the deviant city government under its control (Brenner 88-89). In due consequence Mayor John Gayer (elected in 1646), a Fishmonger and Levant-East India merchant, was ousted from office and replaced by tobacco-dealing Grocer and Parliamentarian John Warner (ibid. 95). The army left London in the spring of 1648 to combat royalist opposition elsewhere and the city took the opportunity to once again re-arrange its government, and even "pressed

---

[1] This despite the fact that, so Brenner, "comparatively few merchants were active in Parliament, at all times a body primarily of the landed class" (95). However, many of London's most prominent magistrates also represented the capital in the House of Commons. Grocer Thomas Moulson (mayor in 1634) became a member of Parliament for the City of London in 1628 as did Christopher Clitherow. Like Moulson, Clitherow sat in the House of Commons until Charles I suspended Parliament in 1629 and began his Personal Rule (Thrush, Moulson n. pag.). Sir John Swynnerton sat in the House of Commons intermittently between 1601 and 1611, Maurice Abbot between 1621 and 1626. Thomas Lowe (mayor in 1604) was MP for the City of London between 1606 and 1622.

Parliament to agree to a personal treaty with the King" (ibid. 88-89); however, when the army returned to London later in the year it once more took control, replacing Mayor Abraham Reynardson, a Levant-East India trader, with colonial merchant – and "East India interloper" – Thomas Andrews, who was to become the first Commonwealth lord mayor (Brenner 88-89, 95, 99). Unlike Reynardson, Andrews was happy to countenance the execution of Charles I and the abolition of the monarchy. "Lord Mayor's Day still took place throughout the Commonwealth period", notes Tracey Hill, but "there is little evidence from Company records that it was accompanied by much in the way of entertainment" (Pageantry 282). Faced with the turmoil and violence of the Civil Wars and the radical Puritan sensibilities of a new regime (that notoriously 'canceled' Christmas), pageantry lost its appeal for most. The wars surely demonstrated the precariousness of a unified commonwealth, so emphatically celebrated in the pre-war Lord Mayor's Show.

The inaugural festivities, in their 17th-century heyday, celebrated an idealized, undivided city using triumphal chariots, elaborate pageant wagons, song and dance, fireworks, and displays on the river. These entertainments have been linked to emblem books and while there are ways in which this may be illuminating, there are also important differences that get lost in the omnipresent comparison. The municipal celebrations for the lord mayor did certainly not consist of sequences of three-dimensional emblems. An examination of early to mid-17th-century Lord Mayor's Shows reveals that a tension between the visual and the verbal, the methodological linchpin of the emblem, is by no means as important in civic pageantry. I described two major factors which cause pageant episodes to be at variance with the 'emblematic' method. Firstly, pageant stages – be they chariots, 'mounts', 'arbors', or 'palaces' – are often (over)crowded with characters whose very presence is a tribute to mayor and city but simultaneously stands in the way of a coherent and cohesive translation of the visual into verbalized moral terms. A case in point is the Chariot of Triumphal Victory in Munday's *Chrysanaleia* which carried an angel, Richard I, personified Truth, Virtue, Honor, Temperance, Fortitude, Zeal, Equity, Conscience, Justice, Authority, Law, Vigilance, Peace, Plenty, Discipline, and, on the diminished opposing side, Treason, and Mutiny. With a cast of 14 characters, among them Fame, Liberality, Meekness, and Simplicity, London's Triumphant Mount in Middleton's *Triumphs of Truth* is also densely populated; as is New Troy's Tree of Honor in Dekker's *Brittannias Honor*, where Minerva, Bellona, personified London, Peace, Religion, Civil Government, Justice, Learning, Industry, and Honor dwell. These figures from the realms of civic history (Richard I, William Walworth, John Norman etc.) and transcendent ideas (Virtue, Justice, London et al.) function as intermediaries between past and present and between the concrete and the abstract. As I argued in chapter three, the feminine gender of the majority of personifications heightens their liminal potential and renders them particularly suitable to function as 'ritual portals', as facilitators of the mayor's passage, and as semi-divine 'cheerleaders' for London and its civic government.

Secondly, a significant percentage of pageants rely primarily on interaction – among characters and between mayor and characters – rather than on the tension between visual and verbal codes characteristic of the emblem. Ships, for example, like the "Barke-Hayes" in Munday's *Himataia-poleos*, the "Ioell" in *Metropolis Coronata*, or the "Fishermongers Esperanza" in *Chrysanaleia* serve as spaces of interaction for sailors, fishermen, and

196

watermen, from which they can also reach out to the mayor and surrounding spectators. Elsewhere shepherds pay their respect to mayor and city (highlighting mutually beneficial trade relations between London and the wider realm), cyclopes work in smithies, former civic dignitaries are resurrected to attend on the new mayor (a strategy especially beloved of Anthony Munday), and 'bards' perform magic tricks. Various characters are engaged in pyrotechnical displays, others throw gifts (coins, spices, fish) to spectators, and gunners fire salutes. Pageant episodes which include these elements highlight the immediacy of the lived experience. It is certainly worth remembering when dealing with the Lord Mayor's Show that while the commemorative pamphlets constitute our best access, they are not one-to-one transcripts of the events, which were primarily ritualistic theatrical occasions to be directly experienced via multiple sensory channels.

Chapter two has demonstrated the often sceptical and world-weary outlook of emblems and contrasted this attitude – exemplified in Jan van der Noot's dictum that "nought in this worlde but griefe endures" (emblem 8, 15) – with the significantly more buoyant and teleological stance of the Lord Mayor's Show. Where emblems (such as Whitney's numbers 22, 161, 185, or Peacham's 76, 153, 155, 159) posit the existence of a chaotic, disinterested, or even cruel world, the Lord Mayor's Show implies cosmic harmony and purpose. Furthermore, human relations are fraught with conflict and abuse in emblems (as, for example, Whitney's numbers 46, 64, 111, 149, or Peacham's 62, 148, 176 attest), while expressions of peaceful (economic) cooperation are a major tenet of the Lord Mayor's Show. Not only Londoners but foreigners, and strangers, even from as far afield as India in the east and America in the west, are presented as sharing in mutually beneficial transactions. Ships play an important part in this narrative as master symbols of merchant culture, whereas they frequently signify instability, danger, and disaster in emblems. The understanding of trade as a facilitator of peaceful and respectful domestic and 'international' relations contrasts with a theme of inherent, racial difference and the contamination of "infected races" present in the anthologies of Alciato, Whitney, Peacham, and others. At the same time, the constant affirmation of pride and ambition, coupled with honesty and industry, in mayoral pageants contrasts decidedly with the increasingly anti-worldly orientation of emblem books in the course of the 17th century. Before this background it is not surprising to find that wealth is seldom if ever positively connoted in emblems. Instead, worldly riches are depicted as a negative influence on character and, moreover, as a mere smoke screen, obscuring the brevity of life and the ultimate vanity and unavailingness of all material objects, including bodies. In the Lord Mayor's Show, on the other hand, wealth is portrayed as a positive force which serves not only those who have immediate possession of it but a much wider community. The positive recognition of manufacture, commerce, and wealth in the Lord Mayor's Show goes hand in hand with an inclination to appreciate material London and with the celebration of the senses as channels of perception.

As discussed in chapter three, material London (in the Aristotelian tradition of feminizing matter) could be metaphorically converted into the bodily shape of a woman – the speaking female city, the inviolate *urbs invictissima*. The discursive association of matter and women – and the alleged bodily determination of women – is one important factor in the conventional construction of feminized territorial personifications, from Italia Turrita to Brute's Britannia or matronly London, dressed as a lady mayoress. The

197

purpose of the personification of London was a collective representation of the diverse constituents of the metropolis in the guise of a manageable, unified organism. "In these events", says Tracey Hill of the Lord Mayor's Show, "the Lord Mayor *became* London" (Pageantry 16). This is true insofar as mayor and city ritually entered into a union and so, metaphorically, formed a single entity from two components, becoming "one flesh" as the Bible required (e.g. Gen 2:24).

We have seen that in Munday's *Chrysanaleia* the inaugural celebrations are explicitly defined as the marriage rites of mayor and city, i.e. "Londons and Lemans wedding day" (C). At the same time, Munday makes clear that the union of Mayor John Leman and London lasts only as long as the magistrate's term in office and that Leman, in his role as ritual husband, is both preceded and succeeded by others. Accordingly, the character of civic hero William Walworth explains to Leman that many officeholders "[h]aue gone before you in this place" but that he "may proue as good as any" (C4). In Middleton's *Triumphs of Love and Antiquity* a personification of "the love of the city to his lordship" salutes Mayor William Cokayne and announces that "[d]esert [the mayor] and love [the city] will be well matched today" but that, sadly, "[t]his match can last no longer than a year" (1399). In other shows the theme of marriage is more implicit but remains detectable. Thus, the mayor is not only confirmed in his new position of authority by his territorial passage across the heart of the city; his political supremacy is also rendered rightful, even 'natural', by his assumption of the roles of husband to the city and fatherly supervisor to his constituents. The Lord Mayor's Show may then be said to function as the post-liminal reintegration of a new office-bearer into society after a status elevation has occurred (following Arnold van Gennep's conception of rites of passage) and the simultaneous integration of the city population into the new equilibrium of political and economic forces. This is achieved, on the one hand, by figuring the proceedings as a (conjugal) union of mayor and London, smiled on by personified virtues and civic forbears. On the other hand, middling and lower segments of urban society are deliberately included in representations of merchant London (in pageant episodes which celebrate labor and enterprise), encouraging these parties to feel included in the livery companies' vision of London and, thus, offering them incentive to recognize and support the new administration. While I see this primarily as confirmation of the inclusive inclination of the Lord Mayor's Show, it remains a fair point that "one should not understate the *latently* coercive elements of civic entertainments, at least in terms of the kind of community they routinely invoked" (Hill, Pageantry 9). Not everyone might have desired ideological integration into the body of the city, under the Aldermen's terms and conditions, and the appropriation of female voices (of personifications) is not itself an innocent strategy.

In *The Triumphs of Truth* personified London tells the mayor that "[a] woman's counsel is not always weak" (969). With these words – supplied by a dominant male culture – the speaking female city calls attention to an important feature of the Lord Mayor's Show and the marriage symbolism which runs through it. London and other feminized personifications (with whom the mayor may also be asked to join) are generally meek and passive but they also wield mystic powers. The paradox may be resolved, or at least better understood, by recourse to Victor Turner's account of "the permanently or transiently sacred attributes of low status or position" (109). Turner's take on the

198

interdependence of worldly powerlessness and mystical potency is anticipated by Simone de Beauvoir who argues in *The Second Sex* that the quality of "mystery" is ascribed to persons of low and marginal status, including women (16). London is both a mighty city with many impressive qualities and virtues, and an inferior woman, placed into the controlling care of the mayor and subordinate to him. The biblical binary of woman as contemptible whore and hallowed virgin – Eve and Mary, Babylon and Jerusalem – plays into this scenario (of the personified city as a deific mediator for the mayor and subject to him), as does the traditional association of women with signs, derivation, and metaphor. The latter allows for feminine personifications to serve as gateways between the material city and a transcendental realm of ideas. His access to these personifications showcases the mayor as the recipient of special sanction, facilitates his ritual passage and confirms his new authority.

Naming and punning also function as strategies of signaling authority and influence. In Munday's *Triumphs of Re-united Britannia*, for example, Britannia gratefully acknowledges her assumption of a new name and identity as Brute's "virgin Queene *Britania*" (B3), echoing Adam's naming of Eve and the more recent case of Amerigo Vespucci's nominal claim to America. In his *Londini Speculum* pamphlet Heywood not only proclaims that London owes her ancient patrimony to Brute and was "first cald by him *Trinovantum*, or *Troy-novant*, *New Troy*" (305), but also reminds his readers that "*Maior* [...] implyeth as much as *the greater*". Punning, of a serious kind, is used further in the Lord Mayor's Show to indicate the inevitability of political developments as they occur and the synthesis of office and officeholders. Anthropologist Victor Turner described the phenomenon of "serious punning" as the ascription of etymological explanations to words used in ritual contexts, often based on "similarity of sound rather than derivation from a common source" (11). From John Lydgate's 1431 entertainments for John Wells, "devised notably indede / For to accordyne with the Maiers name" (qtd. in Hill, Pageantry 163), via John Lyon's 1554 encounter with a pageant lion (qtd. in Lancashire, Comedy 22), to John Leman's identification with the curative lemon tree (1616) and beyond, serious puns (or punning etymologies, often based on homophones) naturalize and justify a new mayor's status elevation and integrate him into his new position.

Finally, even while acknowledging all "latent coercion", idealization and oversimplification, there still remains the fact that the Lord Mayor's Show is a surprisingly worldly affair, free of religious dogmatism (for which it is not generally given credit) and more inclusive in its outlook than the majority of stage plays produced at the time; though its literary merits (regarding plot, coherence, characterization, the quality of dialogue etc.) cannot match those productions, it is ideologically more palatable than most of them.

Works Cited

Primary Sources

André le Chapelain. *The Art of Courtly Love*. Trans. John Jay Parry. New York: Columbia UP, 1941. Print.

Bolton, Edmund. *The Cities Advocate, in this Case or Question of Honor and Armes: Whether Apprentiship Extinguisheth Gentry*. London, 1629. *EEBO*. Web. 4 Mar. 2015.

Booth, Abram. "Abram Booth's Eyewitness Account of the 1629 Lord Mayor's Show." Trans. and ed. James P. Lusardi and Henk Gras. *Shakespeare Bulletin* 11.3 (1993): 19-23. Print.

Busino, Orazio. "Orazio Busino's Eyewitness Account of *The Triumphs of Honour and Industry*." Trans. and annotated Kate D. Levin. *Thomas Middleton: The Collected Works*. Ed. Gary Taylor and John Lavagnino. Oxford: Oxford UP, 2010. 1264-68. Print.

Chaucer, Geoffrey. *The House of Fame*. Ed. and trans. Gerard NeCastro. *E-Chaucer*. U of Maine at Machias, 2007. Web. 29 June 2013.

Cleaver, Robert. *Godlie Forme of Householde Government: For the Ordering of Private Families According to the Direction of Gods Word*. London, 1600. *EEBO*. Web. 25 Feb. 2015.

Combe, Thomas. *The Theater of Fine Devices*. 1593. Ed. Mary V. Silcox. *The English Emblem Tradition: Index Emblematicus*. Vol. 2. Ed. Peter M. Daly, Leslie T. Duer and Mary V. Silcox. Toronto: U of Toronto P, 1993. 325-80. Print.

Dekker, Thomas [?]. *The Blacke Rod and the White: Justice and Mercie: Striking and Sparing London*. 1630. *The Plague Pamphlets of Thomas Dekker*. Ed. F. P. Wilson. Oxford: Clarendon, 1925. 197-217. Print.

Dekker, Thomas. *Brittannia's Honor*. London, 1628. *EEBO*. Web. 24 Feb. 2013.

---. *The Dead Tearme, or, Westminsters Complaint for Long Vacations and Short Termes Written in Manner of a Dialogue betweene the Two Cityes London and Westminster*. London, 1608. British Library. *EEBO*. Web. 4 Sept. 2018.

---. *Londons Tempe, Or, The Field of Happines*. London, 1629. *EEBO*. Web. 24 Feb. 2013.

---. *Newes from Graves-end: Sent to Nobody*. 1604. *The Plague Pamphlets of Thomas Dekker*. Ed. F. P. Wilson. Oxford: Clarendon, 1925. 63-103. Print.

---. *A Rod for Run-awayes: God's Tokens, of His Feareful Iudgements, Sundry Wyes Pronounced upon this City, and on Several Persons, Both Flying from it, and Staying in It*. 1625. *The Plague Pamphlets of Thomas Dekker*. Ed. F. P. Wilson. Oxford: Clarendon, 1925. 135-71. Print.

---. *The Seven Deadly Sinnes of London: Drawne in Seven Severall Coaches Through the Seven Severall Gates of the Citie Bringing the Plague With Them*. London, 1606. *EEBO*. Web. 25 Feb. 2015.

---. *Troia-Nova*. London, 1612. Huntington Library. *EEBO*. Web. 24 Feb. 2013.

---. *The Wonderfull Yeare.* 1603. Ed. G. B. Harrison. London: The Bodley Head Quartos, 1924. Print.

N. D. *Londons Looking-Glasse, or, the Copy of a Letter, Written by an English Travayler, to the Apprentices of London.* London, 1621. *EEBO.* Web. 4 Mar. 2015.

Donne, John. "Epithalamion Made at Lincoln's Inn." *John Donne: Selected Poems.* Select. by D. J. Enright. London: Orion, 2010. 66-69. Print.

---. "To His Mistress Going to Bed." *John Donne: Selected Poems.* Select. by D. J. Enright. London: Orion, 2010. 59-60. Print.

Erasmus, Desiderius. *The Praise of Folly.* 1511. London, 1887. Harvard University. *Internet Archive.* Web. 16 Sept. 2018.

Gascoigne, George. *The Adventures of Master F. J.* 1573. *An Anthology of Elizabethan Prose Fiction.* Ed. Paul Salzman. 1987. Oxford: Oxford UP, 2008. 1-81. Print.

Heywood, Thomas. *Londini Artium and Scientiarum Scaturigo.* London, 1632. *EEBO.* Web. 1 Mar. 2012.

---. *Londini Emporia.* London, 1633. *EEBO.* Web. 1 Mar. 2013.

---. *London's Ius Honorarium.* 1631. *The Dramatic Works of Thomas Heywood.* Vol. 4. Ed. R. H. Shepherd. 1874. New York: Russell and Russell, 1964. 263-81. Print.

---. *Londini Sinus Salutis.* 1635. *The Dramatic Works of Thomas Heywood.* Vol. 4. Ed. R. H. Shepherd. 1874. New York: Russell and Russell, 1964. 283-300. Print.

---. *Londini Speculum.* 1637. *The Dramatic Works of Thomas Heywood.* Vol. 4. Ed. R. H. Shepherd. 1874. New York: Russell and Russell, 1964. 301-18. Print.

---. *Londini Status Pacatus.* 1639. *The Dramatic Works of Thomas Heywood.* Vol. 5. Ed. R. H. Shepherd. 1874. New York: Russell and Russell, 1964. 357-75. Print.

---. *Porta Pietatis.* 1638. *The Dramatic Works of Thomas Heywood.* Vol. 5. Ed. R. H. Shepherd. 1874. New York: Russell and Russell, 1964. 259-74. Print.

Jackson, Abraham. *The Pious Prentice, or, The Prentices Piety.* London, 1640. Bodleian Library. *EEBO.* Web. 25 Feb. 2015.

Jonson, Ben. "On the Famous Voyage." *Ben Jonson: Poems Selected by Thom Gunn.* 1974. London: Faber and Faber, 2005. 56-61. Print.

Keymis, Laurence. *A Relation of the Second Voyage to Guiana: Perfourmed and Written in the Yeare 1596.* N. p.: EEBO Editions, 2010. Print.

Langland, William. *Will's Vision of Piers Plowman.* Trans. E. Talbot Donaldson. Ed. Elizabethan D. Kirk and Judith H. Anderson. New York: Norton, 1990. Print.

Londons Lamentation, or, a Fit Admonishment for City and Countrey: Wherein Is Described Certaine Causes of this Affliction and Visitation of the Plague Yeare 1641 Which the Lord Hath Been Pleased to Inflict Upon Us, and Withall What Meanes Must Be Used to the Lord, to Gaine His Mercy and Favor, with an Excellent Spirituall Medicine to Be Used for the Preservative Both of Body and Soule. London, 1641. *EEBO-TCP.* Web. 30 Aug. 2018.

Lowin, John. *Brief Conclusions of Dancers and Dancing: Condemning the Prophane Use Thereof and Commending the Excellencie of Such Persons Which Have from Age to Age, in All Solemne Feasts, and Victorious Triumphs Used that (No Less) Honourable, Commendable and Laudable Recreation: As Also True Physicall Observation of the Body in Health, by the Use of the Same Exercise.* London, 1609. *EEBO.* Web. 20 Feb. 2015.

Marvell, Andrew. "Upon Appleton House." 1651. *The Poems of Andrew Marvell*. Ed. Nigel Smith. London: Pearson Longman, 2003. 216-41. Print.

---. "On the Victory Obtained by Blake." 1657. *The Poems of Andrew Marvell*. Ed. Nigel Smith. London: Pearson Longman, 2003. 425-27. Print.

Middleton, Thomas. *The Sun in Aries*. 1621. Ed. David M. Bergeron. *Thomas Middleton: The Collected Works*. Ed. Gary Taylor and John Lavagnino. Oxford: Oxford UP, 2010. 1589-92. Print.

---. *Triumphs of Health and Prosperity*. 1626. Ed. David M. Bergeron. *Thomas Middleton: The Collected Works*. Ed. Gary Taylor and John Lavagnino. Oxford: Oxford UP, 2010. 1903-06. Print.

---. *Triumphs of Honour and Industry*. 1617. Ed. David M. Bergeron. *Thomas Middleton: The Collected Works*. Ed. Gary Taylor and John Lavagnino. Oxford: Oxford UP, 2010. 1251-63. Print.

---. *Triumphs of Honour and Virtue*. 1622. Ed. David M. Bergeron. *Thomas Middleton: The Collected Works*. Ed. Gary Taylor and John Lavagnino. Oxford: Oxford UP, 2010. 1719-22. Print.

---. *Triumphs of Integrity*. 1623. Ed. David M. Bergeron. *Thomas Middleton: The Collected Works*. Ed. Gary Taylor and John Lavagnino. Oxford: Oxford UP, 2010. 1768-71. Print.

---. *Triumphs of Love and Antiquity*. 1619. Ed. David M. Bergeron. *Thomas Middleton: The Collected Works*. Ed. Gary Taylor and John Lavagnino. Oxford: Oxford UP, 2010. 1399-1404. Print.

---. *The Triumphs of Truth*. 1613. Ed. David M. Bergeron. *Thomas Middleton: The Collected Works*. Ed. Gary Taylor and John Lavagnino. Oxford: Oxford UP, 2010. 968-76. Print.

Middleton, Thomas, and Thomas Dekker. *The Roaring Girl*. 1611. Ed. Paul A. Mulholland. Manchester: Manchester UP, 1987. Print. The Revels Plays.

Milton, John. "Of Reformation in England Touching Church Discipline in England, and the Causes that Hitherto Have Hindered It: In Two Books, Written to a Friend." *The Prose Works of John Milton*. London: Westley and Davis, 1835. 1-21. Print.

Munday, Anthony. *Camp-Bell, or, the Ironmongers Fair Feild*. London, 1609. *EEBO*. Web. 1 Mar. 2013.

---. *Chrysanaleia: The Golden Fishing, or, Honour of Fishmongers*. London, 1616. *EEBO*. Web. 24 Feb. 2013.

---. *Chruso-thriambos: The Triumphs of Golde*. London, 1611. Huntington Library. *EEBO*. Web. 24 Feb. 2013.

---. *Himatia-poleos: The Triumphs of Olde Draperie, or, the Rich Cloathing of England*. London, 1614. *EEBO*. Web. 24 Feb. 2013.

---. *Metropolis Coronata: The Triumphes of Ancient Drapery, or, Rich Cloathing of England*. 1615. Huntington Library. *EEBO*. Web. 24 Feb. 2013.

---. *Sidero-thriambos, or, Steele and Iron Triumphing*. London, 1618. *EEBO*. Web. 24 Feb. 2013.

---. *The Triumphs of Re-united Britannia*. London, 1605. *EEBO*. Web. 24 Feb. 2013.

---. *Triumphs of the Golden Fleece*. London, 1623. *EEBO*. Web. 24 Feb. 2013.

Nashe, Thomas. *The Unfortunate Traveller*. 1594. *An Anthology of Elizabethan Prose Fiction*. Ed. Paul Salzman. 1987. Oxford: Oxford UP, 2008. 205-309. Print.

Niccholes, Alexander. *A Discourse of Marriage and Wiving and of the Greatest Mystery Therein Contained: How to Choose a Good Wife from a Bad*. London, 1615. Huntington Library. *EEBO*. Web. 4 Mar. 2015.

Nixon, Anthony. *Great Brittaines Generall Ioyes: Londons Glorious Triumphes*. London, 1613. *EEBO*. Web. 4 Mar. 2015.

---. *The Dignitie of Man: Both in the Perfections of His Soule and Bodie*. Oxford, 1616. *EEBO*. Web. 4 Mar. 2015.

Peacham, Henry. *Minerva Britanna, Or a Garden of Heroical Devises, Furnished, and Adorned with* Emblemes *and* Impresas *of Sundry Natures, Newly Devised, Moralized, and Published*. 1612. Harvard College Library. *EEBO*. Web. 1 May 2013.

---. *Basilikon Doron (MS Royal)*. 1610. Ed. Alan R. Young. *The English Emblem Tradition: Index Emblematicus*. Vol. 5. Ed. Alan R. Young. Toronto: U of Toronto P, 1998. 127-205. Print.

Philo of Alexandria. *On the Account of the World's Creation Given by Moses (De Opificio Mundi)*. *Works*. Vol. 1. 12 vols. 1929. Ed. and trans. F. H. Colson, G. H. Whitaker and Ralph Marcus. Cambridge, MA: Harvard UP, 1981. 6-137. Print. Loeb Classical Library.

Plato. *The Timaeus*. Ed. Richard. D. Archer-Hind. Macmillan, 1888. New York: Arno, 1973. Print. Philosophy of Plato and Aristotle.

Quarles, Francis. *Emblemes (1635) and Hieroglyphikes of the Life of Man (1638)*. Intro. Karl Josef Höltgen and John Horden. Hildesheim: Georg Olms, 1993. Print. Emblematisches Cabinet.

Ralegh, Walter. *The Discoverie of the Large, Rich, and Beautifull Empire of Guiana*. London, 1596. *EEBO*. Web. 4 Mar. 2015.

Rous, Francis. *The Mysticall Marriage: Experimentall Discoveries of the Heavenly Marriage Between a Soule and Her Saviour*. London, 1631. Folger Shakespeare Library. *EEBO*. Web. 4 Mar. 2015.

The Run-awyaes [sic] Answer to a Booke Called, A Rodde for Runne-awayes: In Which Are Set Downe a Defense for Their Running, With Some Reasons Perswading Some of Them Never to Come Backe: The Usage of Londoners by the Countrey People: Drawne in a Picture, Artificially Looking Two Waies, (Foorth-right, and A-squint). London, 1625. *EEBO*. Web. 29 Aug. 2018.

Shakespeare, William. *A Midsummer Night's Dream*. Ed. Cedric Watts. Ware, Hertfordshire: Wordsworth, 2002. Print.

---. *Coriolanus*. Ed. Lee Bliss. Upd. ed. Cambridge: Cambridge UP, 2010. Print. The New Cambridge Shakespeare.

---. *Lucrece*. *The Poems*. Ed. F. T. Prince. London: Methuen, 1960. 63-149. Print. The Arden Shakespeare.

---. *Richard III*. Ed. Antony Hammond. London: Methuen, 1981. Print. The Arden Shakespeare.

---. *The Merry Wives of Windsor*. Ed. David Crane. Cambridge: Cambridge UP, 1997. Print. The New Cambridge Shakespeare.

---. *Titus Andronicus*. The Complete Works of William Shakespeare. *Shakespeare.mit. edu.* The Tech, 2015. Web. 2 Oct. 2015.

Squire, John. *Tes Irenes Trophae: The Triumphs of Peace*. London, 1620. Guildhall Library. *EEBO*. Web. 1 Mar. 2012.

Spenser, Edmund. *The Fairie Queene*. Ed. Thomas P. Roche Jr. London: Penguin, 1987. Print. Penguin Classics.

Stow, John. *A Survey of London*. Repr. from the text of 1603. 1908. Ed. Charles Lethbridge Kingsford. 2 Vols. Oxford: Clarendon, 2000. Print.

A Students Lamentation, that Hath in London Bene Sometime an Apprentise: for the Unruly Tumults, Lately in that Citie Hapning: for which Five Suffred Death on Thursday the 24. of Iuly Last. London, n. d. *EEBO*. Web. 25 Feb. 2015.

Taylor, John. "A Navy of Landships." *All the Workes of John Taylor the Water Poet: Being 63 in Number Collected into One Volume by the Author*. London, 1630. *EEBO*. Web. 26 Jun. 2014.

---. *The Triumphs of Fame and Honour, or, the Noble Accomplish'd Solemnity, Full of Cost, Art and State, at the Inauguration and Establishment of the True Worthy and Right Nobly Minded Robert Parkhurst, into the Right Honourable Office of Lord Mayor of London*. London, 1634. *EEBO*. Web. 5 Oct. 2015.

Thomas, Dylan. "A Refusal to Mourn the Death, by Fire, of a Child in London." *Dylan Thomas*. Ed. Walford Davies. London: J. M. Dent, 1997. 69. Print.

Van der Noot, Jan. *A Theatre for Worldlings*. Ed. Peter M. Daly. *The English Emblem Tradition: Index Emblematicus*. Vol. 1. Ed. Peter M. Daly, Leslie T. Duer and Anthony Raspa. Toronto: U of Toronto P, 1988. 1-27. Print.

Webbe, George. *The Bride Royall, or the Spiritual Marriage Between Christ and His Church*. London, 1613. Huntington Library. *EEBO*. Web. 4 Mar. 2015.

Webster, John. *Monuments of Honour*. London, 1624. Huntington Library. *EEBO*. Web. 1 Mar. 2012.

Whitney, Geffrey. *A Choice of Emblemes and Other Devises*. 1586. Ed. Peter M. Daly and Anthony Raspa. *The English Emblem Tradition: Index Emblematicus*. Vol. 1. Ed. Peter M. Daly, Leslie T. Duer and Anthony Raspa. Toronto: U of Toronto P, 1988. Print.

Wilson, Robert. *The Pleasant and Stately Morall of the Three Lordes and Three Ladies of London*. London, 1590. *EEBO*. Web. 4 Mar. 2015.

Wyatt, Thomas. "My Galley Charged." *The Poetry of Sir Thomas Wyatt*. Ed. E. M. W. Tillyard. London: Scholartis, 1929. 65. Print.

---. "Tagus, Farewell." *The Poetry of Sir Thomas Wyatt*. Ed. E. M. W. Tillyard. London: Scholartis, 1929. 119. Print.

Secondary Sources

Aldous, Vivienne. "Cokayne, Sir William (1559/60-1626)." *Oxford Dictionary of National Biography*. Oxford UP, 2004. Web. 24. Sept. 2015.

Alsop, J. D. "A Moorish Playing Company in Elizabethan England." *Notes & Queries* 27 (1980): 135. Print.

Amussen, Susan Dwyer. "The Family and the Household." *A Companion to Shakespeare.* Ed. David Scott Kastan. Oxford: Blackwell, 1999. 85-99. Print.

Appleby, John C. "Watts, Sir John (c. 1550-1616)." *Oxford Dictionary of National Biography.* Oxford UP, 2004. Web. 24 Sept. 2015.

Archer, Ian W. "Swinnerton, Sir John (*bap.* 1564, *d.* 1616)." *Oxford Dictionary of National Biography.* Oxford UP, Sept. 2013. Web. 24 Sept. 2015.

Arendt, Hannah. "The Public and the Private Realm." *The Human Condition.* 1958. *Front Desk Apparatus Library.* Front Desk Apparatus, n. d. Web. 5 Mar. 2015.

Ashton, Robert. "Leman, Sir John (1544-1632)." *Oxford Dictionary of National Biography.* Oxford UP, 2004. Web. 24 Sept. 2015.

Bartels, Emily C. "Too Many Blackamoors: Deportation, Discrimination, and Elizabeth I." *Studies in English Literature, 1500-1900* 46.2 (2006): 305-22. Rice University. *JSTOR.* Web. 28 Aug. 2014.

Baskins, Cristelle. "Shaping Civic Personification: *Pisa Sforzata, Pisa Salvata.*" *Early Modern Visual Allegory: Embodying Meaning.* Ed. Cristelle Baskins and Lisa Rosenthal. Aldershot: Ashgate, 2007. 91-108. Print.

Baskins, Cristelle, and Lisa Rosenthal, eds. Introduction. *Early Modern Visual Allegory: Embodying Meaning.* Aldershot: Ashgate, 2007. 1-10. Print.

Bath, Michael. "Collared Stags and Bridled Lions: Queen Elizabeth's Household Accounts." *The English Emblem and the Continental Tradition.* Ed. Peter M. Daly. New York: AMS, 1988. 225-53. Print.

Beauvoir, Simone de. *Das andere Geschlecht: Sitte und Sexus der Frau.* 1949. Trans. Uli Aumüller and Grete Oswald. 9th ed. Reinbek bei Hamburg: Rowohlt, 2008. Print.

Beaven, Alfred P. "Chronological List of Aldermen: 1601-1650." *The Aldermen of the City of London Temp. Henry III-1912.* London: Corporation of the City of London, 1908. 47-75. *British History Online.* Web. 13 Aug. 2018.

Beer, Anna. "Textual Politics: The Execution of Sir Walter Ralegh." *Modern Philology* 94.1 (1996): 19-38. Print.

Beer, B. L. "London and the Rebellions of 1548-1549." *Journal of British Studies* 12.1 (1972): 15-38. Cambridge UP. *JSTOR.* Web. 5 Nov. 2015.

Beier, A. L. "Social Problems in Elizabethan London." *Journal of Interdisciplinary History* 9.2 (1978): 203-21. The MIT Press. *JSTOR.* Web. 29 Oct. 2013.

Ben-Amos, Ilana Krausman. "Failure to Become Freemen: Urban Apprentices in Early Modern England." *Social History* 16.2 (1991): 155-77. Taylor and Francis. *JSTOR.* Web. 5 Nov. 2015.

Bergeron, David M. "'Are we turned Turks?': English Pageants and the Stuart Court." *Comparative Drama* 44.3 (2010): 255-75. Print.

---. *English Civic Pageantry 1558-1642.* Columbia: U of South Carolina P, 1971. Print.

---. "The Elizabethan Lord Mayor's Show." *Studies in English Literature, 1500-1900* 10.2 (1970): 269-85. Johns Hopkins UP. *JSTOR.* Web. 5 Nov. 2015.

---. "King James's Civic Pageant and Parliamentary Speech in March 1604." *Albion: A Quarterly Journal Concerned with British Studies* 34.2 (2002): 213-31. Print

---. "Middleton's *No Wit, No Help* and Civic Pageantry." *Pageantry in the Shakespearean Theater.* Ed. David M. Bergeron. Athens: U of Georgia P, 1985. 65-82. Print.

---. "Munday, Anthony (*bap.* 1560, *d.* 1633)." *Oxford Dictionary of National Biography.* Oxford UP, 2004. Web. 30 Sept. 2015.

Berlin, Michael. "Civic Ceremony in Early Modern London." *Urban History* 13 (1986): 15-27. Print.

Bindoff, S. T. *Tudor England.* 1950. Harmondsworth: Penguin Books, 1970. Print.

Bliss, Lee. Introduction. *Coriolanus.* Ed. Bliss. Upd. ed. Cambridge: Cambridge UP, 2010. 1-111. Print. The New Cambridge Shakespeare.

Bloch, Howard R. "Medieval Misogyny." *Representations* 20 (1987): 1-24. U of California P. *JSTOR.* Web. 17 Oct. 2014.

Bradbrook, M. C. "The Politics of Pageantry: Social Implications in Jacobean London." *Poetry and Drama 1570-1700.* Ed. Antony Coleman and Antony Hammond. London: Methuen, 1981. 60-75. Print.

Brenner, Robert. "The Civil War Politics of London's Merchant Community." *Past and Present* 58 (1973): 53-107. Oxford UP. *JSTOR.* Web. 28 Dec. 2015.

Bright, David F., and Barbara C. Bowen. "Emblems, Elephants, and Alexander." *Studies in Philology* 80.1 (1983): 14-24. *JSTOR.* Web. 20 Aug. 2015.

Burke, Bernard. *The General Armory of England, Scotland, Ireland, and Wales: Comprising a Registry of Armorial Bearings from the Earliest to the Present Time.* London, 1878. Berwyn Heights, MD: Heritage Books, 2009. Print.

Chalmers Thomas, Tandy, Linda L. Price, and Hope Jensen Schau. "When Differences Unite: Resource Dependence in Heterogeneous Consumption Communities." *Journal of Consumer Research* 39.5 (2013): 1010-33. U of Chicago P. *JSTOR.* Web. 5 Dec. 2014.

Chambers, Robert. *The Book of Days: A Miscellany of Popular Antiquities in Connection with the Calendar, Including Anecdote, Biography, and History, Curiosities of Literature and Oddities of Human Life and Character.* 2 vols. London: W. R. Chambers, 1864. Harvard University. *Internet Archive.* Web. 13 Feb. 2015.

Christie, Sheila. "*Speculum Urbis*: The Chester Cycle as a Tool of Social Cohesion and Transformation." *The Yearbook of English Studies* 43 (2013): 140-55. Modern Humanities Research Association. *JSTOR.* Web. 13 Feb. 2015.

Clermont-Ferrand, Meredith. Rev. of *Festivals and Plays in Late Medieval Britain*, by Clifford Davidson. *The Sixteenth Century Journal* 40.4 (2009): 1160-62. *JSTOR.* Web. 13 Feb. 2015.

Clopper, Lawrence M. Rev. of *Signifying God: Social Relation and Symbolic Act in the York Corpus Christi Plays*, by Sarah Beckwith. *Modern Philology* 102.1 (2004): 97-101. Print.

Coleman, D. C. "Labour in the English Economy of the Seventeenth Century." *Seventeenth-Century England: Society in an Age of Revolution.* Ed. Paul S. Seaver. New York: Franklin Watts, 1976. 112-38. Print. Modern Scholarship on European History.

Cuder, Primavera. "'Spaniard or Moor, the saucy slave shall die': Early Modern English Attitudes Towards the Stranger in Thomas Dekker's *Lust's Dominion* (ca. 1600)." *The Construction of the Other in Early Modern Britain: Attraction, Rejection, Symbiosis.* Ed. Rüdiger Ahrens. Heidelberg: Winter, 2013. 85-95. Print.

Craig, Hardin. "The Corpus Christi Procession and the Corpus Christi Play." *The Journal of English and Germanic Philology* 13.4 (1914): 589-602. U of Illinois P. *JSTOR.* Web. 13 Feb. 2015.

Daly, Peter M. "England and the Emblem: The Cultural Context of English Emblem Books." *The English Emblem and the Continental Tradition.* Ed. Daly. New York: AMS, 1988. 1-60. Print.

Day, J. F. R. "Primers of Honor: Heraldry, Heraldry Books, and English Renaissance Literature." *The Sixteenth Century Journal* 21.1 (1990): 93-103. *JSTOR.* Web. 28 Jan. 2013.

De Certeau, Michel. *The Writing of History.* Trans. Tom Conley. New York: Columbia UP, 1988. Print.

Diehl, Huston. "Graven Images: Protestant Emblem Books in England." *Renaissance Quarterly* 39.1 (1986): 49-66. U of Chicago P. *JSTOR.* Web. 1 Dec. 2015.

Dünne, Jörg, and Stephan Günzel, eds. *Raumtheorie: Grundlagentexte aus Philosophie und Kulturwissenschaften.* Frankfurt a. M.: Suhrkamp, 2006. Print.

Ferrrante, Joan. *Woman as Image in Medieval Literature: From the Twelfth Century to Dante.* New York: Columbia UP, 1975. Print.

Finlayson, Caitlin J. "Jacobean Foreign Policy, London's Civic Polity, and John Squire's Lord Mayor's Show, *The Tryumphs of Peace* (1620)." *Studies in Philology* 110.3 (2013): 584-610. The U of North Carolina P. *Project Muse.* Web. 6 Nov. 2015

---. "Mercantilism and the Path to Spiritual Salvation in Thomas Heywood's *Londini Emporia,* or *Londons Mercatura* (1633)." *English Studies* 91.8 (2010): 838-60. Print.

Foucault, Michel. *Discipline and Punish: The Birth of the Prison.* 1975. Trans. Alan Sheridan. New York: Random House, 1979. Print.

Freeman, Rosemary. *English Emblem Books.* 1948. New York: Octagon Books, 1966. Print.

García, Luciano García. "The Moor in the English Dramatic Mirror 2: The Term 'Moor' in the Secondary Texts of Early Modern English: Plays in which this Term Has a Major Presence." *The Construction of the Other in Early Modern Britain: Attraction, Rejection, Symbiosis.* Ed. Rüdiger Ahrens. Heidelberg: Winter, 2013. 123-52. Print.

Geertz, Clifford. *Local Knowledge: Further Essays in Interpretive Anthropology.* 1983. London: Fontana Press, 1993. Print.

Glanville, Philippa. "The Topography of Seventeenth-Century London: A Review of Maps." *Urban History* 7 (1980): 79-83. Print.

Goffman, Erving. *Frame Analysis: An Essay on the Organization of Experience.* New York: Harper and Row, 1974. Print.

González-Treviño, Ana Elena. "'Kings and their crowns': Signs of Monarchy and the Spectacle of New World Otherness in Heroic Drama and Public Pageantry." *Studies in Eighteenth-Century Culture* 42 (2013): 103-21. Johns Hopkins UP. *Project Muse.* Web. 23 Sept. 2015.

Greenblatt, Stephen. *The Rise and Fall of Adam and Eve.* London: The Bodley Head, 2017. Print.

---. *Tyrant: Shakespeare on Power.* London: The Bodley Head, 2018. Print.

Hadfield, Andrew. *Lying in Early Modern English Culture: From the Oath of Supremacy to the Oath of Allegiance.* Oxford: Oxford UP, 2017. Print.

Hanson, Elizabeth. "The Register of the School's Probation, 1607, from the Merchant Taylors' School London." *The Journal of the History of Childhood and Youth* 6.3 (2013): 411-27. Johns Hopkins UP. *Project Muse*. Web. 28 Dec. 2015

Hardin, William. "Conceiving Cities: Thomas Heywood's *Londini Speculum* (1637) and the Making of Civic Identity." *Comitatus* 28.1 (1997): 17-35. Print.

Harmer, William Scotford. "First Prize Essay." *The Cotswold Sheep Society's Flock Book*, 1982. The Cotswold Sheep Society, 2010. Web. 1 March 2017.

Hartle, Robert, et al. *The New Churchyard: From Moorfields Marsh to Bethlem Burial Ground, Brokers Row and Liverpool Street*. London: MOLA, 2017. Crossrail Archaeology.

Heinemann, Margot. *Puritanism and Theatre*: *Thomas Middleton and Opposition Drama under the Early Stuarts*. Cambridge: Cambridge UP, 1980. Print.

Hicks, Ruth Ilsley. "The Body Political and the Body Ecclesiastical." *Journal of Bible and Religion* 31.1 (1963): 29-35. Oxford UP. *JSTOR*. Web. 8 May 2015.

Hill, Elizabeth K. "What is an Emblem?" *The Journal of Aesthetics and Art Criticism* 29.2 (1970): 261-65. *JSTOR*. Web. 28 Jan. 2013.

Hill, Tracey. *Anthony Munday and Civic Culture: Theatre, History and Power in Early Modern London, 1580-1633*. Manchester: Manchester UP, 2004. Print.

---. *Pageantry and Power: A Cultural History of the Early Modern Lord Mayor's Show, 1585-1639*. 2010. Manchester: Manchester UP, 2013. Print.

Hobsbawm, Eric, and Terence Ranger, eds. *The Invention of Tradition*. Cambridge: Cambridge UP, 1983. Print.

Hollis, Daniel Webster, III. "Whitmore, Sir George (*b*. after 1572, *d*. 1654)." *Oxford Dictionary of National Biography*. Oxford UP, 2004. Web. 24 Sept. 2015.

Homan, Richard L. "Ritual Aspects of the York Cycle." *Theatre Journal* 33.3 (1981): 302-15. Johns Hopkins UP. *JSTOR*. Web. 13 Feb. 2015.

Hotson, Leslie. "Anthony Munday's Birth-date." *Notes and Queries* 204 (1959): 2-4. Print.

Hunt, John Dixon. "Pictura, Scriptura, and Theatrum: Shakespeare and the Emblem." *Poetics Today* 10.1 (1989): 155-71. *JSTOR*. Web. 20 Aug. 2016.

Jager, Eric. "Did Eve Invent Writing? Script and the Fall in 'The Adam Books'." *Studies in Philology* 93.3 (1996): 229-50. U of North Carolina P. *JSTOR*. Web. 10 Aug. 2016.

James, Mervyn. "Ritual, Drama and Social Body in the Late Medieval English Town." *Past and Present* 98 (1983): 3-29. Oxford UP. *JSTOR*. Web. 29 Oct. 2013.

Kathman, David. "Players, Livery Companies, and Apprentices." *The Oxford Handbook of Early Modern Theatre*. Ed. Richard Dutton. Oxford: Oxford UP, 2009. 413-28. Print.

---. "Heywood, Thomas (*c*.1573-1641)." *Oxford Dictionary of National Biography*. Oxford UP, 2004. Web. 30 Sept. 2015.

Keene, Derek. "Henry fitz Ailwin (d. 1212)." *Oxford Dictionary of National Biography*. Oxford UP, 2008. Web. 30 Sept. 2015.

---. "Material London in Space and Time." *Material London, ca. 1600*. Ed. Lena Cowen Orlin. Philadelphia: U of Pennsylvania P, 2000. 55-74. Print.

Kipling, Gordon. *Enter the King: Theatre, Liturgy, and Ritual in the Medieval Civic Triumph*. Oxford: Clarendon Press, 1998. Print.

---. "Triumphal Drama: Form in English Civic Pageantry." *Renaissance Drama* 8 (1977): 37-56. Northwestern UP. *ProQuest*. Web. 13 Feb. 2015.

Kittay, Eva Feder. "Woman as Metaphor." *Hypatia* 3.2 (1988): 63-86. *JSTOR*. Web. 10 Aug. 2016.

Klein, Joan Larsen. "*Hamlet*, IV.ii.12-21 and Whitney's *A Choice of Emblemes*." *Notes & Queries* 23.4 (1976): 158-69. Print.

Knowles, James. "The Spectacle of the Realm: Civic Consciousness, Rhetoric and Ritual in Early Modern London." *Theatre and Government under the Early Stuarts*. Ed. J. R. Mulryne and Margaret Shewring. Cambridge: Cambridge UP, 1993. 157-89. Print.

Korda, Natasha. "Women in the Theater." *The Oxford Handbook of Early Modern Theatre*. Ed. Richard Dutton. Oxford: Oxford UP, 2009. 456-73. Print.

Lancashire, Anne. "The Comedy of Love and the London Lord Mayor's Show." *Shakespeare's Comedies of Love*. Toronto: U of Toronto P, 2008. 3-29. Print.

---. "London Street Theater." *The Oxford Handbook of Early Modern Theatre*. Ed. Richard Dutton. Oxford: Oxford UP, 2009. 323-39. Print.

Landy, Francis. "The Song of Songs and the Garden of Eden." *Journal of Biblical Literature* 98.4 (1979): 513-28. *JSTOR*. Web. 8 Jan. 2016.

Law, Jonathan. *Oxford Dictionary of Law*. 1983. 8th ed. Oxford: Oxford UP, 2015. Print.

Le Corbeiller, Clare. "Miss America and Her Sisters: Personifications of the Four Parts of the World." *The Metropolitan Museum of Art Bulletin* 19.8 (1961): 209-23. *JSTOR*. Web. 20 Aug. 2015.

Levin, Kate D. Introduction. *Triumphs of Honour and Industry*. *Thomas Middleton: The Collected Works*. Ed. Gary Taylor and John Lavagnino. Oxford: Oxford UP, 2007. 1251-54. Print.

Lévy, Carlos, "Philo of Alexandria." *The Stanford Encyclopedia of Philosophy*, Spring 2018. Ed. Edward N. Zalta. Web. 4 July 2018.

Liddy, Christian D. "The Rhetoric of the Royal Chamber in Late Medieval London, York and Coventry." *Urban History* 29.3 (2003): 323-49. Print.

Liggett, Helen, and David C. Perry. Introduction. *Spatial Practices*. Ed. Liggett and Perry. Thousand Oaks, CA: SAGE, 1995. 1-12. Print.

Lindley, K. J. "Riot Prevention and Control in Early Stuart London." Transactions of the Royal Historical Society 33 (1983): 109-26. Cambridge UP. *JSTOR*. Web. 5 Nov. 2015.

Lindley, Keith. "Rainton, Sir Nicholas (1569-1646)." *Oxford Dictionary of National Biography*. Oxford UP, 2004. Web. 24 Sept. 2015.

Lobanov-Rostovsky, Sergei. "*The Triumphes of Golde*: Economic Authority in the Jacobean Lord Mayor's Show." *English Literary History* 60.4 (1993): 879-98. Johns Hopkins UP. *JSTOR*. Web. 29 Jan. 2013.

McGlone, Matthew S., and Jessica Tofighbakhsh. "Birds of a Feather Flock Conjointly (?): Rhyme as Reason in Aphorisms." *Psychological Science* 11.5 (2000): 424-28. American Psychological Society. Web. 8 Jan. 2016.

McGraw, Kathleen M, and Thomas M. Dolan. "Personifying the State: Consequences for Attitude Formation." *Political Psychology* 28.3 (2007): 299-327. *JSTOR*. Web. 20. Aug. 2015.

McIntosh, Marjorie Keniston. "Poverty, Charity, and Coercion in Elizabethan England." *Journal of Interdisciplinary History* 35.3 (2005): 457-79. *Project Muse.* Web. 26 Feb. 2016.

Madelaine, R. E. R. "*The Duchess of Malfi* and Two Emblems in Whitney and Peacham." *Notes & Queries* 29 (1982): 146-47. Print.

Mahood, Molly M. *Shakespeare's Wordplay.* 1957. London: Routledge, 2003. Print.

Manley, Lawrence. "Civic Drama." *A Companion to Renaissance Drama.* Ed. Arthur F. Kinney. Oxford: Blackwell, 2004. 294-313. Print.

---. "From Matron to Monster: Tudor-Stuart London and the Languages of Urban Description." *The Historical Renaissance: New Essays on Tudor and Stuart Literature and Culture.* Ed. Heather Dubrow and Richard Strier. Chicago: U of Chicago P, 1988. 347-74. Print.

---. *Literature and Culture in Early Modern London.* Cambridge: Cambridge UP, 1995. Print.

Manning, John. *The Emblem.* London: Reaktion Books, 2004. Print.

Massing, Jean Michel. "From Greek Proverb to Soap Advert: Washing the Ethiopian." *Journal of the Warburg and Courtauld Institutes* 58 (1995): 180-201. *JSTOR.* Web. 26 Jun. 2014.

Mazza, Ethel Matala de. Introduction. *Der verfaßte Körper: Zum Projekt einer organischen Gemeinschaft in der Politischen Romantik.* Freiburg im Breisgau: Rombach, 1999. 11-47. Print.

McLuskie, Kathleen E. *Dekker and Heywood.* Houndmills: Macmillan, 1994. Print. English Dramatists.

Medine, Peter E. "Object and Intent in Jonson's 'Famous Voyage'." *Studies in English Literature, 1500-1900* 15.1 (1975): 97-110. Rice University. *JSTOR.* Web. 5 Oct. 2015.

Montrose, Louis. "The Work of Gender and Sexuality in the Elizabethan Discourse of Discovery." *Representations* 33 (1991): 1-41. Print.

Morrissey, L. J. "English Pageant-Wagons." *Eighteenth-Century Studies* 9.3 (1976): 353-74. Johns Hopkins UP. *JSTOR.* Web. 28 Jan. 2013.

Muir, Edward. "The Eye of the Procession: Ritual Ways of Seeing in the Renaissance." *Ceremonial Culture in Pre-modern Europe.* Ed. Nicholas Howe. Notre Dame, IN: U of Notre Dame P, 2007. 129-53. Print.

Muir, Kenneth. "Remembrance of Things Past." *Connotations* 6.1 (1969/97): 41-45. Web. 8 Jan. 2016.

Mullaney, Steven. *The Place of the Stage: License, Play, and Power in Renaissance England.* 1988. Ann Arbor: U of Michigan P, 2007. Print.

Nightingale, Pamela. "Walworth, Sir William (*d.* 1386?)." *Oxford Dictionary of National Biography.* Oxford UP, 2004. Web. 24 Sept. 2015.

Northway, Kara. "'To kindle an industrious desire': The Poetry of Work in Lord Mayors' Shows." *Comparative Drama* 41.2 (2007): 167-92. Print.

Oakshott, Jane. "The Fortune of Wheels: Pageant Staging Rediscovered." *The Yearbook of English Studies* 43 (2013): 267-73. Modern Humanities Research Association. *JSTOR.* Web. 13 Feb. 2015.

Palmer, Daryl W. "Metropolitan Resurrection in Anthony Munday's Lord Mayor's Shows." *Studies in English Literature, 1500-1900* 46.2 (2006): 371-87. *Project Muse.* Web. 1 Dec. 2015.

Patterson, Catherine. "Married to the Town: Francis Parlett's Rhetoric of Urban Magistracy in Early Modern England." *Local Identities in Late Medieval and Early Modern England.* Ed. Daniel Woolf and Norman L. Jones. Basingstoke: Palgrave Macmillan, 2007. 156-77. Print.

Paxson, James J. "Personification's Gender." *Rhetorica: A Journal of the History of Rhetoric* 16.2 (1998): 149-79. U of California P. *JSTOR.* Web. 15 Jun. 2014.

Pelling, Margaret. "Apprenticeship, Health and Social Cohesion in Early Modern London." *History Workshop* 37 (1994): 33-56. *JSTOR.* Web. 24 Sept. 2014.

Perreault, Melanie. "'To Fear and to Love Us': Intercultural Violence in the English Atlantic." *Journal of World History* 17.1 (2006): 71-93. U of Hawai'i P. *JSTOR.* Web. 3 Sept. 2014.

Praz, Mario. *Studies in Seventeenth-Century Imagery.* 1939. 2nd ed. Rome: Edizioni Di Storia E Litteratura, 1964. Print.

Read, Sophie. *Eucharist and the Poetic Imagination in Early Modern England.* Cambridge: Cambridge UP, 2013. Print.

Rees, Abraham. *The Cyclopaedia, or, Universal Dictionary of Arts, Sciences, and Literature.* Vol. 3. Longman, Hurst, Rees, Orme and Brown: London, 1819. *Internet Archive.* Web. 9 Aug. 2018.

"Rhyme." *Encyclopedia of Language and Linguistics.* 2nd ed. Ed. Keith Brown. *ScienceDirect.* Web. 26 Feb. 2016.

Rice, Nicole R., and Margaret Aziza Pappano. *The Civic Cycles: Artisan Drama and Identity in Premodern England.* Notre Dame, IN: U of Notre Dame P, 2015. Print.

Robertson, Jean, and Donald James Gordon, eds. *A Calendar of Dramatic Records in the Books of the Livery Companies of London 1485-1640.* London: Malone Society, 1954. Print. Malone Society Collections Vol. 3.

Robinson, Philip. "The Multiple Meanings of Troy in Early Modern London's Mayoral Shows." *Seventeenth Century* 26.2 (2011): 221-39. Print.

Robinson, Phil. "Trading Places: Middleton's Mayor and Middleton's Moor." *The Literary London Journal* 9.2 (2011): N. pag. The Literary London Society. Web. 14 May 2014. http://www.literarylondon.org/londonjournal /september2011/ robinson.html

Rowland, Richard. *Thomas Heywood's Theatre 1599-1639: Locations, Translations, and Conflict.* Farnham, UK: Ashgate, 2010. Print.

Rubin, Miri. *Corpus Christi: The Eucharist in Late Medieval Culture.* Cambridge: Cambridge UP, 1991. Print.

Schöne, Albrecht. *Emblematik und Drama im Zeitalter des Barock.* München: C. H. Beck, 1964. Print.

Schofield, Scott. "According to 'the common received opinion': Munday's Brute in *The Triumphes of Re-United Britannia* (1605)." *Fantasies of Troy: Classical Tales and the Social Imaginary in Medieval and Early Modern Europe.* Ed. Alan Shepard and Stephen D. Powell. Toronto: CRRS, 2004. 253-68. Print.

Schuman, S. "Two Notes Upon Emblems and the English Renaissance Drama." *Notes & Queries* 18 (1971): 28-29. Print.

Schwarz, Norbert. "On Judgments of Truth and Beauty." *Daedalus* 135.2 (2006): 136-38. American Academy of Arts and Sciences and MIT Press. *JSTOR*. Web. 8 Jan. 2016.

Seaver, Paul S. "Middleton's London." *Thomas Middleton: The Collected Works*. Ed. Gary Taylor and John Lavagnino. Oxford: Oxford UP, 2010. 59-73. Print.

---. Rev. of *Popular Politics and Religion in Civil War London*, by Keith Lindley. *The American Historical Review* 103.5 (1998): 1588-89. Oxford UP. *JSTOR*. Web. 28 Dec. 2015.

Simmel, Georg. *Brücke und Tür*. 1909. *Georg Simmel Online*. Soziologisches Institut der Universität Zürich., n. d. Web. 5 Mar. 2015.

Snow, David A., et al. "Frame Alignment Processes, Micromobilization, and Movement Participation." *American Sociological Review* 51.4 (1986): 461-84. American Sociological Association. *JSTOR*. Web. 12 Dec. 2014.

Sontag, Susan. *Regarding the Pain of Others*. New York: Picador, 2003. Print.

Spelman, Elizabeth V. "Woman as Body: Ancient and Contemporary Views." *Feminist Studies* 8.1 (1982): 109-31. *JSTOR*. Web. 8 May 2015.

Swan, Toril. "Metaphors of Body and Mind in the History of English." *English Studies* 90.4 (2009): 460-75. Print.

Teskey, Gordon. "Allegory, Materialism, Violence." *The Production of English Renaissance Culture*. Ed. David Lee Miller, Sharon O'Dair and Harold Weber. Ithaca, NY: Cornell UP, 1994. 293-318. Print.

Thrush, Andrew. "Abbot, Sir Maurice (1565-1642)." *Oxford Dictionary of National Biography*. Oxford UP, 2004. Web. 24 Sept. 2015.

---. "Clitherow, Sir Christopher (1577/8-1641)." *Oxford Dictionary of National Biography*. Oxford UP, 2004. Web. 24 Sept. 2015.

---. "Moulson, Thomas (c. 1568-1638), of St. Christopher-le-Stocks London." *The History of Parliament: British Political, Social and Local History*. The History of Parliament Trust, 2017. Web. 9 Aug. 2018.

Trudell, Scott A. "Occasion." *Early Modern Theatricality*. Ed. Henry S. Turner. Oxford: Oxford UP, 2013. 230-49. Print. Oxford Twenty-First Century Approaches to Literature.

Turner, Victor. *The Ritual Process: Structure and Anti-Structure*. 1969. New Brunswick: Aldine Transaction, 2008. Print.

---. *From Ritual to Theatre: The Human Seriousness of Play*. New York: PAJ, 1982. Print.

Van Gennep, Arnold. *The Rites of Passage*. 1908. Trans. Monika B. Vizedom and Gabrielle L. Caffee. Chicago: U of Chicago P, 1960. Print.

Warncke, Carsten-Peter. *Symbol, Emblem, Allegorie: Die zweite Sprache der Bilder*. Köln: Deubner Verlag für Kunst, Theorie und Praxis, 2005. Print.

Weidle, Roland. *Englische Literatur der Frühen Neuzeit: Eine Einführung*. Berlin: Erich Schmidt, 2013. Print.

Wickham, Glynne. *Early English Stages, 1300 to 1660*. 2 vols. London: Routledge, 1959-72. Print.

Williams, Sheila. "A Lord Mayor's Show by John Taylor, the Water Poet." *Bulletin of the John Rylands Library* 41 (1959): 501-31. Print.

Withington, Robert. "The Lord Mayor's Show for 1590." *Modern Language Notes* 33.1 (1918): 8-13. *MLA International Bibliography*. Web. 14 May 2014.

Witt, Charlotte and Lisa Shapiro. "Feminist History of Philosophy." *The Stanford Encyclopedia of Philosophy,* Spring 2016. Ed. Edward N. Zalta. Web. 4 July 2016.

Zeeden, Ernst Walter. *Europa im Zeitalter des Absolutismus und der Aufklärung.* Stuttgart: Klett-Cotta, 1981. Print.

List of Images

Index

Harper, William (mayor) 166, 167, 175
Harvey, Gabriel 12
Harvey, James (mayor) 27
Harvey, Sebastian (mayor) 27, 28, 48, 59, 160, 171
Hayes, Thomas (mayor) 35, 36, 81, 148, 196
Henry Stuart 105
Henry VII 39, 137, 163
Hercules 32, 43
Heywood, Thomas 10, 14, 19, 20, 21, 22, 23, 35, 36, 38, 44, 45, 47, 48, 49, 58, 59, 64, 65, 66, 74, 81, 82, 83, 84, 85, 87, 100, 105, 110, 111, 112, 114, 116, 126, 127, 141, 144, 145, 146, 147, 149, 150, 160, 161, 162, 163, 164, 165, 171, 175, 176, 183, 188, 190, 192, 193, 195, 199
Hieroglyphica 12, 104
Hieroglyphikes of the Life of Man 57
Himatia-poleos 22, 31, 35, 36, 45, 127, 146, 148, 165, 181, 184, 193
Holliday, Leonard (mayor) 167, 189
Horapollo 12, 104
Iconologia 57, 83, 129
India 68, 78, 90, 95, 98, 99, 100, 105, 150, 155, 191, 197
industry 31, 42, 43, 44, 47, 52, 53, 56, 65, 68, 69, 74, 98, 154, 158, 160, 182, 184, 186, 191, 192, 194, 196, 197
Ironmongers 15, 33, 52, 61, 90, 124, 158, 159, 160, 186, 188
James I 30, 38, 47, 50, 52, 60, 62, 78, 90, 91, 94, 113, 131, 133, 134, 144, 160, 161, 167, 172, 174

Jason 32, 51, 59, 65, 70, 79, 80, 81, 82, 84, 174, 193
Jolles, John (mayor) 32
Jones, Francis (mayor) 74, 141
Jonson, Ben 23, 30, 38, 134, 151, 152
Jupiter 33, 41, 68
King Lud 163
Leman, John (mayor) 17, 38, 87, 117, 138, 139, 140, 142, 144, 145, 146, 147, 169, 170, 175, 176, 198, 199
Liberal Arts 47, 74, 75, 132
limen 48, 136, 137, 141
Londini Artium 19, 45, 48, 59, 64, 65, 66, 81, 85, 105, 114, 144, 145, 147, 190, 192
Londini Emporia 22, 45, 48, 49, 58, 59, 65, 66, 84, 87, 111, 175, 192, 193
Londini Sinus Salutis 45, 47, 126, 188
Londini Speculum 19, 44, 85, 87, 110, 111, 112, 116, 126, 133, 145, 149, 161, 163, 165, 171, 183, 199
Londini Status Pacatus 23, 38, 74, 83, 84, 190, 193, 195
London's Ius Honorarium 48, 65, 74, 82, 146, 147, 149, 150, 151, 163, 164, 165, 175, 192
Londons Tempe 23, 33, 48, 75, 76, 90, 98, 104, 110, 186
marriage 23, 39, 46, 99, 108, 109, 110, 111, 112, 113, 114, 115, 118, 125, 129, 133, 137, 138, 139, 140, 146, 147, 153, 157, 158, 163, 176, 179, 180, 198
Marvell, Andrew 61, 153
Mary (mother of Christ) 137, 147, 148, 175, 179, 199
Medea 32, 65, 81, 84, 193